German Realists in the Nineteenth Century

Georg Lukács

German Realists
in the
Nineteenth Century

Translated

by Jeremy Gaines and Paul Keast

Edited with an introduction and notes

by Rodney Livingstone

The MIT Press
Cambridge, Massachusetts

First MIT Press edition, 1993

English translation © 1993 Libris
Introduction and Notes © 1993 Rodney Livingstone
This work originally appeared in German
under the title *Deutsche Realisten des 19. Jahrhunderts*
Copyright © 1951 Ferenc Jánossy

This book was set in Monotype Postscript Plantin
by Cinamon and Kitzinger, London and was printed and bound
in the United Kingdom

Library of Congress Cataloging-in-Publication Data

Lukács, György, 1885–1971.
    [Deutsche Realisten des 19. Jahrhunderts. English]
    German realists in the nineteenth century / By Georg Lukács;
translated by Jeremy Gaines and Paul Keast; edited with an
introduction and notes by Rodney Livingstone.
    p.   cm.
    Translation of: Deutsche Realisten des 19. Jahrhunderts.
    Includes bibliographical references and index.
    ISBN 0–262–12171–9
    1. German literature—19th century—History and criticism.
    2. Realism in literature. I. Livingstone, Rodney. II. Title.
PT345.L7913 1993
830.9' 12—dc20

Contents

Introduction

BY RODNEY LIVINGSTONE

Georg Lukács is one of the most controversial figures of his own age and of ours. As a Marxist philosopher he has been credited with the most profound development of Marxist theory since Marx. He has been widely regarded as a major influence on writers as diverse as the Frankfurt School, Heidegger, Walter Benjamin and Sartre. In the course of a long life, in which he played an active political role in the Hungarian revolution after the First World War and again in the Imre Nagy uprising in that country in 1956, he has often been subjected to venomous attacks, both for his ideas and his political actions. From inside the communist movements he has been accused of deviations from the current party line as well as attempts to 'revise', i.e. compromise, Marxist doctrine. From outside Marxism he has often been identified as one of the chief spokesmen for the dominant communist cultural ideology and criticized for his failure to speak out against Stalin's crimes.

Lukács is also pre-eminent as a Marxist literary critic. Indeed for many years after 1945 he was the only literary critic who was able to command respect for a Marxist view of literature. More recently his literary writings have been attacked by other, more modern types of Marxist critic, as well as by structuralist and post-structuralist academic critics. At the same time, however, the temperature of controversy has been lowered as Lukács moved from the centre of debate, with the consequence that his views on particular writers have to a certain extent been integrated into the mainstream and have become part of critical orthodoxy – although, inevitably, with the passage of time, many of his particular interpretations and judgements have been superseded. Lukács turned to literary criticism in the nineteen thirties in a move which he has described as a kind of tactical retreat from politics after he was forced to retract views which had been criticized by the Communist International in 1929. It is evident, however, that his withdrawal from politics was involuntary and that he attempted to continue political activity by other, in his case, literary means. His literary writings may be taken at face value, that is, as contributions to our understanding of particular authors or genres (the historical novel, the realist novel). But equally, they may be read as coded interventions in the political debates of the time, such as Stalinism, the ideological implications of modernism or Expressionism, the Popular Front, or the 'Thaw' of the years following Stalin's death.

Finally, Lukács enjoys a third reputation, as a pre-Marxist literary critic. He had turned to Marxism in 1918, in an ethical recoil against what he described as the 'age of total sinfulness' – the effects of capitalism as they became visible in the collapse of Germany and the Austro-Hungarian Empire in the First World War – and in response to to the Russian Revolution. But even before that time he had built up a reputation for three major literary studies: *A History of Modern Drama* (1911), a radical attempt to provide a sociological analysis of the drama; *Soul and Form* (1911), a collection of essays on modern literature which evoked considerable interest at the time, not least on the part of Thomas Mann, who incorporated some of its ideas into *Death in Venice*; and *The Theory of the Novel* (1916). All of these works were later taken up and the ideas they contain flowed into the general corpus of his work. It is notable that while Lukács himself emphasized the discontinuity in his thought and the importance of the rupture involved in the transition to Marxism, as well as the development of his ideas in consequence of his 'mistakes', subsequent critics, most importantly perhaps, Theodor Adorno, Ernst Bloch and Lucien Goldmann, have not hesitated to incorporate the pre-Marxist Lukács into a Marxian framework.

The present collection contains all the major essays Lukács wrote on German nineteenth-century literature, apart from those already published on Goethe.[1] They were all written between 1935 and 1950 and illuminate a side of Lukács previously hidden from the English reader, namely his enduring love of German literature and his faith in the humanist values which are central to the German tradition. With the growth of National Socialism these values had come under attack in Germany itself, and in the eyes of Germany's neighbours the humanist strand in the German tradition seemed to have given way to German militarism and aggression. It was all the

1. See *Goethe and his Age*, translated by Robert Anchor, London, 1968.

more urgent, therefore, to provide a corrective. In some of these essays, notably those on Büchner and Raabe, Lukács sets out to rescue writers from right-wing distortions. Others, particularly the Keller essay, give him the opportunity to work out his own intellectual position and to state his own credo: his faith in democratic socialism even in dark times when such beliefs appeared to face overwhelming odds.

Students of German literature who chance upon these essays may well wonder how important they are today. After all, over half a century has elapsed since they were written and much research has been done on all these authors since then. It may well be maintained that, however important Lukács's voice may be, it can hardly persuade us to ignore the new information about these writers and the new light that has been cast on their works by more recent critical approaches. In reply it can be urged that, despite these real additions to our knowledge, Lukács is still worth reading because he set an agenda which was novel at the time and which endures today. In all of these essays we see him also actively intervening in the debates that were taking place on the left at the time. They concerned the role of literature, of the literary tradition in society, and the relationship between literature and politics. Lukács himself points out in his autobiography that he and Mikhail Lifshitz pioneered discussion of a Marxist aesthetics.[2] Furthermore Lukács was the first critic to ask searching questions about the ideological status of works of literature. At present the critical pendulum may have swung too far against Lukács. Lukács defends the realist classics of the nineteenth century. Modern critics have become suspicious of realism. They deconstruct it, giving realist works a reading which de-emphasizes their 'realism', i.e. their success in reflecting life as it was. To re-read Lukács now is to be reminded of the powerful case that can be made for literary realism and of his continued relevance as a critic.

Georg Lukács was born in 1885 into a wealthy Jewish family in Budapest. His father, József Lukács, was one of the executive directors of the Credit Bank, one of the leading banks in Hungary, and a patron of the arts. His mother Adele, née Wertheimer, was Ger-

2. See Georg Lukács, *Record of a Life*, edited by István Eörsi, translated by Rodney Livingstone, London 1983, p.86.

man-speaking and so German was spoken in the home. She also supported her husband in his enthusiasm for the arts by maintaining a salon. It was here that Georg was able to meet some of the future stars in the Hungarian firmament, most notably Béla Bartók. In 1890 the family Magyarized its name of Löwinger into Lukács and in 1899 József was ennobled. Georg Lukács continued to use the honorific 'von' in his publications up to his conversion to Marxism in 1918. Lukács always played down the Jewish element in his family. Like many of their generation his parents were almost completely assimilated and their Jewishness appeared only at weddings, funerals and similar occasions. Georg was even baptized a Lutheran. While religion played almost no role in his upbringing, it was a fact that the Hungarian bourgeoisie was largely Jewish and the intelligentsia almost exclusively so. Since anti-Semitism was rife among both the peasantry and the aristocracy, it seems likely that his insistence on the unimportance of his Jewishness was a not uncommon defensive reaction – and certainly an understandable one – to an environment that might turn hostile at any moment. In the context of the present book it is noteworthy that Lukács underplays the importance of Heine's Jewishness and completely ignores the question of anti-Semitism in Raabe's *Hunger Pastor*, a significant omission in the general context of his discussion of the reactionary or progressive nature of Raabe's views.

After obtaining his doctorate in Budapest for his book on modern drama, Lukács continued his studies in Berlin (where Georg Simmel, the sociologist, proved an inspiring teacher) and in Heidelberg, where he became friendly with Max Weber, the neo-Kantian philosopher Emil Lask, and the future Marxist philosopher Ernst Bloch. In December 1918 came his conversion to communism and his entry into the Hungarian Communist Party which had just been founded by Béla Kun. In 1919 he took part as a political commissar and as Commissar of Education in the communist uprising in Hungary. In effect he was the leading spirit in cultural and intellectual matters during the brief life of the revolution. After the Soviet Republic was overthrown in September he fled to Vienna. There he was arrested and the Hungarian government under Admiral Horthy sought his extradition. This was resisted after appeals from Thomas and Heinrich Mann, Paul Ernst, Richard Beer-Hofmann and others, and he was released at the end of the year. In 1923 he published his major contribution to Marxist theory, *History and Class Consciousness*.

In 1929 the Austrian government again attempted to expel Lukács. On this occasion too he was rescued by Thomas Mann, this time with an Open Letter in which he pleaded for Lukács to be allowed to remain in Vienna. The plea was successful; nevertheless Lukács decided to go to the Soviet Union, where he remained until 1945 except for the period between 1931 and 1933, which he spent in Berlin. During his first stay in Moscow (1929–31) he worked at the Institute of Marxism-Leninism which was run at the time by David Riazanov, the editor of a planned edition of the complete works of Marx and Engels. Riazanov, later executed during Stalin's purges, showed Lukács the recently deciphered early manuscripts of Marx, a reading of which confirmed Lukács in his Hegelian, humanist interpretation of Marxism. Riazanov also introduced him to Mikhail Lifshitz, a literary scholar who subsequently published an influential two-volume collection of the writings of Marx and Engels on art and literature. Lukács and he became close friends, and Lukács's aesthetic views were strongly influenced by Lifshitz. In 1931 Lukács moved to Berlin having been entrusted by Wilhelm Pieck, later president of the German Democratic Republic (GDR) and Johannes R. Becher, the Expressionist poet and subsequently Minister of Culture in the GDR, with the task of imposing Moscow's latest views on literature. This was to have an important effect in crystallizing Lukács's own convictions. He became active in the BPRS (the League of Proletarian and Revolutionary Writers) which included figures like Becher, Anna Seghers, the dramatist Friedrich Wolf, who was famous for his *Cyankali* (*Potassium Cyanide*), a play protesting against the abortion laws, and Ludwig Renn, who was known for *Krieg* (*War*), a novel about the First World War. Lukács played a leading role in the League and also wrote for its periodical, *Die Linkskurve*. Here he made two significant contributions. In the first, 'The Novels of Willi Bredel', he launched an attack on grassroots working-class writing. In the second, 'Reportage or Portrayal',[3] he attacked a novel by Ernst Ottwalt, a close associate of

3. Both essays can be found in Georg Lukács, *Essays on Realism*, edited by Rodney Livingstone, translated by David Fernbach, London, 1980.

Brecht. This was the first of a number of attacks on literary modernism which form a major theme in Lukács's writing.

In these debates Lukács demonstrated a consistency and a coherence both in literature and politics which marked his position throughout the difficult years of the nineteen thirties and forties. In the *Blum Theses* (1929)[4] he set out the political position that he basically never abandoned. Looking at the situation in Hungary in 1929 he believed that the working class was too small to justify talk of a proletarian revolution. He therefore began to talk not of a 'dictatorship of the proletariat', but of a democratic dictatorship to be based on an alliance of the working class and the peasantry. Unfortunately for him this coincided with a purist phase in the Communist International which had just proclaimed that even social democrats were not to be trusted, let alone the peasantry, since they were in effect supporters of fascism. In the short run Lukács retracted his views, but he never really renounced them. As the party line changed his opinions returned to favour, notably after 1935 when the Popular Front was proclaimed, and again after 1945 when the People's Democracies were established in Eastern Europe, a development he welcomed, hoping for something better than the Stalinist autocracies that emerged.

Lukács's literary views ran parallel to his politics. Here too his opinions were formed during the intense debates about the nature and function of literature which took place in the shadow of the rise of National Socialism in Germany and of Stalinism in the Soviet Union. These debates focused on the attempt to distinguish between reactionary and progressive literature, and the problem of how to judge the European literary tradition which by definition could not have been the product of a socialist society. Lukács reached conclusions which partly overlapped and partly contradicted those of the official party line. The latter crystallized out at the Soviet Writers' Congress in Moscow in 1934 in the doctrine of Socialist Realism, which was now endorsed to the exclusion of other types of literature. The Congress denounced experimental, modernist literature

4. See Georg Lukács, *Political Writings 1919–1929*, translated by Michael McColgan, edited by Rodney Livingstone, London, 1972, pp.227–55. 'Blum' was Lukács's undercover name in the Hungarian Communist Party.

as decadent. Chief among the offenders, according to Karl Radek, the Party ideologist, were James Joyce, Marcel Proust and John Dos Passos. Joyce, for example, was accused of 'filming a heap of dung, crawling with worms . . . through a microscope'.[5]

Lukács accepted the Congress's strictures on modernism. After all he had already attacked avant-garde writing in the *Linkskurve* in 1932. Over the next twenty years he continually renewed the attack, although he tended to provide his own rationale. For example, in 1957 he condemned Joyce, not with Radek's moralizing prudishness, but for making the stream-of-consciousness technique an end in itself, rather than an instrument with which to explore reality.[6] In 1934 he criticized German Expressionism, arguing that the Expressionist movement was the literary parallel to the politics of the Independent Social Democratic Party which had maintained a purely subjective hostility towards the First World War and capitalism, while remaining objectively ineffectual. More recently, he pointed out, Expressionist writers like Hanns Johst and Gottfried Benn had moved towards Nazism. This launched the so-called Expressionism debate which involved him in confrontations with other Marxists, such as Ernst Bloch, for whom Expressionism had been an important inspiration and a phase of their own development. It also triggered a major disagreement with Bertolt Brecht, the so-called Realism debate, whose fundamental importance only emerged years later when Brecht's side of the dispute was published. In Brecht's view the classic realist text was the expression of the dominant bourgeois ideology. It had to be countered by the subversive strategies of the non-realist, avant-garde text. The fact that Lukács is widely felt to have lost that argument is one of the main reasons for his present eclipse as a critic in Britain.[7]

However, Lukács does not simply endorse Communist Party views. Although he shares its dislike of the avant-garde, he does not accept that socialist realism is the only alternative. More specifically, he endorsed it in the hands of Maxim Gorky, its great-

5. See Maxim Gorky, Karl Radek and others, *Soviet Writers' Congress, 1934*, London, 1935 (reprinted, 1977), p.153.

6. See *The Meaning of Contemporary Realism*, translated by John and Necke Mander, Merlin Press 1963, p.18.

7. For Brecht's views see, Ernst Bloch *et al.*, *Aesthetics and Politics*, London, 1977, pp.68–86.

est exponent, but was scathing about its lesser practitioners who wrote propaganda according to the official formula. Instead much of his literary criticism is concerned with the defence of the humanist, bourgeois literary tradition. He undertook the defence of much in the European and specifically the German tradition – the literature of the 'Kunstperiode', the 'art-period', i.e. German literature from Lessing to Heine. More generally, he established a Europewide canon of literary realism: Walter Scott, Balzac, Dickens, Turgenev and Tolstoy. This canon extended into the present, where he defended the tradition of what he termed 'critical realism'. By this he meant writing of a broadly realist kind which provided a critique of modern capitalism, but whose authors refused to move to a communist view of the world. It is this concept that enabled him to endorse the works of liberal humanists like Romain Rolland, Roger Martin du Gard, Anatole France, Lion Feuchtwanger, Arnold Zweig, Heinrich Mann and above all, Thomas Mann, in Lukács's eyes the supreme model for literature in the contemporary world. In short, Lukács's defence of the bourgeois literary heritage can be seen as running parallel to his efforts in politics to achieve an alliance between the progressive bourgeoisie and the left.

During the nineteen thirties Lukács remained in Moscow where he was able to publish his views in _Literaturnii Kritik_ and _Internationale Literatur_, journals which were notable for their relatively liberal policies. He wrote a number of important theoretical articles,[8] and major studies such as _The Historical Novel_ and _The Young Hegel_.[9] However, the Stalin-Hitler Pact put an end to the Popular Front policies which Lukács had supported in these and other writings. _Literaturnii Kritik_ ceased to appear and after the German invasion of Russia in June 1940 the situation of foreign intellectuals in the Soviet Union deteriorated. In 1941 Lukács was arrested and put in the notorious Lubyanka gaol. This can hardly have been pleasant, but in the event the worst that happened to him there was that he was ordered to write his autobiography in considerable detail. Since he did not incriminate himself he was subsequently released,

8. These have appeared in English in _Writer and Critic_, translated by Arthur Kahn, London, 1970.

9. _The Historical Novel_ , translated by Hannah and Stanley Mitchell, London, 1962; _The Young Hegel_, translated by Rodney Livingstone, London, 1975.

thanks to the intervention of Georgi Dimitrov. Following this he was one of the many foreign intellectuals to be sent to Tashkent, probably for their own protection. After staying there a year Lukács was able to return to Moscow where he remained until the end of the war. He then returned to Hungary.

It is important to realize that in all the essays in this book Lukács breaks with the tradition of so-called 'vulgar Marxism'. The essence of this approach was to decode an author's works in terms of his class origins. It was exemplified by Franz Mehring, for example, who had reduced Kleist to 'the Prussian officer'. Although Lukács does not ignore this aspect of Kleist – indeed he stresses it – his approach is fundamentally different: for him art is the reflection of an objective reality, not merely the expression of a particular class psychology (p.49). The chapter on Raabe theorizes this position even more explicitly. In the course of an argument reminiscent of D.H. Lawrence's 'Don't trust the teller, trust the tale', Lukács carefully distinguishes between Raabe's personal views, and the attitudes that emerge from his fictional writings. In his personal opinions Raabe may have leaned towards the conservative wing of National Liberalism; but in his novels we find a critical picture of Bismarckian Germany. Indeed both Raabe's achievement and his limitations are rooted in the creative tension between his political beliefs and his perceptions of social reality. Freed from biographical reductionism, Lukács is able to examine literary works as the contradictory products of the age that produced them. In Kleist's case the 'Prussian officer' is also the precursor of literary modernism, and Lukács traces a line which goes from Kleist to Wagner, Ibsen and Strindberg, to Nietzsche, Hofmannsthal and Wedekind. In what sense is Kleist a 'modern'? For Lukács his modernity is expressed above all in his severing of the link between an individual and the socio-historical context in which he or she lives. This leads to the various Romantic features which Lukács singles out – the emphasis on fate, the expression of subjectivity, the dramatization of the solitary, 'alienated' human being, and the creation of an 'artificial' society in order to depict 'private', often erotic passions.

When Lukács comes to examine German literature, one of his tasks is to trace the origins of that modernist literature he condemns; hence the Kleist chapter is of key importance in the present book. It can be linked to two other themes in his writing. On the one hand, Lukács adopts Goethe's dictum that Classicism is healthy and Romanticism is sick. By and large the progressive tradition as he defines it from Lessing to Heine makes a detour round Romanticism. E.T.A. Hoffmann is the principal exception. On the other hand, he is beginning to develop the view which he would subsequently articulate in *The Destruction of Reason* (1954), according to which National Socialism is a fundamentally irrational ideology whose roots go far back into the German tradition, specifically to Schelling and German Romanticism. His major study of Hegel sets out to distance Hegel from Romanticism (where he has often been situated), and to claim him as the heir to the tradition of Enlightenment and German classicism.

Despite all this, his appreciation of Kleist is by no means wholly negative – indeed, the ambiguity of his title hints as much; the 'tragedy' of Kleist points both to his tragedies and his tragedy as a writer. Lukács clearly responds to Kleist's 'originality', and his praise of *Michael Kohlhaas* and *Der zerbrochene Krug* (*The Broken Jug*) underlines his refusal to reduce Kleist to a single category. At the same time it should be noted that he can accept these works because of their 'social content', that is to say, they come within the ambit of his conception of realism. It should be recorded, however, that not all Marxists have espoused his interpretation of Romanticism. Christa Wolf, for example, who defined the Romantics as the first generation of writers 'whom society did not need', has made Kleist the centrepiece of one of her novels (*Kein Ort, nirgends*) (*No Place on Earth*) in a move which is clearly intended, among other things, as a belated rebuke to Lukács.

Lukács's essay on Eichendorff must come as a shock to anyone familiar with his views on the dire effects of Romanticism in the history of German literature and thought. Eichendorff's conservative attitudes, his 'feudal Romanticism', his Catholic convictions and a lyricism that seems to exclude the social content which alone can qualify as realism, seem designed to invite Lukács's hostility. The fact that he takes a far more sympathetic view suggests that here, as elsewhere in this volume, his ideas are not dictated exclusively by the exigencies of politics or by ideological disputes. On the contrary, it is evident that here, as perhaps nowhere else in his writings of this period, he was able to give free rein to his literary inclinations – and this is all the more remarkable when we reflect that this essay was written in exile in Moscow in the increasingly dark days of 1940.

What is it about 'simple, straightforward Eichendorff' (p.36) that attracts Lukács against all the odds? One factor is that 'the main content [of his poetry] is yearning' ('Sehnsucht', ibid.), a central category of Romanticism and one that never fails to strike a deep chord in Lukács's own soul. In his early writings he had been fascinated by the problem of yearning and he erects it into a master concept of modern life. In *A History of Modern Drama* he had argued that the basis of modern drama was the conflict between the yearning for personal fulfilment and the reified reality of capitalism. In *Theory of the Novel* he maintained that the novel-form expresses the unbridgeable gulf between the individual and the community; it is the 'form of absolute sinfulness'. Both books explore a sense of tragic doom founded on the irredeemable inhumanity of capitalist society and the absence of any adequate way out for the individual. The intervening book, *Soul and Form* (1911) explored various attempts to give yearning a 'form', i.e. to achieve authenticity: Theodor Storm's attitude of resignation, Stefan George's haughty rejection of society, Kierkegaard's cultivation of 'the art of living'. The later critic of Romanticism was profoundly a Romantic at heart. His early rejection of capitalism was Romantic in its origins, and the concept of Romantic anti-capitalism was one Lukács later used frequently, though critically. It refers to a wide spectrum of opposition to capitalism, but an opposition which is not based on the Marxist economic critique. It may contain a rejection of machine-production, the modern division of labour, the depersonalization of individuals (Nietzsche), the growth of large towns and the break-up of small communities (Ferdinand Tönnies) and the inexorable growth of rational calculation (Max Weber). It may be summed up in the polar opposites of 'culture' versus 'civilization', the plea for a universe governed by qualitative values, as opposed to the quantitative logic of rationality and the cash nexus. Unlike Marxism it often looks backward, to the Middle Ages or some other simpler, but ideal society. Thus Lukács begins with a profound Romanticism which he later repudiates as inadequate. His appreciation of Eichendorff exhibits the tensions in Lukács himself.

Eichendorff's *Memoirs of a Good-for-Nothing* is seen as the work of a man who has not really grasped the nature of capitalism, but whose instinctive revulsion from it is basically correct. Accordingly, Lukács emphasizes the gulf separating Eichendorff's hero from the bohemian Romantic intellectual, stressing instead his lower-class origins. Eichendorff's 'fairy-tale idyll' may even be called 'realistic', but this was the last historical conjuncture at which this was still possible, before the inexorable advance of industrial capitalism ruled out such lightheartedness. Despite all this the disparity in Lukács's attitudes towards Kleist and Eichendorff remains startling and requires explanation. It may be found in the idea that Eichendorff's Romanticism is harmless, while, as argued above, Kleist's is held partly responsible for the development of modernism. In other words, Kleist's is a radical right-wing Romanticism, while Eichendorff's is, for all his temperamental and political conservatism, that of a moderate. Lukács's rejection of radicalism is explained in the discussion of Gottfried Keller (see pp.xxi–xxii below).

Lukács's approach to Büchner and Heine is to treat them as transitional figures in the history of ideology: Büchner as a materialist on the road to historical materialism, Heine as a Young Hegelian. This ideological critique is a legitimate approach and Lukács uses it to great effect elsewhere too. However, since it is linked to Lukács's belief in the progressive nature of knowledge, it sometimes sounds complacent: he knows the truths which were denied to them. Because the proletariat did not yet exist, Büchner could not know that salvation lay not with the poor in general, but with the proletariat in particular. This complacency culminates in the Fontane chapter with the assertion that he 'need only have gone into a bookshop to find in the works of Marx and Engels clearly formulated answers to all his questions' (p.300)!

Such facile assertions are a particular danger in the chapter on Büchner, since the issues it raises were uncomfortably close to home, as Lukács must surely have known. His attempt to rescue Büchner from Nazi currents of thought is obviously justified. Karl Viëtor, whose ideas he criticizes, remained influential, despite the present essay, until well into the nineteen sixties.[10] Lukács is also right to focus on *Danton's Death*, with its debate on the morality of revolution. The question of where Büchner's sympathies lie is still debated, compounded, as it is, by the closeness of some of Danton's disillusioned statements about revolution to opinions Büchner expressed in his letters.

It should be recalled, however, that Lukács wrote this essay in 1937, at the height of the Moscow treason trials, and that the theme of the betrayal of the revolution as expressed in the great confrontations between Danton and Robespierre had a direct relevance to events in the Soviet Union. The parallels between the French and Russian revolutions were obvious to the Russian revolutionaries themselves. Isaac Deutscher reports that 'shortly after Lenin's death, the Bolshevik chiefs met and took a secret oath never to fight each other as the Jacobins did and never to guillotine each other. Whether the story was true or not, it is a fact that for a long time Lenin's successors felt bound by the rule that no party member should ever be punished with death for a political offence'.[11] And in 1927, when Stalin attacked Zinoviev, Kamenev and Trotsky, the president of the tribunal, a veteran Bolshevik, Aron Solz, explicitly drew the parallel with the French Reign of Terror:

Do you suppose that Robespierre was not sorry for Danton when he sent him to the guillotine? And yet he did it; and then Robespierre had to go himself. Do you think he was not sorry? But he had to do it – he had to.[12]

Lukács supported Stalin's basic policies, such as 'Socialism in one country', and even the Stalin-Hitler Pact of August 1939 (on the somewhat disingenuous grounds that it brought Britain and France into the war against Nazism). But the political stance he had maintained ever since the Blum Theses and reinforced by the Popular Front meant that he himself was always in danger of falling into disfavour when the class collaborations he favoured were frowned on. His literary views were also out of tune with the rigorous propa-

---

10. It should be noted, however, that in his eagerness to identify and condemn Nazi currents of thought, Lukács oversteps the mark in this essay. However right-wing Viëtor's ideas may have been, he was no Nazi, and in fact he was forced into emigration by Hitler's rise to power. He spent most of the Nazi period in the USA.

11. See Isaac Deutscher & David King, *The Great Purges*, Oxford, 1984, p.34.

12. ibid.

gation of socialist realism. There is no reason to doubt his later claims that he was always critical of Stalin and that he saw himself as involved in 'partisan warfare' for his own beliefs. Lukács broadly approved of the trials, or rather he did not disapprove of them, even though he did not believe in the evidence produced against the accused.[13] The central issue for him was which side would maintain the momentum of the revolution and, above all, which leaders would provide the most effective resistance to National Socialism. For this reason he sided with Stalin despite his reservations. Similar considerations led him to favour the historical Robespierre, even while acknowledging that the case against Danton was trumped up.[14] The parallel between Robespierre and Stalin seems, then, to have been well established in his mind. In Büchner's play Lukács's sympathies evidently lie with Robespierre and the 'plebeian' Saint-Just, and he specifically endorses the latter's blood-curdling justification of the Terror (see pp.81 and 85). In subsequent years Lukács condemned the trials, but even then only because he had decided they were 'superfluous' (because Stalin's position was so strong that there was no danger that an effective opposition could establish itself).[15] He came to perceive the limitations of the parallel with the French Revolution, though mainly because 'Danton was never a traitor and never lost faith in the republic, as Robespierre claimed' (presumably in contrast to the Trotskyite opposition in Russia).[16] Looking at the essay today it is hard to avoid the impression that Büchner was rather more consistent and forthright in his exploration of the conflicts that break out during the conduct of revolution. Lukács's assurance that Büchner could not know the right answer, because he could not know about the proletariat, seems to imply that he does know the answers. But Büchner may have had the greater grasp of the tragic nature of revolution after all. Lukács is on safer ground when he points out that Büchner portrays the contradictions and ideological crises of revolution, than when he offers to take sides. The tortuous nature of some of Lukács's arguments on Stalin

13. See Georg Lukács, *Record of a Life*, edited by István Eörsi, translated by Rodney Livingstone, London, 1983, p.107.

14. See István Hermann, *Georg Lukács, Sein Leben und Wirken*, Vienna, Cologne & Graz, 1986, p.138.

15. *Record of a Life*, op. cit., p.106.

16. ibid, p.107

is reminiscent of those of Brecht. Both men felt it necessary to defend the Soviet Union at all costs because they both regarded Stalin as the most determined and implacable enemy of Nazism. He simply had to be supported even if it meant turning a blind eye to his failings and even if their own intellectual positions suffered in consequence.

Whereas Büchner has the courage of his contradictions, Heine is accused of vacillating. He is caught between the claims of the petty bourgeoisie and the slowly emerging proletariat and cannot decide between them. The importance of Lukács's essay is that, regardless of his particular judgements, he is more or less the first major critic to take Heine seriously as a thinker and as a political consciousness. No less important for Lukács is the position Heine adopted in his various quarrels with Ludwig Börne and the political poets, such as Georg Herwegh and Ferdinand Freiligrath. Lukács sympathizes with Heine's dislike of 'Tendenzpoesie', tendentious poetry, literature with a (political) message, because he is convinced that in great realist writing the message is conveyed through the realism, as part of the fiction itself. It should not be necessary to superimpose it on the literary work and to do so is the mark of the inferior writer. This argument enables Lukács to include Heine in the canon of great realist writers. Even more noteworthy is his argument that Heine's journalistic form is the exact parallel to the achievement of Balzac in France. That is to say, given Germany's fragmentation and economic and political backwardness, a German Balzac who could create an extensive panoramic picture of contemporary society was not a possibility. But Heine's apparently fragmented and unformed technique is the true expression of the Germany of the day. The same argument applies to Heine's achievement as a political poet. Siegbert Prawer has pointed to the embarrassment of liberal critics when confronted by Heine's satirical masterpiece, *Deutschland. Ein Wintermärchen.*[17] In this respect Lukács's essay pioneered a revaluation of Heine as a major poetic satirist.

In some respects the chapter on Gottfried Keller may be regarded as the central essay of the collection, for political as much as for literary reasons. So much may be inferred from the elevated literary status Lukács grants to Keller by claiming for him a place in world literature alongside Tolstoy. As we have seen, the main thrust

17. See S.S. Prawer, *Heine, The Tragic Satirist*, Cambridge, 1961, p.107.

of Lukács's criticism in the nineteen thirties amounted to a defence of realism against modernism. In this chapter, as well as in the chapters on Fontane and Raabe (and elsewhere, in his studies of Goethe and Thomas Mann), he states the claims of German literature to an honoured place in the canon of world literature despite the problems and weaknesses of a tradition which had led to irrationalism and National Socialism.

The key to Lukács's view of Keller lies in the latter's bonds to Switzerland. On the one hand, his experience in Germany introduced him to the most modern brand of humanist theory: the philosophy of Feuerbach. On the other, his return to Switzerland protected him from the worst effects of German social backwardness, the German 'Misere', which is such a crucial aspect of Lukács's view of German intellectual history. Keller's writing is important for Lukács because it embodies Swiss values, that is to say, the values of ethical democracy. For Lukács democracy is not just the political form of capitalism. On the contrary, he praises traditional Swiss democracy because it did not succumb to a developed industrial capitalism until late on in Keller's career. Lukács is able to praise this Rousseauesque form of direct democracy, without confronting the difficulties that present themselves when a state is too large to enable the citizens to be personally involved in the conduct of their own affairs. Three aspects are worthy of comment. First, Keller's art is paradigmatic because it presents an education in democratic values. However this education is not all one way, from top to bottom. Lukács often refers (here p.232) to the episode where the hero, Henry Lee, is rebuked for his 'plebeian haughtiness' towards a girl whom he believes to be a countess, but who is in fact a poor relation. In other words, his democracy is a school in equality, incompatible with class or other forms of prejudice, a school in which Marx's question 'Who shall educate the educators?' receives the reply that there is no privileged elite, not even the proletariat. Second, the concept of direct democracy, with its powerful vision of a self-governing mankind, is clearly intended as a contrast with the burgeoning Soviet bureaucracy under Stalin (Lukács was to criticize Stalin for his 'bureaucratic' methods in 'Tribune or Bureaucrat?' of 1940).[18] Lukács's concept of fighting as a 'partisan' in a 'guerrilla

18. See Georg Lukács, *Essays in Realism*, op. cit., pp.198–237.

war' meant that his fundamental approval of Soviet Russia was qualified by his retention of the right to criticize it by implication, by contrasting the bureaucratic actuality with its democratic 'ideal-type', and to plead for the necessary improvements. He frequently refers (e.g. pp.241 and 242) in the Keller chapter to Epicurus's 'intermundia', intercosmic spaces, where one could find refuge in hard times. This concept evidently applies both to the democratic, but pre-capitalist Switzerland which enabled Keller to flourish, and to Lukács's own situation in Russia in the nineteen thirties. Third, he makes great play with the two endings to *Green Henry*. In the first version the novel ends with Henry Lee's not very well motivated death; the final version concludes with his decision to play an active role in public life. This change is one of the main factors leading Lukács to integrate Keller in the canon of great realist literature. For Lukács the defeat of the democratic revolution in 1848 had led to a split in the middle classes between the 'bourgeois' and the 'citoyen', in other words, the private and the public realms. The private tradition is what fed into the reactionary line leading to modernism. The great literature of the nineteenth century, on the other hand – Goethe, Balzac, Tolstoy – continued to be inspired by the belief that the individual should seek involvement in public affairs. The second ending of *Green Henry*, together with Keller's own practice as a citizen, places him firmly in this tradition. A more negative aspect of the same 'realism' that made Keller and Henry good citizens was the renunciation or mood of resignation this implied. Lukács in the nineteen thirties had abandoned his revolutionary hopes. His turning to literature may have enabled him to conduct his guerrilla warfare, but it is also the construction of a refuge, an 'intercosmic space', an 'internal Weimar', as Ferenc Fehér has termed it, which implies the acceptance, for all his reservations, of a bad reality.[19] In his writings Lukács consistently supports 'realists' who accept the world as against the 'radicals' who are determined to change it. He does so on the grounds that the realists stand a better chance of exerting a practical influence on events than the radicals who refuse to make compromises. Such radicals are doomed to defeat and perhaps to madness or death. Thus he prefers Hegel to Hölderlin,

19. See 'Lukács in Weimar' in *Lukács Revalued*, edited by Agnes Heller, Oxford, 1983, pp.75–106.

Eichendorff to Kleist. The *locus classicus* of this attitude is the much quoted passage in Hegel's *Aesthetics* where heroes of the 'Bildungsroman', such as Goethe's Wilhelm Meister, are praised for their resigned acceptance of necessity (see the discussion on pp.223–5). Of course, these passages are coded too: the reconciliation of Wilhelm Meister with the ancien régime in Germany, or of Henry Lee with traditional Swiss democracy implies a comment on Lukács's attitude to Soviet reality. He had accepted the need to retract both *History and Class Consciousness* and the *Blum Theses*, because to do so enabled him to continue the struggle against fascism within the communist movement, whereas radicals like Karl Korsch were expelled from the party and doomed to isolation.

In the growing tension of the immediate pre-war period and during the war itself anti-German sentiment increased in the Soviet Union. Interestingly, Stalin himself did not abandon the conviction that the war was to be fought against the Nazis, not the Germans. 'Hitlers come and go, but the German people will remain', he said. However, to persuade the Russian people to fight the war meant appealing to their patriotism. Ilya Ehrenburg and others began to argue that the Germans were brutal Nazis because they were German. Lukács's essays on Raabe and Fontane must be seen in this context. They have a dual aim. On the one hand, Lukács was able to use them to point to a humanist, democratic tradition within Germany, broadly identical with the realist tradition. On the other hand, Raabe and Fontane are in different ways committed to Prussia, even though they are critical of it. Lukács is fond of quoting Mirabeau's quip that Prussia went rotten before it was ripe, 'pourriture avant maturité', and extends to Prussia as a whole Bülow's opinion in Fontane's *Schach von Wuthenow* that the army has only a clockwork instead of a soul. In Lukács's view the destructive effects of the Prussian tradition are self-evident. Of the writers he examines here only Raabe and Fontane were fully exposed to the changes that took place in Germany after the foundation of the Empire – the rapid expansion of industry, the persecution of both socialists and Catholics and the development, especially after Bismarck's retirement, of colonial policies. In both cases Lukács attempts to unravel the complexities of their reaction to Bismarckian Germany. He accuses both of them of making significant compromises. For example, both acquiesce in the split between public and private life – a compromise Keller rejected. And in different ways both are ambivalent in their attitudes towards Prussianism; their works contain both criticism and a tendency to idealize Prussia (in Fontane's case), or to fail to provide a sufficiently trenchant analysis of it (in Raabe's). But for all these limitations – and they are perceived as partly inevitable, historical limitations – Lukács defends both of them for promoting the best elements of the humanist German tradition: Fontane, through his ruthless critique of Prussia in a number of novels, *Schach von Wuthenow*, *Effi Briest* and *Irrungen, Wirrungen* (*Errors, Entanglements*); and Raabe, through his portrayal of the inner tragedy of a deformed humanity and through the development of a sense of humour which amounts to a defence mechanism against modern society. Here, as elsewhere, Lukács's praise is dialectical, double-edged. He is anxious to lay bare not just the achievements of the two writers, but also their 'illusions', the necessary limits of their understanding. In this his concept of realism is influenced by the famous letter which Engels wrote to Margaret Harkness in April 1888 and which Lukács had been the first to publish in the *Linkskurve* in 1932. In that letter Engels maintains that Balzac's novels were greater than Zola's despite the fact that Zola had the more progressive political opinions. Even though Balzac was politically a legitimist,

his great work is a constant elegy on the irreparable decay of good society; his sympathies are all with the class that is doomed to extinction. But for all that, his satire is never keener, his irony never more bitter, than when he sets in motion the very men and women with whom he sympathizes most deeply – the nobles. And the only men of whom he always speaks with undisguised admiration are his bitterest political antagonists, the republican heroes of the Cloître Saint Méry, the men who at that time (1830–36) were indeed the representatives of the popular masses. That Balzac was compelled to go against his own class sympathies and political prejudices, that he *saw* the necessity of the downfall of his favourite nobles, and described them as people deserving no better fate; and that he *saw* the real men of the future where, for the time being, they alone were to be found – that I consider one of the greatest triumphs of Realism, and one of the grandest features in old Balzac.[20]

20. See *Karl Marx and Frederick Engels on literature and art*, edited by Lee Baxandall, New York 1974, p.115.

This letter is a foundation document of Lukács's theory of realism. Engels's conception may rest on a dubious premiss: that the great writer somehow has direct access to reality, despite his own judgements and values. But it also has a certain power and it is a key notion in Lukács's attempts to document both the achievements and illusions of German realist writing in the nineteenth century.

Lukács's *German Realists in the Nineteenth Century* may thus be viewed as an attempt to retrieve the 'triumphs of realism' from a Germany whose backwardness and uneven development was at that very moment plunging the civilized world into barbarism. As indicated above, literary realism has been under a cloud lately, because its claim to provide a window onto reality in a direct and unproblematic way makes it susceptible to ideological manipulation. In Brecht's view, for example, Balzac was the outstanding example of an essentially capitalist writer who heaps up the objects of the world in his lengthy descriptive passages, much as a moneylender piles up gold. He was anything but a writer to be held up as a model to the left. However, in Lukács's eyes, as for Engels, realism represented a capitalist truth which ruthlessly swept away the illusions of the ancien régime, rather as Marx describes capitalism itself in the *Communist Manifesto*:

The bourgeoisie, wherever it has got the upper hand, has put an end to all feudal, patriarchal, idyllic relations. It has pitilessly torn asunder the motley feudal ties that bound man to his 'natural superiors', and has left remaining no other nexus between man and man than naked self-interest, than callous cash payment. It has drowned the most heavenly ecstasies of religious fervour, of chivalrous enthusiasm, of philistine sentimentalism in the icy water of egotistical calculation.

Lukács's praise of the 'triumphs of realism' has all the ambiguity of Marx's praise of the bourgeoisie. If capitalism could destroy the illusions of pre-capitalist societies, literary realism was one of the subversive forces assisting in this process. At the same time, potent though realist literature could be, it was as limited as the world view of the bourgeoisie itself. Lukács had maintained in *History and Class Consciousness* that while the bourgeoisie had claimed to speak for the whole of 'mankind' it was creating by its actions an underclass whose interests and perceptions were in conflict with its own. Despite this it could only maintain its hegemony by upholding the illusion that its interests were universal. Realism, like capitalism itself, remains an amalgam of truth and illusion.

It is ambiguities like these that Lukács attempts to define in the present essays. The rejection of realism in the nineteen seventies in favour of experimentalism has now led to something of a reaction. In the women's movement, for example the Lukácsian doctrine of realism was held to enshrine a masculine, patriarchal approach to the novel. Its repudiation implied the rejection of narrativity with its emphasis on closure, in favour of open-ended, experimental, non-narrative writing and film. More recently, however, it has been argued that women should not forego the satisfaction of desire that comes from narrativity.[21] It would be premature to argue that these modern arguments will lead to a reinstatement of Lukács. Nevertheless, it is clear that in our postmodern age the debate between modernism and realism has entered a new phase. It can no longer be claimed that subversiveness lies exclusively with modernism, while dismissing realism as conformist art. In this conjuncture a reconsideration of Lukács's defence of realism could prove timely.

SOUTHAMPTON
JANUARY 1992

21. See the discussion of Teresa de Lauretis in E. Ann Kaplan, 'Feminism/ Oedipus / Postmodernism. The Case of MTV' in E. Ann Kaplan, *Postmodernism and its Discontents*, London, 1988, pp.31–2.

Translators' Note

Lukács has always presented translators with certain problems arising from his frequent use of terminology which either mirrors the particular political debates in which he was engaged at the time of writing or reflects his saturation in Hegelian philosophy. Since these struggles over literary theory were not fought out with the same intensity in an English-speaking context and since Hegelian philosophy has never been particularly at home in the English language, we have assumed that our audience will be less familiar with the ideas expressed by Lukács's terms than German readers. For this reason, certain individual key terms, and our method of conveying the ideas behind them, have been explained below.

Lukács's essays also become more accessible if the general context is borne in mind. The present book marked an attempt to provide fodder for the Comintern's anti-fascist 'popular front' strategy by laying claim to the nineteenth-century 'bourgeois heritage', freeing certain authors from what Lukács saw as their misrepresentation by fascist or reactionary literary historians, who imputed ostensibly conservative contents to books that in Lukács's eyes were basically 'humanist' and 'progressive'. At the same time, this approach allowed Lukács to counter those so-called vulgar Marxists who insisted that literature written by bourgeois authors could not be 'progressive' owing to the respective authors' class origins. In so doing, he was trying to remove the obstacles facing contemporary bourgeois authors who might wish to join forces in combatting fascism alongside the German Communist Party, a line he was to take more explicitly in his *The Historical Novel* (1936–7) and, at a more theoretical level, in *Deutsche Literatur im Zeitalter des Imperialismus* ('German Literature in the Imperialist Period') (1945).
The following are examples of the vocabulary that could give rise to misunderstanding in this context:

volkstümlich – In order to prevent confusion with Brecht's use of the term – to describe literature that adopts the proletariat's means of expression, i.e. the opposite of nineteenth-century realism – we have opted for 'plebeian', which has occasionally been used in prior Lukács translations, or 'popular-plebeian', since the thrust of the word in Lukács's usage is to indicate that particular bourgeois writers' works have roots in the people and can thus be associated with efforts from below to establish true democracy. Lukács deploys the term in such a manner as to expand the alliance of potentially revolutionary classes to include the mass of the population, i.e. not only the proletariat, but also the progressive bourgeoisie, the petty bourgeoisie and the rural population;

Weltanschauung – This denotes a complete system of ideas which defines the way one sees the world. Although modern usage might indicate translation of this by 'ideology', we have preferred to use 'world-view', thus enabling us both to retain the idea that Lukács was combatting Nazi definitions of this particularly German concept and at the same time avoid the untranslated 'Weltanschauung' with its overtly fascist connotations. The adjective 'weltanschaulich' has, for the sake of smooth reading, been rendered as 'ideological';

Tendenz. . . – Other than in the case of the 'thesis play/novel' we have given this as 'tendentious';

Misere – Where Marx uses this it is occasionally given as 'Germany's wretchedness'. We have opted for 'wretched backwardness' as this conveys both the retardation of Germany's economic development compared with other European countries and the negative consequences of this – both actual and psychological – for progressive politics and culture;

gestalten – This Hegelian verb, a signal word in Lukács's essay on proletarian realism 'Reportage oder Gestaltung?' ('Reportage or Portrayal'?), has been rendered variously as 'portray' or 'depict'. It should be borne in mind that these English verbs carry less weight than the German term, which conveys the idea of lending literary – as opposed to theoretical – expression to social phenomena;

Epik/episch – We have given this as *narrative* prose (as opposed to dramatic forms) in order to avoid unwanted confusion with the English term 'epic', which conveys the more specific idea of a story that relates *heroic* actions;

umschlagen – The word used in translations of Hegel's term for the moment at which the thesis becomes its antithesis is 'switch over'. We have avoided this because of its unfamiliarity to English-speaking readers, choosing instead to provide more colloquial verbs, such as 'turn into', 'give way to', etc., to denote the point at which quantitative changes result in a change of quality;

Dichtung and *Poesie* – These terms have generally been given as 'literature', as they do not refer exclusively to poetry but rather to any genre of literature that is of a high standard, as opposed to what Lukács calls *Belletristik* (belles-lettres).

Another minor problem has been Lukács's propensity to quote without giving references. Wherever we – or the editor – have managed to identify the source and locate an existing translation, we have used this. Quotations that are not followed by a reference to an English-language edition are generally our own translations of the original. The titles of works not as yet translated have been left in the original, with a translation supplied where necessary. For quotations from Heine's poetry, available modern English verse translations have been used; other verse is given in the original with accompanying English prose translations.

JEREMY GAINES, PAUL KEAST

German Realists in the Nineteenth Century

Foreword

This collection of essays forms an organic continuation of my book *Goethe and his Age*.[1]* Everything I stated there with regard to the fragmentary manner in which I addressed the subject matter holds all the more true when applied to the present volume. Listing the important authors not dealt with here in detail who nevertheless attract my passionate interest would probably take up more room than the table of contents itself. I would like to take this opportunity to express my particular regret at not yet having been able to engage in a thorough discussion of the works of Friedrich Hebbel and especially those of E.T.A. Hoffmann.

Alongside the subjective reasons for presenting the material in this book in such a fragmentary manner, one must of course appreciate that there is something objectively fragmentary about the development of literature in Germany, an objective lack of continuity. This absence becomes immediately apparent when one compares the development of literature in Russia from Pushkin to Gorky to the German situation. And if one casts a glance over modern French literature, which grew out of the eighteenth century and followed a line leading from Laclos and Constant to Balzac and Stendhal, Flaubert and Zola and then on to Anatole France, Roger Martin du Gard and Aragon, the contrast to German literature is abundantly clear: the latter shows no continuity. A comparison with English literature yields similar results.

What is the reason for this discontinuity in the development of German literature? The answer is, above all, the anachronism of conditions in Germany compared with bourgeois developments in Western Europe. As a young man, in the eighteen forties, Marx had already understood this phenomenon and clearly identified its causes. In the *Contribution to the Critique of Hegel's Philosophy of Law* he wrote as follows:

If one wanted to proceed from the status quo itself in Germany, even in the only appropriate way, i.e., negatively, the result would still be an anachro-

* See Notes on pp.335–354.

1

nism. Even the negation of our political present is a reality already covered
with dust in the historical lumber-room of modern nations. . . . If I negate
the German state of affairs in 1843, then, according to the French computation of time, I am hardly in the year 1789, and still less in the focus of the
present.[2]

The young Marx also recognizes just as clearly what the other side
of the coin of German developments is:

As the ancient peoples went through their pre-history in imagination, in
mythology, so we Germans have gone through our post-history in thought,
in philosophy. We are philosophical contemporaries of the present without
being its historical contemporaries. German philosophy is the ideal prolongation of German history. . . . What in advanced nations is a practical break
with modern political conditions, is in Germany, where even those conditions do not yet exist, at first a critical break with the philosophical
reflection of those conditions.[3]

The full substance of this characteristic of Germany's ideological
condition can be applied to the German literature of the day.
Goethe's disapproving attitude as an old man to the German literature of his time, for which he is so often criticized and which stands
in contrast to the warm appreciation he extended to his English,
French and Italian contemporaries, can also be attributed to this
contradiction between social base and ideology. Goethe as an old
man was painfully aware of this dilemma. In a letter to Knebel he
expressed great enthusiasm for Manzoni's work, adding with a trace
of resignation: 'Oh, why can one not show a German contemporary
the same kindness?'[4]

The most concentrated and heightened form taken by this general anachronism of conditions in Germany is the genesis of a body
of national literature in Germany without there being a unified nation on which it could base itself. This led, first, to German literary
products exhibiting either an over-emphasized individualistic trait
or a provincial character. Second, in the absence of a nation as a real
political entity, the attempts to overcome such provincialism – the
struggles to achieve a national character, a national ethos, etc. –
degenerated into abstract cosmopolitanism or general humanism.
It is perhaps true to say that nowhere else in world literature do
notions such as 'man', 'humankind' and 'the human race' receive
such emphatic expression as they do in German Classicism.

Thus, the great syntheses of German literature come into being:

the Age of Goethe and Schiller in Weimar, and Jena Romanticism. Until now we have stressed only the overall similarity in social base, and thus intellectual and artistic points of departure appear to be similar in formal terms. To put it globally, the greatness of the *Kunstperiode*[5] in Germany rests on the fact that it anticipated the historical development of structures of thought and types of persons in intellectual and artistic terms, although these were based on what were in themselves weak ontological symptoms only barely present in the reality of the time. This same relationship between thought and art on the one hand, and the ontological base on the other, also determined the intellectual and artistic limitations of such behaviour.

However, within what is in general terms an identical ontological base, one must be fully aware of the fundamental differences of content and direction – one might even say opposites – represented by Classical Weimar and Romantic Jena (not to mention Heidelberg). The above quotations from Marx on the ideologically progressive side of an anachronistic Germany are valid solely with regard to Weimar. Romantic Jena is, by contrast, just as much contemporaneous with – and an ideal expression of – the Restoration of the French monarchy as the Weimar of Goethe, Schiller, Fichte, Schelling and Hegel is contemporary with the French Revolution and the rise of Napoleon. Following on from the above, Marx spoke prophetically of the direction in which German society was developing. He stated that Germany had

shared the sufferings of that development without sharing in its enjoyment or its partial satisfaction. . . That is why Germany will one day find itself on the level of European decadence before having been on the level of European emancipation.[6]

In the form of German Romanticism, however, an intellectual and artistic anticipation of this development already existed. The effervescent, sparkling essays and aphorisms of the young Friedrich Schlegel contain a premonition of some elements of the aesthetics and ethics of the decadent bourgeoisie. Moreover, owing to the brilliance with which they are depicted, such decadent[7] traits – both in their general European and in their specifically German variant – come to the fore even more clearly in some of the works of the greatest writer of German Romanticism, namely Heinrich von Kleist.

Having stressed this divergence, let us return to the shared onto-logical base of German Classicism and Romanticism. In all these cases of intellectual and artistic synthesis, we are dealing with an exceptionally weak ontological base in terms of *Heimat*, of a home. The important German figures see the world as a well-defined con-stellation – either from a reactionary or a progressive viewpoint – and capture its essence and lend artistic form to the human types that arise within it. Such thought and such artistic form do not, however, rest on a broad and rich social seam such as existed in England or France at the time, where the multitude of real developmental trends were presented in such a form that their common basis shone through even the most diametrically opposed of solutions. Balzac and Stendhal thus belong together; in this sense Tolstoy, Dostoyevsky and Saltykov-Shchedrin are contemporaries who should be mentioned in one and the same breath. This fellowship, rooted in the objective unfolding of social existence, is lacking in the German literature of the *Kunstperiode*. What makes it great is, as intimated above, the fact that it anticipates developmental tenden-cies on the basis of weak, barely perceptible ontological symptoms. Yet this very same relationship between social base and ideology also determines the limits of thought and artistic characterization. Just as the theoretical syntheses of classical German philosophy could not go beyond an idealistic, mystified conceptual systemati-zation, so too the literary syntheses generated by a similar artistic approach could comprise only the brilliant deeds of isolated person-alities. In his old age, Goethe perceived this weakness in the devel-opment of German literature with great clarity. When talking with Eckermann about Walter Scott's *Rob Roy* he observed, having praised Scott's powers of portrayal:

We see, too, what English history is; and what a thing it is when such an inheritance falls to the lot of a clever poet. Our German history, in five volumes is, on the other hand sheer poverty; so that, after *Götz von Berlichingen*, writers went immediately into private life, giving us an *Agnes Bernauerin*, and an *Otto von Wittelsbach*, which was really not much.[8]

Goethe's observations of course also refer to his contemporary Ger-many as a source of material for literature.

Nevertheless, just because German literature was, of social necessity, so personal in character, it does not by any means follow that it is simply one of great personalities, as chauvinist literary historians are wont to conclude. It may be true that literature is nowhere as peculiarly individualistic as it is in Germany, even when in content it is attempting to provide model exemplars. There is no other great body of literature which, like the German corpus, seems to start at square one with almost every individual writer. Moreover, owing to the social basis involved, this applies to all literary currents, be they progressive or reactionary. *Wilhelm Meister* is just as much an 'isolated' product as is *Michael Kohlhaas, Minna von Barnhelm* just as much as *Prinz Friedrich von Homburg (The Prince of Homburg)*. Even E.T.A. Hoffmann's relationship to the canon of Romantic novella writing is external and superficial.

It would nevertheless be false to see German literature purely in terms of individual personalities or literary currents. Precisely the *Kunstperiode* is, as mentioned above, for all its socio-historical weaknesses, a period of the most violent clashes between progressive and reactionary forces, even if these clashes were confined to the ideological fields of art, religion and philosophy. If they are deciphered in political terms, it becomes clear how exceptionally ferocious they were. And this is no coincidence, for progressive German literature from Lessing to Heine did indeed lay the ideological groundwork for a democratic revolution in Germany.

This whole situation naturally had a profound effect on the choice of artistic form, above all on the genesis of a German realism. The higher the ideological level attained, and the more literary problems reflected the overall European stage of social development, the less the material, i.e. German contemporary and historical reality, lent itself to narrative portrayal. It is no coincidence that hardly any mention was made of German reality in the great German dramas. Between *Kabale und Liebe (Love and Intrigue)* and *Maria Magdalena* there is a vacuum. It is even an exception for the great German dramas to take Germany's past as their subject: *Fiesco* and *Don Carlos, Nathan der Weise* and *Mary Stuart*, the *Jungfrau von Orleans (The Maid of Orleans)* and *Robert Guiscard* are the typical German historical dramas, *Götz von Berlichingen* or *Die Hermannsschlacht* remain exceptions. The situation is similar as regards great narrative prose. Admittedly, in terms of material a specifically German set of themes is in evidence; however, the stylized utopian form adopted in *Wilhelm Meister*, and in E.T.A. Hoffmann's world of fantasy clearly demonstrate the inappropriateness of German life – compared with the reality of France or England – as the subject matter of great prose narrative. All these works were unique, individual syntheses and could thus provide no basis for elaboration and continuation as was the case with literature in France, England or Russia, rooted as it was in the real life of society.

The July Revolution heralded the end of the *Kunstperiode*, although this initially only took the shape of intensified ideological struggle, of a disintegration of the formal syntheses generated by the Enlightenment, Classicism and Romanticism. On the objective side, we can observe a stronger development of capitalism in Germany and the slow but inexorable growth of the *Zollverein* (Customs' Union), which formed the economic basis of a unified Germany. Elements of a unified bourgeois society began to emerge, the basis for a realistic literature in keeping with the nineteenth century. Yet this objective economic growth is at first so slow and weak that it had no immediate impact on the style adopted in literature. A discrepancy remained between, on the one hand, the petty bourgeois German reality of the day and, on the other, the usual all too high-flown general nature of the problems to which literature addressed itself, as well as a tone that seemed lost in the cloudy heights of ideology. Consequently, the historical dramas of the time are still *Danton's Death* or *Napoleon*, *Judith* or *Uriel Acosta*; and for the same reason the most important novel of this transitional period, Immermann's *Münchhausen*, vacillated stylistically between *Wilhelm Meister* and Romanticism, without being able to discover a new realistic form in which to clothe its new contents. As a result – as will be amply demonstrated later – it is left to Heine's *Reisebilder* (*Travel Pictures*) to serve as the German counterpart to Balzac. Hebbel's *Maria Magdalena* – a unique project out of keeping with all that surrounded it – is the exception that only confirms the rule, for the oppressive petty-bourgeois atmosphere characterized there, and the lack of perspective that arises from this, ranks the play well below *Emilia Galotti* or *Love and Intrigue*. It is not only in drama that an expression of this discrepancy is to be found; as I have just mentioned, Immermann's grand project fails precisely when attempting to draw on German reality, the underdeveloped bourgeois society that existed in Germany at the time, as artistic material. The struggle between Goethean or Romantic stylistic elements and realism – as an attempt to describe objective social reality in a general but nevertheless truthful manner – is only a literary reflection of this reality, namely of an economically and socially backward Germany. Such a form of realism restricts an author to portrayals of life and is equally limited in social and intellectual terms. One need only think of the 'Oberhof' episode in *Münchhausen*,[9] or *Die Judenbuche* (*The Jew's Beech*) by Droste-Hülshoff.[10] Similar problems are to be encountered in Willibald Alexis's historical novels.[11]

Thus, owing to objective social realities, the last great period in nineteenth-century German literature to have a progressive thrust was unable to generate a specifically German, contemporary realistic style in the major literary genres, drama and narrative prose.

The defeat of the 1848 Revolution marks a turning point in two ways. First, the struggle of the bourgeoisie, and of the bourgeois intelligentsia at its side, for a democratic revolution, for the radical democratization of Germany, is on the wane, indeed, one might even say it almost completely subsides. Thus, the grand development of literature from Lessing to Heine comes to an abrupt end. To the extent that a certain continuity of style is upheld (the influence of Goethe, Schiller, Platen, etc.), an academic formalism arises: empty, dead and ossified forms, completely devoid of the decisive contents of the Classicist period, namely the struggle for Germany's democratic and national renewal.

Second, the 1848 defeat amounts to a turning-point in the development of capitalism in Germany and by extension in the history of the development of a modern, bourgeois Germany. When reactionary theorists (such as Adolf Bartels, Paul Ernst, and Hermann Glockner) attempt to construct a so-called 'silver age' of German literature out of mid-nineteenth century works, this is precisely the basis of their argument. They combine the growth of capitalism with the reactionary establishment of a unified Germany – viewing this as a new upturn in German literature and philosophy. The problem of German development, however, resides precisely in the fact that economic progress sets in at a time when the bourgeoisie, in particular the German section, has already been transformed into a reactionary class in political and social terms. This situation has a profound effect on German literature. The label 'silver age' entails idealizing this development, tailoring it to suit one's own designs, pasting over the far-reaching contradictions inherent in it, indeed presenting its central ideological and artistic weaknesses as its virtues.

There is no doubt that in a certain sense the age following 1848 constituted progress. Nor is this just the consequence of a now rapid development of capitalism, or just the result of the establishment, at long last, of national unity, albeit in reactionary form, but also in governmental and social terms. Engels emphasizes that the transformation of pre-1848 Prussian absolutism into a 'bonapartist monarchy' amounted, objectively speaking, to a progressive improvement of conditions in Germany. However, recognizing the existence of such progressive elements in a predominantly reactionary course of development means at the same time recognizing the existence of contradictions. Engels occasionally puts this incisively with regard to the German economy and the German novel:

Only with the establishment of the Customs Union were the Germans in a position to comprehend *political economy* at all. It was indeed at this time that English and French political economy began to be imported for the benefit of the German bourgeoisie. Men of learning and bureaucrats soon mastered the imported material and treated it in a way which does little credit to the 'German spirit'. The motley crowd of pen-pushing knights of industry, merchants, schoolmasters and bureaucrats produced a German literature on economics which for triteness, insipidity, shallowness, verbosity and plagiarism, is equalled only by the German novel.[12]

This is an accurate characterization of the average, general state of writing. Of course, such literature is of little interest from today's point of view: it is precisely the most frequently read books of this period that have meanwhile disappeared. But even in the case of those German novels which have entered literary history – Gutzkow's great novels, or the works of Gustav Freytag and, later, Spielhagen – it is the petty bourgeois characteristics of German developments that they stress, the product being an unhappy compromise between a Classical tradition (the novel of educational development, the 'Bildungsroman') emptied of meaning, and the superficial adoption of Western influences (Eugène Sue in Gutzkow, Dickens in Freytag). Moreover, the new turn taken by German life pronounces the death sentence on the previous tradition of great German drama, a form of drama for which the theatre 'was not yet created' in Kleist's words, and, as a result of socio-political developments in Germany, never was created. The great German drama of the old school dies with Hebbel. Richard Wagner's successful stage syntheses were always strongly imbued with dangerous reactionary trends which led German ideology into 1870, 1914 and 1933. (In *Der Untertan* [*Man of Straw*], Heinrich Mann provides a brilliant satirical description of the interconnection between a Wilhelminian bourgeois 'monumentality' and certain traits of Wagnerian drama.) To the extent that a link still obtained between drama and theatre after 1848, it comprised a provincial imitation of the Parisian thesis play.

Heine characterized this transition as follows:

Philosophy and song form the highest pinnacle of German Spirit. This climax has passed, it needed idyllic peace to flourish; Germany is now being carried away by movement, thought is no longer impartial, raw facts have invaded its abstract world, the railway steam engine has thrown us into a fit of trembling mental confusion in which no song can be forthcoming, the coal's steam has scared away the songbirds, and the stench of gas lighting has spoiled the sweet fragrance of a moon-lit night.

German philosophy did indeed not recover after 1848. And the main course followed by poetry is a superficially artificial epigonism. Heine's poems from 'his mattress grave'[13] strike the final chords of what was a past age of a flowering German poetry.

Does this mean that we can write off German literature after 1848? On the contrary; however, it must be said that everything truly valuable and everything that pointed towards a different literary future was squeezed onto the periphery. This is even true in a geographical sense: one need only think of Gottfried Keller and Conrad Ferdinand Meyer – both Swiss – or of Theodor Storm who came from Holstein. Incidentally, the Austrian Anzengruber was the only author of the day to produce original and creative works for the theatre. Indeed, all other literature of lasting value within Germany was also forced onto the periphery – be it the works of Wilhelm Raabe or, despite his successes with the reading public, Fritz Reuter.

It is a moot point to what extent Keller should be regarded as a German rather than a Swiss writer. (The problem will be dealt with in the essay on Keller.) What is certain, however, is that both pre-1848 and post-1848 Germany were decisive for Keller's development and that he had to abandon his émigré existence in Berlin and flee to democratic Switzerland fully to develop his talent as a writer, in order to be able to create great literature in keeping with his democratic convictions. This fact itself passes judgement on the whole development of German literature after 1848. The more eloquent German literary historians are in their endeavours to make Gottfried Keller the key figure in German-language writing after Goethe's death, the harsher their condemnation of the overall development. Keller's Swiss writings demonstrate the course German literature could have taken had the democratic revolution been victorious in 1848. For this would have meant a victory over the ideological ailments of the German mind and thus of German literature.

In their negative aspects, Raabe's and Storm's respective oeuvres show the truth of this statement. What these two authors, and others like them, accomplished – and this was not little – was achieved in opposition to post-1848 German developments. And the fact that their life's work does not figure more prominently in the history of European realism, that it is burdened with provincialism, narrow-mindedness and eccentricity, is a result of the fact that their opposition was neither sufficiently decisive nor sufficiently principled.

This does not stem from some personal weakness on the part of the authors concerned, or at least not solely from a personal weakness. In no other country was bourgeois democracy to decay as rapidly and as disgracefully as in Germany after 1848 and in particular round about 1870 and thereafter. Although Western European writers also stood in conscious or unconscious opposition to their age, and this often led to their isolation, all this took on a much more intensified quality in post-1848 Germany. It was only the working class that posed a true opposition to the Bismarckian system, and as long as their struggle did not touch on literature or influence it, German literature could not escape from the dilemma of either acquiescing in a humiliating deference to the Bismarckian system, with all the intellectual and artistic consequences this would entail, or else of pursuing the solitary existence of an eccentric.

The influence of the working-class movement did not start to make itself felt until the eighteen eighties, when the proletariat's heroism in the struggle against the Socialist Law[14] began to unfold in full force. What was new about the Naturalist movement can without doubt be attributed to this change; as can the fact, however, that the influence of the working-class movement was only fleeting and failed to have a profound effect. This was the result of two equally powerful determining factors, both originating in the same social causes. On the one hand, German writers experienced socialism superficially, as an abstract, utopian way out of the wretched backwardness in Germany, which still existed despite the growth of capitalism and even imperialism (one need only think of Hauptmann's *Emanuel Quint*).[15] On the other, the ever stronger opportunist tendencies within German social democracy prevented the German Social Democratic Party from exercising the same decisive influence on the opposition to the imperialist regime and the culture it spawned as was exerted by the Bolsheviks in Russia. It should also be borne in mind that this inability to make a broad and profound impact was also characteristic of the left opposition within the ranks of the German Social Democrats.

It would go beyond the bounds of this study to describe the German literature of the imperialist period that came about in this fashion. Nevertheless, two observations are warranted in this connection. The first concerns the perspective for the development of the German people. The course followed by the German people since their defeat in the Peasants' War was a false one and, after the failure of 1848, would only ultimately be corrected by taking the road to socialism. A vague intimation of this situation is reflected in all German literary opposition movements in the imperialist period, from Naturalism to Expressionism and beyond. But it remained for a long time no more than a vague intimation. It was the Great Socialist October Revolution, the birth and the external and internal consolidation of the Communist Party, that turned such intimations into more or less clear insights in the heads of writers and that slowly began, after overcoming numerous inhibitions and by a very roundabout way, to influence literary production. Suffice it to mention writers like Heinrich Mann, Arnold Zweig, Johannes R. Becher and Anna Seghers. In this, there is a real sense of German literature being renewed, of a significant form of German realism coming into being – based to an increasing extent on a socialist world-view or at least impressed and influenced by it. For, as the great example of Gorky shows, socialist realism is possible long before a victorious proletarian revolution.

To reiterate: such influences took a long time to assert themselves, and occurred in stages marked by 1918, the Weimar Republic, fascism and its downfall. Just as Germany had for centuries, since the Peasants' War, been the battlefield of European power politics, so too – economically and politically strengthened, yet without having overcome the root causes of the wretched backwardness of Germany – it later became the pivot, the powerhouse of reactionary imperialist ideologies. (And today, American imperialism is endeavouring, with the willing help of its political lackeys in Bonn, to restore the Germany of the Thirty Years' War, the great battlefield of world politics – equipped with the latest industrial and military technology.) Just as, at the time when the ideological preparations were being made for the democratic revolution in Germany, Winckelmann and Lessing, Goethe and Hegel were the leading figures espousing a progressive bourgeois world-view, so in the course of the later, post-1848 imperialist developments, Schopenhauer and Nietzsche and their successors of minor if not puny stature, became patrons of worldwide reaction, became on a world scale the most effective pioneers and promoters of ideological fascism. This new note sounded by German ideology is naturally also to be heard in German literature. The struggle between progress and reaction was never as sharply fought in the field of literature as it was in this period.

This brings us to our second observation. I have attempted to provide a detailed description of these struggles in another context (*Deutsche Literatur im Zeitalter des Imperialismus*).[16] Brief reference must nevertheless be made to the basic battle-lines of this struggle, for what is new about such an interesting transitional figure as Theodor Fontane cannot be correctly understood without a knowledge of this overall framework. And the trends inherent in that framework reach their highest intellectual and artistic pinnacle in the work of Thomas Mann, the greatest figure of present-day bourgeois literature (cf. my little volume *Essays on Thomas Mann*[17]). What becomes visible in the case of Fontane and even more so with regard to Thomas Mann are the detours and modifications by which the best progressive trends in Old Germany were carried over into the realist literature of the age in which the ground was laid for imperialism, and into the age of imperialism itself. Admittedly, in the case of Fontane we can also make out how the same soil brought forth barriers that prevented bourgeois realism from unfolding with the vitality it had in Russia prior to the revolution.

Without such an appraisal of the historical origins and development of German realism in the nineteenth century, one would not be in a position to take a stand on the question as to whether such realism provides a living heritage for the socialist realism that is striving to assert itself in Germany and for progressive literature worldwide. Our observations hitherto have naturally concentrated on vigorously emphasizing the negative elements involved. This is not only the necessary consequence of a concise socio-historical survey, but also imperative in aesthetic terms. For socialist realism can only make that heritage its own in the necessarily critical manner if the traditions of the bourgeois past are subjected to critical discussion at three different levels.

First, a critique is necessary of the bourgeois limitations imposed on the intellectually and aesthetically most accomplished works of art in class society. The new social and human contents of socialism lead necessarily to new artistic viewpoints on a higher plane and demand radically new solutions in the field of artistic form if narrative depiction is to be adequate to its object.

Second, in order to make this transition successfully, an exposure of the specific national weaknesses of every literature, particularly German literature, is urgent and indispensable. However much socialist realism may signify something fundamentally new and of a greater value in the development of literature, however much it thus represents a qualitative leap forward (although, of course, the concrete artistic realization of this leap is only possible in the course of a long evolutionary period of struggle), its concrete point of departure nevertheless necessarily remains the progressive direction of the literature and art of the respective country so far (and of world literature in general). This situation gives rise to those elements which, particularly in the early stages, form some of the central questions in the ideological and aesthetic struggles that follow. Suffice it to refer here to the fact that – even in the field of literature – the specific character of the development of the German people always moves between the wrong poles: a) an abstract cosmopolitanism (as distinct from true internationalism); b) a narrow-minded provincialism which often expresses itself in reactionary chauvinism (as distinct from true patriotism). The struggle to overcome the ideological relics of capitalism is clearly a general phenomenon of every transition to and battle for socialism, while equally obviously, the concrete form it takes everywhere is the struggle against the weaknesses of the development of the specific nation in question.

Third, however – and this can never be over-emphasized – although socialist realism overcomes all the limiting and limited tendencies inherent in the evolution of bourgeois society, it is at the same time the fulfilment of all previous attempts at progress that also arose from this same process of human evolution (i.e. of bourgeois society). It is of decisive importance for literature and art that all struggles to bring about socialism take a particular national form. For it would be wrong precisely in this context to regard the form as something superficial. Lenin remarks that 'Form is essential. Essence is formed. In one way or another in dependence on the essence. . .'[18] The national nature of form in socialist realism, which is to be seen directly in the critical appropriation of the best literary traditions, is therefore something much more profound than external form. If artistic forms possess sufficient vitality to survive this kind of critical reshaping, it is because they are deeply rooted in the best characteristics of a people, those characteristics which enable the people of that nation to find the human resources to aspire to a further and higher development of their own type. These characteristics are, however, subject to incessant change and have radically to turn themselves upside down if they are not only to make possible but also to bring forth socialist individuals. There can indeed be no physical transformation of a substance without recurrent patterns, no higher development in leaps and bounds that does not contain certain elements of continuity. A literature that does not feature such recurrence and continuity will at best be able to depict the new – which has arisen out of the struggle with the old – in abstract but never in concrete terms. It will never truly move the masses, will never be truly plebeian or national. Not least among the exemplary qualities of Soviet literature is the fact that its most prominent works contain in sublated form the best national traditions, sublated in the Hegelian sense of both preservation and of elevation to a higher level.

The history of German literature confronts every German with a whole series of such problems, of which we have mentioned but a very few. These problems are German questions, above all in as much as they are productive and point the way forward. Where real values are concerned, Germanness by no means implies something narrowly national, something provincial when measured on a world scale. For all its weaknesses and limitations, in terms of its discontinuity, German literature – even that of the nineteenth and twentieth centuries – is a high-ranking international phenomenon that demands everyone's critical attention. The more resolutely at least a part of the German people tread the path of liberation and peace, the path to real democracy, the more important such a critical inquiry into the past, present and future of Germanness, of German culture and literature becomes for every person concerned about peace and human liberation. It is obvious that this critical inquiry is a question of intellectual survival for every German.

Even within the relatively narrow parameters we have set for our subject matter, this book can only provide excerpts, fragments – essays in the true French meaning of the word. However, as the approach taken and the problematics of each and every fragment is imbued with an awareness of these overarching problems, the author hopes to have made a modest contribution to clarifying them.

BUDAPEST, JUNE 1950

The Tragedy of Heinrich von Kleist[*]

Kleist is a direct precursor of modern German literature in the strict sense of the term: literature in its later stages, in decline. Kleist's life and work were not understood by his contemporaries. It was not until a relatively late date that he achieved literary fame, which reached a pinnacle during the imperialist period. At this time he was, at least in educated literary circles, the most popular Classical author, and the one felt to be the most modern. It was, above all, the Kleistian drama that was increasingly held up as a model, gradually supplanting the Schillerian drama. Gundolf was already to describe Kleist as the authentic German dramatist, as a writer whose primary instincts were those of a dramatist, and who had not developed into one by way of various complicated detours, as had Lessing, Goethe and Schiller. Fascism has taken this idea still further; for the fascists, Kleist the dramatist becomes the great creative counter-figure to the humanism in the dramas of Goethe and Schiller, the Germanic Dionysian among the dramatists, with whose aid it is possible to overcome the humanist Reason contained in Goethe's and Schiller's plays.

Claims from this quarter regarding Kleist's modernity have some real basis in Kleist's personality. Here, a reactionary history of literature need resort to fewer forgeries, fewer omissions and to suppressing fewer facts than are necessary in the attempt to make Hölderlin, for example, or Büchner out to be the forefathers of reactionary artistic movements.

Franz Mehring gives an essentially accurate assessment of Kleist's personality when he states, in a variation of a remark Treitschke once made in passing, that Kleist 'remained a Prussian officer of the old guard throughout his life'. In so doing, Mehring correctly underlines the word 'remained' and thus rejects the idea that Kleist had ever been in real opposition to the decaying Prussia of his day, a theory constantly put forward by various leftists endeavouring to 'redeem' Kleist.

[*] First published in *Internationale Literatur*, no. 8, 1937.

Even the initial determination of what characterizes Kleist confronts us with a fundamental contradiction: the Old Prussian lieutenant who at the same time has become a precursor of the modern tragedies of monomaniac passions and of the incurable, impenetrable human loneliness of capitalist society; precursor of modern tragicomedies of the hysterical; and pioneer of the Dionysian barbarization of Antiquity, of the destruction of the humanism that drew on that Classical tradition.

A closer examination of Kleist's personality and his fate reveals that these contradictions go even deeper. Kleist represents in the starkest manner and with all its reactionary tendencies the Romantic opposition to the Classical humanism of the Weimar Period of Goethe and Schiller. And yet Kleist remained lonely and misunderstood in an era that indiscriminately brought to the fore mediocre representatives of Romantic thought and feeling, of a blinkered patriotism in the war with France (Adam Müller, Fouqué, etc.). Although Kleist held an extremely reactionary political position, which he championed journalistically with consummate skill in the *Berliner Abendblätter* (1810–11), he also became completely isolated in political terms. At odds with and despised by his family, receiving only very reserved and condescending praise from his political allies among the Romantics (Arnim, Brentano, etc.), he ended his life in misery on the eve of the national stirrings that led up to the 'War of Liberation'.

Kleist's death – he committed suicide jointly with a woman determined to die because of an incurable disease – heightens the eccentricity that characterizes the whole course of his life. All the more so, since joint suicide as a desirable way out of the insoluble contradictions of life had always played an important role for Kleist. Indications are to be found in different periods in his life which suggest that the joint suicide had not occurred at an earlier date only because of the absence of a willing partner. Even in his parting letter to Marie von Kleist, the confidante of the last period of his life, Kleist openly stated that he had only been unfaithful to her, had only gone to his death with another woman, because she, Marie, had turned down his proposal that they should die together.

I

The desolate loneliness of all human beings, the hopelessly opaque nature of the world and all that occurs in it: this forms the mood of the Kleistian tragedy, both in life and in literature. Sylvester von Schroffenstein, a figure in Kleist's first drama, lends what is perhaps the most vivid expression to this feeling:

In your eyes I am probably a puzzle;
Is that not so? Now console yourself, God is one for me.[1]

Kleist himself couches it in similar terms in a letter written towards the end of his life: 'It cannot be an evil spirit at the head of our world; just a misunderstood spirit!'[2]

Seen from the viewpoint of such an attitude to life, death takes on a horrifying and yet seductive shape. For Kleist and for the people Kleist created, death is an omnipresent abyss that is both enticing and at the same time makes the blood run cold. (This attitude to life was later made famous in world literature by Poe and Baudelaire.) The tragic effectiveness of Kleist's scenes can largely be attributed to his superb literary concretization of this attitude to life. Only one scene – recounted by his contemporaries – is known from a tragedy written in Kleist's youth, which has either been destroyed or remained a fragment. In it, Austrian knights are playing dice prior to the Battle of Sempach. Jokingly they wager that whoever throws black will fall in the battle. The first player throws black; there is general laughter and jocularity; the second also throws black and the sneering grows more uneasy, and once every one of them has thrown black a gruesome premonition is given of the battle to come, one in which the Swiss completely annihilated the opposing army of knights. Such scenes are, however, to be found in all of Kleist's tragedies. In his *Hermannsschlacht*[3] the Roman warlord Varus is surrounded by the Teutonic tribes. Fearless Roman that he is, he prepares to take counter-measures. A Teutonic spirit suddenly appears in the forest. The decisive atmospheric part of the dialogue is as follows:

VARUS: Where do I come from?
SPIRIT: From nothing, Quintilius Varus!. . .
VARUS: And where am I going?
SPIRIT: Into nothingness, Quintilius Varus!. . .

VARUS: Where am I?. . .
SPIRIT: Two steps from the grave, Quintilius Varus, close between nothingness and nothingness![4]

It is this depiction of human beings and their fates in terms of a
radical nihilism, of this tension between a horror of death and a
yearning for death, of people's deathly solitude, of their abysmal
separation from one another, that makes Kleist's writing so exceptionally 'modern' in the closing decades of the capitalist world.

But how is this decadent feeling for the world compatible with
Kleist's conservative *Junkerism*, with the fact that he remained an
officer of the Old Prussian school?

This question seems insoluble in abstract terms, for these diametrically opposed poles would seem utterly to exclude each other.
But, as with all questions, its concretization shows that in life these
opposites are connected with one another. It is common knowledge
that even very far-reaching shocks to one's feeling for the world,
deep-rooted crises of the soul that threaten to turn into outright
despair, do not necessarily shake a person's stance towards the social basis he or she has inherited. Indeed, if the crisis has from the
outset taken such a shape that it links a person's purely individual
fate *directly* with the vaguely religious and metaphysically swollen
question as to the 'meaning of the world', such a crisis can in fact
contribute towards the consolidation, the conservation of the person's original social instincts. That is what happened to Kleist.

The underlying Kleistian experience of solitude in itself clearly
arose (although Kleist never understood this) from the position of
the human individual in relation to society under capitalism. It is
striking that Kleist's simplest and most vivid descriptions of solitude stem from his stay in Paris. They describe the loneliness of the
individual in a big city.

People pass each other coldly by; you wind your way through a multitude
of people on the streets, who show nothing but indifference, above all to
their own kind; before you have had time to take in a particular image, a
further ten have rushed by, taking its place; no one has ties with anyone
else, and no one has ties with you; you greet other people politely, but your
heart is as superfluous as a lung in an airless bell-jar, and if for some reason
a feeling escapes it, it finds no echo – like the sound of a flute in a hurricane.[5]

Kleist only sporadically and irregularly subjected the presence of such loneliness to emotional and intellectual scrutiny. To the extent that he was aware of the social roots of his feelings, this consciousness only strengthened his blind and angry hatred of everything new, of the new world of bourgeois society that was dawning in Germany. Thus, he viewed Paris, the French Revolution, Napoleon, Fichte, Smith, Hardenberg etc. with hatred. Yet this hatred remained dull, instinctive, emotional. It never took Kleist beyond the bounds of his original horizon, beyond the horizon of Old Prussia. Indeed, in the course of time, this hatred reconfirmed his ties, which had already begun to loosen, to the Old Prussia of absolutism and the *Junkers*.

In Thomas Mann's profound and perceptive novella, *Tonio Kröger*, the Russian painter Lisaweta calls the hero, a decadent artist, a 'bourgeois who has taken the wrong turning'. By this she means that although all his decadent-refined oppositional tendencies clearly distinguish Tonio Kröger sharply from the average bourgeois and indeed make him appear foreign, eerie, indeed criminal in the eyes of the bourgeois, they nevertheless repeatedly and unerringly lead him back to the fold of the bourgeoisie. One can with the same justification term Heinrich von Kleist an Old Prussian *Junker* who 'has taken the wrong turning'.

Kleist lost his way very early on. Having become an officer owing to a family tradition, he felt himself out of place in the decaying army of Frederick the Great. He found satisfaction in neither war nor peace. He longed for human community, for a world-view which could accommodate his instincts in harmonious equilibrium. First and foremost, this obviously meant having to come to terms with the Enlightenment. In this context it is Rousseau's influence that is decisive for his development. And it is again very characteristic of Kleist's 'modernity' that he was one of the first (at least in Germany) to transform Rousseau's cultural criticism into an unambiguous, reactionary rejection of bourgeois society. Admittedly, as we have already seen, this took on a specifically German form. Indeed, the weakness of the German Enlightenment thinkers is characterized by their disregard for the French philosophers' liberalist critique of society, turning the latters' atheist critique of religion back into a 'religion of Reason'. It is out of this soil that Kleist's Rousseauism arises, out of the earth of a watered-down Enlightenment that had particularly lost its bite with regard to social criticism. Enlightenment thought had even taken root in the *Junker* circles of the Prussia of the day; we know, for example, that Voltaire and Helvétius were the main reading matter of Kleist's favourite sister, Ulrike.

Kleist's critical involvement with the Enlightenment, his attempt by means of an impassioned and arbitrary study of science to acquire a world-view by force, came to an abrupt end with the now-famous 'Kant Crisis'. Reading Kant (or, as Ernst Cassirer believes, Fichte) led to Kleist's hopes suddenly being dashed. All the reactionary, anti-humanist trends in fascist literary theory take this 'Kant Crisis' as their starting point. Werner Däubel, for instance, following Paul Ernst's example, holds Kant to be the great obstacle in terms of world-view to a German tragedy coming into being. Kant, in Däubel's opinion, sounded the death-knell of Schiller the tragedian, and Kleist's 'Kant Crisis' accordingly represents the revolt of healthy Germanic instincts against contamination from this alien Western rationalism. (It is a great shame that at times even anti-fascist writers have fallen for this reactionary argument.)

Lack of space prevents us here from discussing this question of Kant in all its aspects. A few words must suffice to indicate that Schiller's debate with Kant occurs on a fundamentally different plane from Kleist's. Schiller attempted to overcome Kant's subjective idealism by steering it in an objectively idealist direction; as a theorist he becomes one of Hegel's predecessors, as an author – for all their differences in terms of creative leanings – Goethe's companion-in-arms. For Kleist, the great contradictory problems in Kantian philosophy are of absolutely no significance. It is precisely Kant's most incontrovertibly progressive achievement, namely the destruction of the metaphysical proof of God's existence, even in the watered-down form typical of German Enlightenment thought, that had such a devastating effect on Kleist. Kleist had, prior to this period of crisis, pasted together a world-view for himself that centred on a sort of transmigration of the soul, the continuation of human and moral perfection of the individual after death. In a letter to his bride-to-be and sisters he complains of the emptiness and aimlessness that had arisen as a consequence of this belief:

The thought that we on earth know nothing, but nothing of the truth, that what we here call truth is called something completely different after death, and that consequently all striving is completely pointless and fruitless – this thought has shattered me in the very sanctuary of my soul.[6]

We are concerned here with the *immediate* relationship of Kleist the individual to the universe, to a personified God. Kleist himself always described his typical problems with great uprightness and vividness. Very soon after the 'Kant Crisis', he journeyed to Paris, accompanied by his sister. On the way, their coach crashed, an incident from which they luckily emerged unscathed. Kleist writes to his bride-to-be about this incident:

So a person's life hung on the thread of a donkey braying! And if it had come to a close, would *that* have been all I had lived for? Would *that* have been the Creator's intention for this dark and enigmatic life on earth?. . . Is *that* what I should have learned and done in life and nothing else?. . . To what purpose Heaven has chosen to limit life, who can tell?[7]

It is clear from all of the above quotation that the Kleist's 'Kant Crisis' had only shaken a Protestantism somewhat modified by Enlightenment ideas (the human soul's immediate relationship to God).

The radical nihilism we have already encountered grows out of this crisis, the Kleistian mixture of a horror-filled fear of death and a longing for it. And it is of great interest to note how the fundamental structure informing Kleist's relationship to the world is continually reproduced in these crises, namely the question as to the immediate, absolute meaning of Kleist's existence as an individual in the world. All intermediate links, all mediating elements, in particular those of a social nature, are radically excluded from Kleist's sentiment. The fact that his hopes suddenly give way to radical despair does not alter the fact that his fundamental approach is founded on a blinkered religious base. It is precisely this form of intellectual crisis that has made Kleist so popular in recent times, in a period when the bourgeoisie's philosophical world-view has sunk to its nadir. Such crises, subjectively authentically felt but objectively childish, appear to have something especially 'profound' about them precisely in this period.

We can thus now perceive the contours of Kleist's attitude to the world with great clarity. We can see how he reduced the problems of humanism at the time to a monomaniac, individual psychology, and accordingly experienced the illusory problems that this generated with a wild pathos and religious fervour. The key note in his development following the 'Kant Crisis' is that he went to any lengths to be highly disparaging of Reason, which in his eyes was not suitable as a cognitive tool to explain the meaning of his own individuality in the world's scheme. This feud with Reason led to a glorification of unconscious feelings, of instinct and to a contempt for all forms of conscious awareness.

Every spontaneous, involuntary movement, is beautiful, and everything becomes distorted and disfigured, the moment it understands itself.[8]

The pathos of this over-emotional exaggeration was heightened to the point of hysteria, monomania, because what was involved was no longer a truly naïve feeling, no longer an instinctive certainty. Kleist believed his feelings were constantly threatened and struggled incessantly with this threat. For it was only his feelings that could serve him as a compass guiding him through the rest of his life, and he continually sensed, even if only dimly, that these feelings could not be a reliable guide. 'Do not confuse my feelings,' says Kleist's Hermann when a political decision is demanded of him. And all Kleist's heroes live – just like their author – locked away in themselves as if in a dream: a state that permits them, within the vacuum of the utterly self-sufficient ego, to heighten their passions to the point of monomania. But the vague awareness of the external world is always present in them. They are forever shuddering in fear of waking from the dream, and vaguely sense that such an awakening is inevitable.

However, it was precisely this pathos-filled monomania that maintained the presence of an 'Old Prussian *Junker*' within Kleist. Admittedly, the decadent traits thereof made him appear increasingly sinister to his mediocre peers, even to his sisters. Nonetheless, this did not prevent these traits in Kleist from becoming ever more rigid, tense and tenacious: as the pathos-instilled, tragically transfigured instincts of a Prussian *Junker* who had 'taken the wrong turning'.

The collapse of Prussia at the Battle of Jena (1806) suddenly forced its way into this asocial emotional world of Kleist's. This collapse triggered off an important crisis in Kleist, as it did in many of his contemporaries. In the ensuing troubled times in which the national uprising against Napoleonic France was in the making, Kleist's reactionary instincts – of a political and social nature – came strongly to the fore. Kleist's reaction to the events took the form of a dogged anger at all things French, a blind, raging nationalism. He dreamt of Napoleon's assassination. He wrote rabble-rousing poems imbued with genuine emotion, calling upon the German people to slay the French as if they were mad dogs or pestilent beasts. He wrote *Die Hermannsschlacht*, his first drama to go thematically beyond the bounds of subjective passions; the only German drama of the day in which the desire for national liberation – for all its reactionary contents – was magnificently expressed. He made his debut as a journalist and became editor of the *Berliner Abendblätter*, in which he fought, alongside all the advocates of Romantic-Junkeresque reaction, Arnim, Brentano, Adam Müller, etc., against Hardenberg's plans for reform. He turned his newspaper into an organ of the *Junker* opposition to the reforms of Stein, Scharnhorst and Gneisenau.

This, Kleist's resistance to the Prussian party of reform – it would go beyond the realm of this study to analyse the inner contradictions and discord within this party more closely – clearly demonstrates his reactionary leanings. Contradictory, naïve and utopian though the plans of Scharnhorst and Gneisenau may essentially have been, the very moderate, conciliatory reforms they forced through nevertheless afforded the only chance of setting up a Prussian army that would later be able to secure victories over Napoleon. The politics professed by Kleist and his like-minded companions would ineluctably have led to a new Jena.

Yet, seen from the point of view of Kleist as a person and as a poet, this development was a great step forward. For the first time, Kleist was deeply moved by national, by general, indeed by social problems. For the first time in his life he acted within a community. 'He who had taken the wrong turning' had, as it were, found his way home.

Finding his way home should also be set in quotation marks. For the real *Junkers*, Kleist remained a down-at-heel man of letters, as he did for his family. Having visited his family following the collapse of the *Abendblätter*, Kleist wrote to Marie von Kleist of the impression he had of this visit. He would rather die ten deaths, he said, than have to experience another such meeting. In the government's eyes, a government that had suppressed the *Junker* opposition to the *Abendblätter* by ruthless application of the censorship laws, Lieutenant Kleist, although retired, was nothing but a troublesome petitioner. For his Romantic comrades-in-arms he was a stubborn lone wolf. Arnim and Brentano's pronouncements on him are very reserved and circumlocutory; they are sparing with praise and combine it with such a degree of reservation that, given that Kleist towers above them in poetic stature, they appear almost comical today.

Kleist was shipwrecked, both in his personal and his public life. Prussia allied itself with Napoleon for the campaign against Russia. The party that espoused war with Napoleon had thus suffered a defeat.

It is really not our purpose here to try to specify which of the many motives was the main one that drove Kleist to suicide following this collapse. Each sufficed to make him feel there were no prospects for his future life.

Kleist, however, went to his death at the height of his maturity as a writer. His last drama, *Prinz Friedrich von Homburg* (*The Prince of Homburg*), is also a further step forwards to the extent that here the passions of the characters are not only – as in *Die Hermannsschlacht* – imbued with and focus on national, social content. In his last play Kleist, for the first time, portrays a conflict between individual and society, a conflict between opposing social forces. Admittedly it is at precisely this dramatic climax in his development that his Prussian *Junkerism* comes most clearly to the fore: the objective social power which he dramatizes and glorifies is none other than that of Old Prussia.

II

The psychology of Kleist's plays, and that of his novellas as well, is based explicitly on the solipsistic isolation of human passions and, as a consequence, on the insurmountable *mistrust* that the characters in his writings feel towards each other. The fact that all of Kleist's dramas are filled with a burning but unfulfillable longing to burst through the bounds of solitude and overcome the feeling of mistrust serves merely to accentuate the predicament, for such longing is necessarily condemned to failure in Kleist's work. In keeping with this psychological basis, the plot adopted in Kleist's plays and novellas centres on delusion, misunderstanding and self-deception. The plot is always patterned on the continual exposure of these misunderstandings, although in a highly original and complex manner. Namely in such a way that each case of exposure renders the tangled web of misunderstandings all the more opaque, that with each further step the thicket of misunderstandings becomes all the more impenetrable and only the final catastrophe – which often occurs suddenly and without connection to what went before – brings the true state of things to light.

Die Familie Schroffenstein (*The Schroffenstein Family*), the work with which Kleist made his debut as a writer, already contains all these tendencies in a sharply contoured, artistically mature form. This exceptional level of maturity in artistic and especially in dramatological terms clearly distinguishes this play from the first works of other dramatists. The author's youthfulness is only evident to the extent that the specifically Kleistian problems are lent expression in a completely bald manner, without resort either to some human, social background or to an attempt to portray a real basis for them. The medieval world, knighthood, the bloody feuds between the two branches of the Schroffenstein family are drawn in a purely conventional manner, are reduced to what is necessary for the denouement in purely technical terms.

The theme of this play bears a close resemblance to that of Shakespeare's *Romeo and Juliet*. Yet precisely this thematic relatedness is well suited to illuminate the originality inherent in Kleist's conception. The difference is visible in the way the plot unravels. In Shakespeare, there is a real bloody feud between the two houses (Tybalt kills Mercutio, Romeo kills Tybalt, these acts ensuing directly from the family feud). In Kleist, the murder – which the plot takes as its point of departure – is not the real result of a struggle between the two branches of the family, but is rather only perceived as such by those involved. The blood feud that ensues on the basis of this misunderstanding produces a series of similar misunderstandings that are not cleared up until the end. Only then do the remaining family heads realize that they have been killing each other off, exterminating each other's children, for absolutely no reason. In Shakespeare, furthermore, we are dealing with the tragic conflict between, on the one hand, new, humanist passions and the right to individual love and, on the other, the medieval barbarism of a blood feud. In Kleist we encounter the portrayal of a 'fatefulness' that grows out of a confused web of misunderstandings that cannot be disentangled.

This fundamental difference is reflected in the psychology of the main heroes, the lovers from the feuding families. Romeo and Juliet's love for one another is an eruptive passion that sweeps away all else in its wake, and which is, regarded in isolation, something completely pure and unproblematical that leads to tragedy only because of a social conflict. Kleist, however, even embeds the general mistrust in the psychology of the lovers themselves. They demand, in truly Kleistian fashion, absolute trust from one another and yet their relationship is constantly steeped in mutual distrust. In Shakespeare's play a magnificent tragic mood is created: the lovers' passion sweeps like a purifying storm through the rotten remnants of feudalism. The individual tragedy of love reveals – without any explicit commentary to this effect – an enormously liberating insight into the course of human development. In Kleist's drama, by contrast, a storm-laden, sultry and brooding atmosphere is created: the eruption of dark, passionate feelings interlaced with self-torment, sophistry and hypercritical reflections.

By virtue of the plot's structure, Kleist's first drama is not far removed from the 'fate tragedy' so fashionable at the time. Bourgeois literary historians have racked their brains over when and where the 'fate tragedy' first arose and whether Schiller's *Bride of Messina* can be considered one or not. A somewhat closer examination of the world-view underlying the 'fate tragedy' clearly reveals the unfathomable and therefore fetishized necessity of all social occurrences in nascent capitalism. At the beginning of the development of capitalism, following the collapse of the primitive medieval religious notion of a well-disposed God-Creator intervening directly in the course of the world, the Calvinist mythology of an unknowable pre-determination of human fate (predestination), the mythology of a hidden God, arose. This mythological conception of a world whose course was unfathomable gained aesthetic form in the age of ideological crisis in which Kleist lived: namely the 'fate tragedy'.

The seemingly remorseless necessity of this 'fate' – blindly following its course, utterly indifferent to all human concerns – reveals itself in its aesthetic form to be mere illusion. Hebbel places his finger on this accurately when he writes of *The Bride of Messina*:

Why does this all happen? What is to be washed away by this blood?. . . One asks oneself to no avail! In this drama, Fate plays blind man's buff with human beings.[9]

Hebbel's criticism pierces to the very heart of Kleistian drama.

It would nevertheless be wrong to judge the different 'fate tragedies' of this period mechanistically according to some preconceived pattern. For Schiller, the tragedy of fate consisted in man becoming embroiled in guilt from socio-historical necessity, i.e. without him willing it, indeed against his will. This is why he is successful in portraying this feeling in *Wallenstein*, and why it is only the abstract depiction in *The Bride of Messina*, ignoring as it does the social aspect, that has such absurd consequences. This absurdity, which was necessarily only an isolated experiment in Schiller's work, forms the central problem in the Romantic treatment of the theme of fate. In Zacharias Werner's work, for example, to name the most important representative in this connection, this absolutely meaningless and incomprehensible aspect of fate has become the sole theme.[10] All human and social agencies have been occluded, the necessity inherent in the capitalist present has been reduced to a pale shadow, a blind, fatalistic, exaggerated 'world'. Intentionally, it is purely superficialities (certain dates, specific objects) that have become the vehicles of a fate that always has dire consequences.

Kleist's conception must be distinguished from those of both Schiller and the Romantics, although the common social basis for the respective conceptions does bring forth a certain number of common traits. For, as we have seen, in Kleist it is the individual psychology of each person through which a cataclysmic fate is seen to act. Kleist became a forerunner of the modern drama in the narrow sense of the term precisely by virtue of this. The fatalism that reigns, for example, in Strindberg's later plays has a very similar structure, a very similar combination of penetrating individual psychology and mystical belief in the inevitability of fate.

The basic dramatic problems inherent in the composition of *The*

Schroffenstein Family also form the underlying scheme for Kleist's later dramas. We come across similarly fateful secrets everywhere. That is to say, we encounter unsettled situations, which, owing to the mutual, insurmountable mistrust of human beings, develop into ever greater entanglements, a web that can only suddenly be resolved in the tragic end. However, the product is something organic and original, because in Kleist's work the plot structure and the psychology of his characters form a perfectly unified whole within his perception of the world; because, in other words, psychology and plot are not just attuned to one another but arise spontaneously from the same well of sentiment.

The shape Kleist gives his dramas is the diametrical opposite of the Classical Greek mode of composition. The Classical 'recognition scenes' of which Aristotle speaks and which also play a great role in Shakespearean drama, are always the revelation of a previously unknown, but rational interconnection. The route, along which they are but points of intersection, leads from darkness into light, from confusion into clarity, even if the final light is the merciless highlighting of an insoluble, tragic contradiction. This insolubility is, in the case of the Greeks and Shakespeare, clearly portrayed as an important crossroads in the historical course of humankind. Behind its insoluble contradictoriness lurks the real contradiction of human progress. In Kleist's work, each 'recognition scene' leads but further into the webs of confusion. It may clear up a misunderstanding between the people in the play, but at the same time it creates a new, deeper-seated, even more calamitous misunderstanding. The 'recognition scenes' do not reveal the dialectics of socio-historical progress, but only the ever deepening emotional abyss that we constantly find between the solitaries who inhabit the Kleistian world.

In the course of Kleist's development, the conflicts, both inner and external, depicted in his work become ever more important. The weighting given to the humanness of the characters increases, and the portrayal of their passions becomes ever stronger, more intensive, richer and more varied. In his great, unfinished work, *Robert Guiscard*, Kleist attempted to find for his conception of fate a vehicle of expression that was of true significance in terms of human history. It is the plague that is the fate threatening Guiscard, leader of the Normans. The Kleistian 'secret' of the plot consists in the fact that Guiscard has himself been struck down with the plague, but his affliction is kept strictly secret. Here, Kleist wanted to imbue his conception of fate with a Classical simplicity, grandeur and generality. In the introductory scenes that have been preserved, he does indeed attain a level of greatness that neither he nor modern drama as a whole otherwise achieved.

One must ask, however, whether there is not a connection between such futile wrestling with this theme – which finally led to the playwright's breakdown and attempted suicide, to his destruction of the existing manuscript – and the nature of the theme itself. In Sophocles's *Oedipus Rex*, on which the Kleistian play is clearly based, there is also an outbreak of the plague. But in Sophocles's drama the plague is only a point of departure in terms of mood and denouement, only the cause that triggers off the real Oedipus tragedy, which then takes place on a completely different plane. In the Kleistian version, however, the disease is the hero's real antagonist. And since this 'antagonist' is not a social force, it cannot don the guise of a personified opponent, cannot result in an intensification of the plot. Guiscard struggles with an invisible ghostly antagonist.

The fundamental weakness – which was always regarded as a particular 'profoundity' – of Kleist's world-view consists in his bypassing all social mediation in his direct juxtaposition of people and fate (i.e. mythical and fetishized social forces which he elevates to the status of supra-social status). Such a world-view makes the dramatic portrayal of this tragedy (*Robert Guiscard*) impossible. The profound indifference that Kleist at that time showed towards the socio-historical occurrences of the age is to be seen in his suicide attempt following his failure to complete this play. Although he was already clearly hostile towards Napoleon, he nevertheless wished to participate as a volunteer in the latter's expeditionary force against England, and dreamed of his own death being bound up with the glorious sinking of the Napoleonic fleet. For Kleist, the historical events form but a background to his purely individual fate. Their meaning has no relevance for him.

The great dramas involving erotic passions on which Kleist embarked following the failure of *Guiscard* (*Amphitryon*, *Penthesilea*, *Das Käthchen von Heilbronn*) continue in this subjectivist direction.

In none of these plays does the conflict between objective socio-historical forces, nor that between the passions of an individual and one such objective force, take on central importance. On the contrary, the centre of the drama is shifted quite consciously and radically to focus on the inner dialectic of purely subjective, purely erotic passions.

Kleist had, however, developed substantially as an artist since writing *The Schroffenstein Family* and was no longer able to content himself with the purely conventional surroundings of his first play. Admittedly, the medieval world of chivalry in *Käthchen of Heilbronn* is still painted with fairly conventional strokes. Yet, the fairy-tale like, fantastic elements of psychology and plot lend the whole a different, much more lively atmosphere than was exhibited by Kleist's earliest play. In the other two erotic dramas Kleist takes a new tack, one that was to have serious consequences for German drama as a whole. In order to be able to give graphic shape to completely eccentric individual passions, intensified to the height of monomania, Kleist creates his 'own', self-invented, purpose-built social world as a basis and background for these plays. The state of the Amazons in *Penthesilea* is an example of such an exotic world. Penthesilea's passions do not arise out of a specific world, as do passions in Shakespeare's or Goethe's work. Her passion is the product of the self-contained and solitary soul of Kleist, the isolated, self-isolating poet who cut himself off from the world. And – quite unlike the great writers of the past – a suitable 'social environment' is fabricated for this passion that supposedly 'explains' it.

In this connection, Kleist had only one precursor in the history of the German drama, namely Schiller's *Bride of Messina*, where a fantastic mixture of the Orient, Classical Antiquity and the Middle Ages was tailored to fit Schiller's conception of fate. In later German drama, this artificial form of a socio-historical environment, this artistic inversion of the relationship between society and passion, comes to play an important role. One need only think of Hebbel's *Gyges and his Ring* or Grillparzer's *Libussa*, etc. The effect this form of dramatic composition had, however, extends far beyond its immediate function. After all, in Kleist's writings this compositional mode springs from the endeavour to create a social background for a very eccentric passion. With the spread of decadent feelings among wide sections of the bourgeoisie, this form of stylization became at least externally superfluous. It proved possible to replace it with a factually existent milieu consisting exclusively of decadent emotional eccentrics, which had isolated itself from the overall life of society and magnified its internal problems to the status of the great conflicts between man and fate. The 'special' world of emotional eccentricity is, in other words, no longer an artist's stylized construct, but has been brought about by capitalism itself. However, this 'proximity to life' only seemed to exist. For such a circle of eccentrics was even more hermetically isolated from the major problems of social life than their artificially-created predecessors had been. The latter had at least been concerned with questions of real life, even if these were subjectivistically distorted; now everything became reduced to the quaint particularities of outsiders who were completely detached from the life of society. In this sense, plays such as Wedekind's *Erdgeist* (*Earth Spirit*) and *Die Büchse der Pandora* (*Pandora's Box*) are the modern, naturally minor and subaltern great-grandchildren of this period of Kleistian drama.

In addition to this formal, compositional aspect, the structure of the dramatic plot, *Amphitryon* and *Penthesilea* also mark a change in the history of German drama in another respect. Their themes are drawn from Classical Antiquity. However, these dramas modernize Antiquity, and *dehumanize* it: they transpose the emotional anarchy of a new nascent barbarism into the world of Antiquity. Here Kleist is the forerunner of those trends that culminated in theoretical terms in Nietzsche and in practical, dramatic terms in the imperialist period, for example in Hofmannsthal's *Electra*. (It surely need not be pointed out here that culmination is used here in the sense of the climax of the barbarization of Antiquity and not in aesthetic terms; in aesthetic terms Hofmannsthal is so far inferior to Kleist that a comparison would be an insult to the latter's memory.)

Penthesilea is also a typical product of this stage in Kleist's development to the extent that here the most radical and consistent emphasis is given to the purely subjective, monomaniac nature of individual passion. Penthesilea and her Amazons burst in like a meaningless whirlwind in the middle of the Trojan War. Neither the Trojans nor the Greeks know for or against whom the Amazons are fighting. And within this berserker-like, meaningless struggle, Penthesilea detaches herself from the Amazons, and Achilles detaches himself from the Greeks. They play out their tragic love-hate relationship, the tragedy of two lovers in the air-tight vacuum of isolation from their peoples, in the air-tight space of solitude and mutual misunderstanding. The grandiose and grotesque quality of this drama consists in the fact that two respective armies with their battle-wagons, elephants, etc., play the role of mere props. The furious Penthesilea throws her army into battle against Achilles, in a manner similar to the despairing captain in Strindberg's work who throws his lantern at his wife.[11]

Kleist repeatedly stresses the purely subjective nature of the dramatic necessity that prevails in the play. Penthesilea and her Amazons are, for example, meant to flee from the Greeks:

MEROE: Was it impossible for her to flee?
THE HIGH PRIESTESS: Impossible,
    Since nothing holds her from without, no fate
    Nothing but her foolish heart -
PROTHOE: That is her fate.[12]

Since both protagonists are now isolated from their surroundings and from one another by their passion, since both are completely ensnared in their obsessive state of mind, the action can again, in truly Kleistian fashion, consist only of a chain of major misunderstandings. Penthesilea, vanquished, sees herself as the victor in the battle with Achilles, and on this basis Achilles is ready to play the great lovers' scene with her. Once this fraud has been uncovered, and Penthesilea angrily thirsts for revenge, Achilles, blindly in love with her, thinks that the duel with Penthesilea is only for the sake of appearances, a sham that serves only to fulfil the laws of the Amazons in order for him, now effectively vanquished, to enjoy matrimonial happiness with Penthesilea. And then, in this duel, Achilles is killed. Penthesilea, jarred out of her bloodthirstiness, commits suicide.

The awakening of Kleist's patriotic feelings at the time of his fight against Napoleonic France instils a new, more objective quality into his plays, for they now begin to portray significant national events. A decidedly upward trend is to be detected in Kleist at this time. *Die Hermannsschlacht* may still essentially be a drama in the old Kleistian vein, but the protagonist's passion is now focused on an objective, national entity, namely the liberation of the Germanic tribes from the Roman yoke. A new quality now informs the maze of misunderstandings and delusions, which once again provide the basis of the plot: it now involves Hermann consciously and craftily deceiving the Romans, in other words a successfully applied chain of conspiratorial dupery. As a consequence, these deceptions only result occasionally in Kleistian tragic disillusionment and the latter is only pivotal in the Thusnelda/Ventidius episode. It is highly revealing of Kleist the playwright that we find here a premonition of Hebbel's and Ibsen's tragedies of the relationship between man and woman, namely the woman's indignation that the man treats her as an 'object' (Hebbel), and the form taken by tragic disillusionment – Thusnelda throws Ventidius to a starving bear – is truly Kleistian. We see here in concentrated form all the contradictions of Kleistian poetics precisely as a result of the national hatred which figures in this love affair: an extremely modern refinement of feeling, a dialectic of emotions, combined with the most brutal and refined barbarism.

The Prince of Homburg is Kleist's first and only play to hinge on the conflict between an individual and society. His participation in the cause of national liberation is reflected in his progress as a dramatist, even though Kleist championed the most reactionary side in the struggles. For the dramatic question at the centre of *The Prince of Homburg*, the conflict, is intimately bound up with the efforts of the Prussian reformers, with the attempt to rejuvenate Prussia from within on the basis of a newly kindled national feeling.

Precisely here, however, the consequences of Kleist's Old Prussian *Junkerism* become most apparent. Kleist is unable to furnish this idea of rejuvenating Prussia through the mobilization of popular feelings with any objective historical contents – it remains at the level of subjective individualist indignation and intensifies to the point of subjective individualist affirmation and enthusiasm. The endeavours of Stein, Scharnhorst and Gneisenau undoubtedly contributed to this mixture of 'reaction and regeneration' which Marx speaks of as being characteristic of all uprisings against Napoleonic France. Their plans for Prussia's rejuvenation were accordingly contradictory and utopian. However, when, in a memorandum to the King of Prussia, Gneisenau writes, 'The security of the throne is founded on poetry,' he has something concrete in mind, both politically and socially, namely the true national enthusiasm brought about by the reforms, the cessation of the indifference hitherto shown by the population towards the absolutist monarchy.

Kleist was, as we know, an enemy of all such reforms (his personal liking for Gneisenau in no way altered this fact). Thus, he can only portray the social ambience of the ossified Old Prussia. Admittedly, this Old Prussia, the Prussia of the Great Elector, appears in the drama not only as a social force but, without it having been changed, is also glorified as such, as Old Prussia, at the end of the play.

This world is contrasted to the purely individual, solipsistically secluded passion of the Prince of Homburg. It is characteristic of Kleist that he equips his hero with a far-reaching personal psychological motivation for his breach of military discipline, which forms the main conflict in the play. He first presents the prince in a somnambulist state and then shows us how the latter pays no attention whatsoever when the battle orders are issued and in fact does not in any way register what the plans are. (It is interesting to note that this scene is prefigured in *Penthesilea*, with regard to both the heroine and Achilles.)

The conflict can, as a result, unfold exclusively within the soul of the hero. In Kleist's conception it can, moreover, only end with the prince grasping the absolute necessity of discipline, assessing his own breach of discipline as a crime against the state, a crime for which he deserves, in his own opinion, the death penalty.

Old Prussia unchanged thus triumphs over the individualistic revolt of the emotions. Clearly, Kleist was so much under the sway of the currents of the day that he nevertheless sought to find a balance. Since, however, his hero's emotions have no social content, this balancing act is bound to be eclectic. The prince's bride lends clear expression to the eclectic nature of Kleist's chosen solution when she attempts to save Homburg in her conversation with the Elector:

Yes, I know, I know: the rules of war must never be allowed to fall into contempt – nor must our tender feelings. . .[13]

By virtue of this conception of the conflict, this, Kleist's last and most mature drama, is, despite the marvellous dramatic quality of its scenic structure, imbued with the inner character of a *Bildungsroman*. It takes as its subject the education of the Prince of Homburg – from a fanatical anarchy of emotions to an acceptance of Prussianism. Kleist was unable to lend true dramatic expression to the drama which was inherent in the historical transition of the time and which made it possible to write such a play in the first place. This was because he had not understood the clash of the opposing social forces of his age, and what he had experienced of it he was only able to recast in this essentially narrative, novelistic form.

It may sound paradoxical, considering that Kleist is generally regarded as the sole truly 'born' German dramatist, yet the fact remains: Kleist the playwright progressed from taking the novella as the basis of his earlier plays, to adopting the novel structure for his later dramas. The contradiction between this and the conception of drama dominant today soon resolves itself for the reader if one bears in mind that the current bourgeois theory of drama completely ignores the substance of drama, namely the collision of opposing *social* forces, of great *historical* contradictions. Instead it claims that the inner dialectic of heightened individual passions suffices, if taken to a sufficiently sharp point, to constitute a drama, indeed even generates a 'deeper' form of tragedy than that which is 'only' based on social conflicts.

The problems do not reveal themselves clearly until we take the case of such an unusually gifted playwright as Kleist. The majority of his successors cannot aspire to the creative powers that would justify a comparison with the truly great dramatists of the past. Kleist, however, is one of the greatest masters of the theatre, of theatrically effective yet nevertheless intellectual dialogues, in world drama. Dialogues that in a flash illuminate convoluted situations between people in a crystalline, concise and concentrated fashion and at the same time further the action of the plot, dialogues such as the retorts that are forthcoming on Guiscard's appearance or when the orders are issued in *The Prince of Homburg* – these are only to be found in the works of the greatest playwrights. Furthermore, we should bear in mind Kleist's exceptional ability to create characters: he was a master of both the great and the lovable, the gruesome and the comic, drawing on the same simple but by no means trivial techniques of characterization. What he lacked in order to become – as Wieland hoped – a new Shakespeare was 'only' the clarity of world-view and 'only', as a necessary consequence of such clarity in great writers, the healthy, the rational inclination to conceive of passions normally. However, a whole world is concealed in this 'only'. Kleist's Käthchen is, for example, in terms of disposition, one of the simplest and most lovable figures in German drama, almost attaining to the status of Goethe's Gretchen and Klärchen. Yet, simply because Kleist bases her beautiful strength and her ability to make sacrifices on a Romantic-pathological rather than a normal, human foundation, the figure becomes stunted and distorted.

Such flaws on the part of someone of Kleist's greatness demonstrate where the real problems in tragedy and drama lie. The Kleistian conception of passion brings the drama close to the novella: an over-exaggerated individual case finds radical presentation *in its arbitrariness*. This is quite a legitimate approach in the novella for it is precisely there that the enormous role which chance plays in human existence is supposed to be made palpable to the senses. If, however, the occurrences thus portrayed remain at the level of such arbitrariness – and Kleist in fact even exaggerates this individual, arbitrary nature of the characters' psychology and of the events of the plot – in order to be lifted to the heights of the tragic without being portrayed in terms of its being objectively necessary, then something contradictory and dissonant is the inevitable result.

Kleistian drama is, in other words, far removed from being able to illustrate the great path taken by modern drama. This path extends from Shakespeare via Goethe and Schiller to Pushkin's *Boris Godunov*, and later, owing to the ideological decline of the bourgeois class, finds no worthy successor. Kleist's dramas, by contrast, constitute an *irrationalist byeway* taken by drama, which, as we have shown, is precisely why they serve as a model for the plays of the period of decline and have received a belated popularity in it.

For encapsulated, individual passion tears asunder the organic link between individual fate and socio-historical necessity. The ideological and poetic foundations of a true dramatic conflict are destroyed with the severing of this link. Drama is given a narrow, confined basis that is purely individual and private. This contradiction is particularly marked in the case of Kleist's work, for in the course of his development he learned to bestow objective form on the external expressions of inner tragedies with great plasticity: in dramatic scenes, in dramatic dialogue. As, however, major dramatic conflict was lacking, these expressions have no truly living, historical life. Only in *The Prince of Homburg* are there intimations, but no more than intimations, of such a great, generalizing dramatic-historical portrayal of a stage in the development of humankind. Kleistian passions are admittedly typical passions within bourgeois society. Their inner dialectic reflects typical conflicts of the individuals in bourgeois society, individuals who have seemingly become 'windowless monads'.

In the process, however, Kleist – and this is true of all modern drama in the narrow sense – goes into depth only in psychological terms: socio-historically he stops short at the immediate, given form these conflicts take and does not portray those social forces that in reality generate such a psychology and its conflicts, albeit unknown to the individuals concerned. Kleist is thus the first important nineteenth century dramatist to start privatizing the drama, the social form of poetry *par excellence*. For this reason he is the greatest ancestor of modern drama in the narrow sense, an exemplary model for the distortion and dissolution of dramatic form in bourgeois literature's period of decline.

III

Only twice was Kleist as a writer confronted with conflicts which situated the passions he portrayed in powerful, generalized contexts that placed the individual passions within the great frame of historicity: in *Michael Kohlhaas* and in *Der zerbrochener Krug* (*The Broken Jug*). What is noteworthy in this connection and of particular importance with respect to the problem of Kleist the tragedian is that these great masterpieces are not tragic dramas but rather a novella and a comedy.

In *Michael Kohlhaas* Kleist again describes an exclusive, all-consuming passion that leads to ruin. Yet, firstly we are not presented with a passion that is the already fully developed characteristic of a strange individual, but rather the passion arises and unfolds before our eyes and is heightened to the point of raging pathos only gradually. Secondly, the object of this passion is from the outset something social. A *Junker* has illegally seized hold of the horses that belong to Kohlhaas, a horse trader. All he demands is what is rightfully his, and it is not until all the peaceful means to achieve this have failed that, bitterly angry, he turns on the violent and corrupt *Junker* society of the sixteenth century. In other words, Kohlhaas's passion is from the outset – precisely owing to its social and not purely individual roots – rational in the sense of great tragic writing.

Kohlhaas's fate is indeed unusual and above-average, as is every truly tragic fate. And Kohlhaas's psychology also departs from the average course, reaching the heights of tragic tension. Yet it is never pathological in the sense that Penthesilea's passions or those of Käthchen were. Kohlhaas is a normal person who makes very modest, very moderate demands of society. Every reader can well comprehend and appreciate that the frenzied rage with which he takes matters into his own hands is the result of these demands not being fulfilled, and in particular of the violent and corrupt manner in which the *Junker* society treats him.

Kohlhaas's tragic fate fits organically into the series of what may be considered the most important pieces of modern prose: that is, into the series of prose writings that attack what is in bourgeois society the insoluble dialectic of justice, texts in which the insoluble contradictoriness of the legality of class society is powerfully expressed. These contradictions culminate in the realization that it is typical of class society that the individual must either submit unconditionally to the injustice and lawlessness of the ruling classes or is forced to become a criminal in the eyes of society, indeed in terms of his or her own conception of morality.

Kleist depicts this great tragedy in the framework of an exceptionally evocative account of Germany in the sixteenth century, one that is profoundly accurate in historical terms. As a politician, Kleist was an ally of the most reactionary Romantics. Politically speaking, he was a party to Romanticism's reactionary falsification of history, the transformation of feudal relations into the harmonious idyll of the landowner and his serfs, the idealization of the Middle Ages. But the disintegrating medieval world of *Michael Kohlhaas* has nothing of Fouqué's, or Arnim's social idyll about it. With unsparing energy, Kleist portrays the criminal brutality, the barbaric, cunning trickery of the *Junkers* of that age. He shows how all the public authorities and the courts are but a nepotistic arm of the *Junkers* and corruptly cover up and support their crimes. Kleist even has an intimation of the limitations of the ideological leader of that age, namely Luther. Naturally, the conversation with Luther has a decisive influence on Kohlhaas. But this is historically correct. Objectively speaking, the Lutheran *Junkers* – despite all of Luther's pronouncements – did as they wished. They felt no inner obligation to Lutheranism.

Thus, a significant historical narrative was created; although we must particularly emphasize that Kleist's treatment of historical objectivity follows quite an idiosyncratic tack. The only model on which he could orient himself – just as did, at a later stage, Walter Scott – were the dramas of Goethe's early period. It is only regrettable, however, that this masterpiece should have been disfigured by some cranky Romantic elements that Kleist incorporated into it.

Bourgeois literary history is forever trying to equate Kohlhaas with the obsessive heroes of Kleist's love plays. This is, as we have seen, a completely erroneous approach. Indeed, the contrary is true, for the narrative achievement of this novella is intimately connected with the fact that its hero is by no means as close to Kleist's heart as were Penthesilea and Käthchen. As a consequence, Kohlhaas passion does not live itself out to the full in scenic lyricism but rather fits itself neatly into the objective framework of events told with masterly concision. The perfection of the story resulted precisely from the fact that the Kohlhaas problem obviously touched Kleist less directly, less lyrically and tragically, than did the love tragedies of his heroes and heroines, because for him it was more an objective occurrence than a passionate experience, more something observed than something felt, more a reflection of reality than an expression of his inner being. This discrepancy shows all too clearly the tragedy of Kleist as an author. In sharp contrast to the greatest authors in world literature – whose heights his powers of artistic description occasionally matched – he came closest to the deepest problems of reality the more distanced his passions, his innermost feelings, were from the reflection of precisely this component of reality. His most deeply felt experiences did not – as they did in the case of Goethe and Pushkin – lead Kleist onwards to the core of reality; the opposite is true: the more deeply personal they were, the further away from this kernel they bore him.

This interconnection is even more evident in *The Broken Jug*. We know something of the history of this comedy, certain extraneous factors that prompted Kleist to write it. On the one hand, as Kleist himself tells us, an engraving he saw in Switzerland and, on the other, a sort of literary competition he held with some of his colleagues of the time, some unimportant writers. Without wishing to overestimate the importance of these causes, it is nevertheless noticeable that the comedy arose from a creative mood quite unlike the violent and painful eruptions that led to the lyric tragedies. Even Gundolf perceives that *The Broken Jug* cannot be included among the list of Kleist's normal works but rather occupies a special place in his oeuvre.[14] However, because Gundolf views Kleist's hysterical barbarism as the starting-point of the Germanic drama, he quite consistently belittles the value and significance of this outstanding comedy. He views *The Broken Jug* as the 'isolated work of an expert, executed solely with his talent, as a test of his technical ability'; a stylistic exercise using odd and remote subject matter... What public interest was attached to this strange special case in which a roguish judge tries to save himself from a shameful discovery by resorting to all sorts of evasive measures?

It is obvious that Gundolf stands the objective context and all objective evaluation on its head. One should not, however, forget that Gundolf is, after his own fashion, quite consistent in approach and radically follows through to its logical conclusion a viewpoint that is widespread in literary history today. If one were namely to view (as Gundolf does) literature solely as the *expression* of the author's individuality or (as does vulgar sociology) to regard it as the expression of a class psychology and not the reflection of *objective reality*, then Gundolf would be right. As an expression of Heinrich von Kleist's personality, *The Broken Jug* is indeed but an episode, a mere testing of his powers of artistic description following the tragic collapse in *Guiscard* of his attempt to depict his perception of the world as a major tragedy, and prior to the great lyrical eruptions of his erotic passions in *Penthesilea* and *Käthchen of Heilbronn*. Moreover, *The Broken Jug* can in no way be explained in terms of the 'class psychology' of Kleist, the *Junker* of Old Prussia.

What is decisive for a Marxist view of literature is the artistic work and its relation to objective reality. In *The Broken Jug* we have a magnificent canvas of the Prussia of the day, presented to us – be it for political or aesthetic reasons – as patriarchal Holland. The Dutch setting is, however, only secondary and serves as artistic decoration. What is of the essence here is, as in *Michael Kohlhaas*, the artistic destruction of the Romantic idyll of the 'good old days'. The despotism of patriarchal jurisdiction outside the towns, the authorities' maltreatment of farmers, the farmers' deep mistrust of everything that came from 'above', their feeling that one could only protect oneself from the authorities by bribery and fraud, irrespective of whether such bribery took the form of money, presents or sexual compliance: all of this merges to form an outstanding picture of rural Prussia at the time. And it is very interesting to note how Kleist's favourite psychological motifs are imbued here with social content. Kleistian mistrust also plays a strong role in the heroine of this comedy. She is mistrustful of the authorities, even of the 'good' auditor who unmasks the village judge and finally restores order. It would be unjust to admonish Kleist for this optimistic ending. A comedy was only possible in the first place on the basis of the illusions expressed by such optimism. Here Kleist shares the illusions of Molière and Gogol.

Artistically, *The Broken Jug* is Kleist's most accomplished work. The gradual unravelling in the final twist of the tangle of misunderstandings on which the situation rests is not discordant or out of place as it is in Kleist's tragedies; rather, it heightens the comedy's wonderfully structured composition and its smooth progression to the climax.

It is, however, instructive to cast a glance from the vantage point of such perfection back over the structure of Kleist's dramas. We have already stressed their novella-like foundations. If we study the action more closely then we can determine the existence of a *comedy-like* quality in the structure and the plot of all Kleist's dramas. Let us bear in mind that *Amphitryon*, Kleist's pathos-laden mystical drama, takes over the structure and denouement of Molière's comedy almost unchanged. Kleist's changes consist solely of the tragically deepened psychology of the main characters, that is, in the intensification of their erotic experiences to the point of the mystical. The main factor underlying the plot in *Käthchen of Heilbronn* – namely that Käthchen is in reality not the daughter of a simple artisan but rather of the emperor – also has a certain comic touch about it. Hebbel, who was a passionate early champion of Kleist's fame as a writer, and who in some respects continued in the Kleistian dramatic tradition himself, took passionate exception to this motif and condemned the drama, despite some individual felicities, precisely because of it. For he correctly argued that the true drama resided in the fact that the human power of Käthchen's love triumphed over feudal prejudices; the drama was destroyed as a drama when Käthchen is declared daughter of the emperor. This is true. But it is also obvious that such a motif, the clarification of existing confusion by virtue of a fact unknown to the participants, can indeed function as the basis for a comedy.

This analysis could be applied to all Kleist's dramas. Suffice it for us to refer to our observations on the structure of *Penthesilea*. And it is highly characteristic of Kleist that he dealt with a similar plot in the novella *Die Verlobung in St. Domingo* (*The Betrothal in Santo Domingo*). Here the negro uprising and the massacre of the whites form the background to the plot. A white man flees into the house of a black, who by chance is not at home. There, a mestiza falls in love with the white man, and the love is, as is always the case in Kleist, magnificently portrayed by means of the dialectics of misunderstandings and mistrust on the verge of a tragic abyss. The negro returns home. The mestiza wants to save her beloved but uses means that only reinforce his mistrust of her. As a consequence, he kills her, only to feel truly Kleistian remorse at the side of her corpse on realizing that her help has been instrumental in securing his liberation. Theodor Körner, a very mediocre contemporary of Kleist's, turned this novella into a comedy with a 'happy ending'. The comedy is bad, and Hebbel is quite right to reject it with the utmost contempt.[15] Yet it is very characteristic of the problem at hand that Körner was able to take over the plot of the Kleist novella almost unchanged and only had to remove and water down the psychology of mistrust in order to arrive at a comedy.

Naturally, a flaw repeated so consistently in the conception of his works is no accident in the case of such an important writer as Kleist. This is all the more true in that precisely his proclivity, and the lyrical-ecstatic means adopted, to cover over the objective fragility of the dramatic structure of his plays was of great importance for the development of the drama from the middle of the nineteenth century onwards. It would seem to me that this form of dramatic construction is intimately linked with that crisis of world-view that was first given expression in major dramatic form by Kleist.

The problem in question is that, for these more modern writers, the tragic and the comic cease to be objective categories of reality and increasingly become subjective viewpoints from which the phenomena of life are explained. It is only at a relatively late stage that writers become conscious of this subjectivization and relativization of the tragic and the comic respectively. One could say that they are first present in a conscious form in Ibsen's work, which in turn influences Strindberg and particularly Shaw. Kleist still regarded his subjective, tragic feeling as something absolute. However, that is merely fanatical conviction and changes nothing substantially with respect to the objective fact that the tragic conflict does not arise in his works from the events portrayed, from the exposure of its socio-historical roots. The objective dilemma which arises here as a consequence of a purely individualistic, asocial and ahistorical dramatic approach, influences the style of the Kleistian drama throughout.

Here we are once again dealing with a fundamental trend in the drama of the second half of the nineteenth century, a trend of which Kleist was the most important forerunner. The ever more pronounced loss of the objectively tragic, parallel to a strengthening in the deeply subjective experience of the tragic nature of personality in the contemporary bourgeois world, gives rise to a unique dramatic style. In short, a *theatrical and lyric* substitute is forthcoming for the objectively tragic, for the tragic as embedded in the action.

This lyricism functions in the case of Ibsen or Strindberg via the atmospheric values of specific, realistically observed details, which are, however, always stylized and over-stressed in theatrical and lyric terms in relation to this tragic (or tragi-comic) mood. In Kleist's work, the tragic mood emerges solely from what could be called the musical effect of these theatrical and lyrical elements. It is of great interest and not unimportant that in his anti-Wagner period, Nietzsche viewed *Penthesilea* as one of the great precursors of Wagner's musical dramas. The exceptional international impact of Wagner's opera can be attributed precisely to the fact that he was successful in devising a musical theatre to replace the objectively dramatic, objectively tragic properties that had been lost. There can be no doubt that the psychological characterization of Wagner's heroes is very closely connected with the dramatic writing of Kleist and Hebbel (and with analogous trends in the development of the French novel and French poetry, with Flaubert and Balzac). We cannot, of course, go into the problematics of Wagner's music dramas here. Suffice it to state that, from the point of view of the development of drama itself, Wagner's work represents the most effective use of theatrical lyricism as a substitute for dramatic action. And, as an examination of the theatrical values in the 'leitmotif technique' adopted by Ibsen and others clearly shows, we are concerned here with a lasting trend in the development of drama.

In the case of Kleist, of course, all these problems and contradictions exist only in a germinal form. On the basis of the above remarks, the reader will, however, realize that it is the entrancing lyrical pathos of *Penthesilea* that makes it inconceivable for this work to be transformed into a comedy or tragi-comedy. This relativism is to be seen much more clearly wherever Kleist is forced by the form of the novella to refrain from deploying this lyrical machinery – indeed, this would seem to have gradually dawned on Kleist himself when he takes over Molière's *Amphitryon* almost unchanged. In the manner outlined above, the mystical love poetry sets the protagonists on a plane beyond that of the comic or the tragi-comic. The sub-plot, which Kleist took from Molière and made even more coarse and plebeian emphasizes this relativity; it is at times clearly expressed in some of the retorts by Sosias, Amphitryon's servant. Mercury namely disguises himself as Sosias, Jupiter as Amphitryon, and the confusing mix-up leads in the domain of the servants to purely comical, coarse effects, whereas in the case of the protagonists it results in a tragic mysticism of love. After being given a sound thrashing by Mercury in the guise of Sosias, the real Sosias, believing the other to be himself or at least his double, says:

That's the way it is. If it's my mouth it comes out of, it's childish nonsense, pay it no attention. But if it'd been a great one flogged himself himself, you'd hear the whole world crying miracle.[16]

Here, Kleist inadvertently and unconsciously arrives at a plebeian-realistic self-criticism of his own dramas. For, in the case of the 'great persons' in this drama Kleist does in fact himself 'proclaim a miracle'. And Kleist, in this realistic self-criticism, portrays, unconsciously, the plebeian critique of the social foundations of his dramatic approach: he illustrates the emotional and objectively false over-exaggeration and distortion of the 'great persons' who, detached from the healthy life of the people, experience their individual problems in a state of obsessive, mystical eccentricity.

All Kleist's works are full of such outbreaks of realism. Suffice it to point to a few examples. As we have seen, Kleist does not treat the liberation of old Germany as an idyll in *Die Hermannsschlacht*. And in addition there is the daring realism with which Kleist transforms Thusnelda, the Teutonic national heroine, into 'a silly goose' to use his own words. The most important realistic intrusion occurs in Kleist's last play, in the renowned and much criticized scene centring on the fear of death in *The Prince of Homburg*. Here, although it was his intention on the one hand to glorify Old Prussianism and on the other to express the somnambulist pathology of his hero, Kleist in fact offers a shatteringly true and authentic picture both of the fear of death and of the inner moral conquest of such momentary cowardice. Heine rightly held these scenes to be a major and humanly authentic protest against the conventional Prussian notion of the hero.

What is only to be seen in the occasional intrusion of realism in the other dramas appears in perfected form in Kleist's masterpieces, *Michael Kohlhaas* and *The Broken Jug*: namely his magnificent ability to create an objective and critical realism, the ability to reflect reality in a rich and three-dimensional vein, with unabashed authenticity and veracity. These masterpieces signify for Kleist, the *Junker* of Old Prussia, that 'triumph of realism' which Engels spoke of with regard to Balzac the royalist.

Yet such a 'triumph of realism' never occurs by a miracle, but always on the basis of subjective and objective preconditions. The subjective preconditions comprise the writer's talent and honesty, i.e. his ability to grasp and depict reality in all its complexity as well as his courage to portray that world which he has really seen and in the manner in which he has really seen it. There is no need for us to discuss Kleist's talent here, although we should briefly emphasize his unabashed subjective honesty. Kleist admittedly fought politically on the side of the extreme reactionaries, yet in terms of character he contrasts very sharply and very favourably with the adventurist rabble alongside whom he fought his battles. The contrast in terms of humanness and morality between Kleist and Adam Müller, his most intimate friend during his final years, is particularly striking. Adam Müller participated in the reactionary campaign waged by the *Abendblätter*. But, on the one hand, he at any case secured through the agency of Gentz the backing of the Court in Vienna and, on the other, a submission he made to Prime Minister Hardenberg still exists, in which he proposes both to open an 'oppositional paper true to the cause of the government' and to be remunerated for his loyal services. He did in fact receive a regular allowance from Hardenberg. Kleist, by contrast, brusquely rejected all attempts at bribery by the government and went to ruin, both materially and morally, in his reactionary struggle, but as a subjectively honest man.

This honesty that characterized Kleist is one of the important subjective conditions for the 'triumph of realism' in his masterpieces and in some parts of his overall output.

The reason why the 'triumph of realism' did not constitute the principal characteristic of Kleist's entire oeuvre – as Engels had found it to be in that of Balzac, and Lenin in that of Tolstoy, where expressions of narrowly reactionary class psychology formed mere sunspots – is to be sought in the Germany of the day. Balzac experienced the tremendous chain of violent fluctuations between revolution and reaction in France up until 1848; Tolstoy lived through the contradictory developments of rural Russia from 1861 to 1905. These major revolutionary developments, these turning points in the progress of society, made great realists of Balzac and Tolstoy. Although Kleist also experienced a period of upheaval, it was one that took place under the most confused and atrocious conditions, namely that transformation of Prussia of which Mehring with great acumen remarked that the ignominious defeat at the Battle of Jena was Prussia's equivalent of the liberation of the Bastille. The objective power of this reality was not sufficiently unambiguous and strong to transform Kleist's reactionary outlook and decadent individualism into an objective overall artistic portrayal of reality. His masterpieces thus remain but isolated cases in his total oeuvre.

Yet it is only from an understanding of these works that the real tragedy of Heinrich von Kleist is to be appreciated. In terms of 'class psychology' he was a blinkered Prussian *Junker*, in terms of literary intentions he was an exceptionally forceful pioneer of most of the decadent currents in later bourgeois literature. And in the few cases where, counter to his actual intentions, reality caused a 'triumph of realism' he was one of the most important realists in the whole of German literature. Goethe who, on account of his healthy distaste for decadence, did not like Kleist, calls him a 'body that nature had intended to be beautiful in the grip of an incurable disease'.[17] It was the Germany of the day that was afflicted with this incurable disease, and no avenue was open to Kleist by which he could overcome it. It was Germany's wretched backwardness, as well as his own reactionary and decadent instincts, that led to his tragic end.

1936

Eichendorff[*]

Wir sehnen uns nach Hause,
und wissen nicht, wohin. . .
We long for home
and know not whither. . .

EICHENDORFF

There are writers of whom it can be said that their entire oeuvre or at least a large proportion of their writings forms part of the living body of literature, and there are others who have only produced isolated works that have survived the test of time. Eichendorff belongs to the latter category. Very little nineteenth century German literature is as popular as his poetry and his *Aus dem Leben eines Taugenichts* (*Memoirs of a Good-For-Nothing*). His other writings – novels, novellas, plays, literary history – have fallen deeper into the realms of oblivion than most of the other products of German Romanticism. They do not even have admirers among the specialists, as do many of Arnim's or Brentano's works; they are for the most part genuinely dead, that is to say, compulsory reading only for literary historians.

The varying literary fortunes of his works can only be explained with reference to Eichendorff's social situation and personality.

He came from an ancient aristocratic line and was raised in his family's Silesian castle. His student days coincided with the heyday of Romanticism, and he studied in the intellectual centres of the period, Halle (1805) and Heidelberg (1807). It was here that he met and became friends with numerous leading Romantic thinkers and poets (Steffens, Schleiermacher, Arnim, Brentano, Görres, etc.). In the course of his travels to Paris and Vienna he came into contact with Friedrich Schlegel, Adam Müller and Gentz. He saw active service as an officer in the Wars of Liberation and subsequently entered the Prussian civil service (until 1844). He died in 1857, after the political movements of the eighteen forties and the 1848 revolution had led him to develop increasingly conservative views.

[*] First published in *Internationale Literatur*, no.6, 1940.

We are, in other words, clearly dealing with an example of feudal Romanticism in its purest form. This impression is strengthened by the fact that Eichendorff was a Catholic from birth, and that the most extreme reactionaries among the Romantics, Görres and Friedrich Schlegel, influenced his intellectual development.

On closer inspection, however, this apparently simple picture becomes more complicated. Eichendorff may indeed have been a practising Catholic with all the accompanying reactionary traits, yet his Catholicism was not problematical, having been a part of him from birth. It had not presented itself as the solution to a severe inner crisis, as it had done for many Romantics. Eichendorff's Catholicism did not mean that he had reneged on earlier ideas of religious and political freedom, as had Friedrich Schlegel, which is why his Catholicism did not exhibit Brentano's pathological ecstaticism or Görres's fanatical propagandistic streak. His Catholicism was more cheerfully conventional, a part of his everyday life; it narrowed his philosophical horizon but made very little difference to the normal conduct of his outer and inner life.

Eichendorff was, furthermore, a Prussian Catholic, and thus belonged to a religious minority, indeed at times a persecuted minority. This fact played an important role in Eichendorff's career in the civil service. He very bravely defended Catholics against all attempts at repression and his resignation was the result of one such conflict.

There is also something in Eichendorff's biography that differs completely from that of most leading Romantics: a straightforward, unproblematical decency, a solid, often blinkered outlook. This is far removed from the disoriented, hypocritical or cynical adventurism of an Adam Müller or a Gentz. It is equally remote from the instability and inner strife of the Romantic type, as embodied in Brentano. Eichendorff was a conscientious and capable official; he married early, and lived an unproblematical, exemplary family life. His work as an author fitted smoothly into the given framework of his life.

This (often narrow-minded) stability and straightforwardness of public and private lifestyle was thoroughly un-Romantic. Nonetheless, all his works are spontaneous, profound and typically Romantic in a completely unaffected way. Recognition of this contradiction is important if we are to understand his works and their fate.

The manner in which Eichendorff rejected all capitalist prose, which from the outset took on ossified, philistine forms in the Germany of that period, was particularly Romantic. In Germany, the narrow-minded, hidebound philistines of the declining guild system were slowly turning into the capitalist petty bourgeoisie. Engels makes a point of emphasizing this quirk of German history which had such a crucial influence on the form taken by the Romantic protest. He regarded German philistinism not as a normal historical phenomenon, but as a 'caricature carried to extremes, a piece of degeneracy', and offered a clear historical explanation for this abnormal phenomenon.

In Germany, philistinism is the fruit of a failed revolution, of interrupted and repressed development, and took on its abnormally marked characteristics – cowardliness, narrow-mindedness, helplessness and inability to take any kind of initiative – during the Thirty Years War and the following period, when nearly all other major nations were making rapid progress.[1]

Therefore, if Romantic anti-capitalism in Germany was primarily a struggle against philistinism, this was not merely the predilection of writers of cheap and obvious satire, but rather – albeit unknown to the Romantics themselves – a necessary consequence of Germany's historical development. Recognition of this historical necessity does not alter the fact that the struggle was one-sided and often bore the features of a literary clique, but merely demonstrates that the more vigorously most Romantics attack German philistinism, the more they remain imbued with this very philistinism, albeit in a different way.

German Classicism also fought against philistinism, but this was in the main a struggle for great historical progress. Little as Goethe may have been an advocate of the plebeian methods of the French Revolution, he nonetheless strongly opposed philistinism as an element of the old order, of resistance to the development of the new bourgeois society. Even when he portrays the new type of capitalist philistine, the contrast results from the diametrical opposition between the humanist ideal of a universal development of humankind on the one side and, on the other, blinkered specialization and slavish subordination to the social division of labour under capitalism (*Werther* and *Wilhelm Meister*).

In the Romantic polemic against philistinism, however, art – or life transformed into art – is posed as the alternative to petty bourgeois narrowness. This gives rise to a one-sided irony that reverts from one philistine extreme to the other, in contrast to the Classicists, for whom art was only one factor – albeit an important one – in the humanist universal education of humankind. These Romantic tendencies are to be observed most clearly in the work of Novalis, who also displays the greatest degree of vagueness regarding ideals and their transformation into mysticism and magic.

Eichendorff's novel *Ahnung und Gegenwart* (*Premonition and Actuality*) also takes up the struggle against philistinism.

Most people's lives consist of continuous business journeys from the butter market to the cheese market; the life of poetic souls, by contrast, is a free, endless journey to heaven.[2]

That is thoroughly Romantic, very much in line with Novalis's sentiments. It is, however, characteristic of Eichendorff's pervasive sobriety that one of the novel's figures, who is very close to the writer himself, replies to this claim with the following remark: 'These travelling poetic souls are like the birds of paradise who are wrongly believed not to have any feet.'[3] And it is interesting to observe that this novel, in which Eichendorff depicts his youth, is a constant satire on philistinism and in equal measure a polemic against certain distorted features of Romanticism. Thus Eichendorff frequently criticizes Romantic irony for degenerating into an empty game, and demands from poetry profound subjective honesty and human simplicity.

How can you expect people to admire your works, to refresh and edify themselves, when you do not yourselves believe what you write, and try with fine words and artistic thoughts to outwit God and Men?[4]

He is similarly outraged at all Romantic trifling with religious feelings and notions. 'Scarcely have we rid ourselves of sophistry in religion, than we begin again to poeticize and evaporate its firm dogmas, miracles and truths.'[5] Eichendorff sees in this a regression from true Romanticism as he understands it, from a true revival of poetry out of a spirit of genuine religiosity. He who

thinks he can survey religion like any other poetic subject . . . is just as inclined to believe in the Greek Olympus as in Christianity and to confuse or transpose one with the other until heaven in its entirety becomes frightfully barren and empty.[6]

It is obvious here that Eichendorff is polemicizing against the concept of Romantic Christianity which A.W. Schlegel occasionally termed 'une prédilection artistique'. It also seems that in the figure of Countess Romana Eichendorff is criticizing the abhorrent aspects of that Romantic over-excitability and instability of which Bettina von Arnim is perhaps the most striking example.

Eichendorff is therefore searching for a genuine, a religious Romanticism. His religiosity is less problematical and thus more uncritical and even more blinkered than that of the dishonest ironists or strife-ridden despairers among his contemporaries. He is no more capable than they of finding a solution, of stating clearly what a world corresponding to his ideals would actually look like. Romantic perplexity, the inability to come to terms with the problems of modern life, indeed of even grasping their true nature, stands out even more saliently and more bewilderingly in his case than in that of his poetic comrades-at-arms because this perplexity exists in such strange and completely unresolved contradiction to his human stability, to his unshakable belief in those Romantic ideals. But the power of facts, the power of the real, extant contradiction between being and consciousness constantly comes to the surface, and Eichendorff is often forced to behave just as nihilistically towards the problems of life as do many other Romantics of quite a different personality. Like them, he often has to admit that he does not comprehend the essence of life, that reality appears to him to be unfathomable and unknowable.

Life, however, ... with its colourful pictures, is to the poet what an incalculably vast book of hieroglyphs written in an unknown, long dead primeval language, is to the reader.[7]

Even the plot of the novel cited earlier expresses involuntarily, but therefore all the more strongly, this despairing nihilism. Eichendorff portrays three people with whom he inwardly sympathizes. None of them finds his place in life. One emigrates in desperation to America; the second retires to a monastery; the third even goes to Egypt to devote himself to magic.

Admittedly, the despair in this novel is to a certain extent historically determined. The book was written in 1808, when Germany was at its most down-trodden and fragmented, and in the metaphysical despair vis-à-vis life in general there is much genuine patriotic despair at the fate of Germany. This is revealed in the only bright, optimistic pages of the book, when the Tyrolean popular uprising is enthusiastically described. The manner in which Eichendorff contrasts the simple, self-sacrificing heroism of the peasants with the vacillations and perplexity, indeed the treachery of the genuinely Romantic figures, is highly characteristic of his work.

There are, however, deeper reasons for Eichendorff's inability to comprehend life's new developments, an inability which persists even after the end of the Wars of Liberation, albeit with less despairing overtones. The later Eichendorff is by no means one of the disillusioned reformers, yet his estrangement from bourgeois life remains essentially unchanged, despite the slowness of Germany's bourgeoisification and despite the unproblematical way in which Eichendorff is able in practical terms to adapt his private life and public activities to this world.

Like all of his poetry, this feeling of perplexity and dissatisfaction later becomes a kind of musical accompaniment to life. It is expressed by harking back to 'nature', to 'the good old days', when life still had meaning and was unproblematical. And this yearning sometimes takes on overtly religious, overtly Catholic forms. In this sense, Eichendorff is truly a feudal Romantic.

However, in the absence of a programme, his yearning remains very indistinct. Indeed, when as a creative writer he harks back to the 'good old days', he comes into barely resolvable conflict with his philosophy of life. As long as only the landscape of the 'good old days' is described, everything is fine: old castles in beautiful parks; ruins surrounded by romantic forests; the sound of horns; jovial postilions on the highway; carefree wanderers – all this makes for a rapturously beautiful landscape of days gone by. But as soon as people are depicted living their concrete lives, this feudal idyll goes up in smoke. Eichendorff, for all his Catholic narrow-mindedness, for all his feudal sympathies, is much too honest to violate the truth by idealizing the life of the old nobility, the nobility of the ancien régime. He is naturally a passionate opponent of the French Revolution. Yet whenever he addresses this or the pre-revolutionary period as a writer, the dreadful atrocities of the aristocracy are immediately brought vigorously to the fore, and the Revolution appears, much against the writer's conscious philosophy, as the oppressed masses' thoroughly justifiable reaction to such arbitrary, cruel treatment. (See *Das Schloß Durande*, 1839 and the much more reactionary verse novella, *Robert und Guiscard*, 1833/34.) The beauty of the 'good old days' in such works by Eichendorff is the beauty of the landscape, of the interiors and of a still life, but not of life itself, which he too finds in no way attractive. This contradiction in the composition, which Eichendorff never becomes aware of and which stems from the disorientation of his philosophy, gives such works an indistinct tenor, lacking in contours and, despite the beauty of details, remaining basically formless and unartistic.

Eichendorff is a true poet only when he expresses this dissatisfaction with present-day life, this unease, in general terms, as a feeling without a concrete object, only when he foregoes trying to give form to the causes and effects of his attitude to life, and instead lets his feelings flow freely – which he does, above all, in his lyric poetry. In his verse we find the purest expression of the folk-song like strain in Romantic poetry. He very rarely lapses into the kind of archaism and formal sophistry that made Tieck's poetry seem so quickly outdated; he avoids that subjective arbitrariness that so often distorts even the deeply felt and powerfully eloquent poems of Brentano. Simple, straightforward Eichendorff, who despises all trifling with forms and especially with feelings and ideas, instinctively follows the line of reviving the folk-song tradition which began with Herder and Goethe and received new impetus with the publication of Arnim and Brentano's collection of folk songs, *Des Knaben Wunderhorn*.[8] We have already observed the nature of his poetic feeling in his prose writings: it is an instinctive empathy with the people and plebeian characters, the instinctive feeling that they are morally superior, richer in human terms than the aristocratic intelligentsia whose fate is at the centre of his stories. We have already mentioned that the rebellious Tyrolean peasants are the only positive figures in his youthful novel; and it is no coincidence that the hero of the only one of his novellas still popular today, *Memoirs of a Good-For-Nothing*, is also a peasant's son, albeit a somewhat stylized, fairy-tale one. This instinctive, genuine feeling makes Eichendorff's poetry overwhelmingly popular.

Its main content is yearning. A yearning to escape 'normal', modern bourgeois life; a yearning for the free nature of the forests, for rambling, for distant lands; in Germany for the beauty of Italy, in Italy for the familiarity of home; a yearning for the 'good old days', which, as we have shown, constantly recurs in stylized form and the social content of which is present in the writer's head as a confused idea, bereft of form and free of contradiction, yet from which he is able, if only in his poetry, to recreate the natural, the general yearning for a simpler and more meaningful *condition humaine*. This gives rise to poetry with the simplicity, authenticity and profundity of folk-song, poetry whose many repetitions are no more monotonous than the constantly recurrent themes in folk-songs themselves.

These simple and genuine feelings form the poetic basis for the truth of the folk-song as an artistic form. The special place Eichendorff's poetry occupies in the Romantic movement, the freshness it still holds today is based precisely on the fact that his recourse to the folk-song form is in no sense a formalistic contrivance, as it is in the work of many others. Eichendorff is a poet who uses universal contents and radically new forms to evoke world-historical changes in human feelings, as did Goethe or Heine. Yet he can be counted among the ranks of genuine poets who have given expression to specific, at times narrowly limited feelings with steadfast poetic honesty in both content and form. He stands in a line of poets extending from Matthias Claudius, his boyhood favourite, to Theodor Storm.

Unproblematical simplicity is an essential feature of this poetry. However, although this observation is basically correct in itself, one should be wary of mechanistically carrying it too far. We have already shown the problematic aspects of Eichendorff's relationship to reality. They are not completely absent from his poetry; they simply take on a lyrically freer form which, by virtue of their composition, detaches them from the problematical nature of Romanticism. Yet the contents themselves remain problematical, indeed it is their presence and constant intrusion into the poems which gives Eichendorff's verse its true profundity. Yet it follows from the nature of Eichendorff's poetry as we have described it that everything problematical – uncomprehended and unknowable life, unalterable human solitude, the hopelessness of any desire for a meaningful existence – is only expressed in moderate tones and does not destroy the unity of content and form. We can illustrate this point with a typical example, the major part of the poem 'Eldorado':

> Es ist von Klang und Düften
> Ein wunderbarer Ort,
> Umrankt von stillen Klüften:
> Wir alle spielten dort.

> Wir alle sind verirret;
> Seitdem so weit hinaus
> Unkraut die Welt verwirret,
> Find't keiner mehr nach Haus.

> Doch manchmal taucht's aus Träumen,
> Als läg es weit im Meer;
> Und früh noch in den Bäumen
> Rauscht's wie ein Grüßen her.

> Ich hört den Gruß verfliegen,
> Ich folgt ihm über Land
> Und hatte mich verstiegen
> Auf hoher Felsenwand.

> Mein Herz wird mir so munter:
> Weit hinten alle Not,
> Als ginge jenseits unter
> Die Welt im Morgenrot.

> Der Wind spielt in den Locken,
> Da blitzt es drunten weit,
> Und ich erkannt erschrocken
> Die alte Einsamkeit.

There is a place full of wondrous sounds and scents, surrounded by silent chasms. That's where we all played.

Now we have all parted; weeds have sown confusion throughout the world, so that no one can find his way home again.

Sometimes, though, it surfaces in our dreams, as if it lay in the ocean's depths; and in the early dawn it comes wafting through the trees like a greeting.

I heard the greeting float past. I pursued it over land and lost my way clambering up a steep, rocky slope.

My heart leapt; all misery lay beneath. It was as if the whole world were setting yonder in the dawn.

The wind plays in my hair, suddenly lightning flashes far away below, and with a start my loneliness returns.

In accordance with this conception of the world, Eichendorff's poetry does not lack the Romantic horror of unknown forces, the dark, sinister nature of the 'unfathomable' that intervenes in men's lives, shaping their destiny. But if Eichendorff's utopian dream does not take on the magical, mystical form of Novalis's, neither do his bad dreams, his nightmares give rise to the grotesque and ghostly reality of Hoffmann. Heine rightly regards Novalis and Hoffmann as the opposite poles of Romantic inventiveness. Eichendorff represents a kind of 'happy medium' somewhere between the two. This delivers him from Novalis's eccentricity and disintegration of form, yet at the same time bars him from attaining Hoffmann's realistic depth and accuracy. For all that, it would be wrong to overlook the similarity between certain perceptions, a similarity which is not the result of one writer influencing the other, but rather is deeply rooted in the state of German society at that time.

> Dämmrung will die Flügel spreiten,
> Schaurig rühren sich die Bäume,
> Wolken ziehn wie schwere Träume –
> Was soll dieses Graun bedeuten?
>
> Hast ein Reh du lieb vor andern,
> Laß es nicht alleine grasen,
> Jäger ziehn im Wald und blasen,
> Stimmen hin und wider wandern.

Dusk makes to spread its wings, the trees stir awesomely, clouds come like heavy dreams – what means this dusk and dread?

If you have a fawn you favour, let her not graze alone. Hunters range in the forest, bugling; voices flit here and there.

Eichendorff's dreams of a better reality and of life's frightening abysses are in fact daydreams. Reality is neither overpowered by dream fantasies and de-objectified, as in Novalis's work, nor do the really inhuman abysses of life under capitalism appear in fantastic form, as in Hoffmann's tales. We encounter here a subjectively genuine, profound yearning, but one which nevertheless has a faint awareness of its own dreamlike unreality, a vague intimation of the fact that it is no more than the musical accompaniment to real life.

Memoirs of a Good-For-Nothing is just such a daydream – a stroke of genius on the part of the writer, who grasps such profound emotional strands of the German people that the work's popularity has remained unshaken to the present day. Very few characters were formed in nineteenth-century Germany without the *Memoirs of a Good-For-Nothing* playing some part in their development. It remains one of the most widely read and best loved German books, above all among young people.

This qualification does not, however, detract from the work's importance, it merely defines it more concretely. Goethe believed that his *Werther* expressed and accompanied a certain stage of development of every person, and when Schiller spoke of the justification for 'sentimental poetry', and especially of the idyll, he emphasized that every person has his 'golden age', as does humankind as a whole.

The Good-For-Nothing lives as a manifestation of this 'golden age'. It is not a 'young person's book' in the transient sense of one that is devoured at a certain age only to be forgotten later without trace, but rather an expression of a crucial stage of the development of German youth. (The reference to Goethe's view of *Werther* at this point was, of course, only intended to define the general location of Eichendorff's novella. In comparison with the global significance of *Werther*, *Memoirs of a Good-For-Nothing* remains no more than a happy reverie.)

Memoirs of a Good-For-Nothing is an idyll with almost fairy tale-like features, shadowy dangers and unexpected strokes of good fortune. It contains no direct social criticism, no direct polemics (at least, only very occasionally and sporadically), yet it owes its continued success to the polemics nonetheless intrinsic to it.

Above all, the form of the idyll is polemic in itself. According to Schiller's definition, the idyll, the elegy and the satire each give artistic form to the confrontation between ideal and reality, nature (in Rousseau's sense) and society. What distinguishes the idyll within this system of 'sentimental' forms of writing, is that here nature, the ideal, is portrayed as a reality, not as something lost and thus an object of mourning, as in the elegy. That is why Schiller regarded the portrayal of the dawn of culture as the natural subject of the idyll. He appreciated, however, that this choice of subject was by no means exclusive and obligatory. In his great premonition of the integral development of the human race and its abbreviated expression in the life of the individual, he stated, as we have already indicated, that every people, every individual has a 'golden age', an idyllic state, a 'state of harmony and peace with oneself and the environment'.

Memoirs of a Good-For-Nothing is at once fairy tale and reality. Here the golden age appears in the midst of the present. And this is – in the artistic sense – not at all stylized. Viewed individually, the portrayal of people, landscapes and towns is completely realistic and true to nature. Here again Eichendorff comes very close to the problems of composition experienced by Romanticism's realist current. We find this pointed realism of all the individual details at the heart of fantastic events in Chamisso's *Peter Schlemihl* and in Hoffmann's works. In their case, however, realism serves the function of heightening the uncanny, the fantastic, whereas its narrative purpose for Eichendorff is to make a dream appear true. Only the situations and especially the interconnections between them remain beyond the scope of the typical causality of the modern world. Yet within any given situation – disregarding the way it came about – a genuine realism, both internal and external, holds sway.

The fairy tale was revived by the German Romantics and is one of the movement's favourite genres. Here the situation is similar to that of their poetry in that the pseudo-archaic narratives which affect the childlike tone of some popular fairy tales are for the most part utterly forgotten. *Memoirs of a Good-For-Nothing*, by contrast, although it bears no similarity to fairy tales in formal terms, possesses the irrepressible vitality of genuine popular fairy tales. Eichendorff keeps to only the most essential stylistic elements used specifically to depict a fairy-tale world, but he does so in a completely naïve, contemporary way and is thus able to conjure the fairy-tale atmosphere into the present. It would be interesting to trace how and where Eichendorff completely transforms individual popular fairy-tale themes and incorporates them into his story. The main theme in *Memoirs of a Good-For-Nothing*, for example, bears a distant relationship to the traditional story of the Grimms' 'Lucky Hans'.

All this idyllic formal conjuring is, however, pervaded by a strong, genuinely modern polemic feeling. Taken as a whole, this beautiful, untendentious idyll rebels against the pointless and inhuman bustle of modern life, against the 'efficiency' and 'diligence' of the old and new philistine.

The struggle for a meaningful life of human dignity under capitalism is to a large extent a struggle for leisure. Marx says: 'Time is
the space (*Raum*) of human development. A man who has no free
time to dispose of, whose whole lifetime, apart from the mere physical interruptions by sleep, meals, and so forth, is absorbed by labour
for the capitalist, is less than a beast of burden. He is a mere ma-
chine for producing foreign wealth, broken in body and brutalized
in mind. Yet the whole history of modern industry shows that capital, if not checked, will recklessly and ruthlessly work to cast down
the whole working class to the utmost state of degradation'.[9] And in
his famous observations on freedom and necessity, Marx indicates
exactly how this question is resolved by socialism. He identifies
social control over production as being of primary importance for
human relations and man's relationship to nature.

But it nonetheless remains a realm of necessity. Beyond it begins that
development of human energy which is an end in itself, the true realm
of freedom, which, however, can blossom forth only with this realm of
necessity as its basis. The shortening of the working-day is its basic prerequisite.[10]

The capitalist world of free competition, of bourgeois freedom,
means increasing destruction of this (in the Marxian sense) free
space for free, universal human development. Marx and Engels
repeatedly show that this process of man's slavish subordination
to the capitalist division of labour with all its consequences affects
not only the exploited but also the exploiters.

This question plays an extremely important role in all forms of
Romantic opposition to the nascence of capitalism, which was in
full swing after the victory of bourgeois society in the French Revolution and as a result of the industrial revolution in Britain. And it
is obvious that the Romantic opposition in the economically and
politically more advanced western countries was able to formulate
its dissatisfaction with the economic and social ills of capitalism
much more clearly than in backward Germany, where capitalist
production was still in its infancy. The Romantic opposition in
Germany is therefore much vaguer than parallel movements in
Britain and France. It would, however, be wrong to let these important differences make us lose sight of the common features.

The ability at times to expose with great accuracy the contradictions of capitalist society and to combat them with genuine bitterness and hard-hitting scorn is characteristic of every Romantic opposition, as is its inability to grasp the essence of these contradictions. In most cases this results in an exaggerated distortion of the problems, a point at which correct criticism turns into social untruth. Thus, their exposure of the contradictions of the capitalist division of labour turns into an uncritical glorification of the social conditions which existed at a time when this division of labour was still unknown. This is at the root of the Romantic enthusiasm for the Middle Ages.

All these weaknesses and distortions inherent in the Romantic opposition manifest themselves in the question of leisure, in combining meaningful and useful labour with the conditions necessary for humankind's all-round development. The opposition posed by German Romanticism turns into a glorification of idleness. Criticism of inhuman and pointless labour under capitalism becomes a rejection of all useful labour whatsoever. The golden age of every popular legend is a period without private property. The paradise of German Romanticism is an age without labour. This tendency finds its most exaggerated and paradoxical expression in Friedrich Schlegel's *Lucinde*. Schlegel incorporates his own 'idyll of idleness' into his book. In it he initiates a 'hymn to idleness', to the 'only fragment of divinity that we have retained from before the Fall'.[11] He continues to attack the destructive impact of capitalist labour on culture, 'for industry and utility are the angels of death who, with their swords of fire, bar humankind's return to paradise'.[12] And in conclusion he portrays the positive figure of Hercules, whose aim in life, for all his great feats, was a noble form of 'idleness', posing him as an alternative to the constantly active Prometheus, the 'inventor of education and enlightenment'[13] and thus – in Schlegel's eyes – of all evil.

It is not difficult to expose the one-sided, paradoxical distortion latent in these ideas. It is not even necessary to refer to Marx' observations cited earlier. In his *Phenomenology of Spirit*, Hegel, Friedrich Schlegel's contemporary, treats human beings as the product of their own labour, and the greatest fictional compositions of this period, *Wilhelm Meister* and *Faust*, express the same basic idea. Moreover, the biographies of the advocates of Romantic paradoxes,

Friedrich Schlegel himself, Clemens Brentano and others, provide a frightening cautionary lesson as to the human demoralization caused by this Romantic opposition when it turns into falsehood, even if such opposition is subjectively justified in the first instance.

It is important, however, to emphasize this justified core. For a bourgeois thinker or writer who is not able to see beyond the capitalist horizon, and especially for a Romantic who is not even capable of grasping the essential elements of capitalist progress, it is impossible to arrive at the full truth on this question. However, capitalist society not only subjects workers by means of the blind force of economic necessity to slave-like discipline, but also uses every available means of ideological propaganda to glorify this new form of dehumanizing serfdom. In the eighteen eighties Paul Lafargue aimed his witty essay, *Le Droit à la Paresse* (*The Right to Laziness*), at this capitalist 'religion of labour'. Admittedly, the emphasis and the proportions are completely different in Lafargue's work from those of the Romantics. Knowledge of the relations that actually obtained should not, however, prevent us from recognizing the correct and progressive core in the Romantic critique of capitalist labour even in its unconscious forms, and from distinguishing this from manifestations that had turned into total falsehoods (*à la* Friedrich Schlegel).

Eichendorff's *Memoirs of a Good-For-Nothing* is a graphic demonstration of how utter lack of clarity at the level of ideas can go hand in hand with a correct instinct at the human and artistic level. Judged in terms of its external form, this novella could be seen as an artistic paradigm of Schlegel's paradoxes. Eichendorff's sobriety and diligence, known to us from his biography, is clearly expressed both in the conception of the work as a whole and in individual compositional details. The fairy-tale plot transports the hero into the kind of paradisal situation glorified by Schlegel. For a while he feels very contented, yet the other side of the coin soon reveals itself.

So one day after another went by, until at last I began to grow quite melancholy from all this good food and drink. My limbs fairly began to drop out of their joints as a result of this everlasting idling, and I felt as if indolence might make me simply fall apart.[14]

Thus the Good-For-Nothing is not just a simple (or romantically idealized) lazybones; indeed this is not even the main side to his character. Rather he is a vagabond who is unable to fit naturally into the sober order of bourgeois life. He is lively, sensitive, a gifted poet and musician, at times even intelligent. In spite of his dreamy nature he is capable – if only briefly – of vigorous, self-sacrificing activity. But he is neither able nor willing to fit into the order of the 'world of industrious philistines'. He is by character one of those peasant boys who, while not being geniuses, do nonetheless possess a certain primitive talent, but who are mostly degraded by the 'normal' running of capitalist society to the level of average worker ants.

The strength of Eichendorff's story lies precisely in the typicality of the character, and the typicality of his fate is brought about by creating a fairy-tale polar opposite to the average, through which the typical, as a backdrop, as a contrast emphasizing general truth within the atypical, shines through. This representation is successful only because Eichendorff, with his correct human instinct, constantly appreciated and exposed the dangers of the Romantic philosophy of which he was in theory a follower but which he did not apply to the conduct of his own life. His hero is a vagabond, but he has nothing of the declassed, intellectual, bohemian-anarchistic opposition about him. This kind of opposition starts at the level where the process of social declassment resulting from the capitalist division of labour is already complete, and therefore combats it in an unproductive and distorted way. Because Eichendorff's hero is a fairy-tale peasant boy at a time *before* this declassment, a deeper and more correct kind of Romantic opposition is developed in which the core of truth contained in this tendency is expressed in much purer and more powerful form, and is freer of distortions than in earlier and later bohemian rebellions against capitalist labour.

Eichendorff's – in human terms – more correct form of opposition is also expressed in his keen sense of the social dangers of this behaviour, and although he seeks and finds a fairy-tale-like happy solution to all problems, he is continually aware of the threat to humanity of such a rebel. He therefore realizes that this kind of rebellion can make a person unsocial, indeed antisocial, and does not try to console himself with the illusion that it might be possible to create a Bohemian 'society' of antisocial anarchists. He experiences the isolation of unsociability as a real existential danger. Thus, on the occasion of a festival, he has his hero remark:

Everyone is so merry, and nobody cares about you. And that is my lot always and everywhere. Each one has his plot of ground staked out, has his warm stove, his cup of coffee, his wife, his glass of wine in the evening, and is thoroughly content. . . For me there's no happiness anywhere. It's as if I had always come just too late, as if the entire world had not counted me in at all.[15]

Such remarks and similarly critical observations recur in Eichendorff's story again and again. Yet they are only a shadow, as is the element of the uncanny in his poems. But this shadow has an important literary function: to lend the world of daydreams, which would otherwise have remained flat and two-dimensional, the contours of reality.

There is therefore a profound literary truth in the fairy-tale form of Eichendorff's writings. Moreover, the plot lends expression in genuinely epic, truly literary fashion, to Eichendorff's wishful dream, to his utopia. In addition, owing to the hero's sane, realistically popular and sober attitude, the work as a whole bears a strong affinity to true popular fairy tales, precisely because the story almost entirely lacks any of their external characteristics.

However it is a thoroughly modern Romantic story. Its essential characteristic is a gentle oscillation between dream and reality. Dreamlike contents take on a realistic appearance, real people find themselves in dreamlike social circumstances, wonderfully naturalistic landscapes, gardens, palaces and towns are so nostalgically exquisite as to be almost dreamlike. The perpetual atmosphere of the whole story is determined by this kind of beauty, and this is precisely what makes it so unique and its popularity so lasting.

Memoirs of a Good-For-Nothing is a genuine idyll, more genuine and lasting than the eighteenth-century pastoral. Eichendorff's very lack of clarity, which makes his other narrative and dramatic works so vague and featureless, is here just a silver mist of unspoken melancholy which makes the inner lightheartedness of the idyll profound and attractive. Only here – apart, perhaps, from in his very best poems – does Eichendorff's confused, rebellious yearning find adequate and artistically profound formal expression.

The profundity and truth of this idyll do not just surpass Romanticism in the narrow academic sense. We can perhaps best describe its essential contents using Schiller's words, written some thirty years before Eichendorff's *Memoirs of a Good-For-Nothing*:

We can then perceive irrational nature as our more contented sister, who remained behind in the maternal home whence we, intoxicated by our freedom, sallied forth into the unknown. As soon as we begin to experience the ordeals of culture, we suffer pangs of desire to return thither, and in the distant realm of art we can make out the sweet voice of our mother calling.[16]

Eichendorff's Good-For-Nothing is of course hardly aware of this problem. At most he experiences it as an indefinite feeling, for he is, after all, a naïve child of the people. Yet for this very reason this figure and his fate portray so poignantly the situation of unbroken humanity, of the Schillerian 'naïvety' in capitalist society. Schiller says of such people that in a modern society

they are scarcely possible, or at least only possible if they *run wild* in their time and are preserved by some happy fortune from its mutilating influence.[17]

That the hero remains unspoilt and unmutilated as he 'runs free' in his fairy-tale idyll is the truly realistic and truly rebellious content of this idyll. The literary truth of the idyllic form shows that this salvation can only be imagined and portrayed realistically as a fairy tale, a dream.

Eichendorff's dream was shared by many of the best nineteenth-century Germans. But with the increasing capitalization of Germany, the fairy-tale happy ending, the realistic lighthearted idyll, increasingly became a literary impossibility. It reappears in much of Mörike's poetry; but in Storm's works it has already become a novella-like lyrical elegy, in which objective fulfilment is mourned as something destroyed and irrevocably lost. And in the imperialist period, Thomas Mann's youthful novellas take place against the backdrop of such a heap of rubble that this can hardly be termed a ruin any longer, which is why their elegiac mourning takes on an ever stronger satirical tone. The recognition that the dream is but a mere dream, mere yearning, takes on an increasingly conscious form, and thus its treatment becomes increasingly elegiac and satirical. The rebellion contained in the works of later writers is therefore much more decisive than in Eichendorff's. (The extent to which this heritage of Eichendorff's dream helped particular writers to a solution, to an understanding of the capitalist nature of this destruction, cannot be discussed here.)

It is no coincidence that this line is often pursued by writers who reject capitalist and philistine 'industriousness', yet whose life-styles and writings are equally remote from any bohemian rebellion. In this way they are able, like Eichendorff, to maintain a degree of human industriousness and poetic sanity with regard to their own dreams. This both allows them to live the dream out fully on a literary level, while at the same time enabling them to preserve instinctively, and to express artistically, what they are unable to grasp intellectually, namely the right proportions between dream and reality.

1940

The Real Georg Büchner and his Fascist Misrepresentation

On the hundredth anniversary of his death, 19 February 1937[*]

I

The unbiased reader of Georg Büchner's work will find it completely improbable that fascism could even attempt to lay claim to Büchner for its own devices. (For example, even the old-fashioned reactionary Treitschke recognized the revolutionary nature of Büchner's writings and so rejected them.) And yet such improbability has become fact. Just as fascist German 'literary history' has tried to turn Hölderlin, the late Jacobin, into a prophet of the 'Third Reich', so too it has now dared to turn its attentions to Büchner.

The method adopted by this fascist falsification is essentially the same as that applied to Hölderlin and other great transitional revolutionary figures. The aim has been to interpret away everything revolutionary from their work and lives by means of falsification and ingenious misinterpretations. In Georg Büchner's case the fascists have again found precursors in the literary scholars of the imperialist period, notably Friedrich Gundolf. He admittedly makes Büchner out to be 'only' a belated Romantic, a poet of 'mood'. By concentrating on mood Gundolf deliberately loses sight of Büchner's entire social critique: 'The social stratum in *Woyzeck* is *mood*. . . Here, it is the landscape of fate and its spiritual essence that are the main protagonists.' Everything which would otherwise have been social criticism in the drama 'glows in *Woyzeck* down into the realm of primordial powers. No German who has tried to portray poverty, evil and gloom has ever come so close to their foundations as Büchner'.[1]

The German fascists carry this train of thought even further. Precisely Büchner the revolutionary writer is claimed to be the

[*] First published in *Das Wort*, no.2, 1937.

forerunner of their 'revolution'. This has been attempted in recent years in two larger-scale treatises.[2] Both approach the matter 'scientifically', that is, they resort to complicated detours in an attempt to render Büchner somehow fascist. For even the most refined fascist falsifications would not suffice to make Büchner a direct forerunner of the Führer.

Both treatises take as their point of departure Büchner's alleged *despair*, inserting him in a line extending from Schopenhauer, via Kierkegaard, Dostoyevsky, Nietzsche and Strindberg to Heidegger. There are echoes of Heidegger when Viëtor claims that Büchner's greatness resides in 'his placing himself resolutely in nothingness'. Equally, Pfeiffer remarks of Büchner's conception of history:

Man stands in history as if exposed to the force of inconceivable higher powers, which with utter irresponsibility and cruelty cause man to fall victim to an abominable addiction or mood.

According to Pfeiffer, Büchner's participation in the attempted uprisings in Hessen after the July Revolution is the expression of a transient 'alienation from reality'. Here we can see quite clearly that even such a 'refined' fascist interpretation uses blatant lies as its method. Pfeiffer goes on to 'prove' this assertion by pointing to the fact that, as a student at the University of Giessen, Büchner kept his distance from the goings-on of the *Burschenschaft* (student societies). Luckily, in a letter to his family, Büchner gives a very clear account of his position: he hated such people because of their conceit and vanity, because they despised the great mass of their fellow men on the basis of a laughable pseudo-education.

Aristocracy is the most disgraceful contempt for the Holy Spirit in man; I turn its own weapons against it: arrogance versus arrogance, scorn versus scorn.[3]

Büchner's *Danton* came into being following the defeat of his revolutionary endeavours, indeed, in the interpretation given it by the above-mentioned fascists, as an expression of his disillusion. Both of them term Büchner a great writer precisely because he gave artistic form to *disillusion with the revolution*.

This is why Viëtor gives his study the title 'The Tragedy of Heroic Pessimism'. He describes Danton as:

. . . someone who does not *want* to act because he has been overcome by the great disillusion. Who *no longer* wishes to act – it is this that is decisive. . .The drama commences at that moment when Danton's revolutionary faith is broken by the recognition of the hopeless unfreedom of humankind and the irredeemability of life.

What does this disillusion consist of? Viëtor offers a clear answer in his analysis of the scene with Robespierre:

Robespierre is naïve enough to believe that the revolution's sole purpose is to create better conditions for the people. . . Danton's enmity is roused by this dangerously obtuse terrorist dogma.

Danton – and with him Büchner – is more profound and more 'realistic' than Robespierre precisely because of his disillusion. As to the substance of this disillusion:

It was a religious truth – one that referred to the ultimate, eternal questions of humankind. . . a recognition . . . in the face of which all action appears meaningless.

Büchner, in other words, depicts

a religious truth taken from history. *Danton's Death* is the tragedy of a great politician who is destroyed in the very moment when, following the intoxication of radical action, he regains his statesmanlike levelheaded-ness and regenerative power.

The disillusionment with the revolution, and the despair that arises from this are, in other words, in Viëtor's eyes the real basis of a positive development, of 'statesmanlike levelheadedness'.

Pfeiffer is even more radical. His book is based on a new 'philosophy of the history of drama'. This theory hinges on the claim that the drama is heroic, demonic and Germanic, whereas the epic is Judeo-Christian in origin. There is no point in entering into a factual discussion of this theory. In order to elucidate his method, suffice it to emphasize that Pfeiffer is of the opinion that he is entitled to claim Schelling's support, which he does in the following manner. Pfeiffer terms the epic, using Schelling's words, 'the presentation of the finite *in* the infinite'; and he goes on to quote Schelling's statement on Christianity: 'The direction innately present in Christianity moves *from* the finite *to* the infinite' [my emphasis, G.L.]. It is obvious from the grammatical sense of both sentences, without even considering Schelling's conception of the infinite, that Schelling here says the opposite of what Pfeiffer claims he says. Schelling accordingly regarded Homer as a typical representative of the epic, and outlines the dissolution of the old epic in Christianity. This contrast between Pfeiffer and Schelling in fact extends even further, for Pfeiffer perceives rhyming couplets as the cohesive factor of the epic, whereas for Schelling the hexameter was the metre typical of the epic. If, in other words, Pfeiffer wants to cite Schelling's authority in support of his theory, then he can only do so by speculating on the uneducated and inattentive nature of his audience.

Yet there is method behind all this nonsense. Pfeiffer wants to be able to grant only the old Germanic adages and songs the status 'dramatic' in the sense he attaches to the word. And he claims that throughout modernity the form of the drama has become more and more narrative, even in Shakespeare's work, and especially in German Classicism. Thus, it is not until Kleist that a truly Germanic-demonic drama is forthcoming. Here, Pfeiffer continues in the field of literary history the line laid down by Alfred Bäumler, the official philosopher of the 'Third Reich', who in his inaugural address at Berlin University, decreed that the ideological struggle against the humanism of the German Classicists was the main task facing 'political educationalists'. Pfeiffer wished to fit Georg Büchner into this demonic-dramatic lineage.

Danton has fallen prey to 'demonic inbetweenness'. He is heroic in an unheroic age. Democracy is the obstacle to his heroism: 'Danton recognized that a heroic step was not open to him because of the superior strength of the unheroic spirit among his contemporaries.'

According to Pfeiffer, Danton's tragedy consists in the fact that the latter has to act with the masses, but the masses cannot keep pace with his 'heroic' aims. His tragedy resides in his not yet being able to apply the fascist methods of social demagogy successfully. It is this that is his tragic disillusionment and despair. Viëtor, more open and blunt, gives the game away more imprudently. His comments on Robespierre's words in Büchner's play are as follows:

When is a revolution completed? That is not a condition that can be asserted objectively, this state of completion; a revolution is complete when a state has been reached which fulfils the basic demands of the *revolutionary leaders* (Führer) [my emphasis, G.L.].

'Scientific proof' is provided in this manner and with such methods to show that Büchner was a tragically despairing, hitherto unrecognized forerunner of the 'National Socialist revolution'.

II

What is it then that constitutes Danton's real tragedy in Büchner's play? As Arnold Zweig very perceptively remarked of it:

Büchner makes the dramatic error of taking for granted the overwhelming necessity and laudability of the revolution as such, as he himself felt it.

Irrespective of whether or not Zweig's demand can be fulfilled within the framework of Büchner's conception of Danton's tragedy, Zweig is absolutely correct with regard to the playwright himself and goes to the core of his being. Büchner always remained a consistent revolutionary, was astonishingly mature and lucid for his age, and exhibited an astonishing consistency in the ebb and flow of his fate as a revolutionary, human being and playwright.

This is not the place to give even a sketchy biography of Büchner's life. We must limit ourselves to presenting isolated statements from different periods of it in order to dispel the myth of his 'disillusion with the revolution'. Büchner's basic trait was a burning revolutionary hatred of all exploitation and suppression. At an early date, in a speech held at grammar school he glorified Cato at Caesar's cost. He wrote to his family while a student in Strasbourg:

Young people are condemned for their use of violence. But are we not in a constant state of violence? Because we were born and brought up in prison, we no longer notice that we are stuck in a hole, chained by our hands and feet, and with a gag in our mouths. What do you call *a state of law*? A *law* that reduces the great mass of the populace to oppressed beasts in order to satisfy the needs of an insignificant and pampered minority?[4]

Such convictions led Büchner to join a secret revolutionary organization in Hessen, although while in Strasbourg he had on occasion expressed great scepticism as to whether a revolutionary uprising were possible in Germany. The fascists who seek to misrepresent him regard it as a 'contradiction' that he nevertheless placed himself at the head of the secret revolutionary organization. This 'contradiction' can be very easily resolved if we consider Büchner's *special position* within the ranks of the German revolutionary movement. Büchner was perhaps the only one of the revolutionaries of the time to place the economic liberation of the masses at the *centre* of his revolutionary activity. This was the cause of bitter conflicts with his comrades. Throughout Büchner's draft of the *Hessische Landbote* (*The Hessian Courier*), Weidig, the leader of the secret revolutionary organization in Hessen, changed the word 'rich' to 'noble' and thus reoriented the pamphlet in a liberalist direction, levelling it exclusively against the vestiges of feudal absolutism. In Büchner's conception, however, the revolution stood and fell with the question of whether the mass of the poor would rise up against the rich. Thus, the court testimony given by Becker,[5] a friend of Büchner's, explains the latter's participation in the attempted revolution in Hessen better than any commentary:

By means of the pamphlet [i.e. *The Hessian Courier*] he had written he wanted initially to sound out the mood of the people and of the German revolutionaries. When he later heard that the peasants had handed over to the police most of the leaflets they had found, and when he learned that the patriots had also spoken out against his leaflet, he gave up all hope of political change.

Where is the evidence of the 'disillusion' with the revolution to be found in this? *Prior* to his revolutionary activity Büchner wrote to his family that:

I will always act according to my principles, however I have *recently* learnt that only the essential needs of the masses can bring about change, and that all the activity and shouting of *individuals* is a foolish waste of time.[6]

And *after* fleeing the clutches of the authorities, in other words at the time of his 'disillusion' he wrote to Gutzkow:

The whole revolution has split into liberals and absolutists and will have to be gobbled up by the poor and uneducated classes. The relationship between rich and poor is the only revolutionary element in the world, hunger alone can become the goddess of freedom.[7]

There are without doubt few examples in history of a young revolutionary having adopted such an advanced political line between the ages of twenty and twenty-four and having followed it through so consistently.

Büchner is thus a *plebeian revolutionary*, who starts to perceive with clarity the economic foundations of a liberation of the working masses. He is an important figure in the sequence that leads from Gracchus Babeuf to Blanqui (in the June Uprising of 1848).

In keeping with this concrete historical position, the clarity of Georg Büchner's opinions cannot be measured using the yardstick of later struggles waged by a proletariat organized on a class basis.

Büchner, although a contemporary of Chartism in England and the Lyons Uprisings in France is, as a practical German revolutionary, not yet in a position to see and recognize the proletariat as a class. As a true plebeian revolutionary he concentrates on the economic and political liberation of the 'poor'; in line with conditions in Germany he naturally focuses his main attention on the peasants. That he consistently held true to his opinions brought him into insoluble theoretical and practical conflict with the liberals among his contemporaries whom he – as important revolutionary democrats were later also to do – repeatedly criticized with biting irony.

It is self-evident that such a state of affairs meant that Büchner's revolutionary perspective was still very unclear on many issues. Thus, he writes in the letter to Gutzkow cited above:

Give the peasants a square meal, and the revolution would die of apoplexy. A *chicken* in every peasant's pot would soon stop the Gallic *cock* crowing.[8]

These unclear tendencies can be seen even more clearly in another letter to Gutzkow written somewhat later. Following a trenchant critique of the 'uncomfortable relationship' between the educated liberals and the people, Büchner writes:

And the masses themselves? They know only two levers, material suffering and *religious fanaticism*. Any party that knows how to put pressure on these levers will succeed. Our age needs weapons and bread – and then a cross or something similar.[9]

The fact that Büchner, a consistent and pugnacious materialist, was able – if only temporarily – to arrive at such views on the revolutionary role of religion, or of a substitute for religion, shows how deep and unresolved the contradictions were in the transition that was occurring during his age.

And by no means just in Büchner's head, but generally, in the overall historical sense. The capitalist productive forces unleashed by the French Revolution and the industrial revolution in England caused the contradictions in society to emerge in a quite different fashion than had been the case in the eighteenth century. Isolated great thinkers had already drawn socialist conclusions from the contradictions of capitalist society; admittedly utopian conclusions, admittedly without even sensing the significance of the proletariat as the revolutionary agent that would turn these demands into reality. The followers of Ricardo, the great theorist of the capitalist economy, started to draw socialist conclusions from the theory of surplus value not long after their master's death; again admittedly without a dialectical recognition of the laws governing the dynamics of society, without recognizing the role played by the proletariat in the revolution, but rather with an ethical interpretation of the theory of surplus value. Those thinkers and politicians who were, on the other hand, directly involved in the early specific struggles of a proletariat in the process of organizing itself as a class, attempted to conceptualize the particular aims of proletarian class struggle by contrasting these sharply with the aims of all previous uprisings; in this period, however, their efforts got no further than the level of such a direct, crass contrast (from the Luddites to the beginnings of syndicalism). Yet the determined plebeian revolutionaries sought a way, via a rigorously pursued democratic revolution, of abolishing by revolutionary means the socio-economic contradictions of capitalist society. However, it was impossible for them to perceive the problem clearly until such a time as in reality and thus in the minds of the revolutionaries, the 'poor' had become a true proletariat.

The more profound, radical and comprehensive the questions put by a revolutionary democrat at this stage of developments, the more profound and insoluble the contradictions he found himself embroiled in. Notice the way in which Büchner expresses himself when telling Gutzkow of his positive perspective:

I believe that in social matters one must proceed absolutely from the principle of *justice*, and seek the creation of new spiritual life in the *people* and let this superannuated modern society go to the devil. What is the point of such individuals continuing to live? Their whole existence consists of trying to rid themselves of the most terrible boredom. They may die out, that is the only novelty they may still experience.[10]

Blanqui, France's great democratic revolutionary, managed in the course of his long life to press forward from a notion of the 'poor' to the proletariat, from Babeuf to a recognition of Marxism. The twenty-four year old Büchner died at the beginning of the same path. He is, however, with the exception of Heine, the only person in Germany who took this path. He is, with Heine, the only person among the ranks of German writers who can even be compared with the later, greater and more mature revolutionary democrats, with Chernyshevsky and Dobrolyubov.

III

It is not difficult to appreciate that one of the most important questions posed by this transitional crisis in the revolutionary movements on the Continent was that of the critical analysis of the French Revolution. After all, this had not only shaken the life of the French people to the core, but had given all Europe a completely different appearance: namely an appearance riddled with those deep contradictions, the ideological expressions of which we have just alluded to. It is only natural that two diametrically opposed views should emerge. On the one hand, a rejection of all political, democratic revolution was deduced from the fact that this convulsion in the world had only made the material conditions of the nascent proletariat worse (this conception, which found its crassest form in Proudhon's work, had in Büchner's day, however, many antecedents in France). On the other, the democratic-plebeian revolutionaries were under the illusion that if the Jacobin terror were only taken to its logical conclusion then this would inevitably lead to the masses' salvation from material impoverishment. The depth and significance of this antinomy can be seen in the history of the French workers' movement, in which even as late as the imperialist period the two extreme poles of this antinomy still have representatives in the persons of Sorel and Jaurès.

This antinomy is the tragic contradiction underlying Büchner's *Danton's Death*. In other words, this tragedy did not lend artistic form to a young person's subjective experiences ('disillusion', 'despair', etc.); rather, Büchner attempted with the great instinct of a true, epoch-making tragedian to depict the major contradiction of his age in the light of the French Revolution. And yet not in a fashion that involved his imposing the problems of his time onto that period and thus using the revolution as a mere costume. On the contrary, he recognized with the astute eye of the great tragic poet that this problem of his epoch first arose precisely in the French Revolution, where it took on a significant historical and polemical form.

With a clarity and vehemence reminiscent of Shakespeare, this problem is exposed in the very first scenes of the drama. Danton and his friends speak of the fact that the Revolution must be brought to an end. 'The Revolution must end, and the Republic must begin,' says Hérault. Very soon afterwards Büchner shows, in a turbulent and realistic scene involving the ordinary people of Paris, what the poor think about the achievements of the revolution hitherto.

They [namely, the rich – G.L.] have no blood in their veins but what they've sucked from ours. They told us: Kill the aristos, they are wolves. So we strung up the aristos. They told us: The veto is taking the bread from your mouths. So we killed the veto. They told us: The Girondins are starving you. So we guillotined the Girondins. But they pulled the clothes from the dead men's backs and left us freezing and barefoot as before.[11]

In all the plebeian scenes Büchner shows this deep bitterness on the part of the pauperized masses. Moreover, as a great realist, he simultaneously shows how these masses cannot yet have a clear awareness of what purposeful actions that embitterment could be converted into. The insolubility of the objective contradictions in reality (and also in Büchner's head) are reflected in the fact that the people's bitterness is still without direction, oscillating from one extreme to the other. The only firm characteristic that remains is the embitterment itself and a cynical but sincere statement of the immediately visible causes of the masses' disillusionment. Büchner is, in other words, completely consistent in artistic terms in that he portrays this plebeian scene with a grotesque, realistic form of bitter humour, a humour learned from Shakespeare.

However, the significance of this plebeian scene within the overall composition extends beyond the Shakespearean model. The people's role as a chorus providing a social basis for the protagonists' respective personal tragedies and commenting on it both in social terms and in terms of the plot, increased substantially in the period of development in the drama preceding and following the French Revolution. The plebeian scenes in Goethe's *Egmont*, Schiller's *Wallenstein's Camp*, etc., demonstrate this development clearly: it consists of a close interlinking of what occurs at the *top* of society, in the tragic intertwining of the fates of the main protagonists, with the movements, developments *below*, in the life of the people itself.

Büchner, however, takes things one step further: in his work, material conditions as well as the resultant spiritual and moral state of mind of the Parisian populace are the ultimate fundamental reason underlying both the conflict between Robespierre and Danton and the course it takes, namely the downfall of Danton's supporters. This chorus is thus more active than that of Classical Greek theatre, and intervenes directly in the action. Yet Büchner restricts – with very conscious artistry – the role of the plebeian scenes to a chorus-like intellectual and atmospheric accompaniment to the tragic fates of the leading, 'world-historical figures'. For it was indeed in the struggles between Robespierre and Danton that the historically decisive awareness of the world crisis we have been describing found its greatest expression. The people's bitterness, as yet without direction, is therefore both superior and inferior to the tragic individual struggles that occur at the top of society. Büchner gave an overwhelmingly powerful dramatic form to this profound and accurate historical insight with his original, Shakespeareanized chorus-like portrayal of underlying social conditions, an approach that nevertheless went beyond Shakespeare's own conception of the people.

It is on this ground that the major political conflict within the play, namely that between Danton's supporters on the one hand and those of Robespierre and Saint-Just on the other, occurs. Danton wants, as we have seen, to end the revolution, whereas Robespierre wants it to continue – on his own terms. Danton's demand that revolutionary terror be renounced is simply the logical consequence of his premises. He thus states at the outset of his decisive audience with Robespierre: 'Where self-defence ends, murder begins.' Robespierre answers:

The social revolution is not yet accomplished. To carry out a revolution by halves is to dig your own grave. The society of the privileged is not yet dead. The robust strength of the people must replace this utterly effete class.[12]

The common view of this decisive scene in the play is that, with his objective intellectual superiority, Danton contemptuously rebuts the moralizing of the narrow-minded and limited Robespierre. It is true that Danton treats Robespierre with contempt. It is also true that Büchner shares Danton's philosophical-ideological viewpoint – epicurean materialism – and therefore, as we shall see, shows dramatic-lyrical sympathy for his character. The real intellectual and dramatic course of this dialogue is, however, completely different, and demonstrates precisely Büchner's great talent as a tragedian. Danton at no point disproves Robespierre's *political* stance. Rather, he evades a political discussion, he has no argument to counter Robespierre's political remonstration, to counter his political conception, which, as we may recollect from the last letters of Büchner cited above, is essentially that of Büchner himself. Danton transfers the conversation to the level of a discussion on principles of morality, and as a materialist scores an easy victory over Robespierre's Rousseauesque moral principles. However this cheap victory in the discussion contains no answer to the central political question, the question as to the antagonism between rich and poor. Here Büchner shows himself to be a born dramatist, for he embodies the great social contradiction, which resided as an insoluble contradiction in his own feelings and thoughts, in two historical figures – each endowed with the necessary level of greatness and narrow-mindedness.

Danton's evasiveness is no accident, but rather the kernel of his tragedy. In Büchner's play Danton is a great bourgeois revolutionary who, however, does not wish to go beyond the bourgeois aims of the revolution in any respect. He is an epicurean materialist, fully ensconced in the eighteenth century tradition of Holbach or Helvétius. Such materialism is the sharpest and most consistent ideological form witnessed in pre-revolutionary France; it is a world-view that provides the *ideological preparation* for the Revolution. Marx characterized this philosophy as follows:

Holbach's theory is the historically justified philosophical illusion about the bourgeoisie just then developing in France, whose thirst for exploitation could still be described as a thirst for the full development of individuals in conditions of intercourse freed from the old feudal fetters. Liberation from the standpoint of the bourgeoisie, i.e. competition, was, of course, for the eighteenth century the only possible way of offering the individuals a new career for freer development.[13]

However, new contradictions in society arise precisely by virtue of the victory the Revolution scored over the monarchy and the feudalists, a victory in which Danton played a leading role – contradictions foreign and abhorrent to Danton, to which his ideology has no answer. Robespierre and Saint-Just wish to press ahead with the revolution, yet for Danton such a continuation is no longer *his* revolution. He fought for society's liberation from feudalism, but delivering the poor from the yoke of capitalism no longer has anything in common with his aims. He says of the people in a dialogue immediately prior to the great debate with Robespierre: 'They hate libertines as eunuchs hate whole men.'[14]

For this reason he feels alienated from the people and from politics. In conversations with his friends one repeatedly hears that he is a 'dead saint' of the Revolution. It is no coincidence that memories of the September murders, and the connected pangs of conscience, arise in Danton directly before his arrest. As long as the revolution had still been his own, i.e. in September, he had acted decisively and courageously and viewed the September murders as a natural, necessary means to save the Revolution. If the Revolution, however, goes beyond this, if it follows the plebeian course advocated by Robespierre and Saint-Just, then Danton's alienation from this revolution will of psychological necessity result in a conflict of conscience.

And Danton does not simply imagine this alienation from the people, as his supporters would have him believe. After the debate with Robespierre he goes to the *sections* to warn them of Robespierre's intentions: 'They were very respectful – just like undertakers,' says Danton himself.[15] His entrancing eloquence when in the dock admittedly makes a great impression on his listeners. But this is only a passing impression; he is unable to change the fundamental mood among the broad masses of the people.

Büchner appends a plebeian scene outside the palace of justice immediately after Danton's last great speech. In it one of the citizens says:

Danton has fine clothes. Danton has a lovely house. Danton has a beautiful wife. He takes his bath in burgundy, he eats venison off silver plates and sleeps with your wives and daughters when he's drunk. Danton was as poor as you are. Where did he get all this from?[16]

Danton's cynical apathy, his world-weary boredom, his reluctance to act, all appear in this light not as the contradictory psychological characteristics of a once vigorous revolutionary, but rather as the necessary mental reaction to his situation. One must not forget in this context that Büchner conceives of this boredom as the predominant trait of the satiated bourgeoisie (we refer here to the letter to Gutzkow cited above, and also to the figure of Leonce in his later comedy [*Leonce and Lena*]).

However, Büchner's Danton is no reactionary bourgeois. He cynically mocks Robespierre's theory of morality – but he has no sympathy for his supporters (with the exception of Camille Desmoulins). What should he fight for? Whom should he fight alongside? Lacroix, one of his followers, refers to himself as a villain; General Dillon wants to free Danton with a band of such followers: 'I'll find support enough. Old soldiers, Girondists, ci-devant nobles.'[17] The fact that he does not wish to enter such a struggle with such allies demonstrates that the revolutionary remains latent in Büchner's Danton.

The strange manner in which Büchner spreads his political and his personal sympathies is mirrored in the whole structure of the play. Robespierre and in particular Saint-Just are real figures, full of dramatic action, and the ones who actually drive events forward. In the first half of the drama and at the end, Danton is admittedly the focus of attention, but more as an object than as the motor behind the action. It is no accident, but rather a credit to Büchner's powers of dramatic composition, that the first act closes with the discussion between Robespierre and Saint-Just following the Danton-Robespierre dialogue, and the second with the scene in the National Convention and the speeches by Robespierre and Saint-Just. And we have seen that even the third act, in which Danton's speeches in his own defence also place him on a central platform in dramatic-scenic terms, does not close with these great rhetorical outbursts, but rather with the scene from which our earlier quotation of the people's condemnation of Danton is taken. And the play itself finally closes with the small scene in which Lucile Desmoulins, who has gone mad, cries out 'Long live the King' on the square where the guillotining has taken place. Danton's *fate* is in other words the centre of the action, but it is not the hero's activities that motivate the drama. Danton is a passive victim of his fate.

IV

Nevertheless, it is the tragedy of Danton and not that of Robespierre and Saint-Just that is at the centre of the drama. A decade later, Karl Marx was to sketch the tragic conflict between these Jacobins in *The Holy Family*. Büchner hinted at various human conflicts in his figure of Robespierre (and unfortunately – this is one of the few inconsistencies in the characterization – he includes what bourgeois historians saw as Robespierre's 'jealousy' of Danton); Saint-Just has few psychologically individualized traits: he is the embodiment of the active, unbroken, plebeian revolutionary, more an ideal figure than a fully developed character. In dramatic terms, he functions as a foil to Danton, not unlike – *mutatis mutandis* – the relationship of Fortinbras to Hamlet.

The central dramatic and tragic significance of the figure of Danton resides in the fact that Büchner, showing exceptional depth of poetic insight, not only laid bare the socio-political crisis in eighteenth century revolutionary endeavours at its turning-point in the French Revolution but – and the two are inextricably bound up with each other – at the same time portrayed the *ideological crisis* of this transition, the crisis of the old mechanistic materialism as the ideology of the bourgeois revolution. The figure of Danton, indeed Danton's fate, is the tragic embodiment of the contradictions generated by historical developments in the period between 1789 and 1848, contradictions which the old materialism was not able to resolve.

The social character of epicurean materialism gets lost along the way. As a result of the objective situation, eighteenth century materialists were in a position to believe that their theory of society and history – and both are essentially idealist in philosophical terms – arose from their materialist epistemology; indeed they believed that they could really derive the course their actions should take from their epicurean materialism. Helvétius says: 'Un homme est juste, lorsque toutes ses actions tendent au bien public' ('A man is just when all his actions promote the public good'). And he judged himself to have derived the substance of such sociality, and its necessary connection with an ethics of the individual, from Epicurean egotism.

The bourgeoisie's victory in the Revolution tears these illusions asunder. The contradictions within the *bien public* emerge sharply at precisely the stage in developments at which Danton is called upon to act. Simple egotism is transformed into capitalist rascality, into cynical moral nihilism. Büchner describes this process with deep irony and superb, discreet poetic force, always confining himself to objective portrayal and never resorting to subjective commentary. Barrère, a common upstart, says: 'The world really would be topsy-turvy if the so-called rascals were to be hanged by the so-called honest men.'[18] And Laflotte, an informer, who is about to betray General Dillon, defends such an action with Dantonesque, with epicurean and egotistical arguments: 'No, pain is the only sin, and suffering the only vice. I'll stay virtuous.'[19]

Robespierre and Saint-Just, at least in comparison to *these* characters, retain a yardstick for their actions in that they wish to see a plebeian revolution, admittedly on the basis of a rejection of philosophical materialism, and on the basis of a Rousseauesque idealism which – in itself, viewed in isolation from the political situation of his immediate actions – Danton's irony and intellectual superiority is easily able to refute, particularly in the moral sphere. As, however, political action is the order of the day, Danton is not helped by the philosophical superiority of materialism. He has lost all direction as a politician, as a thinker, and as a human being.

Old materialism's inability to make sense of *history* is pushed to the foreground of this great tragedy. Büchner himself experienced this conflict to the core without being able to resolve it in philosophical terms. He writes on his studies of the history of the Revolution (from Giessen to his fiancée):

I felt shattered by the terrible fatalism of history. I find in human nature a terrible uniformity, in human relationships an irrepressible force, shared by everyone and no one. The individual just foam on the wave, greatness mere chance, the rule of genius a puppet play, a laughable struggle with an iron law; to recognise this is the highest insight, to control it impossible. It no longer occurs to me to bow down before the monuments and bigwigs of history. . . 'Must' is one of the words of damnation with which mankind is baptised. The saying, 'It must needs be that offences come, but woe to that man by whom the offence cometh', is terrible. What is it in us that lies and murders and steals?[20]

It is of exceptional interest to see how and with what variations this outburst finds its way into Büchner's *Danton* in the scene of his arrest. Büchner makes almost verbatim use of various statements from the letter, putting them into the doubting, despairing Danton's mouth. One readily perceives the extent to which the figure of Danton is the poetic expression of these contradictions which

Büchner experienced so profoundly. Nevertheless, close attention needs to be paid to the differences in the formulations, differences in stress. Danton arrives at a mystical agnosticism, is confronted by his own despairing inability to understand history. For Büchner, the cognition of historical necessity, even if one cannot control it, remains of paramount importance. Thus, Büchner's 'must' is not used despairingly, pessimistically as is Danton's. In the play, Büchner uses compositional means to provide an answer to Danton's doubts: namely in the form of Saint-Just's great speech to the National Convention in which he passionately affirms and glorifies the unyielding and inhuman necessity of history, the march of revolution which grinds underfoot whole generations that stand in its way, likening its effects to the irresistible eruption of a volcano or to an earthquake.

Here, we again see how the two protagonists in the drama embody the contradictions, the crisis in Büchner's life and thought. But it is only both together, in their tragic interplay, that they embody Büchner's thoughts; neither Danton nor Saint-Just is, taken on his own, Büchner's mouthpiece. Admittedly, Saint-Just's point of view is closest to Büchner's own conception of the solution to the 'bread-and-butter issues' of the day. It is likewise the case that the figures of both Robespierre and Saint-Just are equipped with rhetorical features which can be traced back to Büchner's speech on Cato. But Robespierre and Saint-Just are no more identical with Büchner than is Danton. Yet emotionally Büchner is closer to Danton than to Saint-Just, with whom he feels a greater political affinity, precisely because in this major intellectual crisis he steadfastly clung onto materialist philosophy and never lost faith in the possibility of applying it to solve the great problems of life.

The contradiction which is dealt with in the tragedy in relation to the materialist affirmation of life, to the philosophy of enjoyment, is equally a major ideological problem of the transitional period. Camille Desmoulins says in the first scene of the play: 'Divine Epicurus and sweet-buttocked Venus – these must be the doorkeepers of the republic, not Saints Marat and Chalier.'[21] This sounds fairly Thermidorian. But, in the period in question, the *joie de vivre* of the bourgeois class once they have become rulers, repeatedly intermingles with the longing for a new and better world in which no ascetic restrictions are placed on human virtue. Heine also proclaims this *joie de vivre* in his poetry and prose; in fact he almost always proclaims it in such a manner as to incorporate both currents.

The blossoming flesh of Titian's paintings is thoroughly protestant. The thighs of his Venus are much more convincing theses than those which the German monk pasted on the church door in Wittenberg.[22]

However, in the case of Heine a path leads directly from here to that other 'better song' which proclaims the *joie de vivre* and worldliness of a liberated humankind.

This contradiction is nourished, seen from the other end of the spectrum, by the nascent revolutionary working class movement. Babeuf is the heir to both the old materialism and the revolutionary asceticism of Robespierre. Great poets like Heine and Büchner, great thinkers, such as Fourier, are convinced of the inadequacy of *both* approaches; none of them is capable of reaching a solution free of contradictions. Even the early Marx and Engels still find it necessary, having reached a position of dialectical materialism, to fight against the ascetic conception of the revolution.

Heine's outlook is broader, more flexible and richer than Büchner's; he processed Hegelian dialectics in his own way, rather than ignoring it, as did Büchner. Yet even he is only able, both in intellectual and poetic terms, to express the contradictory trends in all their contradictoriness, and remains unable to reveal their uniform driving principle. Of course, Büchner also fails to find a solution. What he seeks politically, the concretization of the 'poor' in the revolutionary proletariat, does not exist in his reality, the reality of Germany. He cannot therefore find a dialectical conception of history even in his consistent materialism. Büchner's personal uniqueness, however, consists in his having gone all the way down a contradictory path unwaveringly, in a straight line and without being troubled by the contradictions, instead of vacillating to and fro between the contradictory extremes, as did Heine.

V

It is this that makes Büchner's realism, trained in the tradition of Shakespeare and Goethe, so significant. Politically, he longs for the 'poor' to attain consciousness, to be aroused to political activity. As a great realist, however, the literary figure he portrays is Woyzeck: helpless, exploited, ceaselessly hounded back and forth, kicked around by everyone – the greatest depiction of the German 'poor' of that time.

Gundolf and Pfeiffer wish to falsify this magnificent social portrait by making it out to be a study of mood, whereby Pfeiffer adds 'depth' to Gundolf's aestheticizing forgery by claiming that Büchner's atmospheric art was the expression of his demonic nature. 'Mood is for him the constant presence of the demonic. Mood means the demonic constantly breathing down our necks.' The purpose of these analyses is to turn Büchner into a literary precursor of Strindberg and Expressionism. Here again, historical truth is being stood on its head. Büchner portrays Woyzeck's physical and ideological helplessness in the face of his oppressors and exploiters; in other words, real social helplessness, depicted from the viewpoint of existence, the essence of which Woyzeck at least senses, even if he does not clearly perceive it. When his captain rebukes him for immorality, Woyzeck answers:

Us poor people – you see, Captain: money, money. If a man has no money – just let him try to reproduce his kind in a moral sort of way! We're made of flesh and blood like other people. Our sort will always be unblessed in this world and the next. I think that if we went to heaven, we'd have to help make thunder.[23]

Strindberg, by contrast, depicts the profound experience of his own helplessness in the face of the unleashed powers of capitalism; he does not see through them and therefore has to mystify them. He does not portray concrete existential helplessness, but rather the ideological reflections of his own experience of helplessness. Thus in literary terms, he is not Büchner's successor, but rather a diametrical opposite.

Büchner incessantly and openly promulgated his realistic inclinations on a high theoretical level. His theory of realism is: poetic reflection of life in all its dynamism, vitality and inexhaustible richness. He demanded of the drama that it adhere to historical fact. In *Danton's Death* Desmoulins already lambasts artistic idealism. And in *Lenz*, the unfinished novella, Büchner has his hero, the famous friend of Goethe's youth, profess the following allegiance to true realism:

'This idealism is the most shameful contempt for human nature. If only artists would try to submerge themselves in the life of the very humblest person and to reproduce it with all its faint agitations, hints of experience, the subtle, hardly perceptible play of his features. . .' He himself had tried something of the kind in his *Private Tutor* and *The Soldiers*. 'These are the most prosaic people in the world, but the emotional vein is identical in almost every individual; all that varies is the thickness of the shell that this vein must penetrate. All one needs for these things is eyes and ears in one's head.'[24]

The ideological connection between Büchner's endeavours to achieve a consistent, plebeian democracy and his literary realism is clear here.

Thus, we now have a clear picture of Büchner before us: as a revolutionary and a great realist in the wretchedly backward Germany of the eighteen thirties. How was he supposed, in the face of such a miserable reality, not to suffer outbursts of rage and embitterment? Yet, seen in the context of his life as a whole, these do not even lead to such vacillations as they did in the case of Heine, let alone give way to 'disillusion' or 'despair'. In his short life, Büchner acted consistently and without vacillating: as a plebeian-democratic revolutionary in his political activity, as a philosophical materialist in the field of ideology, and as the successor to Shakespeare and Goethe as a great realist.

VI

To what end does fascism need to falsify Büchner, why does it transform Büchner into someone who 'despaired'? Despite all their efforts at forgery, neither Viëtor nor Pfeiffer were able to turn him into a herald of the 'Third Reich'. What then have they gained by falsely transforming the revolutionary into a representative of 'heroic pessimism', the realist into the 'atmospheric artist of the demonic'?

One should not underestimate the political effect such demagogy has on literary history, however crude and obvious these forgeries may be.

Most assuredly, the whole fascist German press never ceases to profess its belief in the future of fascist Germany. But it is only a belief, indeed blind trust, rather than a certainty or a real perspective for the future. It is not thinking individuals but rather people who have been *hypnotized* to the point of lacking any individual will who are meant to clamour round the 'Führer'. To this end, an atmosphere of blind faith has to be created, in which context the annihilation of each and every rational conception of nature and history is imperative. Every philosophy of the past that has been misappropriated by German fascism (Schopenhauer, Romanticism and Nietzsche) denies the cognizability of the world. People are meant to be saved from chaos, from nothingness, from the dark depths of despair by a 'miracle', by the 'Führer'.

What is more, National Socialism came to power as a result of the masses' despair (including the mass of the intelligentsia). This despair had very real economic and ideological reasons: the impending collapse of the capitalist system and then the real collapse in the life of millions of working people, the collapse of the hitherto dominant bourgeois ideology. The despair of the masses that arose on such a breeding ground can provide the starting-point for a revolutionary uprising, but at the same time offers openings for the most devastating and crudest demagogy. Lenin wrote the following on the despair of the masses on the eve of the victorious October Revolution:

Is it any wonder that the crowd, tired out, and made wretched by hunger and the prolongation of the war, clutches at the Black-Hundred poison? Can one imagine a capitalist society on the eve of collapse in which the oppressed masses are *not* desperate? Is there any doubt that the despair of the masses, a large part of whom are still ignorant, *will* express itself in the increased consumption of all sorts of poison?[25]

The despair of the German masses was systematically stirred up by the Nazis' social and national demagogy; all forms of thought or pursuit of truth were suppressed in order to prepare the way for the 'miracle', in order later to throw those who, as a consequence of the further deterioration in their material and ideological situation remained desperate and could no longer be fully anaesthetized by the opium of Nazi propaganda, into torture chambers and concentration camps.

The crisis in every social system is always accompanied by a major crisis in ideology; one need only think of Ancient Rome, or of the dissolution of feudal society. It is precisely at the moment of their breakdown that economic categories prove themselves to be the 'basis of existence', the 'existentially determining factors': when the material, social existence of the broad masses is uprooted, this necessarily gives rise to a world-view of rootlessness, despair, pessimism and mysticism.

The ugliness, mendacity, uncertainty and injustice, indeed the senselessness of life under capitalism, appear at an early date in the works of a series of poets and thinkers as the senselessness of *life* as such, in the works of writers and thinkers who cannot even imagine that there is a perspective for rejuvenation. The despair thus generated, often honest, critical and even rebellious, is forever being exploited by the sycophants of capitalism in order at least to induce those who cannot be won directly for the cause of capitalism to be paralysed in a directionless and goalless state of despair that therefore poses no danger to capitalism. Such desperate persons are harmless to capitalism, and a large proportion of them will, as experience shows, sooner or later give in. Dostoyevsky says that the true atheist is only one step from God.

The deeper the crisis in the capitalist system, the greater the social significance of this despair, for it forces its way into ever broader sections of the masses, influencing ever more profoundly the thought and life of human beings. And as its social importance increases, the ideological level of the despair declines, taking on ever more feverish, ever more virulent forms that eventually give way to mysticism. One need only think of the series comprising Schopenhauer, Kierkegaard, Dostoyevsky and Nietzsche.

The deeper the crisis, the less able are simple apologetics to provide an ideological defence of the capitalist system. The senselessness, the cruelty and bestiality of life, man's exposure to the chaos of life, and pessimism as the adequate ideological reaction to this chaos, all have to be taken into account and affirmed; and the apologetics consist in educating the masses, on the basis of this uncritical affirmation, to expect a miracle, to distract them from an unbiased investigation of the concrete social causes of this situation. This new period of capitalist apologetics commences with Nietzsche. The so-called philosophies put forward by Spengler, Klages, Bäumler, etc., are a repeated call for despair – in the service of a reactionary capitalism.

The despair of the masses themselves is, however, honest, even rebellious. It is simply diverted by fascist demagogy in a reactionary direction. And in the process, as Dimitrov has so excellently shown, fascism appeals not only to the backwardness of the intellectual and emotional life of the masses, but also to the searching, still unclear instincts that even tend in the direction of true liberation.[26] It is in fascism's vital interest to confine the despair of the masses to such stultification, darkness and fruitlessness.

In other words, by encouraging such despair and denouncing any examination of the economic basis of the existential collapse of the masses as shallow, crude, un-Germanic, etc., fascist philosophy performs the same demagogic propagandist function for fascism in certain circles as does Streicher's crude anti-Semitism. It is therefore not enough simply to look down arrogantly on the inferior content of this ideology of despair. Of course, Pfeiffer's theory of the demonic is pure nonsense. But such nonsense skilfully latches onto the immediate ideological situation of broad sections of the intelligentsia, distracts them by demagogic means from a true understanding of their situation, leads them into the false depths of an inescapable darkness, into a world of chronic desperation, into Heidegger's 'nullifying nothingness'. In this manner a psychology is cultivated that perceives even in despair a sign of the superior race of human beings which – precisely by means of despair – isolates people, casts them in upon themselves, and teaches the intelligentsia arrogantly to turn their backs on the masses.

In other words, such coarse and crude falsifications have a very concrete social basis and political purpose, and in our struggle to win back the seduced intelligentsia we must work unceasingly to unmask such falsifications. Dostoyevsky was wrong to perceive atheism as the penultimate stage before a perfect faith in God, yet his atheists do adopt such a position. However, the path taken by Jacobsen's Niels Lyhne[27] or Turgenev's Basarov can never lead to any kind of belief in God. If one were to rewrite the history of atheism in such a manner that it culminated in Ivan Karamasov as its pinnacle, this would constitute just such a falsification of history. This is the method used to transform Jacobins such as Hölderlin, revolutionary democrats such as Büchner, indeed even disillusioned rebels such as Flaubert and Baudelaire, who had become sceptical or at times gripped by mystical impulses, into victims of despair *à la* Klages or Heidegger.

Their despair – admittedly a concrete reality in every case – and also their pessimism, their scepticism have nothing in common with such imperialist demagogy. Their thought is, as we have shown in the case of Büchner, *concrete*, *historical* and *social* and its thrust is, precisely because of this, profoundly and comprehensively human. If Büchner 'despairs' at the fact that plebeian-democratic revolution could not be sparked off in the Germany of the eighteen thirties, then his embitterment bears the seeds of future greatness within it, because it is – in his case with lucid awareness, and in that of others more or less unconsciously – directed towards the real future of humankind, the real liberation of human beings from society's yoke. Such a tendency is, however, latent at least as a possibility within every despairing mood of the masses when confronted with the collapse of their material and ideological existence. And this possibility can be brought to life, brought to light by a Büchner or a Hölderlin. This is why the great writers and thinkers of the past pose such a threat to fascism if understood correctly. That is why they have to be falsified, so that the despairing present-day intelligentsia can see a precursor for its own muddle-headedness in Büchner rather than viewing him as an aid in achieving clarity, in entering the fray.

The battle against such falsifications can only be that of the *historically concrete*. For only if an eternally human, supra-historical, meta-social form of despair is ingeniously devised, can the path to real knowledge be blocked. It is our task to make certain that this open and clear language of historical reality can make itself heard. This language is, however, in the case of the truly great figures of the past, that of the concrete struggle for humankind's liberation. Of the legends contrived by German literary history, one is that Lenau, an older, softer and more confused contemporary of Büchner's, was a 'pessimist'. Yet Lenau stated very clearly what the real causes of his 'pessimism' were. In the closing verses of his *Albigenses* he says of his own situation:

> Geteiltes Los mit längstentschwundnen Streitern
> Wird für die Nachwelt unsre Brust erweitern,
> Daß wir im Unglück uns prophetisch freuen

Und Kampf und Schmerz, sieglosen Tod nicht Scheuen.
So wird dereinst in viel beglücktern Tagen
Die Nachwelt auch nach unserm Leide fragen.

Woher der düstre Unmut unsrer Zeit,
Der Groll, die Eile, die Zerrissenheit? –
Das Sterben in der Dämmerung ist schuld
An dieser freudenarmen Ungeduld;
Herb ist's, das langersehnte Licht nicht schauen,
Zu Grabe gehn in seinem Morgengrauen.

A fate shared with fighters long since passed away will expand our breasts
for posterity so that in our misfortune we can rejoice in advance and have
no fear of struggle and pain and death without victory. Thus in far happier
days to come posterity will ask after the sources of our grief.

Whence springs the dark discontent of our age, the anger, haste and divi-
siveness? Dying in the twilight is to blame for this impatience so bereft of
joy; it is a harsh fate not to glimpse this long-awaited light, to go to the grave
by the grey light of dawn.

And even though Lenau has clearly shown throughout his poem
what he understands liberation to mean, he nevertheless supplements this in the last stanza by listing the long series of struggles by
the Albigenses for liberation right up to the storming of the Bastille.
He adds the words 'and so forth' ('und so weiter') in order to say
quite unequivocally that his 'despair' is of a concrete, historical
nature, namely indignation and impatience at the fact that the
democratic revolution in Germany has been so long in the making,
and that his 'pessimism' is levelled at the wretched backwardness of
Germany in his time and bears within it a ray of hope for the future,
for the final realization of the revolution.

A certain sense of guilt must make itself felt in us when considering this blatant contrast between the historical facts and their
falsification by the fascists. All the more so as these crude fascist lies
are based on 'more refined' forgeries of history in earlier periods, in
periods when the legal avenue was still open to us to combat each
and every forgery. Undoubtedly, the narrow and rigid method of
vulgar sociology, ignoring as it does the richness and complexity of
great historical figures, bears some of the responsibility for the failure of the correct Marxist conception of history to have sufficiently
reached the masses, or to have had a profound enough impact on a
sufficiently broad section of the intelligentsia. But our anti-fascist

friends among the writers and literary theorists should also devote some thought to this. They should examine whether they did not in fact make too many concessions to those dangerous ideologies that prepared the way for fascism out of some misunderstood 'modernity', out of an uncritical collaboration with philosophical currents of the day. Whether they did not for their part – to remain with the case in point – promote dehistoricization, desocialization, the abstract eternalization of 'despair' in the field of literary history. Is the linking of Büchner to Kierkegaard, Dostoyevsky and Heidegger really a purely fascist invention, or were the fascists able to pounce on 'preparatory works' which, although intended as quite the opposite, nonetheless pointed in this direction?

Unmasking fascist demagogy means to scrutinize the intellectual weaponry everywhere, not only among Communists, but also among all honest anti-fascists.

1937

Heinrich Heine as National Poet*

Marxists generally pay far too little attention to the lives of the great writers and artists of the bourgeois era. However, it is by no means the case – as most bourgeois literary historians would have it – that biographies provide the true key to understanding individual writers. On the contrary, the writer's biography and the nature of his writings can only be properly understood if viewed from a vantage point that both takes the society of the time into account and is based on a knowledge of that period's major social tendencies, struggles and contradictions. In this sense a Marxist study of writers' biographies is able to provide exceptionally sharp insights that hold true for capitalist culture as a whole. A close study of many such personal histories would reveal that the lives of almost all the major writers of the capitalist age are one long tale of martyrdom, by which we do not just mean that a large number of major writers have physically perished as a direct result of their impoverishment during the age of capitalism. Even those who had the good fortune to be born into a life of material security often paid for this with severe damage to their personality and their development as authors. Moreover, most of the major writers whose fate lay somewhere between these two extremes of absolute poverty and a sheltered life on private means were subjected to a whole range of gruesome, humiliating circumstances that stunted and deformed their development. The immediate material and moral conditions of their lives severely hindered all of them, preventing them from developing their abilities to the full.

I

The circumstances of Heine's life are determined by the fact that he lived in Germany during the dawn of the capitalist age and came from a poor family which was nevertheless related to multi-millionaires. Heine lived at a time when in Germany the economic precon-

* First published in *Internationale Literatur*, nos 9/10, 1937.

ditions for an independent career as a writer already existed, when a productive and popular writer already had the material means with which to forego the patronage of petty princes, state employment, etc. by living on the proceeds of his work as a writer. Heine was without doubt the most popular and widely read German author of this period. His writings, poetry as well as prose, were printed in larger editions than had ever been known in Germany before, and his publisher, Campe, became a rich man thanks to Heine's works. Heine himself, however, was never able to live on the proceeds of his writing. For him, writing was always a very uncertain secondary source of income and every new book, every new edition involved an unpleasant, ugly and humiliating struggle with his publisher. It was a struggle not only to secure at least a small part of the fee due to him, but also to prevent the original text being mutilated by alterations. Indeed, the publishing house treated the original text in a most scandalous fashion (ostensibly to avoid official censorship, but very often for unscrupulous reasons in connection with the literary politics of a clique). In order to save his honour as a writer, Heine repeatedly had to resort to appeals to the public, subjecting his publisher to public exposure. Although we do not have the space here to describe these petty wrangles which accompanied Heine throughout his life, suffice it to say that in the eighteen forties, because Gutzkow and his clique objected to it, the publication of Heine's second collection of poetry was delayed for years.[1] The very same Gutzkow clique arbitrarily altered the title of Heine's book on Ludwig Börne, only then to attack Heine publicly for this 'presumptuous' title. And so I could go on.

The impossibility of material independence as a writer had a disruptive influence on Heine's private life and greatly endangered his political effectiveness. It meant humiliating dependence on his wealthy relatives, the family of the Hamburg millionaire Salomon Heine. Admittedly, this dependence dated from his early youth – Heine's studies had been supported by his rich uncle – but even as a famous writer the circumstances described above forced him into this humiliating dependence on his relatives. The petty-bourgeois moralists among Heine's biographers accuse him of irresponsibility and extravagance in this matter, portraying Heine himself as the guilty party. It is true that Heine never became an ascetic. Born and raised in the Rhineland, the part of Germany which had at that time experienced the greatest degree of capitalist development, into a class that was on the point of seizing economic and political power, he remained throughout his life a person of effervescent *joie de vivre*. His rejection of petty-bourgeois asceticism is, as we shall see later, an essential and decisive element in his ideological and literary impact. Leading a life of comparative material well-being lay in the nature of Heine's talents. We have seen that his writing could have provided him with the necessary means. It failed to do so by reason of the capitalist social order. The funding he received from his relatives, a means of support which assumes such significance in the eyes of petty bourgeois moralists, was a mere bagatelle, a tip, compared to the fortune owned by the Hamburg millionaires. The maximum amount received by Heine from his relatives was an allowance of 4,800 francs. Here again it is impossible to describe the extent of the tragi-comedy of Heine's relationship to his rich relatives. Heine himself gave this poetic description of his uncle's mansion and garden, the scene of his adolescent love affair with Salomon Heine's daughters:

> Accursed garden! Ah, there was
> No single spot throughout the years
> In which my heart had not been torn,
> My eyes not blinded by my tears.
>
> There wasn't a single tree, in truth,
> Beneath whose shadow an affront
> Had not been flung at me, by tongues
> Refined or crude, and suave or blunt.[2]

Heine's uncle had promised to leave him an allowance in his will. On Salomon Heine's death this promise turned out to be untrue, and for many years the heir refused to make any payments. Only after frightful humiliation was Heine able to secure the 'clemency' of being allowed to continue to draw on this allowance and – following his death – to ensure that his wife continued to receive half the amount. Poor Heine wrote the following about his 'reconciliation' with his cousin Karl Heine in his own will:

Yes, he [the cousin, G.L.] showed once again all his noble spirit, all his love, and as he gave me his hand to put the seal on his solemn promise, I pressed it to my lips, so moved was I, and how he resembled his late father in this

moment, my poor uncle, whose hand I had often kissed like a child whenever he showed me favour![3]

There is a poetic commentary by Heine on this disgraceful act of
ceremonious 'reconciliation' in which, however, Karl Heine is not
mentioned by name:

> Heart, my heart, let plaints and protests
> Stream in torrents burning hot,
> But of *him* be never mention –
> May his memory be forgot!
>
> May his memory be forgotten,
> – Nor recalled in prose or verse –
> Dog, you'll lie obscure in darkness,
> You will rot beneath my curse![4]

The price for this 'family generosity' was the destruction of Heine's
memoirs. This work, to which Heine attached the greatest importance throughout his life, vanished because his relatives were afraid
of the poet's true living conditions being revealed.

> When I die, they'll cut my tongue out
> From a corpse untenanted;
> For they fear I'll come back – talking –
> From the Kingdom of the Dead.[5]

We must constantly bear Heine's living conditions in mind if we
are to give a fair assessment of his journalistic and political career.
For this career is full of rather shameful attempts at compromise
with the powers of feudal absolutist Germany that Heine despised
and fought against. Even as a young man – already a successful
writer – Heine applied for a professorship in Munich and had his
publisher Cotta intimate to the government that at heart he was not
as radical as he seemed. Before and after the July Revolution he had
his friend Varnhagen von Ense inquire of the Prussian government
whether it might not be possible to find some kind of *modus vivendi*
between Prussia and Heine. And so on. His acceptance of sponsorship by the Guizot government may have been the greatest public
scandal in Heine's life, but it was still far less shameful than those
failed attempts at compromise. When the sponsorship affair was
made public in 1848, Heine referred to Marx in order to justify
himself. Marx never publicly disowned him, but wrote to Engels
about the matter:

I now have Heine's 3 volumes at home. Amongst other things he retails at some length a lie to the effect that I, etc., went to console him after he had been 'attacked' in the Augsburg *A.[llgemeine] Z.[eitung]* for having accepted money from Louis Philippe. The good Heine deliberately forgets that my intervention on his behalf took place at the end of 1843 and thus could have no connection with facts which came to light *after* the February revolution of 1848. But let it pass. Worried by his evil conscience – the old dog has a monstrous memory for such things – he is trying to ingratiate himself.[6]

The existence of these dark shadows in Heine's character cannot be denied. However, on the one hand mention must be made of the material background of his life in order to pass fair judgement on them and, on the other, they must be fitted into the totality of Heine's literary activity. It would of course be wrong to attribute in mechanistic fashion these waverings, compromises and corruptions, etc., solely to the insecurity of his material means of subsistence. It is quite another question, however, to what extent and in what measure the epicurean instability and lack of scruples, the personal 'Machiavellianism' with which he conducted his life, was developed and cultivated from this material base. Rahel Varnhagen criticizes young Heine's instability in the severest of tones: 'Don't become like Brentano, I couldn't bear it! . . . Heine must become "substantial", even if it has to be beaten into him.' And in one of his later letters to Marx, Engels compares Heine's character with that of Horace:

Old Horace reminds me in places of Heine, who learnt a great deal from him and was, *au fond politice* no less common a cur. Remember how the sterling fellow challenged the *vultus instantis tyranni* and licked Augustus' boots. And the old goat is quite charming in other respects, too.[7]

For all his grandiloquent public denials Heine was of course relatively well aware of the weakness of his political character. When defending Voltaire's character against Alfieri's attacks, one can tell from the tone that it is an act of self-defence:

Voltaire is done an injustice when people claim he was less enthusiastic than Rousseau; he was merely cleverer and more dexterous. Clumsiness always seeks refuge in stoicism and moans laconically at the sight of the elegance of others. Alfieri holds it against Voltaire that he attacked the mighty in his philosophical writings yet was prepared to be their torch-bearing courtier. It escaped the notice of this dismal Piemontese that

Voltaire, by obligingly holding the torch up to the mighty, was illuminating their vulnerability for all to see.[8]

This type of ironic 'tactic' of polemical assassination by false praise is of course no excuse for the gross political indecencies in Heine's life. On the other hand, one must never lose sight of the fact that, despite his various successful and unsuccessful attempts at compromise, the basic tenor of his writing shows that he fought intelligently and relentlessly against German feudal absolutism, and that even the 'praise' he gave the 'July Monarchy' was written with easily discernible irony in nearly every case. Prince Metternich's intelligent and unprincipled secretary, Friedrich Gentz, always understood this and put unofficial pressure on Cotta to suppress Heine's reports on France for the *Augsburger Allgemeine Zeitung*. In his journalistic activity Heine was constantly engaged in guerrilla warfare with the censors in order to gain access to a mass audience. He always dismissed the small émigré newspapers with very small circulations in both Germany and France; he was fighting to gain a mass audience and developed a special ironic style in order to smuggle his criticism of the political and social situation past the censors. His socialist leanings, which grew more pronounced during his time in Paris, and his indifference to bourgeois forms of government, which intensified under the influence of Saint-Simonism, helped him to develop this kind of literary tactic. In a letter to his friend Laube he gives the following advice:

In political questions you can make as many concessions as you wish, for the diverse political forms of state and the governments are but means; monarchy or republic, democratic or aristocratic institutions are of no importance as long as the primary principles of life, the idea of life itself, remain undecided. . . By distinguishing between these two aspects of the question one is also able to appease the censors; for discussion of religious principle and morality cannot be denied without rendering null and void the *protestant* idea of freedom of thought and freedom of opinion; even the Philistines are bound to concur on this point. . . You follow my meaning.[9]

That Heine was not talking about a real political compromise is clearly shown by his later letter to Laube: 'We must harmonize with the *Hallische Jahrbücher* and the *Rheinische Zeitung*, we must never make a secret of our political sympathies and social antipathies. . .'[10]

When judging the basic tenor of Heine's journalistic activity,

admission of his vacillations and compromises should not, therefore, lead to concessions to the contemporary petty bourgeois
critics, who accused him of 'indifferentism', and even of turning his
back on the liberation movement, reverting to monarchism, etc.
There are of course innumerable passages in Heine's writings which
could justify such allegations when quoted in isolation. However,
when one reads them in context one generally sees that they
are partly ironic, partly expressions of the political tactics Heine
adopted (though it must be conceded that this was often a question-
able 'private tactics'). In Paris, Heine often confessed his allegiance
to monarchism, to the July Monarchy, but the intelligent reactionaries have always been better able to judge the true worth of such
'confessions' than the narrow-minded petty-bourgeois republicans.
Thus Friedrich Gentz, in his letter to Cotta about Heine's newspaper reports from Paris mentioned earlier, writes:

The clergy and the aristocracy have long since fallen from favour, they have
been done away with: *requiescant in pace!* But when more scorn is heaped on
men like Périer and their followers, i.e. employees, bankers, landowners
and shopkeepers than on the former princes, counts and barons, who is it
then who is to govern the nations?[11]

And for this reason he demands that Cotta should suppress the
reports by that 'disreputable adventurer' Heine. So in spite of all his
ironic and tactical manoeuvering, Heine was able to regard himself
as an honourable soldier of the liberation struggle.

> 'If ever I put sheep's clothing on,
> it was purely a practical measure,
> it kept me warm, but I never felt
> that Sheepdom afforded much pleasure.
>
> 'I'm not a sheep, I'm not a dog,
> not after high rank, not selfish –
> I've always remained a wolf, my heart
> and these teeth of mine are wolfish.'[12]

At the same time, however, the ironic and tactical stance Heine
took on many current political affairs does have an essential objective reason closely bound up with his best qualities. Heine's life
presents the moderately attentive observer with a strange paradox.
Heine is without doubt the most popular and most widely read
German writer of his time, and yet one notices, when one reads his

intimate confessions, that almost his whole life was spent in appalling isolation and loneliness. Most of his friendships (Varnhagen von Ense,[13] Immermann,[14] Laube,[15] Meissner,[16] etc.) could only be kept up, if at all, by extremely careful diplomacy on Heine's part. The source of this loneliness and the diplomacy which became necessary as a result of it lies not in any of Heine's personal psychological characteristics, and certainly not in his Judaism, to which his anti-Semitic critics and Zionist defenders attach such importance. We believe, in opposition to both camps, that Heine the writer and thinker was intimately connected with the development of Germany, that his isolation had nothing to do with his Jewish origins, a problem which, after all, does not arise in the lives of either Börne[17] or Marx. The reason is simply that Börne was deeply involved in the movement of the German radical petty bourgeoisie and Marx in that of the German proletariat, so that each, in different ways, experienced the life and development of a class. Heine, however, had no links with any class or party in Germany. His development took him far beyond the horizon of the radical petty bourgeoisie to a relatively high level of understanding of the historic mission and the historic role of the proletariat, yet without enabling him to throw in his lot with the revolutionary proletariat. Heine therefore remained throughout his life in a position that wavered between bourgeois and proletarian democracy. Although he realized very early on that the struggles between political parties and the class struggles underlying them had reached a significance that transcended national differences, he could never commit himself completely and unreservedly to one class or one party. As a bourgeois intellectual Heine is at times very conceited about this independence, this non-partisanship. For example, he describes a conversation with his mother in a boastfully ironic tone:

> But my mother began her questions again –
> you know how an old girl natters –
> a thousand things she wanted to know,
> among them some delicate matters.
>
> 'My dear boy! how do you see things now?
> Do you still have your addiction
> to politics? Which party now
> commands your whole-hearted conviction?'

'These oranges, mother dear, are good,
so rich in tasty juices.
But I'm not inclined to swallow the peel,
the wrapping they come in is useless.'[18]

However, in the fierce political and literary feuds which filled Heine's life it turned out to be impossible to maintain this 'splendid isolation'. He needed comrades and allies. And wherever he could find a certain amount of agreement on political, philosophical and literary ideas, Heine desperately seized hold of this common ground and tried for as long as humanly possible to overlook the existing differences of which he was constantly aware. Only at times does it become apparent that the bond was built on objectively very insecure foundations. Wienbarg describes a conversation with Heine during the course of which he asks if Heine really considers Immermann to be a great poet. Heine praises Immermann at first. 'After a short silence he added, "What do you expect? It is so awful to be completely alone!"'[19] A similar story could be told of all of Heine's friendships.

Intellectually speaking, Heine had outgrown bourgeois democracy; in Germany he alone had, before Marx, recognized the role and the significance of the proletariat, yet he never became a proletarian revolutionary. This is the real key to understanding his isolation. This is the reason why, as a lone revolutionary with no class, no party to turn to for support in his struggle against the state and bourgeois society, he was forced into so many vacillations and so many ugly compromises. But for all that Heine still remained faithful to the basic direction of his life. He was justified in saying of himself in one of his later poems:

I fought to hold positions that were lost
In Freedom's War for thirty faithful years:
Without a hope to win, despite the cost
I battled on, expecting only tears.[20]

II

Heine's profile is determined by his position as a pre-1848 German revolutionary. The July Revolution and the move to Paris made him a revolutionary journalist of European standing and significance. Heine's poetry and journalism constituted a very early anticipation of the Franco-German idea nurtured by the most left-wing revolutionaries of the eighteen forties. But the European, Franco-German nature of his journalism does not detract from the central importance in Heine's work of the ideological preparation of the German revolution. On the contrary, a growing and deepening recognition of the class structure of society and the role of the proletariat in the revolution made Heine a clearer and more determined German revolutionary. As we shall see in due course, however, the deeper Heine's insights became, the deeper, at the same time, became the contradictions that tore his thinking and his life into irresolvable dissonances.

In the *Deutsch-Französische Jahrbücher* – written at the time of the close personal friendship between Marx and Heine – the former gives an extremely detailed analysis of the German situation which is very useful for an understanding of Heine's method of journalism and its contradictions. Marx proceeds from Germany's economic and political backwardness, but examines this backwardness in the greater international context of perspectives for the coming revolution. Germany is on the eve of a bourgeois revolution, yet at a time when in the more developed countries, France and Britain, the class struggle between the bourgeoisie and the proletariat has become the central question in the development of society. The German situation is therefore in Marx' words an *anachronism*:

Even the negation of our political present is a reality already covered with dust in the historical lumber-room of modern nations. . . If I negate the German state of affairs in 1843, then, according to the French computation of time, I am hardly in the year 1789, and still less in the focus of the present.[21]

In the course of his later development this profound assessment of Germany's national and international position very quickly leads Marx to the *Communist Manifesto*, to the recognition of the revolutionary role of the proletariat in the bourgeois revolution, to the perspective of a revolutionary transition from the bourgeois to the proletarian revolution. From this standpoint Marx determines the tasks facing revolutionary journalism with respect to Germany. He places the critique of ideology, particularly critique of German philosophy, at the heart of this struggle and thus retrospectively justifies Heine's journalistic activity in the eighteen thirties.

As the ancient peoples went through their pre-history in imagination, in *mythology*, so we Germans have gone through our post-history in thought, in *philosophy*. We are *philosophical* contemporaries of the present without being its *historical* contemporaries. German philosophy is the *ideal prolongation* of German history. If therefore, instead of the *oeuvres incomplètes* of our real history, we criticize the *oeuvres posthumes* of our ideal history, *philosophy*, our criticism is among the questions of which the present says: *That is the question.*[22]

The contradictions of the German situation and the contradictory tasks that emerge from it no doubt determined Heine's journalism even before he became acquainted with Marx. Heine's political journalism follows two paths. On the one hand it is a description and a critique of the social, political and cultural development of France under the July Monarchy, in which Heine's central interest becomes increasingly directed towards the class struggle of the proletariat against the bourgeoisie. On the other, Heine's comprehensive and popular description and critique of the development of German idealistic philosophy and of German Classical and Romantic poetry elaborates their political significance in terms of world history, 'revealing the school secret'[23] of Hegelian philosophy, as Heine himself says. And the political point made by this popular history of ideology is, for Heine, that the philosophical cycle comes to an end with Hegelian philosophy, that Germany has fulfilled the intellectual preconditions for revolution, that in Germany the time is ripe for the transition from philosophy to action, to practical revolution, to the smashing of rotten feudal absolutism.

Heine's journalism therefore lends expression to the same contradictions in Germany as those Marx outlines in the form of a fully-fledged theory and takes as the basis of his revolutionary tactics. The 'only' difference is that Marx is aware of the dialectical interconnection of all these contradictions and recognizes the contradictions themselves as the objective motor of the revolutionary movement, whereas Heine can go no further than to point out the contradictions and is hurled in his helpless intellectual brilliance from one extreme to the other. Heine clearly sees the necessity of the coming proletarian uprising. He sees in the universal development of capitalism, the growth and strengthening of the proletariat, an internationally necessary process. He also sees the infinitely great gap between Germany's level of development and that of

France and Britain, but he is unable to draw from these facts any real concrete conclusions with regard to the prospects of a German Revolution. And this uncertainty also manifests itself in the way he sees perspectives for France. It is all too easy today to sneer in conceit at the 'political inexperience' of the poet Heine. But if we look at Germany's political journalism in the eighteen forties after Marx and Engels had entered the arena (not to mention the eighteen thirties), we cannot find a single journalist who can match Heine's contradictory magnitude. Germany's radicals are either vulgar, narrow-minded political revolutionaries (*à la* Heinzen), for whom the abolition of petty-state absolutism completely obscures all social questions, or they are vague, idealistic reactionary utopians ('The True Socialists'), for whom all the concrete revolutionary tasks of sweeping away the remnants of feudalism vanish behind the dream of a 'purely socialist' revolution. By comparison with both these tendencies, Heine's journalism is of an extremely high level. Heine comes closer to the revolutionary standpoint of Marx and Engels than any other contemporary with the exception of a very few of the most conscious members of the Communist League.

Enthusiasm for the French Revolution is a decisive experience in Heine's youth. In a surviving fragment of his memoirs he speaks of two passions to which his whole life was devoted:

... the love of beautiful women and the love of the French Revolution, with the modern *furor francese* which also took hold of me in the struggle with the mercenaries of the Middle Ages.[24]

Heine was from the Rhineland and spent his boyhood days in Napoleonic Düsseldorf, so his enthusiasm for the French Revolution is very strongly mingled with an enthusiasm for Napoleon. Indeed, Rahel Varnhagen criticizes some passages in the *Reisebilder* (*Travel Pictures*) for being bonapartist. However, under the influence of journalistic struggles in Germany prior to the July Revolution, Heine's ideas, although still unsettled, are already developing more and more clearly in the direction of revolution. Even before he moves to Paris, Heine declares that he only admires Napoleon up to Brumaire, that is to say he only affirms the latter in the role of executor of the French Revolution. The revolutionary side of Heine assumes an increasingly strong plebeian accent. In the drama of his youth, *Ratcliff*, we already encounter, albeit in very confused and episodic form, the 'bread and butter question' which is later to become so decisive for Heine's world-view. And when he greets the July Revolution with enthusiasm directly before his move to Paris, he does so with the words he puts in the mouth of a Heligoland fisherman: 'The poor people have won,' an admittedly naïve exclamation.

Nonetheless, even at that time Heine no longer fully shares the illusions of the Heligoland fisherman. Although he still considers it tactically correct, particularly in Germany, to concentrate the revolutionary struggle exclusively on smashing the remnants of feudalism, he already knows that the revolution must grow beyond this framework and enthusiastically welcomes this expansion. Before leaving for Paris he writes to Varnhagen about the last volume of his *Travel Pictures* to be published in Germany:

The book is deliberately so one-sided. I know very well that the Revolution unites all social interests, and that the aristocracy and the church are not its sole enemies. However, to make it more easily comprehensible, I have depicted these two institutions as the only members of the enemy alliance in order to consolidate initial forms of opposition. I personally despise the *aristocratie bourgeoise* far more deeply.[25]

Heine's anti-capitalist tendencies, which had already manifested themselves during his stay in England before the July Revolution, were further strengthened and given a more general form through observation of the July Monarchy in Paris. Heine comes to perceive with increasing clarity that in all previous revolutions the proletariat, the plebeians, the people had only been used as cannonfodder in the interests of another class, the bourgeoisie. Nine years after the July Revolution Heine makes the following comment on the line about the poor people having won:

The story goes back a long way. Not for themselves have the people, since time immemorial, bled and suffered, but for others. In July 1830 they secured the victory of a bourgeoisie which is just as worthless as the nobility it replaced, and filled with the same egotism. . . The people have nothing to show for their victory but regret and even greater poverty. But you can rest assured that the next time the bells ring out to signal the attack and the people take up arms once more, they will be fighting for themselves and for the reward they so richly deserve.[26]

French society under the slogan 'Enrichissez-vous' provides infinite scope for Heine's venomous irony. He observes and mocks not only the general corruption of the July Monarchy, of railway speculators, etc., but at the same time exposes the petty grocer-shop mentality of French capitalism which subordinates all major national interests to the stock dealing interests of a bourgeois aris-tocracy. 'Casimir Périer has humiliated France in order to raise stock exchange prices.'[27] He observes, at the same time as Balzac, the growing subordination of literature and the press to capital and their consequent increasing corruption. He observes and derides capitalism's depravation of love in its various forms of legal and illegal prostitution. He observes how former fighters are gradually swallowed up by the dirty flood of capitalism, how for example Saint-Simonists, once victims of persecution who suffered coura-geously, become capitalist speculators. He describes with irony the Paris Bourse, 'built in noblest Grecian style and devoted to the most unworthy of affairs, the bartering of state bonds'. It was built by Napoleon at the same time as, and in a similar style to, a 'temple of glory'.

Alas, the Temple of Glory has not been completed . . . but the Bourse stands completed in the most perfect splendour, and it is no doubt due to the latter's influence that its noble rival, the Temple of Glory is still unfinished . . .[28]

Heine the poet, like most of his great contemporaries, like the important poets of the period following the French Revolution, despises capitalism above all because it radically eliminates or sul-lies every kind of heroism, any true human greatness. He attributes the demise of tragedy to the rule of the bourgeoisie.

The belittlement of all true greatness and the radical annihilation of all heroism is the particular achievement of the bourgeoisie, that class of citi-zens which succeeded to power here in France after the fall of the heredi-tary aristocracy and which has forced the victory of its blinkered shopkeeper mentality on every facet of life. It will not be long before all heroic thoughts and feelings in this country, insofar as they have not been snuffed out completely, will have been made to appear ridiculous. . . The eighteenth century men of ideas who so untiringly paved the way for the Revolution would blush with shame if they could see the sort of people whom their work has served. . .

Heine's enthusiasm for Napoleon which, as we have seen, is sub-stantially qualified as he matures politically, nonetheless remains alive in him as opposition to the petty baseness of the Louis

Philippian present, as a glorification of that heroic period of bourgeois development which began with the Renaissance and reached its climax in the French Revolution. He once pointed out that without the French Revolution and Napoleon, classical German philosophy would have been nipped in the bud by the reactionary petty despots. He emphasizes that Napoleon and the French were not merely fighting to defend their own hearths at Waterloo, but that Napoleon and Wellington opposed each other as the standard bearers of democracy and autocratic reaction.

However, Heine's loathing for capitalism, for its destruction of culture and human greatness, is nevertheless not Romantic. Heine always contrasts the wretchedness of the capitalist world with the great revolutionary upsurge in the bourgeoisie's heroic period and the prospect of the heroic greatness of future revolutions, but not with the musty idylls of primitive pre-capitalist conditions. In the *Travel Pictures* he already mentions the quiet contentment of the Middle Ages and the significant advances made by art during that period, yet he says that intellect has strode on inexorably beyond this situation. One can pose the question as to whether there is more happiness today than in former times, and it is not easy to answer in the affirmative,

but we also know that happiness based on a lie cannot be true happiness, and that we can experience more happiness in the few isolated moments of a godlike state of mind, a higher order of intellectual dignity, than in all the long years of clinging to a stultifyingly naïve faith.[29]

Heine later poses this question in much more materialist form. He realizes how the development of industry undermines the basis of feudalism and its ideology, especially religion, and for all the harsh criticism of capitalism he unconditionally welcomes this development. He once refers to the Rothschilds as the strongest promoters of the revolutionary cause.

I regard Rothschild as one of the greatest revolutionary founders of modern democracy. For me, Richelieu, Robespierre and Rothschild are the three terrorist names that stand for the gradual destruction of the old aristocracy. Richelieu, Robespierre and Rothschild are the three most dreaded levellers of Europe.[30]

Heine's critique of capitalist society and its culture develops into an increasing certainty that the days of this society are numbered.

In the hurly-burly of festivities, the new bourgeois society is in a hurry to drink the last glass dry, just like the old aristocracy before 1789 – it can already hear footsteps echoing in the marble corridors, made by the march of new gods who, without waiting to knock, will kick down the doors to the banqueting-hall and overturn the tables.

Heine's hatred and contempt for the bourgeoisie is so great that he underestimates the bourgeoisie's capacity for resistance in the event of a proletarian revolution.

The bourgeoisie will put up much less resistance than the former aristocracy; for, even in spite of its pathetic weakness, in spite of the atrophy brought on by its lack of morals, in spite of its degenerate recourse to courtesans, the old nobility was nonetheless inspired by a certain *point d'honneur*, which is totally absent in the case of our present bourgeoisie, who have risen to power with the spirit of industry but who are doomed to perish.[31]

According to Heine, the bourgeoisie lacks faith in its own legitimacy, lacks self-respect: its society will easily crumble.

His underestimation of the difficulty of overthrowing the bourgeoisie emanates not only from his well-justified contempt for those representatives of the bourgeoisie whom he was able to observe at close quarters, but at the same time from his enthusiasm for the only true heroes of this period, for the democratic-plebeian and proletarian revolutionaries. In Heine's view, the only true act of heroism of his time is the defence of the Saint Méry monastery.[32] At a later date he is equally enthusiastic about the heroic uprising of the Silesian weavers, and even at the time of his greatest disappointment over the February Revolution he continually emphasizes the heroism of the workers. He sees in these heroes the worthy successors to the great figures of the heroic period.

However, his healthy historical instinct and his literary sensitivity make him suspicious of the attempts of bourgeois-democratic revolutionaries to recreate the heroic period of the National Convention in the present day. Although he probably could not explain the fact, he senses that the Jacobins of the July Monarchy are 'plagiarists of the past'.[33] At the beginning of the eighteen thirties he listens to a speech given by the great revolutionary Blanqui, agrees completely with the contents, yet summarizes his impressions as follows: 'The assembly smelt just like a grubby, worn out copy of the *Moniteur* from 1793.'[34]

As far as Germany is concerned, Heine is equally distrustful and contemptuous of the imitators of Jacobinism. The essential political difference between him and Börne derives from the fact that Heine had a broader and deeper conception of revolution than the rigidly Jacobin Börne. Yet at the same time Heine knows that the *Moniteur* of 1793, although scoffed at in Paris, represents for Germany a revolutionary banner;

It is full of rousing slogans. . . Slogans to raise the dead from their graves and send the living into mortal combat, slogans to make giants out of dwarfs and send giants crashing to the ground, slogans that cut through your power like a guillotine through the neck of a king.[35]

He also understands, again with an instinctive feel for the contradictions rather than the ability to combine them into a dynamic unity, the national character of the coming German Revolution. He never tires of mocking Barbarossa-Romanticism, the Romantic dreams of reviving a Germany of the past and the colours black, red and gold. However, in the preface to *Deutschland, Ein Wintermärchen* (*Germany, A Winter's Tale*), where his scorn is at its most scathing and most comprehensive, he writes on this question:

I will respect and honour your colours when they deserve it, when they are no longer the plaything of some idle or subservient game. Raise the flag of black, red and gold at the peak of German thought, make it the standard of freedom for all humanity, and I will serve it with the blood of my heart.[36]

He explains to the Germans that they can only regain Alsace-Lorraine if a German revolution can offer the Alsatians greater freedom than France offers them. This broader and deeper conception of the content of the German Revolution is evident in all questions on which Heine's position is diametrically opposed to that of Börne and the other blinkered vulgar democrats. Heine realizes that the creation of national unity is the central question of the German Revolution. He scoffs, as does Börne, at the servility of the so-called 'Wars of Liberation', but he sees that the representatives of German nationalism were obliged by a certain political necessity to join forces with the liberal movement during the Age of Restoration and that they had to distance themselves from the progressives only in the course of a long period of development as a result of differences brought to the fore by defeats.

Yes, the army of German revolutionaries was teeming with former German patriots, who mouthed the modern slogan with twisted lips and even sang the *Marseillaise*. . . Yet all that counted was the common struggle for a common interest, for the unity of Germany. . . Our defeat is perhaps a blessing. . .[37]

This is why Börne condemns Menzel from a merely moralistic standpoint as a renegade, whereas Heine, whose literary demolition of Menzel contains at least as much devastating scorn, is also aware of the socio-political movement of which this betrayal is a consequence.[38]

Heine's attitude towards the republic – even if we ignore his general or private, tactical monarchism – is riven with a whole series of contradictions. A part of the crucial contradictions lies, however, in the nature of the beast itself. Marx later wrote, summing up the experiences of the 1848 revolution, that

the republic signifies in general only the political form of the revolutionizing of bourgeois society and not *its conservative form of life*, as, for example, in the United States of America. . .[39]

Heine senses that the relationship of the bourgeoisie to the republic does not depend on the abstract nature of the republican form of state.

Indeed, the French bourgeoisie would not be frightened of a republic of the old sort, even if it involved a bit of Robespierrism; they could easily make their peace with this form of government and would be happy to take up guard duties outside the Tuileries, regardless of whether a Louis Philippe or a Comité du santé publique were in residence there. For the bourgeoisie is interested above all in maintaining order and protecting existing property rights – interests that a republic is just as capable of upholding as a monarchy. But, as I have said, these shopkeepers sense instinctively that the republic of today is no longer willing to stand up for the principles of the nineties, but would instead be the form of state enabling the implementation of a new, unprecedented rule of the proletariat with all its principles of common ownership. They are conservatives out of external necessity, rather than by nature, and fear is their driving force.[40]

In this context, Heine grasps the significance of Louis Philippe as 'the grand master of the hosepipes, quelling the flames and preventing the world from catching fire'. The question of the republic is therefore, for Heine, directly linked to the 'second act' of the revolution which will bring the proletariat to power.

This question most clearly brings forth the deepest conflict in

Heine's world-view, the intellectual expression of his vacillation between the two major social classes. The dreadful outcome of the February Revolution is one of the most bitter disappointments in Heine's life. He has nothing but utterly biting scorn for the Louis Blancs, Lamartines, etc. However, his sorrow not only has to do with the fact that all expectations he had of a 'second act' of the revolution were dashed in the June Days, but is also rooted in the fear that it could take place after all. He sees the victory of the proletarian revolution as an inevitable necessity, but at the same time trembles at the thought of this victory as the downfall of culture, although, as we have seen, he harbours no doubts as to the daily and hourly destruction of culture that occurs under capitalism.

The contradiction between insight into the necessary demise of bourgeois culture and the view that this demise is tantamount to the end of the world is not an isolated phenomenon among the great writers of this period. Balzac is also aware of the inner contradictions of bourgeois society which drive it towards its own downfall, and sees in this downfall the end of all culture. Heine's case is, however, much more acute and complicated, because unlike Balzac, Heine by no means fails to understand the development and the necessary demands of the proletariat. He not only realizes that the proletarian revolution is by historical necessity the inevitable product of capitalist development and the successive stages marked by bourgeois revolutions, he also sees and understands the foundations and the justification of this revolution. His special position among the important bourgeois ideologists of this period results precisely from the fact that he has a deeper understanding of the material foundations of the proletarian revolution. He understands full well that no Declaration of Rights, no matter how radically Jacobin its implementation, can satisfy that most elementary of human rights, the right to food. The irrefutability of communism is for Heine based precisely on the existence of this right and the fact that modern capitalist development provides the material preconditions enabling it to be satisfied. In his later poem 'Die Wander-ratten' Heine makes fun of the philistines' fear of the proletarian revolution and the illusions they harbour of being able to counter it with arguments or by force of arms.

No blaring bells or priestly prayers,
No councillors or decrees of theirs,
No cannon, not the biggest guns,
Can help you now, my pretty ones!

No fine spun talk can help, no trick
Of old out-dated rhetoric.
Rats are not caught with fancy issues –
They leap right over syllogisms.

When bellies are hungry, they only make sense
Of soup-bowl logic, breaded arguments,
Of reasoning based on roast beef or fish,
With sausage citations to garnish the dish.[41]

But Heine does not stop short at the recognition of this material necessity and the possibility of satisfying the demands of the proletariat. He also follows with utmost attention the ideological reflections of the development of the proletariat during the July Monarchy from Saint-Simonism to Proudhon. He is perhaps the only bourgeois ideologist of this time to grasp the necessary link between the proletarian movement itself and the utopian theories with which it was not connected, and to prophesy at a very early stage that the proletarian movement and socialist theory must unite with one another, and that this unity was bound to mark the end of all utopian sects. In his reporting from Paris, especially in the early eighteen forties, the proletariat is thus the main protagonist. Louis Philippe is, according to Heine in a letter about his *Lutetia*, mere decoration. 'The hero of my book, the true hero is the social movement. . .'[42] And elsewhere he describes ironically his position as that of a reporter. He likens it to that of a Roman correspondent who does not write about the great intrigues of state at the imperial court of Rome, but rather about the obscure persecuted handful of early Christians. And he singles out the Communists as the 'only party in France worthy of serious attention'. Considering this relatively high level of understanding for the revolutionary movement of the proletariat, the contradiction contained in Heine's fear that its victory will mean the end of the world is all the more crass and remarkable.

Uniting socialist theory with the revolutionary workers' movement remains for Heine a purely theoretical postulate, at best an aphoristic statement of necessity, but it never becomes a concrete conclusion that could be implemented in practice. Heine's socialist perspective thus hovers in mid-air. He is a penetrating observer of facts and trends in the development of bourgeois society, and concludes from these that a socialist revolution is necessary. Yet in his thoughts, regardless of whether they are enthusiastic or horrified, this appears as a fantastic twilight of the gods for bourgeois society, as the sudden arrival of a new age. All the concrete intermediary stages are missing. Heine has no conception of socialist revolution as a concrete historical process. In this connection he remains throughout his life, methodologically speaking, a utopian: socialism is for him a state of being, a future world condition. No matter how far beyond Saint-Simonism he may have travelled in other respects, no matter how clearly he realizes the necessity of revolution as a precondition for the socialist world condition – in this regard he remains a Saint-Simonian Hegelian.

As we already know, Heine borrows very important patterns of thought from Hegelian philosophy, especially from the philosophy of history and also from aesthetics. However, unlike Hegel he does not stop short at the present, but endeavours to use the Hegelian dialectic of history as a means of understanding the developmental tendencies that point to the future. Saint-Simonism played an important part for Heine in this extension of Hegelian philosophy, this extension of its progressive methodological strands. It is well known that Hegel, following his youthful revolutionary period, believed Antiquity to be a thing of the irretrievable past. According to Hegel, Christianity had irreversibly, and of historical necessity, superseded Antiquity. Heine, by contrast, under the influence of Saint-Simonist sensualism, hopes that the revolution he prophesies and expects will bring a revival of Antiquity's joy of the senses and love of life, irreversibly superseding all forms of Christian asceticism. By linking this new period in human development with the preceding revolution, following the Hegelian method, he goes beyond Saint-Simon's concept of history – although for Heine, as for the utopians, socialism is an anticipated future condition which does not develop organically out of the process of liberation of the proletariat.

Despite having had an extremely broad education and wide-ranging interests, Heine never examined problems of political economy. His estrangement from the concrete basis and the historical specificity of the proletarian revolution reflects his estrangement from the workers' movement itself. For all the sympathy he shows for the socialist revolution, for all his enthusiasm for the heroic deeds of workers in struggle, Heine found it impossible to build a bridge to the movement. It would of course be gross oversimplification, indeed a vulgarization of the problem, if we were to see this merely as the intellectual 'aristocratism' of the poet. Rather, this antagonism also emanates from the objective contradictions within the development of the revolutionary workers' movement at that time. The workers' movement was on the verge of overcoming the primitive Jacobinist puritan asceticism of its early days, yet this was a complicated, laborious and contradictory process. (One need only think of Engels's struggle in Paris against primitive 'Knotentum'[43] and artisanal communism.) Thanks to his Hegelian reworking of Saint-Simonism, Heine has gone beyond this primitive asceticism, but only on a purely *intellectual* level.

We [the German pantheist philosophers, G.L.] promote material well-being, the material contentment of the people. . ., because we know that Man's divinity is also expressed in his physical appearance and that poverty destroys or abuses the body, the image of God, and that this in turn causes the demise of the spirit. . . We do not want to be sans-culottes, nor frugal citizens, nor cheap presidents. We aim to found a democracy of equally glorious, equally holy, equally inspired gods. You demand simple clothes, abstemious morals and unseasoned vegetables; we, however, demand nectar and ambrosia, purple robes, delicate perfumes, lust and splendour, the laughing dance of nymphs, music and comedy – do not let that annoy you, ye virtuous republicans! In reply to your reproachful censorship we quote one of Shakespeare's fools: 'Dost thou think because thou art virtuous there shall be no more cakes and ale?'[44]

Heine's conception here is double-edged, and all the contradictions of his position, wavering as it does between the bourgeoisie and the proletariat, are tangled up in it. For Heine the sensualist anti-ascetic conception of socialism does not preclude heroism in struggle. On the contrary, as we have seen, Heine's desire for socialism arises in part precisely from his sorrow at the passing of the bourgeoisie's heroic period. Directly before the passage quoted above he says: '. . . and now the truly great deeds of true heroism shall glorify the earth.' There can be no doubt that, by going beyond the primitive asceticism of the early workers' movement, Heine takes an objective step forward: the dawning awareness, in spite of all pantheistic religious vagueness in the formulations, that the true realization of the human personality is only possible under socialism; on an anticipatory intellectual level, this supersedes all primitive Phalanstèrist and barrack-house conceptions of socialism.

However, this conception also harbours, inextricably linked to the progressive socialist tendencies, a bourgeois, post-Thermidorian element, namely the bourgeois form of overcoming the heroic asceticism of the revolutionary period, an intellectual tendency which was also present in all the currents that had a decisive influence on Heine's thought – in Goethe, Hegel and Saint-Simon. It is no coincidence that Heine occasionally refers even to Napoleon as a Saint-Simonist emperor. And when viewed in this light, Heine's vacillations on the question of socialism appear to be the regression of any utopian to the bourgeois standpoint that necessarily sets in when he tries to imagine in concrete terms the conception of socialism in its final form without taking into account the real, concrete, historical-dialectical intermediate links. This intellectual movement naturally reflects a real shying away from the difficulties and from the ugliness of the intermediary stages. Heine's utopian vision of socialism in its final form can offer him no assistance, no orientation with which to cope with these difficulties. On the contrary, the contrast between the final goal and the present situation only serves to deepen his despair.

The vacillating and contradictory character of Heine's position should not, however, be allowed to mask the fact that his polemics against primitive asceticism, the vulgarizing narrow-mindedness of ascetic Jacobinism and the asceticism of the primitive workers' movement are often justified. He is completely justified in his criticism of the republican limitations of Börne's conception and in his passionate defence of the great bourgeois heritage (Goethe, Hegel, etc.) against Börne's short-sighted attacks. It is surely no coincidence that Marx as a young man had intended to defend Heine publicly in the Börne debate. Heine's criticism of the primitive workers' movement is incorrect insofar as he is unable to comprehend the inner tendencies of the workers' movement that would necessarily overcome this stage of development in a real, non-utopian way.

Heine's dualism gives rise to his well known and much discussed vacillation between enthusiasm for socialism on the one hand and a shocked abhorrence of the reality of proletarian revolution on the other. Heine comes closest to embracing socialism on the eve of the upsurge that led to revolution in the 1840s. The *Lutetia* reports, the book levelled against Börne, *Atta Troll* and *Germany, A Winter's Tale* are journalistic and poetic documentation of this proximity. On a personal level, this development culminates in Heine's close and intimate friendship with Marx during the latter's stay in Paris (1843), a friendship which is kept up until the 1848 Revolution. The period of friendship with Marx even produces moments in which Heine's poetry and thoughts become linked in a concrete way to the revolutionary movement itself (see his poem 'The Silesian Weavers'). And Heine's affirmation of socialism now takes on the overtones of unconditional, sensualist, materialist enthusiasm:

> A different song, a better song,
> will get the subject straighter:
> let's make a heaven on earth, my friends,
> instead of waiting till later.
>
> Why shouldn't we be happy on earth,
> why should we still go short?
> why should the idle belly consume
> what working hands have wrought?
>
> There's bread enough grows here on earth
> to feed mankind with ease,
> and roses and myrtles, beauty and joy,
> and (in the season) peas.
>
> Yes, fresh green peas for everyone
> as soon as the pods have burst.
> Heaven we'll leave to the angels, and
> the sparrows, who had it first.[45]

Only after the February Revolution do Heine's remarks on this question take on a thoroughly gloomy and despairing tone. The fact should not be overlooked, however, that only the colour of the painting, only the tone of the song changes, but not the social content. This remains the same in the gloomily ironic verses of the 'Wanderratten' quoted earlier and in the joyous hymns quoted here. Heine, by this time terminally ill and confined to his bed, virtually isolated from the outside world, experiences the disappointment of the February Revolution, the defeat of the proletariat in the June Battle, the crushing of the revolution in Germany, Austria and Hungary, and the whole period of reaction following 1848 under such adverse circumstances that he himself was his only source of strength: the strength he needed to swim against the tide of despair. This mood of despair did indeed take a grip of him too. Lacking a knowledge of the concrete inner strength of the workers' movement, or of the concrete revolutionary theory of the necessity of a new revolutionary upturn, he is unable to combat this mood of despair within himself. His loneliness, the effects of which we have already observed even during the period of upsurge and struggle, now acts upon him with redoubled force. However, one only need compare Heine's drift towards despair with the mass defection of socialists and quasi-socialists from the ideals of revolution following the defeat to see how (relatively) faithful Heine remained to the great ideal of his life.

In the loneliness of his 'mattress grave', in the stifling atmosphere of Bonapartist reaction, Heine loses his faith in the revival of culture through socialism, in the sensualist paradise of maximum physical and intellectual development of the personality under socialism. In the preface to the French edition of *Lutetia*, only a few months before his death, he expresses this traumatic vision with disgust and horror:

. . . they [the communists, G.L.] will chop down my laurel trees and plant potatoes in their stead. . . The roses, those carefree brides of the nightingales, will suffer the same fate; the nightingales, those useless singers, will be chased away, and, I fear, my *Book of Songs* will be used by the grocer to make paper funnels which he will fill with coffee or tobacco for the old women of the future.[46]

Yet in spite of all these horrific visions, communism still holds an irresistible fascination for Heine. He brings forward two arguments which, as he says, he cannot resist.

The first of these voices is the voice of logic. Dante once said that the devil is a logician. I am caught up in a frightful syllogism, and if I am unable to refute the claim that all people have the right to eat, then I am forced to accept all the consequences that follow from it. . . This old society has for a long time stood accused and condemned. Let it suffer its just deserts! Let it be smashed, this old world, where innocence perished, selfishness flourished, where man was starved by fellow man. . . And blessed be the grocer, who will make paper funnels out of my poems to fill them with coffee and tobacco for the poor, old, good women who had to do without such luxuries in this present, unjust world – *fiat justitia, pereat mundus!*[47]

The second argument brings out perhaps even more clearly and more concretely the old revolutionary in Heine. He sympathizes with the communists because they are the enemy of his enemies, the Christian German Nationalists.

I have despised them and fought against them all my life, and now that the sword is falling from the hand of the dying man, I feel consolation in the certainty that communism, upon finding them on its path, will put an end to their miserable lives, and not with the blow of a club, oh no, the giant will crush them with a simple stamp of his foot, as if he were crushing a toad.[48]

And Heine professes his sympathy with a communism that he views as the representative of the internationalist idea against narrow bourgeois reactionary nationalism.

The overt message contained in this last profession of faith is unmistakable. It also shows that the same motives and contradictions in Heine's relationship to socialism are at work here as in the period of hymnic affirmation. In essence, the changed circumstances merely give rise to a shift of emphasis. Against this underlying tack it is of no great significance that Heine occasionally toyed with reformist projects. They are just as abstractly utopian as his radical visions (e.g. the mosaic 'Social Policy' of the jubilee year in the *Geständnisse – Confessions*). It is of equally little significance when Heine, on his death bed, refers to the communists as his enemies, for even here he talks repeatedly of the inevitability of the victory of communism. All these vacillations take place within the same framework. Heine is the last great poet of the bourgeoisie in whom all the underlying currents of social development converge in the attempt to create an integral and comprehensive view of the world, and in whom the living memory of the duties of the bourgeois intelligentsia as ideological leaders of the general social revolutionary movement have remained alive. These currents necessarily lead Heine to recognize communism as the victor of the future, yet they are not strong enough, for all his embittered criticism, to tear him away from the bourgeois class altogether and to allow him to take root concretely and actively in the new revolutionary class, the proletariat. Thus a space opens up in which Heine moves back and forth between jubilant optimism and inconsolable despair depending on the development of the revolutionary movement.

Heine's significance for the preparation of revolutionary ideology in Germany remains a complete mystery to German literary historians. In that they either ignore or underestimate the significance of the disintegration of Hegelianism, the revolutionary transformation of Hegel's idealistic dialectic and the creation of the materialist dialectic which Marx' work represented, they remain in the dark with respect to this entire, crucially important ideological development. In his historical account of the transitional period, Engels determines Heine's position within this development with great historical fairness. He describes the paradoxical situation in which the German reaction was temporarily able to think of Hegelian philosophy as its own world-view while the party of progress saw in Hegel nothing but a reactionary. 'However,' says Engels, 'what neither the Government nor the Liberals saw, was already seen at least by one man as early as 1833, and this man was indeed none other than Heinrich Heine.'[49]

It is impossible to overestimate the importance of the role played by Hegel in Heine's development. One should not confine one's analysis to the few passages where Heine expressly refers to Hegel. Heine's overall conception of history (his assessment of Classical Greece and Christianity, the historical significance of the Renaissance, the Reformation, the French Revolution, Napoleon, etc.) and Heine's entire theory of art (the contrast between Antiquity and Modernity, his assessment of Romanticism, etc.) are influenced by Hegel. That all this is ignored by standard German literary history is mainly attributable to the literary historians' complete ignorance in the field of philosophy. Nonetheless, the – albeit scarce – explicit references by Heine could give an indication both of how much he owes to his teacher Hegel and of how his interpretation attempts to overcome Hegel. In this respect Heine is a very advanced precursor of the radical Young Hegelians. In his early days in Paris he already has such a liberal and broad conception of Hegelian philosophy and applies it to politics in such a radical way, that only the most left-wing Young Hegelians are later able to match him. It is true that Heine never went as far as the materialist inversion of Hegel's idealist dialectic. Despite his intimate friendship with Marx in Paris he never appreciated the philosophical significance of Marx's writings in the *Deutsch-Französische Jahrbücher* to which he also contributed. Just as, politically speaking, he remained on the threshold of distinguishing between bourgeois and proletarian revolutionary democracy, so too he transformed the conservative elements of Hegelian philosophy into social and religious radicalism, only to remain poised on the threshold of completing this restructuring process. As can easily be seen, both movements are ideological reflections of the same social dichotomy in Heine.

The central problem in restructuring Hegelian philosophy lay in overcoming its innate conservatism, its glorification of the status quo. Heine often openly attacks this side of Hegelian philosophy. His main line of argumentation is, however, the one generally taken by the radical Young Hegelians, namely to interpret the conservative side of Hegelian philosophy as a 'screen' made necessary by the circumstances and then to proclaim the revolutionary side as the essence of Hegel's esoteric theory. (*The Trump of Doom* by Bruno Bauer,[50] for which Marx did some preliminary work as a young man, marks the climax of this form of radical re-interpretation of Hegel.) Heine once describes a conversation with Hegel in which he gives very clear expression to this tendency of Hegel's on questions of politics and religion.

Once when I was perturbed at the saying, 'Everything that exists is rational,' he smiled enigmatically and remarked, 'It could read: Everything that is rational must exist'. . . It was not until later that I understood such phrases. And I only understood later why he had claimed, in *The Philosophy of History*, that Christianity represented a step forward for the sole reason that it taught the existence of a god who had died, whereas the heathen gods had not known death. Just think what a great step forward it would be if the god had never existed at all![51]

Heine therefore interprets Hegelian philosophy in terms of atheism under the guise of pantheism, in terms of its total worldliness. On the strength of the religious core which still remains even after this radical transformation, Heine draws from this worldliness the conclusion that Man is the true God. 'I was never an abstract thinker,' he says ironically in his *Confessions*,

and I uncritically accepted the synthesis of the Hegelian doctrine because its conclusions flattered my vanity. I was young and proud and it was a tonic for my conceit when I learned from Hegel that God did not reside in heaven, as my grandmother had told me, but that I myself was God living on the Earth.[52]

In disclosing the school secret of Hegelian philosophy in this way Heine was fully aware of the ideological and political consequences of this newly interpreted Hegelian philosophy. Following on from the conversation with Hegel quoted above, Heine writes:

The destruction of a belief in heaven carries not only moral, but also political significance: the masses no longer bear their worldly misery with Christian patience, they thirst for happiness here on Earth. Communism follows as a natural consequence from this changed world-view, and is spreading all over Germany. Another, equally natural phenomenon is the fact that the proletarians, in their opposition to the existing order, are led by the most progressive minds of today, the greatest philosophers; the latter have moved on from pure doctrine to the actual deed, the ultimate goal of all thought, and are formulating the requisite programme.[53]

Merging this interpretation of Hegelian philosophy with Saint-Simonism was merely one step further in the radicalization of Heine's thought. As we have seen, this provided him with the perspective of proletarian revolution as the realization of Hegel's concept of 'Reason'. It also provided him with the weapons he needed to combat the idealistic asceticism of the remains of Jacobinism and the primitive workers' movement.

There is no doubt that the main thrust of Heine's synthesis of Hegel and Saint-Simon is anti-religious. Heine regards the entire history of the world as a struggle between the Hellenics and the Nazarenes (a term he uses to refer to both Jews and Christians), he sees in all of modern intellectual and political history a struggle between spiritualism and sensualism. In the idealistic Young Hegelian fashion, therefore, he regards revolutions, historical upheavals – as did Ludwig Feuerbach, incidentally – as upheavals of ideas, philosophy and religion. He thus correctly discerns the materialist, sensualist elements in all earlier revolutionary movements (e.g. in the Peasant Wars), and recognizes the intellectual and political superiority of the Renaissance over the Reformation. Both are, according to Heine, the beginning of the destruction of the Middle Ages.

Leo X, the splendid Medici ruler, was just as fervent a protestant as Luther, and whereas in Wittenberg this protest was expressed in Latin prose, in Rome it was expressed in stone, colour or *ottave rime*. The polemics of Italy's painters against the clergy may even have been much more effective than those of the theologians of Saxony. The blossoming flesh in Titian's paintings is thoroughly protestant. The thighs of his Venus are much more convincing theses than those which the German monk pasted on the Church door in Wittenberg.[54]

This polemic against Christianity is in Heine's view the precondition for social revolution. The social revolution is the realization in this world of that which religion promises in the hereafter. Heine therefore argues:

Mankind is perhaps destined to eternal misery, maybe the peoples of the world have been condemned to be crushed by despots, to be exploited by the despots' accomplices and to be ridiculed by their lackeys for all eternity. Ah yes, in that case it would be necessary to uphold Christianity, even though we know it to be a fallacy. . . The ultimate fate of Christianity thus depends on whether or not we still need it.[55]

Heine's answer goes without saying. Having come to regard Christianity as the necessary ideology of enslaved humanity, and pantheistic atheism as the philosophy of liberation, it is understandable that he should pour bitter scorn on Börne who in Paris became a follower of Lamennais' 'Christian Socialism'.

At the same time, however, Heine's Saint-Simonism reinforced the perpetuation and further development of the religious remnants in his pantheism. Although Heine knows full well that pantheism is merely a concealed form of atheism, he nonetheless retains an indestructible religious core. Heine opposes revolutionary worldliness to religious other-worldliness, yet this opposition is itself based on a religious deification of this worldliness. Just as the most important successor to Hegel before Marx, the materialist Ludwig Feuerbach, had at times to shroud his own world-view in the mist of a 'new religion', so Heine is even less capable of eradicating the religious remnants of his Hegelianism. (The development of Saint-Simonism into a new religion clearly shows the general necessity of this tendency.) Heine – again following Hegel – sees philosophical materialism as the philosophy of the French Revolution. Therefore, whenever he wants to portray the proletarian revolution as going beyond the bourgeois revolution, he also feels an understandable urge to go beyond the philosophical limitations of the old school of materialism. However, since he is incapable of overcoming mechanistic materialism with dialectical materialism, he is forced to consecrate the proletarian revolution in an idealistic, religious way.

That great slogan of the Revolution, as proclaimed by Saint-Just, *le pain est le droit du peuple*, has been changed in Germany into: *le pain est le droit divin de l'homme*. We are not fighting for the human rights of the German people, but for the divine rights of man. We differ in this and in many other respects from the men of the Revolution.[56]

This is followed by the polemic against Jacobin asceticism with which we are already familiar.

It is easy to see the philosophical weakness in Heine's position. He substitutes the contradiction between sensualism and spiritualism for the contradiction between materialism and idealism, which he formally recognizes as being valid for a theory of knowledge, though his conception of it as the contradiction between *a priori* and *a posteriori* is vague and erroneous. With his sensualist philosophy, Heine attempts both to overcome the mechanistic character of early materialism and to banish the idealistic reactionary tendencies of Hegelian philosophy from his thought. This attempt to bring Hegel and materialism closer to each other is not merely Heine's personal philosophical inclination, but is a necessary part of the general philosophical ferment of the age culminating in its ripest fruit, namely Marx's dialectical materialism. When describing the importance of scientific and industrial progress for the development of philosophy, Engels remarks:

. . .the idealist systems also filled themselves more and more with a materialist content and attempted pantheistically to reconcile the antithesis between mind and matter. Thus, ultimately, the Hegelian system represents merely a materialism idealistically turned upside down in method and content.[57]

This situation becomes even more acute once Hegelianism as a movement begins to disintegrate. Engels says of this:

. . .the main body of the most determined Young Hegelians was, by the practical necessities of its fight against positive religion, driven back to Anglo-French materialism. This brought them into conflict with their school system.[58]

This conflict never breaks out openly in Heine; at least, not before 1848. Pantheism is for Heine a veil woven by poetry that even conceals the contradictions of his philosophical position from himself. As long as optimistic revolutionary prospects remain alive in him, as long as love of life and the drive towards revolution are the twin motors propelling his life forward, he considers sensualist pantheism as the non-religious atheistic religion of the age, as the world-view that unites early materialism with newly revolutionary Hegel-ianism, at the same time overcoming the errors and limitations of both.

In his post-1848 writings Heine announces his 'conversion', his radical break with this past. In his postscript to *Romanzero*, he him-self protests at the insinuation that he had been converted to a belief in God because of his illness. He also protests at the claim that he had returned to some kind of church, be it Christian or Jewish. It is of great importance for our overall picture of Heine that we ascertain the exact nature of his 'conversion'. Above all, in spite of Heine's assurances, it would be wrong to dismiss completely the significance of his illness and the other unfortunate private cir-cumstances of his life. In this regard, Heine makes the following declaration in his *Confessions* after speaking of Hegelian Man as God, as we have quoted earlier:

But the expenses incurred by a god who does not wish to appear tight-fisted and who has a complete disregard for his physical health and that of his purse are absolutely enormous. In order to play this kind of role in a befitting manner, two things in particular are indispensable: a great deal of money and a sound constitution. Unfortunately it came to pass one day – in February 1848 – that these two things were mislaid, and my divinity began to look very shaky as a result.[59]

For Heine, therefore, the necessity of a personal God arises from this material collapse of his own 'divinity'.

I am only a poor man, and furthermore one who is not in the best of health, who is in fact very ill. In this condition I find it very soothing to know that there is someone in heaven to whom I can keep on reciting the litany of my woes, especially after midnight, when Mathilde has retired – to the rest of which she is often in great need. Praise God that in such moments I am not alone, and am able to pray and weep as much as I want without feeling embarrassed, to pour out my heart to the Almighty and confide to him many a secret that we would normally keep even from our own wives.[60]

Heine expresses himself even more openly and cynically in vari-ous conversations. In conversation with Adolf Stahr and Fanny Lewald he once says:

But I also have my faith. Don't think that I have no religion. Opium is a religion too. When some of that grey dust is sprinkled on my frightfully painful burning sores and the pain immediately ceases, who is to say that this is not the same soothing power as that which is at work in religion? Opium and religion are more closely related than most people could ever imagine. . . . If I am unable to bear the pain any longer, I take morphine; if I am unable to destroy my enemies, I pass them on to God for him to take care of – except. . .

He paused, then added with a smile,

Except that I still prefer to deal with my money matters myself.[61]

Or, in conversation with Alfred Meissner, Heine declares that, were he able to walk on crutches, he would go to church. Upon Meissner's amazement he replies:

No, no! Of course I would go to church! Where else should one go on crutches? Of course, if I could go out without crutches, I would rather go for a stroll along the happy boulevards and join in on the Bal Mabille.[62]

Heine's 'conversion', as we can see, is not all that serious. The prayers he directs to his new-found God have very little religious content:

> Dear Lord, just leave me here below,
> I think it would be none the worse;
> But cure my ailments first, you know,
> And spare some money for my purse.
>
> Just health and extra cash – Lord, give
> No more than that, please! Oh, bestow
> A brace of more good days to live
> Beside my wife in statu quo![63]

Or, in a more serious, plaintive, ironic poem:

> Permit me, Lord, I'm shocked at this,
> I think you've made a bloomer:
> You formed the merriest poet and now
> You rob him of his good humour.
>
> The pain has dulled my sense of fun,
> I'm melancholy when sick;
> If there's no end to this sorry jest,
> I'll end up a Catholic.
>
> Like other good Christians, I'll fill your ears
> With wails – if I persist,
> O Miserere! You will lose
> Your very best humorist![64]

Heine is therefore always aware of the fact that for him religion is not something to be taken seriously as a world-view, but in reality a mere anaesthetic for his pain, opium for his growing despair. However, just because opium cannot be taken seriously as a world-view, and never was taken really seriously by Heine himself, it does not follow that his despair itself was not serious, profound and honest. And not just his despair at his own terrible personal fate, but, as we have seen, at the same time despair at the fate of the most profound content in his life, the perspective of the development of human-kind. There is deep, despairing irony in his words to Meissner:

I believe in a personal God again! That's what happens when you get ill, fatally ill and demoralized. Don't hold it against me like some crime! If the German people in their hour of need accept the King of Prussia, why should I not accept a personal God?[65]

And in another conversation with Meissner he reads, as he puts it, religious poems to him:

Drop those holy paraboles and
Pietist hypotheses:
Answer us these damning questions
No evasions, if you please.

Why do just men stagger, bleeding,
Crushed beneath their cross's weight,
While the wicked ride the high horse,
Happy victors blest by fate.

Who's to blame? Is God not mighty,
Not with power panoptical?
Or is evil His own doing?
Ah that would be vile indeed.

Thus we ask and keep on asking,
Till a handful of cold clay
Stops our mouths at last securely –
But pray tell, is that an answer?[66]

Upon Meissner's surprised question: 'You call that religious? I call it atheist,' Heine replies with a smile, 'No, no, religious, blasphemously religious.'[67] And there is no doubt that Heine understands his meaning better than his insignificant, shallow admirers.

Doubtless these poems of Heine's are not without their religious core, even though any religion would hardly be pleased with such a form of religiosity. Heine errs only to the extent that he sometimes overestimates and stylizes the religious nature of his 'conversion', drawing much too clear a line of distinction between the 'conversion' and his earlier, ostensibly irreligious, Hellenic, pantheistic period. In our analysis of this period we have already revealed the residual religious content concealed within Heine's pantheistic worldliness. This residual religiosity comes to predominate in the post-1848 period – that of the declining revolutionary movement – in which Heine, in his sickness and isolation, was bound to be incapable of recognizing even the seeds and strands of a new upturn. Heine's despair, which takes on such a compelling tone in his last collection of poetry, *Romanzero*, is not, therefore, private despair brought about by his own personal fate; at least it is not only private despair. It is despair at the course of the world, at the development of humankind, at the fate of reason and justice, at the fate of the revolution. The basic motif running through almost all the romances and histories in *Romanzero* is mourning at the fact that Evil always and everywhere triumphs over Good in this reality. It is the desperate search for hope, for a brighter perspective, the desperate clutching at any illusion and finally the courageous, rational and ironic destruction of this self-made illusion that he never fully believed in. The meaninglessness of the course of the world causes Heine in desperation to create a personal God in puppet form for his own personal use, although he is intelligent enough at least to be constantly aware that it is only puppet. Nonetheless, this same intelligent Heine cannot help but play with the puppet in his hour of despair and seek consolation in this game. After the defeat of the revolution, the course of the world becomes meaningless for Heine. He sings of the defeat of the Hungarian Revolution in 1849, the last armed struggle in this revolutionary wave:

> When I hear Hungary's name outcried,
> My German jacket binds too tight,
> I feel a rousing sea inside,
> I hear the call of trumpets in the night!
>
> Again within my soul I hear
> Old sagas they no longer tell,
> Wild battle songs of sword and spear –
> The song of how the Nibelungen fell.
>
> . . .They also have the same old fate:
> Though banners proudly wave, of course,
> The hero must, as customs state,
> Be overthrown by raw and brutish force.[68]

Evil triumphs over Good, reaction over revolution. The troops of the revolution are smashed, the best revolutionaries killed or on the run, and many of the old fighters have become traitors to the revolution. Heine's later poems deal bitterly with the behaviour of Dingelstedt, Herwegh and others.[69] Nowhere does Heine glimpse a ray of light, nowhere does he see people to whom he could feel attached, nowhere a country in which he could live. In the poem 'Jetzt wohin?' ('Now Where?') he has all the countries march past without finding a home for himself in any of them:

> Sadly gazing to the sky
> I see stars in thousands there –
> But the star that is my own,
> I can't see it anywhere.
>
> Maybe it has lost its way
> In a maze that's silver-pearled,
> Just as I am lost
> In the tumult of the world.[70]

Even the beauty of nature can offer this Heine, unlike the youthful Romantic, no consolation, no exaltation, nor even a means of forgetting his sadness and his songs. (Even this consolation was always problematical, torn apart by irony.) On the contrary. The more beautifully the sun shines, the crasser the contrast between beautiful yet insensate Nature and the disconsolate gloom within the poet's soul.

> The sweet spring blooms. The greenwoods ring
> With merry birdsong echoing,
> Flowers and girls wear a virginal smile –
> O beautiful world, you're hideously vile.[71]

The God of Heine's own invention is an opium with only a passing effect on the spiritual suffering of a despairing and dying man.

Nevertheless, in spite of the inner continuity between Heine's earlier and later period with respect to religion, his 'conversion' still constitutes a breakdown, a typical tragedy: the tragedy of the bourgeois atheist. Heine's fate shows with particular clarity that a consistent atheism which takes a stance on the great questions of humanity, on the question of the development of human society, which is not vulgar, complacent and shallow like that of the 'vulgarizing hawkers' in the Germany of the eighteen fifties and sixties, is necessarily linked to the fate of the revolutionary liberation of humankind. It is no coincidence that the shining and powerful figures of bourgeois atheism from Vanini to Diderot were active during the period between the Renaissance and the Great French Revolution. Even though their hopes of a renewal of humankind were full of illusions – these illusions did not at that stage of development reveal themselves to be illusions; they were still necessary and productive vehicles of the progressive development of humankind. Not until the nineteenth century does it become impossible for rigorous and honest thinkers to live with these illusions of a renewal of humanity. The real perspective of genuine human liberation comes to the fore with the appearance of the revolutionary proletariat on the scene. We saw how Heine's atheism was necessarily linked to his perspective of proletarian revolution. The vagueness of his perspective left a religious aura clinging to his atheistic worldliness. The loss of his perspective brought with it the breakdown of this atheism. It is a breakdown even though the faith that ostensibly arises is worthless, even though, subjectively, it does not signify a genuine return to religion.

In his later years Heine therefore becomes the ideological precursor of the despairing 'tragic' religious atheists of the latter half of the nineteenth century. They live in a world that has become meaningless for them, and are honest enough to do without the old religions as they would do without decaying rubbish. However, atheism is also incapable of providing them with any sustenance, any ideological support. Whether Jacobsen's Niels Lyhne breaks down at his child's deathbed and, like Heine, pleads for help from a God he does not believe in, or whether he resolutely abides by his atheism on his own deathbed – in neither case is there a way out of the hopelessness of the situation. In all these doubting and despairing atheisms there thus remains, consciously or unconsciously, an element of religion. 'The religious reflex of the real world can, in any case, only then finally vanish, when the practical relations of every-day life offer to man none but perfectly intelligible and reasonable relations with regard to his fellowmen and to Nature.'[72]

IV

In his *Confessions* Heine calls himself the last Romantic poet in Germany; 'I mark the end of the old school of poetry in Germany, while at the same time the new school, modern Germany poetry, started with me.'[73] This definition of his own position in literary history as that of a borderline phenomenon bridging the gap between two periods is correct, with the proviso that modern German poetry went a very different way from that which Heine thought it would and was able to foresee, namely in accordance with the socio-political development whose tragic effect on Heine's world-view we have been analysing so far.

Heine's basic conception of literary history takes as its point of departure the idea of 'the end of the *Kunstperiode*':[74]

My old prophecy of the end of the *Kunstperiode*, which began with Goethe's cradle and will end with his grave, seems to be approaching fulfilment. Present-day art will inevitably perish because it is rooted in the principles of the *ancien régime*, in that past which belongs to the Holy Roman Empire. This is why, like all the withered remains of this past, it stands in uneasy contradiction to the present. It is this contradiction, and not the advance of time itself, that is so harmful to art; on the contrary, the advance of time should actually help art to flourish, as it once did in Athens and Florence. . .[75]

Heine goes on to explain how the link with the great inter-party struggles, with the politics of the day, formed the basis of artistic progress in past ages. He continues his description of the perspective for new developments in Germany's art as follows:

However, the new age will give birth to a new art, which will be in inspired harmony with it, which will not need to borrow its symbols from the faded past and which is certain to engender new techniques different from any hitherto developed. Until then, may the colours and sounds of the most egocentric subjectivity, may individuality freed from all worldly constraints, and may the love of life of a personality freed from all gods hold sway – which is after all more productive than the sterile pseudo-existence of the old art.[76]

Heine therefore regards the literary stylistic period that he himself represents as transitional. Just as he has the highest admiration for the great epic and dramatic artists of the past, the Cervantes and the Shakespeares, just as he detects in Goethe's lyrical character the result of Germany's development, yet also sees Goethe's greatness in his objectivity ('a mirror of Nature', 'the Spinoza of poetry', he says of Goethe), he regards his own subjectivism as the necessary transition to a new art. It is clear that Heine's perspective on this new art is very closely linked to his socio-political view of a new period of human development.

It necessarily follows from this position that the struggle against the literature of the preceding period, against German Classicism and especially against Romanticism, is central to Heine's literary activity. This struggle – viewed abstractly – does not afford him a special position in the overall development of German literature. All progressive German literary criticism had, since the eighteen twenties, been working to overcome the *Kunstperiode* and in particular to deal a death blow to a Romanticism which was becoming increasingly reactionary (Börne, Menzel, Ruge, etc.). What makes Heine's position special is that, on the one hand, his interpretation of the Classical and Romantic period is broader, deeper and more historical than that of these critics, and that on the other, his critical evaluation of the present potential open to the new poetry is much more accurate. His criticism is more radical, and made from a left-wing standpoint. The liberal critics are also critical of the new literature, but their main objection to it is that it is too "demoralizing", not positive enough. (Friedrich Theodor Vischer, and most of the Young German critics from the eighteen forties onwards.) Heine, by contrast, criticizes progressive German literature for being too abstract, for harbouring too many illusions, for being insufficiently concrete in its criticism.

Heine's critique of Romanticism, the central focus of his critical activity, is inseparable from his political critique of the development of Germany. Heine is right to consider the struggle for national unity as the central problem of the coming bourgeois revolution in Germany. At the same time he sees that in modern times this question was first put on the agenda on a large scale by the so-called 'Wars of Liberation'.[77] The Romantic literary movement, in particular those currents of Romanticism that dominated the reactionary ideology of the pre-1848 period and that experienced a special renaissance in the eighteen forties, are rooted in the Wars of Liberation. Heine therefore concentrates his critical irony on exposing and pouring scorn on the ideology of the Wars of Liberation. Above all he attacks German servility, which became evident at that time. When Napoleon was defeated in Russia, Heine says:

We Germans received orders from the highest command to liberate ourselves from the yoke of foreign occupation, and a manly rage welled up within us at the oppression we had suffered for far too long. We allowed ourselves to be inspired by the rousing melodies and rotten lyrics of Körner's songs, and we won the struggle for our freedom; for we do everything that our princes order us to do.[78]

The blinkered nationalistic narrow-mindedness, the politically and socially reactionary nature of Romanticism, the dominant ideology of this period, all arose from this servility. Romanticism seeks to perpetuate the wretched, subservient, petty-state condition of Germany. Its admiration for German history is admiration for the backwardness of Germany's historical development. It glorifies the Middle Ages, Catholicism and later even the Orient in order to create a literary ideological model for the conservation of the wretched German condition.

Heine stands shoulder to shoulder with most of the progressive critics in this criticism of the reactionary nature of German Romanticism. Yet his critique goes beyond them in two respects. Firstly, Heine is the first and for a long time the only critic in Germany to recognize the bourgeois nature of the Romantic movement, to discover and expose the liberal-reactionary traits of those Late Romantics who belonged in political terms to the liberal wing of the bourgeoisie. This incisive criticism, which mainly concentrates on the struggle against Uhland and the 'Swabian School of Poetry'[79] and which occasionally even goes so far as to foresee the liberals' coming betrayal of the bourgeois revolution, was not at all understood in Germany for a very long time. In his critical elaboration of the bourgeois nature of Romanticism Heine does not stop short at a criticism of the poetry of the liberal bourgeoisie and the liberal petty bourgeoisie. In his critical poetic struggles against the period of reaction under Frederick William IV, Heine concentrates his satirical attacks on the Romantic King of Prussia precisely on the fact that the latter's flirtation with the Middle Ages was nothing but a pathetic bourgeois reactionary parody of the Middle Ages. In *Germany, A Winter's Tale*, Heine ironically demands of Emperor

Barbarossa, the legendary Romantic patron saint of German unity, that he should create genuine Middle Ages, because:

> 'The Middle Ages, well, I suppose
> if you give us the genuine article,
> I'll put up with that. Just rescue us
> from all this hybrid, farcical,
>
> 'revolting, pseudo-knightliness
> which, under its Gothic cover,
> is just a lot of modern deceit,
> neither one thing nor the other.
>
> 'Throw out that pack of comedians
> who parody times long gone,
> and shut down their theatres once for all –
> how long, O Emperor, how long?'[80]

Secondly, however, Heine spots the inner connection between Romanticism and the modern literary movement much more clearly than do any of his contemporaries in Germany (here too Heine is influenced by the Hegelian conception of history). He is, for example, one of the few who realized the ideological and methodological significance of the German philosophy of nature. He also realizes that Romanticism's recourse to the plebeian was indispensable for the development of modern literature and culture in Germany, despite all the reactionary tendencies it contained. Tendencies are expressed in Romanticism which were initially confused and were misunderstood by the Romantics themselves, only to become overtly and clearly reactionary ideologies in the later stages of development.

Indeed, our first Romantics acted out of a pantheistic instinct that even they themselves did not understand. The feeling which they mistook for a yearning for the Catholic mother-church was in fact of a more profound origin than they imagined . . . it was all due to a suddenly re-kindled but still uncomprehended inclination to return to the pantheism of the ancient Germans.[81]

Finally Heine focuses on the central literary-philosophical concept of German Early Romanticism, romantic irony. He purges the concept and use of irony from any purely artistic trifling – which was what irony had become in the hands of the Romantics themselves, particularly Tieck – and places irony at the centre of the critical and artistic method he adopts to come to terms with modern reality.

Heine transforms irony into the principle with which to destroy bourgeois illusions of an ostensibly harmonious reality. In the foreword, already written in Paris, to the second edition of the *Travel Pictures*, he makes a point of emphasizing this contrast between himself and Late Romanticism as represented by Uhland:

Admittedly, these pious and chivalrous tones, these echoes of the Middle Ages, which only a short while ago, in the period of patriotic narrow-mindedness, resounded from all quarters, are being drowned in the noise of the latest struggles for freedom, in the tumult of a general fraternization of the European peoples and in the sharp jubilation of pain of those modern songs that refuse to create a false, Catholic harmony of emotions, but rather, in their remorseless Jacobinism, cut through all emotions for the sake of truth.[82]

For Heine, therefore, the ironic destruction of all false harmony, the ironical, cynical emphasis of the strife-ridden present is part and parcel of his Jacobin struggle to destroy the remnants of the Middle Ages. And indeed at the same time to destroy all the false ideologies of the bourgeoisie, who have cobbled together a world of false harmony out of elements of feudal and capitalist ideology. This is why the young Engels accurately characterizes Heine's ironic style thus:

In Heine's case, the raptures of the bourgeoisie are deliberately high-pitched, so that they may, equally deliberately, then be brought down to earth with a bang. . .[83]

That is why, so Engels says, the bourgeois reader of Heine is so outraged, whereas the playful irony of other poets has a soothing effect and confirms him in his illusions. Heine too is aware of the apologetic nature of merely formal, artistically playful irony and always directs the most violent satirical attacks against it.

Heine's irony therefore goes far beyond the general practice of Romanticism. Yet it nonetheless has its source in Romanticism. Young Friedrich Schlegel, and, in his wake, Solger in particular conceived of irony in a profound, philosophical way as the self-dissolution of ideals.[84] The contradiction, Solger says, which becomes apparent in irony, is not only the destruction of a detail, not only the transience of things earthly, but 'the vanity of the idea itself, which together with its embodiment was subjected to the common fate of all mortal things'. This conception of irony is of great historical significance for the whole literary epoch between the French Revolution and 1848, especially in Germany. Reality exposed the illusory nature of the heroic illusions with which the bourgeois class had hitherto conducted its revolutions. However, the German bourgeoisie, while preparing itself for its own revolution, also needed heroic illusions if it were to carry out the bourgeois revolution as the true leader of overall social progress. As is well known, the retarded development of capitalism in Germany did not permit the bourgeois revolution to be carried through in this way. The German situation, which already cast a shadow on the ideological preparation of the revolution even though the progressive elements of the bourgeois class were by historical necessity arming themselves for a German 1789, made it constantly necessary both to create illusions and to destroy them.

Hegel thought his conception of historical development overcame Solger's irony, which he was fully prepared to acknowledge as occupying a legitimate place as an element of that development. However, the Hegelian solution could no longer satisfy the progressive intelligentsia of the eighteen thirties and forties, for that 'positive' element of philosophy in Hegel which overcame the 'negative' in Solger's irony is based on the notion that the period of bourgeois revolution had already been completed. Germany's progressive intelligentsia, however, who were preparing themselves for a revolution, could not possibly be satisfied with this Hegelian conception. Heine's return to the deepest sources of Romantic irony is not therefore antiquarian reversion, but rather the revitalization of a tendency of his day that arose out of the deepest contradictions of the special situation of German class struggles. Heine already acknowledges his approval of this most profound form of Romantic irony at a relatively early date. In a review of Ludwig Robert's Romantic comedies he provides – in letter form – the clearest formulation of his opinion on this. He criticizes the comedy for lacking 'the grand world-view, which is always tragic', for not being a tragedy. Heine does not of course make this 'outrageous demand that a comedy should be a tragedy' of the usual comedy of the French type, but expressly only of the Romantic comedy. At the same time he praises another Romantic comedy – that has not survived – by the same author, *Pavian* (*The Baboon*), and writes:

Much as we may initially laugh at the baboon, who complains bitterly at the oppression and insults he suffers at the hands of more privileged creatures – on closer examination of the play we are greatly moved by the aweful truth of the fact that this complaint is actually justified. Therein lies the irony, which is always the main element of the tragedy. The most horrifying, appalling, frightening situations can only be depicted in the colourful patchwork coat of the ridiculous if they are not to become unpoetic.[85]

Marxism, of course, overcomes this tragicomic self-production and self-destruction of illusions, right from the start, in quite a different way from Hegelian philosophy. The essential element of the Marxist conception of revolution is precisely the critical dissolution of the heroic illusions of past revolutionary periods and their replacement with the soberly practical heroism of an accurate assessment of the facts and tendencies of economic development itself. From our examination so far, it is clear why Heine was incapable of reaching a Marxist conception of how Romantic irony could be overcome. However, from the situation of Germany it is equally clear that his reversion to Romantic irony, his critical and literary renewal and intensification of Romantic irony, constituted not a regression behind Hegel, but on the contrary a revolutionary step beyond Hegel. The transitional period of extreme subjectivity, which in Heine's literary works is mainly expressed by precisely such irony, was the highest philosophical and literary standpoint that Heine could hope to attain. It was the highest standpoint attained by any writer in the Germany of this period. It was the final form of a bourgeois and yet nevertheless overall social assessment of all the contradictions of the historically possible development in Germany. That it took place in this paradoxical, ironic subjectivist form is a consequence of the uneven development, the special position of Germany within the development of international capitalism. Heine is, precisely because of his ironic subjectivism which some reactionary critics attack as 'un-German', *the most German writer of the nineteenth century*. His problems of style are the most appropriate and the most artistically valuable reflection of the great turning-point in the German development before and during 1848. To call Heine 'un-German' is an expression in literary history of those reactionary tendencies which culminated in fascism, which wanted to eradicate everything revolutionary from German history in order to be able to glorify its most wretched aspects.

Contradictions are not overcome in the realm of ideas, as Hegel believed. 'The differentiation of commodities into commodities and money does not sweep away these inconsistencies, but develops a *modus vivendi*, a form in which they can exist side by side. This is generally the way in which real contradicitons are reconciled.'[86] The way in which contradictions are resolved in reality is bound to determine the particular forms taken by the literary reflection of such contradictions. Heine, alongside Balzac, becomes the last great writer of the Western European bourgeoisie to attain world-wide significance, because he, like Balzac, found a particular form in which the contradictions could move in a dynamic way. The old apologetic form of bourgeois literature aimed at freezing the contra-dictions in a fictitious and false harmony. Late bourgeois, post-1848 literature was no longer able to ignore the insolubility of the con-tradictions as completely as did the earlier apologists. It therefore created a new form in which the contradictions *are frozen as contra-dictions*, just as in earlier literature they had been frozen in harmony.

Heine stands at the centre of this development, at its turning-point. He combats all false harmony. He uses literature to destroy any such deceitful unity. He seeks beauty in the dynamic of contradictions, he seeks the beauty of the transitional age of the bourgeoisie before the revolution, the beauty of pain, of sadness, of hope, of the illusions that necessarily arise and necessarily dis-integrate. Heine's contemporary, the important German dramatist Friedrich Hebbel, Heine's contemporary, sees this very clearly and very accurately:

In poetry, Heine found a form in which the most disparate tones, the expression of a world caught in a fit of apoplexy, come together in a cacophony, only to depart again as enchanting music; his collection of songs is a stern reminder of the mythical iron bull of Phalaris, which, according to legend, was so designed that the despairing cries of the slave who perished in the glow of its belly were transformed into flattering har-monies for the pleasure of the king, and in Heine's case this pleasure is all the more justified when one remembers that the perpetrator and victim of torture are one and the same person.[87]

The living dynamic of contradictions in Heine's poetry distin-guishes it from the late bourgeois verse which he comes so close to, especially in his final period. This dynamic derives from Heine's perspective of the revolution as the deliverance of humankind from the suffering of the present. And in spite of the fact that, as we have already seen, for Heine in his final period this concrete perspective has dissolved almost into nothingness, it still remains alive as a negative element, as a driving force of disquiet, of concrete social outrage, and prevents the contradictions from freezing to an apologetic pessimism, to an empty declamation against 'humankind's eternal and unalterable fate'. There is no question, however, that the later Heine does indeed stand on the threshold of this development. This point of contact makes Nietzsche, for example, such a great admirer of Heine that he extols him as the last German writer of European significance. It is necessary from Nietzsche's standpoint that he should do so by juxtaposing Heine with Baudelaire, and although this is an unbalanced appraisal of the later Heine, it is nonetheless not entirely inappropriate.

Our earlier juxtaposition of Heine with Balzac is based only on their place in the development of Western European nineteenth century bourgeois literature. They are the last two great bourgeois writers for whom comprehensive portrayal of dynamic contradictions was possible; both adopted the most profound form for overcoming Romanticism; while overcoming the Romantic heritage, both carried over its best aspects into their own work; yet both were unable to overcome Romanticism completely. For the impossibility of completely overcoming Romantic ideology on bourgeois terrain is the same problem as that of the 'tragedy' of bourgeois atheism that we have already analysed. Admittedly, in stylistic terms, Heine and Balzac, who admired each other personally and artistically, are absolute polar opposites. Balzac depicts the autodynamic of contradictions in the real world itself. He paints a picture of the real dynamic of real social contradictions. Heine's form is that of extreme subjectivity, reducing the literary composition of reality to the living and contradictory interplay of the reflection of reality in the mind of the writer.

It is no coincidence that Heine, with the exception of two unsuccessful dramas written in his youth, was incapable of completing any dramatic or narrative prose works. This is by no means the result of his lacking the necessary powers of composition. The fragment *Der Rabbi von Bacharach* and individual episodes of the *Travel Pictures* (in particular *Die Bäder von Lucca* [*The Baths of Lucca*]) show that Heine was thoroughly capable of portraying living people. There are deeper, socio-historical reasons why, with increasing maturity, he tended more and more consciously towards a lyrical ironical form both in poetry and prose; and why, in spite of his admiration for and deep understanding of its greatest exponents, he resolutely renounced narrative and dramatic realism in the classic sense. Heine was searching for a kind of poetry in which it was possible to portray the deepest contradictions of the epoch at the highest intellectual level of the epoch. In France and Britain, realistic portrayal of the real processes of social life enables Balzac or, at a lower level, Dickens to portray the real contradictions in this direct way. The 'anachronism' of the German situation, the young Marx's identification and critique of which we have already mentioned, renders a great German realism in this period impossible. The German realists of the day (Immermann, for example) are of necessity stuck fast in their depiction of the petty wretchedness of German social development. If Heine wanted to present criticism in literary form of the German situation on a level with contemporary international standards, i.e. that was really contemporary, as opposed to German-anachronistic, it was impossible for him to find a plot taking place on German soil which, combined with a realistic portrayal of the German situation, would adequately and realistically convey this criticism so that it could be tangibly experienced by the reader. It is therefore neither a lack of poetic skill nor Heine's personal whim that made him choose the correspondingly modified lyrical-ironical, fantastic-ironical, extremely subjectivist form of the poetic *Travel Pictures* for his great poetic criticisms of Germany, *Atta Troll* and *Germany, A Winter's Tale*. The form he chose was at that time the only possible *German form* for expressing the social contradictions on the highest literary level.

Heine also understood the necessity of this German development.

Philosophy and song form the highest pinnacle of the German Spirit. This climax has passed, it needed idyllic peace to flourish. . .

Poetry and philosophy (followed in the second rank by idealistically stylized drama and the fantastic novella) are the typical forms of German ideological development prior to Heine. The period between the revolutions of 1830 and 1848 brings with it the dissolution of both great forms. As we have seen, Heine takes an active part as a precursor in the dissolution of the idealistic philosophy of the Classical period. As a writer he carries out the testament of Classical and Romantic German poetry.

However, what Marx said about the dissolution of philosophy also applies – *mutatis mutandis* – to this dissolution of the highest German poetic form. In the essay from the *Deutsch-Französische Jahrbücher* to which we have already made repeated reference, Marx emphasizes that, on the one hand, one cannot supersede philosophy without first making it a reality, and that, on the other, one cannot make it a reality without superseding it. By the same token, Heine's ironic destruction of the German song is not merely destruction. That would have simply meant replacing the obsolete idyll of mood with dry capitalist prose. In such a case Heine would have been no more than a versifying Gustav Freytag – without Freytag's hidden and dishonest liberal Romanticism. Heine's greatness resides precisely in the fact that he did not succumb to either of the false extremes of late bourgeois development: he is neither a blinkered Romantic elegist of the destroyed idyll of pre-capitalist Germany, nor is he a trite apologist for the 'splendour' of nascent capitalism. He is neither a Mörike nor a Freytag, but rather, on the basis of the specifically German development, a great European writer of the profundity and stature of Balzac.

The overcoming of the Classical and particularly the Romantic heritage is in Heine's case a complete critical succession to this heritage. His poetry grows organically out of Romantic poetry; Brentano, Wilhelm Müller, etc., are the models for the poetry of his youth. He also succeeds to the Romantic heritage in so far as he takes up the threads of the Romantic polemic against the flood of capitalist prose. His deep-seated antipathy towards modern England at times takes on an almost Carlyle-like accent, although Heine, as we know, was never a Romantic anti-capitalist. However, his succession to the Romantic heritage lies precisely in the fact that he was able to use the Romantics' brilliantly colourful ironic outrage at capitalist prose as a component in his writing, without joining in the chorus of blinkered elegies about the disappearance of pre-capitalist conditions.

The most important Romantic heritage which Heine makes his

own is, however, the popular plebeian strand in Romanticism. For in spite of all the predominantly reactionary elements in the German national movement against Napoleonic oppression, it was still a national mass movement which for the first time in centuries had a profound effect on broad sections of the people. It is a consequence of the wretched backwardness of German developments that all the historically necessary illusions to which this struggle gave rise necessarily look backwards in the reactionary direction of the Middle Ages. However, the reactionary nature of their basic tendency, the reactionary exploitation of these tendencies (the Historicist School of Law, etc.) does not alter the fact that as far as literature was concerned, a continuation of popular plebeian traditions (folk songs, fairy tales, popular sagas) was sought and found. And Heine, both as a critic and a poet, picks up precisely these plebeian elements of the German development from the Classical and Romantic period. The vigour with which he stands up in particular for Germany's plebeian writers – Voss versus Menzel, Bürger[88] versus A. W. Schlegel – is extremely characteristic of Heine the critic and literary historian. And in his crushingly bitter polemic against the Romantic school he always defends and salvages this popular plebeian heritage. (For example in his appreciation of the anthology *Des Knaben Wunderhorn*.)

His literary practice takes as its point of departure this Romantic tradition of the German folk song. In his youth he even participates in the themes of Romantic poetry, at times going as far as to embrace Catholicism (e.g. 'Die Wallfahrt nach Kevlaar' ['The Pilgrimage to Kevlaar']). But even in Heine's youth all this is superficial and episodic, really just a 'prédilection artistique', as A.W. Schlegel once said. Heine's poetry very soon transcends this subject matter and uses it merely in order to overcome it ironically. In a letter to Wilhelm Müller in which Heine pays him tribute for inspiring his poems, he emphasizes at the same time the profound difference:

How pure, how clear your songs are, and every one of them a folk song. In my poems only the form is somewhat folksy, whereas the content belongs to conventional society.[89]

It should not be forgotten, however, that the problem of 'metropolitan poetry' also emerges in Romanticism, albeit in an often false, often reactionary polemical way. As a poet Heine may be the first great pioneer. In the field of the fantastic novella, however, E.T.A. Hoffmann precedes him.

Only when this relationship to the Romantic heritage is taken into account do Heine's polemics in literary criticism, the fundamental importance of which has only been understood by a very few of his biographers, appear in its true light. Heine must, admittedly, bear some of the blame for these misunderstandings, for he conducts most of his polemics in such a passionately personal way, destroying the private personality of the writer he is attacking, that the principles at stake, the depth of literary theory contained in the polemics, are far from obvious. Throughout his life Heine wages a battle on two fronts in his literature. On the one hand, he combats the narrow-minded, petty bourgeois vegetation of Romanticism, the reactionary ideology contained in the idyllic glorification of German backwardness. In principle he is certainly quite right to attack the liberal provincialist Late Romantics if anything with even more venom than the narrow-minded open reactionaries (his struggle against the 'Swabian School'). On the other hand, Heine fights against any false, lifeless, non-plebeian classicism in German poetry.

This struggle begins with his annihilating polemic against Platen[90] and ends with his biting critique of Herwegh, Freiligrath and the 'tendentious poetry' of the eighteen forties. It is highly revealing and important that all these 'classicists' attacked by Heine were politically progressive poets. However, this fact in no way detracts from the literary-political correctness of Heine's polemic. On the contrary, it highlights the deeper context of these literary struggles: they are the literary-political counterparts to Heine's political and ideological struggle against Börne. (It is no coincidence that Platen, Herwegh and many others sought theoretical support precisely from Börne.) The essential literary content of these struggles is a criticism of the abstract narrowness of those poets and at the same time, intimately connected with this, a criticism of the non-plebeian, the unspontaneous nature of their lyric form. Heine continually makes fun of Platen's 'metrical mastery'. He is the sworn enemy of that artificial virtuosity with which Platen attempts to compress the German language into classical metres. Heine regards this tendency as fundamentally wrong, as a tendency that contradicts the essence of the German language, of German verse, the plebeian nature of German verse. The greater the virtuosity, the greater the damage done to German verse by this developing tendency. In spite of his ironic dissolution of Romantic contents, in spite of the cosmopolitan primacy of content in his poetry, Heine is anxious to preserve the effortlessness and spontaneity of the folksong form. He regards metrical affectation as a dangerous obstacle to this plebeian form. And the development of German literature after 1848 certainly bore out his fears: from the derivative Munich poetry of Geibel[91] to the imperialist-reactionary park-bench poetry of Stefan George, Platen's tendency comes to triumph for what is now a reactionary bourgeoisie, denying German poetry any chance of the popular mass appeal which Heine saw as its aim. And it is surely no coincidence that of the ideological representatives of the democratic movement in Germany, people such as Ruge, Lassalle, etc., were the greatest admirers of the Platen-Herwegh line within German poetry, and that only Marx and Engels saw in Heine and his even more popular, even more plebeian successor Georg Weerth, the correct path along which poetry should develop. Only if viewed superficially does it seem paradoxical that Börne, who fraternized with the Parisian German artisans, stood for a less popular, less plebeian tendency of literary politics than Heine, the 'aristocrat'.

Heine's plebeian literary orientation is closely connected with his broader, more dialectical, less sectarian conception of the revolutionary tasks. And here we come upon the political content of Heine's polemic against these poets. Heine attacks their empty and abstract pathos, their disregard for the concrete conditions, the concrete enemy and the real fight to the death to be waged against him. As soon as Herwegh appears on the scene, and when he celebrates his great triumphs, Heine senses at once his rigidity, his narrowness, his ignorance of the real conditions, his sectarian naïvety and narrow-mindedness.

> Herwegh, you lark of iron:
> With a clang you soar to a jubilant sphere,
> To the holy light of the sun!
> Is wintertime really close?
> Is Germany's springtime really here?[92]

And Heine expresses his rejection of this kind of political poetry with even harsher irony in the poem 'Die Tendenz':

> Blare out, bellow, thunder, man –
> Till the last oppressor flees!
> Make your verses strong and biting. . .
> But make sure you keep your writing
> Just as general as you can.[93]

This polemic by no means comprises the full sweep of Heine's position on tendentious poetry. It would be a complete misinterpretation of his *Atta Troll*, were one to believe his ironic assertions that this poem was written against tendentious poetry and in defence of the arbitrariness and independence of poetry. *Atta Troll* contains a double-edged polemic: Heine derides narrow tendentious poetry just as much as the social and ideological contents that such poetry proclaims. Indeed, he derides tendentious poetry mainly because it only possesses character, i.e. staunch sectarian narrowness, but no talent, no ability to see things in their complexity, from their many sides, in their dynamic state. Nobody has yet doubted the tendentious nature of *Germany, A Winter's Tale* which followed *Atta Troll*, and yet Heine says of this poem: 'It is politically Romantic and I hope it will deliver the death blow to prosaically bombastic tendentious poetry.' Heine's struggle against tendentiousness is therefore a thrust in the direction of true, genuine and deep political poetry in which the tendentiousness develops organically out of the subject itself, rather than being plastered over the contents in abstract and prosaic manner.

The defence of the independence of poetry is in no sense a contradiction of poetry as an instrument of struggle. Heine's affirmation of the independence of poetry has nothing to do with *l'art pour l'art*. It is an expression of Heine's strangely isolated position within the German inter-party struggles of the eighteen thirties and forties. He wants to fight, but he is neither willing nor able to join forces with the narrow-minded political and literary representatives of the democratic movement any more than to make ideological concessions to the reactionaries. In his book against Ludwig Börne, Heine jokes that at times both camps have dismissed him as a mere poet.

Yes, I was, so to speak, given my political marching orders and was sent to retirement on Mount Parnassus. Anyone who is familiar with the two parties in question will readily appreciate the magnanimity they showed in allowing me to retain my title as a poet. The one side see in the poet nothing more than a courtier who wastes his time idly dreaming of ideals. The other side see nothing at all in the poet: poetry is unable to bring forth even the slightest echo in their sober emptiness.[94]

Heine's defence of the independence of poetry is therefore a defence of the right of great poetry to combat attempts on the part of the reactionaries and narrow-minded 'progressives' to restrict the scope of its impact.

In the struggle against the two false extremes, Heine's subjectivist poetry fights to achieve a high aim: a popular plebeian poetry whose contents express the deepest problems of the age. Heine sees clearly the value and significance of the great objective poetry of past ages. In spite of the correct criticism he levels against Goethe's various philistine traits, Goethe occupies a position that is similarly central to his view of literature as Hegel's in his philosophy and Napoleon's in his view of history. However, he recognizes at the same time that for Germany, historically speaking, the Age of Goethe belongs to the past, that the high, contemporary poetry to which he aspires can only be realized by applying a completely different creative method. When Heine affirms radical subjectivism on this question, he is on the one hand fully aware that this style is of necessity the transitional style of a transitional epoch; on the other hand, he senses the danger of a mannered style of writing which always accompanies the consistent use of any subjectivist style. Heine himself very often falls victim to this danger of mannerism. His 'private tactic' described earlier, the exaggeratedly personal nature of his polemics, his efforts to make a broad impact at all costs and to create a popular form of expression without possessing a secure class base which could have served him as a guide for content and form, etc. – all this was bound to make Heine prone to a mannered style. Thus he complains to Wienbarg, who praises his poetry:

You are still a free stallion, but I am a victim of my own dressage. I have fallen into mannerism, of which I am scarcely able to rid myself. How easy it is to become a slave to the public. The public expects and demands that I continue in the same vein as I began. If I change my style, people will say: that's not Heineian, Heine isn't Heine any more.[95]

Heine's dependence on the capitalist market for literature is clearly expressed in this self-criticism.

However, in Heine's case the danger of mannerism has deeper causes, which stem from the roots of his dissonant world-view. He is completely right to challenge Börne's narrow-minded contrasting of 'talent' and 'character'. He is absolutely correct to emphasize, as we have seen, the freedom of the poet because he recognizes in this freedom the free association of the poet with the great political currents of the age. Nonetheless, in the polemic against Börne's narrow-minded conception of steadfastness of character he often falls into a position of nihilistic scepticism. This scepticism is then reflected in his style as mannerism, as vacuous intellectualism.

However, for Heine the danger of adopting a mannered style emanates not only from this aspect of intellectualism but also from that of lyricism. Heine is in constant danger of allowing his genuine, deep lyrical feeling to turn into a mannered sentimentality. He senses this danger and generally dissipates such examples of senti- mentality by means of witty, ironical punch-lines. Nonetheless, the ironic dissipation of feeling is only profound, and therefore justified irony, if the poet's feeling is itself genuine. The witty dissipation of false sentimentality remains nothing but an empty witticism. (It is, admittedly, quite a different matter when Heine derides the philis- tines' expression of feelings which are falsely sentimental to begin with.) This false sentimentality is also ideologically rooted in Heine's inability to gain a fully dialectical understanding of the social proc- ess. When evaluating the material problems of social development he generally remains at the standpoint of mechanistic materialism, and because he senses that this results in a rigid and insufficient explanation of the dynamic and because he is incapable of intellec- tually discovering the true driving forces, he 'supplements' the mechanistic explanation with sentimental emotional additives. Heine himself very clearly appreciated this limitation of mechanistic materialism:

Sentimentality is the desperate attempt of the material world, dissatisfied with itself alone, to venture out into the realm of uncertain feelings in search of something better.[96]

It is necessary to emphasize these weaknesses of Heine so sharply because his popularity among the shallow liberal publicists (as 'father of the feuilleton')[97] and the liberal petty bourgeoisie is based precisely on these affectations. Heine's isolation in spite of his great popularity is expressed here in a particularly extreme form. He is popular with a social stratum to which he is bitterly opposed, and is popular in such a way that all his great, profound and revolutionary qualities are completely extinguished, leaving only his affectation. That all the reactionary literary historians (from Pfizer, the theoretician of the 'Swabian School', to Bartels, the fascist) should attack him from this angle and that even significant critics (such as Karl Kraus, for example) have fallen prey to this reactionary prejudice, has been less harmful to the memory of Heine than the fact that he should achieve such popularity among the type of people whom he held in the deepest and most justified contempt.

The underlying thrust of Heine's poetry – far from this mannerism – moves in the direction of a compositional form that is at the same time both popular and profound, grasping all the important questions of the epoch at their roots. As a poet too, Heine wanted to reveal the school secret of Hegelian philosophy and saw in this school secret the relentless and bitter struggle against the economic and political wretchedness of the old society, against the economic and political vileness of nascent capitalism, the struggle to awaken the masses to a revolutionary uprising:

> Go drum the people up from sleep,
> Drum reveille with youthful fire,
> March onwards drumming, on and on –
> That's all the knowledge you require.

That's Hegel's philosophy in short. . .[98]

The profundity of Heine's poetry is derived from a historically correct understanding of the present in its major developmental tendencies, from a legitimate assessment of the victory of capitalism, with all its prosaicness and its atrocities, over the now false idyllic poetry of the Middle Ages and its surviving remnants. This correct evaluation therefore goes hand in hand with a harsh criticism of capitalism and its culture, and a merciless recognition of capitalism's destructive effect on culture, despite the fact that its emergence and expansion are historically necessary and progressive. On the other hand, Heine's criticism of the Middle Ages and of medieval remnants never takes the form of a negligent philistine dismissal of the popular plebeian poetry that grew from this soil. The young Marx once refers to feudalism as 'the democracy of unfreedom', and Heine, as we have seen, had a very keen sense of the need to oppose the unfreedom of feudalism, while at the same time salvaging for his creative method the popular plebeian democratic poetic traditions of this period as living elements of literary portrayal. Thus, like the great writers of this period, he neither descended to the level of an apologist of capitalism, nor did he become bogged down in a narrow-minded Romantic critique of capitalism, in a narrow-minded glorification of the poetry of pre-capitalist conditions.

Heine thus wants to lend poetic literary expression to the real dialectic of the real development of his period. And even if we take into account the fact that this dialectic is merely that of Solger, a tragicomic dialectic, and not the complete and comprehensive materialist dialectic of Marx, we are still forced to recognize that Heine approaches the problems of the present with a degree of perspicacity and an ideological arsenal matched by only one contemporary, Balzac, whom Heine, despite his problematical relationship to the workers' movement, far excels when it comes to an understanding of the revolutionary role of the proletariat. The stylistic struggle of the great nineteenth century writers involves overcoming the prosaic nature of capitalist life, an endeavour which is constantly prone to the danger of seeing everything through Romanticism's rose-coloured spectacles or succumbing to the prosaic. Stylistic success always depends on the extent to which the writers are able to understand from an ideologically correct standpoint the elements of the disappearing poetry of life and to incorporate this very poetry as a correctly understood and therefore *poetically legitimate* component into their overall view. The great writers of the pre-1848 period, including Heine, were historically fortunate in that they were still able to portray capitalism as being in the process of emerging, rather than as something which had already emerged, and pre-capitalist poetry as being in a process of decline rather than something which had already been destroyed. In this way Heine is able to make a historically legitimate link between his work and the magical mood of Romantic folk poetry, and even though he dissolves it through irony – which is also historically legitimate – he is able, in spite of this dissolution, indeed precisely in and through this dissolution, to make use of this magical mood as the most legitimate literary medium available. This special lyrical peculiarity of Heine's is not some purely personal peculiarity. It is, as we have seen, a consequence of Germany's historical situation that Heine resorted to the lyrical medium, to the ironic exploitation and salvage of folk-song poetry. But the poetry of Balzac, the prose narrator, is also largely derived from the historically legitimate compositional treatment of pre-capitalist remnants, the historically necessary destruction of which he portrays with elegiac melancholy, yet in a way that is historically fully justified.

We have seen that Romanticism in Germany arose as a consequence of the French Revolution and that its central problem was the dialectic of the necessary creation and necessary destruction of the illusions held by the bourgeoisie, which was still an objectively revolutionary class. The central theme of its poetry is the question of the unity of man and nature, and man's search for refuge in this unity in the face of capitalism's cruel destruction of all ideals. The inner dialectic of Romantic poetry consists in the latent awareness that this unity of man and nature is merely a projection of subjective desires and aspirations onto nature, and that the reality behind this imagined unity of man and nature is nature's cruel indifference to man's yearning. The accentuation of such a cruel indifference is in turn an unconscious and itself Romantic projection of the inhumanity of capitalist laws onto nature. The victory of Evil, the basic motif of Heine's *Romanzero* cycle, is only the pessimistic culmination of this development. Its seeds are not only present in the young Heine, but in all Romantic poetry. According to proletarian consciousness, the objective independence of the laws of nature from human consciousness is not coloured by this idea of 'cruel indifference', since socio-historical reality loses its impenetrability when viewed with proletarian consciousness. This Romantic empathy, this sentimental oneness with nature does not even arise as a problem. Both the longing for such a unification and the necessary impossibility of realizing this longing stem solely from the ground laid by nascent capitalism. The more strongly capitalist society develops, the more empty and untrue this desire becomes.

Heine's relationship to Romantic poetry therefore represents a uniquely fortunate transition: he can, with complete clarity and remorselessness, destroy these illusions as illusions, and at the same time make poetically legitimate use of this longing in his poetry. In his *Confessions*, he relates a very interesting conversation with Hegel:

... I spoke rapturously of the stars, calling them the dwelling-place of the saints. The master, however, muttered to himself, 'The stars, tut, tut! The stars are nothing but a shining leprosy in the sky.' 'Good gracious,' I cried, 'you mean there is no place of contentment up there with which virtue will be rewarded after death?' The master, looking askance at me, said cuttingly, 'So you expect a tip for having looked after your sick mother and for not having poisoned your brother?'[99]

In the course of his development Heine goes further and further in the direction of this duality: the poetic portrayal of Romantic moods, of the historically necessary illusions and their ironic destruction. He constantly discovers new and more wonderful sides to nature's magical mood – for example, it is he who discovers German monumental sea poetry – yet at the same time he shatters with ever increasing violence the dishonest Romantic harmony, the illusory unity between man and nature.

> The waters murmur their eternal murmur,
> The wind is blowing, the clouds are fleeting,
> The stars are gleaming indifferent and cold,
> And a fool waits for an answer.[100]

Heine had of course written many poems in which he simply mocked the shallowly sentimental and ridiculous illusions of the philistine. His most profound poems, however, were founded on the dialectic of the historically necessary creation and historically necessary destruction of illusions. Heine's poems derive their lyrical legitimacy and their inimitable magic from precisely this source, from the fact that Heine himself is caught up in the very illusions he cruelly destroys. In the course of this development, as Heine's insight into social relations grows and deepens, these illusions become more and more faded as the poet's own belief in them becomes weaker and weaker – but they can never be completely eradicated from Heine's heart. Indeed, what characterizes Heine's final period is precisely the fact that, as a consequence of his political and ideological despair, both contradictory tendencies become stronger. The illusions become even more faded, they are even more plainly experienced as mere illusions from the very beginning, yet in spite of this the desperate poet clutches at these illusions that he no longer believes in himself and that have been inwardly destroyed even before their conscious poetic destruction. Thus the ironic dissolution of illusions takes on a particular inwardness. The dissolution does not have to take the form of punch-lines, as used particularly by the young Heine, since it is inherent in the melancholy disbelieving tone in which the illusions themselves are portrayed. This lends Heine's later poems their peculiarly inimitable tone, perhaps most vividly expressed in the poem 'Bimini':

> Bimini! At that sweet-sounding
> Name my heart leaps in my bosom,
> Youthful dreams I thought had faded
> Now awaken in my breast.
>
> On their heads the withered garlands
> Gaze at me with melancholy,
> And dead nightingales are fluting
> Tender sobs as if in pain.
>
> And I jump in startled panic,
> And my sick limbs are all trembling
> With such violence that seams of
> My clown's motley burst wide open. . .[101]

This shows very clearly the fact that Heine can be characterized as a *borderline phenomenon* between the periods of the bourgeoisie's ideological advance and decline. For by using this compositional form to portray disbelieved or half-believed illusions, he is able to influence the poetry of the late bourgeois age, a poetry which was consciously anti-Romantic yet which was in reality deeply ridden with Romanticism not yet overcome. This explains why Heine had such a strong and lasting influence on French poetry, why Richard Wagner was able to take the subject and conception of the *Flying Dutchman* and *Tannhäuser* from Heine, etc. This after-effect of Heine's, which – except in the case of French poetry – was subterranean and indirect, can be traced through to the end of the nineteenth century. The later Heine's compositional form of portraying disbelieved and aborted illusions is still reflected in Ibsen's *Hedda Gabler* ('Vineleaves in his hair').[102] In this respect he is, therefore, the first truly modern poet – or at least, one of the first – although this development does not follow the course anticipated by Heine himself when he saw himself as the forerunner of a new age.

However, this is not the only direction followed by Heine's poetic use of the Romantic heritage of mood. By reawakening the democratic-plebeian element in the 'democracy of unfreedom', Heine is inwardly able to deploy the atmospheric content of this poetry directly, albeit with a similarly contrasting dissolution of the self-created moods, in the service of popular revolutionary poetry. Particularly in the period when his revolutionary feelings ran high, Heine is successful – in the incomparable poem, 'The Silesian Weavers', and in many parts of *Germany, A Winter's Tale* – in transposing the plebeian-democratic tone of romantic folk poetry directly onto a revolutionary indictment or a song of victory. And even his later writings are full of examples of how he makes use of this poetry either directly or, for the most part, in ironized form, for revolutionary ends, for a screaming indictment of the poetically veiled wretchedness of social reality.

> In woods the quiet rillets run
> Soft moonlight bathes the garden plot,
> But sometimes *bang* – Was that a gun? –
> Perhaps it is a friend who has been shot.[103]

Heine also succeeds in adapting the themes of this plebeian democratic element of poetry – this poetry of the declining Middle Ages, destroyed by the development of the bourgeoisie – in such a way as to turn the melancholy of transience directly and ironically into the triumph of the popular revolution, as to make not the prose of capitalism the victor over the passing Middle Ages but the poetry of revolution. The finest example of this is perhaps his later poem 'Karl I':

> In a simple workman's hut in the woods
> The king sits lone and dreary;
> He rocks the workman's child, and sings
> In a monotone wintery and weary:
>
> '*Lullaby, baby, what stirs in the straw?*
> *The ewe-sheep are lowing and leaping* –
> You bear the mark upon your brow,
> And smile so fiercely when sleeping.
>
> '*Lullaby, baby, the kitten is dead* –
> The mark on your brow is aquiver –
> You'll grow a man and swing an axe,
> Already the oak trees shiver.

'The workman's older faith is dead:
His child is no standard-bearer
(*Lullaby, baby*) of faith in God,
And faith in the king even rarer.

'*The kitten is dead, the mice are glad* –
We'll come to grief and woe here –
(*Lullaby, baby*) in Heaven the Lord
And I the king below here.

'My heart is faint with sorrowing,
And daily grows my sorrow –
– (*Lullaby baby*) – You, my child,
Will be my headsman tomorrow.

'My funeral hymn is your cradlesong –
(*Lullaby, baby*) – It's pricking
The hair on my neck, you'll shear it first –
I can hear your scissors clicking.

'*Lullaby, baby, what stirs in the straw?* –
The realm is yours – ironhearted
You smite the head from off my trunk –
The kitten is dead and departed.

'*Lullaby, baby, what stirs in the straw?*
The ewe-sheep are lowing and leaping.
The kitten is dead, the mice are glad –
Sleep, little headsman, keep sleeping!'[104]

In this revolutionary poetry Heine really is, as he says himself, the last Romantic writer and the first modern poet. But here he had no successor, indeed the development of the revolutionary movement in Germany meant that he could not have had a direct successor anyway. Georg Weerth[105] is alone in continuing Heine's democratic-plebeian line, less hampered by a bourgeois-romantic past and thus in a more healthy, unproblematically sensual, plebeian way. Although he must be treated critically, Heine offers proletarian poetry, and not only that of Germany, an extraordinarily great and fertile poetic heritage, one which is only beginning to be discovered and elevated now that the development of proletarian class struggle has spread to the domain of literature and has begun to eradicate the abstract formalistic preconceptions of the early period and its stylistic limitation to the forms of late bourgeois, imperialist poetry.

German Reaction has always been instinctively aware of Heine's greatness and fertility and has always gone to the greatest lengths to erase Heine's name from German literary history. It is no coincidence that even in Germany, with its passion for monuments, Heine was never – despite his popularity – to receive an official monument. And reactionary literary history has always been at pains to accord the greatest German writer since Goethe an episodic role, replacing him with people like Mörike who were, by comparison, quaint little dwarfs.[106] Fascism, correctly sensing that the lethal irony Heine levelled against the parody of the Middle Ages is capable of dealing an even more lethal blow to the 'Third Reich' than to pre-1848 Prussia, wants to erase Heine, together with Marx and Engels, Lenin and Stalin, from the consciousness of the German people. The hatred of these enemies – who represent in their most horrifically wretched form of development the same forces that Heine always opposed – is justified. With their struggle to destroy Heine they have built for him the most fitting monument possible, until such time as the victorious German Revolution is able to express its gratitude to him in adequate fashion.

1935

Gottfried Keller[*]

Keller, one of the greatest narrative writers of the nineteenth century, clearly ranks among the leading authors in world literature. This, the objective state of affairs, is not altered by the fact that he has not until now, or at least only partially, received international recognition. However, it would seem to be time to view Keller's work from the vantage point of world literature and to determine the historical place he deserves to occupy among the world's truly great writers. The following study thus follows a course which deliberately runs contrary to the majority of appreciations of Keller, which tend to view him from a narrowly provincial German or Swiss perspective.

Today, however, there is a particularly topical reason for turning our critical attention to that classic champion of democracy. The misuse of all of what were once revolutionary democratic ideals for the purposes of imperialism has inevitably shed an especially harsh light on all the limitations of bourgeois democracy. It is, however, instructive and useful in precisely such a situation to concern oneself with the honest and important representatives of democracy in past ages. The example they set, their intellectual, ethical and artistic culture, constitutes a clear unmasking of the depravity and barbarism of the egotistical imperialists of the present-day, for whom the word democracy has become hollow and hypocritical. At the same time, such investigations return the heritage of our classics to their true home: to the liberated people of today, whom every true freedom fighter loves and honours as his ancestors.

I

HISTORICAL SITUATION

The defeat of the bourgeois-democratic revolution in 1848 signified a major turning-point in German literature. Let us emphasize but two aspects of this: first, the break in that revolutionary-democratic

[*] First published in *Internationale Literatur*, nos 6/7, 1939.

line of development that starts in the preparatory years of the Great French Revolution and reaches its climax in the eighteen forties. The political significance of this turning point can best be characterized by the fact that, whereas the democrats of 1848 had wanted to bring about the national unity of Germany by achieving freedom, the intellectual leaders of the bourgeoisie – which was increasingly developing into a camp of National Liberals – now wished to accord 'unity' absolute priority over 'freedom' even with regard to their chronological sequence. In other words, they prepared the way for the German bourgeoisie's capitulation in the face of the Prussia of Bismarck and the House of Hohenzollern.

This development culminated in the patriotic jubilation at the victories over France. Indeed, if one investigates the intellectual developments of this time more closely, one notices that this jubilation was objectively justified to the extent that the Hohenzollerns' military victories did in fact result in the realization of the central goal of the bourgeois revolution in Germany, namely the creation of national unity. However, the manner in which this desire was fulfilled meant at the same time breaking with Germany's best social and ideological, political and artistic traditions. For this reason, these victories were prepared intellectually and emotionally both by an unprincipled subservience to the House of Hohenzollern and Prussia, and by a deep depression, an embitterment filled with resignation on the part of the best and most honest of the leading intellectual figures of the day. It is no coincidence that the decades after the defeat of the revolution are the age dominated by Schopenhauer's philosophy.

Second, this period involves the first major upturn in German capitalism. However, given that Germany's development lagged behind that of the other Western European countries, it lacks the sombrely unfolding grandeur of developments in England and France. Here as there, the transformation of semi-patriarchal into capitalist relations results in the massive pauperization of wide sections of the working people. Whereas the history of capitalism in England and France reads like a storm that sweeps away the rotten remains of the Middle Ages, in the Germany of the Reaction the most wretched and confining remnants of the pre-capitalist period remain intact; the only phenomena that gradually disappear are those which are economically incompatible with the development of capitalism. German capitalism erodes the more primitive social relations which had provided the momentum of democratic revolution in seventeenth century England and eighteenth century France and had in Germany formed the social basis for developments in philosophy from Leibniz to Hegel and in literature from Lessing to Heine.

Germany's economic and political backwardness determined the way in which its literature developed. Given its social backwardness and national disunity, no actions were forthcoming in the life of the country which could have been taken to embody major national and social problems in the form of the fates of individual persons. Hand in hand with the economic and social consolidation of capitalism, the abstract-fantastic universality of social criticism (e.g. the works of Swift or Voltaire) in the literature of the Western countries increasingly gave way to a panoramic realistic reproduction of everyday life in bourgeois society, a development which reached its climax in the first half of the nineteenth century in Dickens and Balzac. The novel as the typical form of bourgeois life necessarily became more and more urban, increasingly metropolitan, because the city epitomized in reality the most profound and typical problems of the whole nation. A corresponding development was impossible in Germany prior to unification. But even when the political unity of the nation had been achieved and Berlin had become a true metropolis, the manner in which unity had been achieved remained as a damaging heritage. Wilhelm Raabe said pertinently: 'France's conscience resides in Paris, England's in London, but the German conscience is by no means Berlin.'

It would be all too one-sided and thus false only to see the negative sides of culture and literature in the backwardness of pre-revolutionary Germany. The early Marx rightly pointed to the fact that German conditions prior to 1848 lagged behind the times and demonstrated that even their complete negation would only correspond to a 1789 compared with developments in Western Europe. In the same context, however, he showed that intellectual life in the Germany of the day, particularly German philosophy, was abreast of the great events of contemporary Europe.

In keeping with the backwardness of capitalist developments in

Germany, there is nothing commensurate with the development of economics in England from Petty to Ricardo and in France from Boisguillebert to Sismondi. At the same time, however, Germany sees the genesis of Classical philosophy from Leibniz to Hegel, which, at a high scientific level, posits the universal laws of the opposition between being and consciousness, linking them profoundly, if often covertly, with the contradictions of bourgeois society. This is the highest intellectual expression of bourgeois thought *per se*.

The literature of Germany's Classical period gives poetic expression to this large view, this concrete universality of the greatest problems of bourgeois Humanism. It is – in terms of content – completely up-to-date. Germany nevertheless lagged behind the times, and this is expressed by the specific approach to formal questions adopted by its literature, by the fact that its form of realism was unable to describe directly the life of bourgeois society in Germany in the sense of the English and French realism of the age; by the fact that particular forms of realism, such as monumental and fantastic realism, had to be found in order to pour the concrete universality of Humanism's contemporary problems into a vivid, poetic mould. In other words, German developments are anticipated in German literature; the greatest examples of this are the narrative prose of Goethe, the historical monumentality of the dramas of Goethe and Schiller and the genesis of the modern novella, in particular as developed by E.T.A. Hoffmann. However, the more the relations of production in Germany develop, the less tenable this style becomes and the more such disintegrative trends as arise are geared towards realism in the Western European sense. The more the objective conditions for a bourgeois-democratic revolution in Germany develop, the stronger these endeavours become. The literary struggles in the eighteen thirties and forties can almost without exception be traced back to this. When Heine speaks of the 'end of the *Kunstperiode*' in Germany, he doubtless has such a new literary development in mind.

Obviously, Germany's continuing economic and social backwardness strongly inhibited the development of this realism. Heine's oeuvre and Immermann's novels, the most important attempts in this direction, still bear the mark of the self-dissolution of the *Kunstperiode* rather than the traits of a new realist art. This is particularly true in the case of Immermann, who worked very consciously and energetically to achieve a new form of realism and whose 'Oberhof' episode in *Münchhausen* accords him a pioneering role in German literature in this respect.[1] His literary generalization, by contrast, was poor and contained an exaggerated amount of fantasy, a sign that he was still unable to conquer the concrete social problems with directly realist means.

The collapse of the 1848/49 Revolution meant for Germany not just the collapse of the Classical traditions in philosophy and literature, but at the same time the death of those healthy buds that had promised new blossom, buds that had burst forth in all areas during the preparatory phase leading up to the revolution, despite the problems inherent in them. Thus, Feuerbach signified for Germany the end of Classical philosophy.

The calamitous caesura in German literature, which still makes itself felt today, began with the defeat of the 1848 Revolution. We know that the Age of Reaction was simultaneously one of strong capitalist growth, that the gradual spread and victory of capitalism in Germany constituted only a restructuring, and thus in the final instance brought with it a consolidation of the old political structure. Since this development required the German bourgeoisie's betrayal of the bourgeois revolution, its consent to the politically reactionary solution of national unity, this compromise and capitulation leave their mark on the whole development of German literature.

On the one hand we see the evolution of a literature of a Germany that is in the process of becoming capitalist, from Gutzkow via Freytag and Spielhagen right up to the shallowness and hollowness of Paul Lindau's Berlin novels.[2] By participating in and affirming the German bourgeoisie's class compromise, this literature can only describe the genesis of capitalism in Germany by embellishing it, by serving as an apology for it. It fails to encapsulate the truly profound national and social problems. Despite passing successes, it remains foreign to the life of the German people.

On the other hand, literature becomes more provincial. We do not just mean thematically, but we refer also to the increasing inability of even highly talented writers to consider local events in the provinces from the perspective of the overall national and social framework. Immermann was the first to try something in this direction, and Otto Ludwig[3] recognized correctly that the German 'village story', beginning with the 'Oberhof' episode, provides a healthy basis for the development of the German novel. He also proclaims Dickens as an artistic model for such a development. He overlooks the fact, however, that this question is not purely one of art; that is, he overlooks the social and ideological preconditions for the greatness of Dickens's description of society compared with the narrowness and pettiness of German narrative prose as it gradually becomes more provincial. For the true realism of a Balzac or a Dickens does not mean the loss of high humanistic standards in the generalization of types and fates, but rather their transformation, their conversion into objects of everyday society, and thus something openly critical of that society.

Why, for example, is a writer so artistically talented as Fritz Reuter,[4] with such a powerful and humorous gift for portraying people, hopelessly provincial? Let us make the point again: not because of his provincial themes. When Reuter deals with the 1848 Revolution and himself says that he does not wish to take a stance on the revolution, that he only wishes to describe that part of the revolution which directly affects his characters, then this would appear to be his perfect right as an author. The awful truth, however, is that he actually carries this intention out in his work. The 1848 Revolution is not described in the villages and small towns of Mecklenburg in such a way as to show how the great problems involved actually became apparent through these small surroundings – as major national and social problems. Instead he only allows that part of the revolution to become visible which an average Mecklenburg petty bourgeois contemporary of it would have experienced. In other words, nothing but a tumultuous chaos full of comical episodes. If one thinks of the reflections of the French Revolution in Goethe's *Hermann and Dorothea*, then one realizes why Reuter's powerful realism remains provincial, why his direct plebeianism had to accelerate the atomization of the German people and the extinction of a unifying democratic spirit. And yet Reuter has a very forceful and healthy plebeian instinct which his successors were increasingly to lose sight of.

This provincial German literature is at the same time an expression of the opposition to nascent capitalism. This could have formed the healthy seed from which a critical realist description of society could have evolved. All the great French, English and Russian realists are, after all, full of Romantic feelings of opposition to capitalism. But the provincialism in Germany is to be seen in the weakness of such criticism. It is not that the feelings behind the opposition are weak, but that it lacks a deeper knowledge of the object criticized.

The weaknesses of such an exceptional writer as Wilhelm Raabe do not reside in the fact that he described every capitalist milieu in caricature – Dickens often does the same – but that these caricatures remain pale and are kept at a general level, do not illuminate decisive traits in the baseness of the opponent thus criticized, that they are generated from a distance, without incisive knowledge or intellectual superiority. The only – politically speaking – significant, lively depictions in Raabe's work are those of Old Germany in its slow process of decline. Raabe describes with a unique, bitter lyrical humour of the highest literary standard the complete foreignness experienced by the best surviving moral representatives of that Germany in the new capitalist-reactionary reality. This is the last, desperate rearguard action of German Humanism. Raabe has often been compared with Jean Paul. And in essence wrongly so. For Jean Paul's humour amounts to the effort to break with the narrowness of Germany's wretched backwardness; behind the failure of each individual fate, behind the resignation of each individual figure, there is nevertheless a bright overall perspective for the future. Precisely this past, this small-town, idyllic closeness is, however, in Raabe's work the last salvation of humanity; it has become the abandoned hut in which German Humanism, crippled and senile, ekes out its last, sad days.

It is interesting that immediately after the defeat of the revolution, Keller foresaw – with misgivings – the genesis of this kind of humorous literature in Germany (1851). He stated that a writer of the people should not write in the style of Sterne or Jean Paul, adding that:

It was an unhappy and troubled age in which consolation had to be sought in such literature, and may the Gods preserve us from its renewed blossoming following the Preliminary Treaty of Olmütz and the Dresden Conferences.[5]

Naturally, the literature handed down by the German Classical and Romantic periods did not disappear after 1848. Yet its continued existence signified, with respect to the broad mass of literature, an increasingly hollow and soulless academicism with its nurturing of form for form's sake. Acquiescence in the Reaction, with opposition confined to the feeble efforts of the National Liberals, led to a paucity of thought and feeling, which thus became the diametrical opposite of the conventional Classical forms and transformed the humanity of the latter into resounding empty phrases.

In Germany, however, authentic writers continued to exist in whose works the furtherance of Classical forms had deep-seated ideological reasons, writers who in terms of their approach to problems and character portrayal matched the heights attained elsewhere in the Europe of the day. Yet we notice precisely here the extent to which the Classicism of the Age of Weimar was a specific, temporally-determined stage in German history, precisely because the form of poetic generalization it deployed grew organically out of the state of society at that time. The less artists of the Age of Reaction lagged behind historical developments – seen in an overall European context – the greater the dissonance between the *Classical* monumentality of the form of depiction and the *modern* psychology of the characters.

Nietzsche in his later period had already discovered the affinity between Wagner's heroines and Flaubert's *Madame Bovary* and *Salammbô*, and it is not difficult to detect the Dostoyevskian traits of Hebbel's heroes behind his pathos-laden iambic verse.[6] A discussion of the tragedies of Wagner, Hebbel, etc., would go beyond the bounds of the present study, yet we must nevertheless point out that even in the case of the most honest and important artists of this time a strong tendency already existed to link monumental form with the decadent psychology of individual fate, a linkage bereft of all good taste and later to have such fateful consequences.

A thorough investigation would show that the defeat of the 1848 Revolution signified a fissure in the artistic development both of Hebbel and of Wagner; a rupture that caused this trend towards *tastelessness* to become even more pronounced. Hebbel, as a result, drifted increasingly further away from a truly plebeian approach. Passing successes owing to the whim of fashion are of no import here. And the great popularity of Wagner's art has predominantly to do with events that have in common the tragic compromise of the later Wagner and the anti-democratic tendencies in Germany under the Hohenzollern dynasty. Heinrich Mann's *Der Untertan* (*Man of Straw*) is a brilliant satirical critique of these influences and a trenchant literary exposure of their social roots.

II
DEMOCRACY

Gottfried Keller stands in conscious opposition to all these currents. No one will be surprised at the fact that he despised Gutzkow and the Young Germans. It may be more striking that he criticized Adalbert Stifter for philistinism and polemically contrasted Stifter's descriptions with Gotthelf's truly epic greatness.[7] He always had a deep antipathy for Hebbel, despite the latter's early works having had a profound influence on him; he recognized Hebbel's great talent but strongly rejected all the contrived elements in Hebbel's works. In Zurich he was for a time on very good personal terms with Richard Wagner. However, in a letter to Freiligrath he characterized him as follows: 'a very talented person, but also something of a charlatan, and somewhat on the make.'[8]

Keller's rejection of the literary currents that predominated in Germany is not of literary origin. The fact that Keller was able to polemicize against both the petty bourgeois constrictions of provincialism and against ingenious, individualistic exaggeration is, after all, a result less of a personal idiosyncrasy and much more of the deep attachment he felt towards Swiss democracy, whose natural roots were still largely intact.

The German liberation poetry of the eighteen forties had a very strong influence on Keller as a young man; he was swept along with the tide of democratic developments which even led all the way to his making the highest conceptualization of German revolutionary democracy, namely Feuerbach's philosophy, his own. Consequently, Keller stood at the pinnacle of philosophical and literary developments in Germany prior to the 1848 Revolution.

He was idiosyncratic in that he did not participate in the retrograde movement following the defeat of the revolution. It was Swiss democracy that preserved him from doing so. Whereas he had until then taken an active part in the intellectual struggles in the German cultural region, he now increasingly became a mere observer of German developments. He studied them carefully, with deep sympathy, with sharp indignation at the Reaction, but they no longer represented a fundamental element in his intellectual existence, and changes in them no longer affected his own development.

One need only read carefully the notes and letters Keller wrote in Heidelberg (1848/50) and Berlin (1850/55) to see this difference, this change in his entire attitude. While living in Heidelberg he participated in the events with deep personal commitment, whereas in Berlin he lived as a Swiss democrat on a study tour in order to be able to return, politically active, to public life in his home country. And as Keller's major works were produced during this time, even though the themes used often rely on the author's experiences as a young man, it is this turning away from a Germany that had become reactionary, this exclusive occupation with Swiss democracy, that determines the contents and form of his whole oeuvre.

Viewed superficially, there is something about this withdrawal that could remind us of the retrograde line adopted in the provincial German literature described earlier. And the deep congruity with the best representatives of this trend – one thinks above all of Theodor Storm – clearly have their roots in this withdrawal. But although these two kinds of withdrawal were both caused in the final analysis by the defeat of the 1848 Revolution, they are similar only at a formal level. For Keller did not bury himself in some provincial German cranny in order to turn his back in disgust or self-satisfaction on a public life that had become reactionary. Rather, he returned to his democratic home and took up a central place in its public life, both as a writer and a citizen.

This decisive difference is emphasized even further by the fact that the development of capitalism in Switzerland occurred later and was by no means as tempestuous as in Germany. Of course, capitalism destroyed all the natural social relations in Switzerland – and its impact is also portrayed negatively in Keller's writings, as we

shall see. First, however, it was not until much later that these negative effects of capitalism became significant and obvious enough in
Switzerland to have a decisive influence on Keller's output (*Das
verlorene Lachen* [*The Lost Smile*], 1874 and *Martin Salander*, 1886).
Second, and more important, the development of capitalism in
Switzerland did not occur under politically and socially reactionary
conditions that degraded the democratic bourgeoisie. Keller only
experiences the beginnings of the capitalist destruction of traditional Swiss democracy.

It would thus seem that in the shape of Keller we have a Swiss
national writer before us, whose idiosyncrasies can be derived from
and understood in terms of his Zurich roots. Throughout his life
Keller protested sharply against such a conception. There is a
revealing discussion between the hero and the Southern German
Count, a democratic disciple of Feuerbach, at the beginning of the
first version of *Der grüne Heinrich* (*Green Henry*). The protagonist
(and via this mouthpiece, Keller too) passionately declares his
allegiance to democratic republicanism in Switzerland and is prepared to defend its independence from Germany with his own life.
On the question, however, of whether he was then a supporter of
Swiss national literature, of a Swiss national culture, he answers
(and here again, he answers for Keller as well) as follows:

Many of my fellow countrymen do indeed believe in Swiss art and literature, and even in a specifically Swiss science. The glow of the Alps and the
poetry of the Alpine roses soon grow stale, and odes to the few great battles
do not take long to sing. And to our shame, all the toasts, mottoes and
inscriptions used at our public ceremonies still have to be borrowed from
Schiller's *William Tell*, as this is still the best source for such occasions.[9]

In Keller's eyes, science and literature need the wide field constituted by more global contexts; each part of Switzerland consequently belongs in terms of literature to the respective large country
with which it is linked in terms of language and intellectual culture:
to Germany, France and Italy.

This stance that Keller took with regard to his own Swiss literature remained unchanged. It is highly characteristic that he only
once permitted a few of his poems to be published in a Swiss anthology. He justified his concurrence by referring to the 'impotence at
present in evidence in Germany' (meaning the years following

1870) only to add immediately: 'But I in no way wish thereby to support the eternal founders of a Swiss literary cottage industry.'

Keller, in other words, viewed Swiss belles lettres as part of German or French literature respectively. He was just as much a German writer as Rousseau, who came from Geneva, was a French author.

He was, however, at the same time a Zurich democrat, just as Rousseau was a supporter of Geneva democracy. That is to say, he polemically contrasts Swiss, Zurich democracy with the Germany of petty princedoms, which was slowly and painfully extricating itself from a semi-feudal condition, and the later unified Germany of Bismarck and the House of Hohenzollern, just as previously Rousseau had contrasted democratic Geneva with French absolutism.

Admittedly, the contrastive conjunction *just as* must be italicized. For in the case of Rousseau the social and political model of Geneva democracy – strengthened and underpinned theoretically by the Plutarchian ideal of Sparta and Rome – became the banner of French radical democracy and, through it, of the democratization of all Europe. The ideal of Geneva democracy forms not only the annihilating polemical contrast to the feudal absolutism of the Bourbons, but also to those members of the Enlightenment who believed that the introduction of the constitutional monarchy in England might provide a solution which could save French society. This contrast later developed into one of the most important characteristics of the difference between radical democrats and conciliatory liberals, between Jacobins and Girondists.

Keller's allegiance to Zurich never had such a world-historical significance, even in terms of the development of German culture, not to mention international culture. For Keller, Zurich democracy was but one humanly and artistically healthy means of withdrawing from the pestilence of the German Reaction. His support for Zurich democracy was Keller's salvation as a major plebeian and realistic writer, but it simultaneously gave him a unique and isolated place in the history of German literature. The defeat of the democratic revolution in Germany, the reactionary manner in which German unity was brought about, Germany's subsequent undemocratic development: all were decisive in determining not only the course taken by the culture of the German Reich, but also its relationship to those German-speaking areas that lay outside the borders of what had constituted itself as the German nation. The hopes for a democratic Greater Germany were dashed in 1848/49. Only now did German-speaking areas, such as Switzerland and Austria, truly detach themselves from overall developments in Germany, and start energetically to nurture the existing seeds of an independent culture.

Keller stands at the point at which this division occurs. His world-view remains that of a radical 1848 democrat (and, among other things, his rejection of an independent, national body of Swiss literature is linked with this), but his political and literary life becomes decidedly Swiss. This contradiction affects all his areas of activity. Thus, Keller's democracy – just as is, ideologically, his Feuerbachian materialism – is neither aggressive, propagandistic, nor universalistic as were Rousseau's social, political and ideological convictions.

It would be a shallow, one-sided explanation of this contrast if we were to regard Keller solely as an artist and Rousseau solely as a political theorist and journalist. For on the one hand, Rousseau's theoretical and artistic oeuvre forms an indivisible whole and has had worldwide impact as such. One cannot detach his novels and his autobiography from his *Social Contract*. And contradictory though the unity of this oeuvre might have been, it nevertheless had an effect only as a unified whole precisely by virtue of its inherently contradictory nature. For this contradiction was intrinsic to life itself, was a fundamental contradiction of radical democracy before and during the Great French Revolution.

On the other hand, only in a very limited sense can Keller only be considered a mere artist. His fifteen years work in the high and responsible position of head clerk of the chancellery of democratic Zurich (1861–1876) are much more than a passing episode in his biography. *Green Henry*, the great autobiographical novel of his younger years, takes as its basic theme a multi-talented and problematical person growing up to occupy his place in public and political life. Here, as in the greater part of his writings, Keller portrays the positive and negative human characteristics which determine whether or not one is suited for public office. Education for public activity: this is the basic notion underlying all of Keller's work as a writer.

Keller has a far-reaching and profound conception of the interdependence of public and private life. He lambasts the reactionary political opinions of Jeremias Gotthelf, a Swiss plebeian author whom he held in high regard, yet decidedly approves of the fact that the latter took a passionate political stance. Keller writes:

For today everything is politics and depends on it, from the leather that soles our shoes to the uppermost tile on the roof, and the smoke that wafts up from the chimney is politics and hangs in hazardous clouds above the huts and palaces, drifting back and forth between the towns and the villages.[10]

It would, however, also be incorrect to find fault with the sincerity and level of Keller's political convictions, and not to understand them from the point of view of his specific historical situation. Clearly, Keller is no plebeian democrat; in particular he shows little understanding for the socialist workers' movement. If one compares the narrowness of his conception of democracy with that of Rousseau and the Jacobins, one should never forget that the latter were active in a society in which the classes were far less differentiated, in an age when the proletariat had not yet constituted itself as an independent class. Clearly Keller is no enthusiast of revolutionary upheaval and prefers peaceful legal political changes to revolutionary coups. But on this question again there is much greater agreement between him and Rousseau than one might imagine at first glance. One must distinguish sharply between a general abstract opinion on this subject and actual behaviour once a revolution had broken out. How Rousseau would have acted when confronted with the reality of a democratic revolution we cannot know. We do know, however, that Keller participated actively in the democratic struggle against the Swiss Separatist League and had the liveliest sympathy for the democratic wing during his revolutionary years in Heidelberg.

An extensive profession of faith from this Heidelberg era has survived in the form of drafts for *Green Henry* written at that time. We believe that it is sufficiently important to be reproduced here in full despite its length:

Patriotism and Cosmopolitanism

Each gains its true position only via the correct unification of both. The advice and actions of the limited, one-sided patriot will never be of true service nor bring fame to his fatherland; if the latter comes in contact with the century and the world, then he will find himself in the predicament of a hen fearfully watching the hatched ducklings waddling into the water, whereas the one-sided cosmopolitan, whose heart is not rooted in one particular fatherland, who does not stand with both feet on one concrete piece of earth, is never able to fight for the influence of his ideas and can be compared with that fabled bird of paradise which has no feet and can therefore never descend from its lofty domain.

Just as a person only knows his fellow-beings if he explores himself, and only then gets to know himself completely if he explores others, just as he only serves others if he keeps himself in order, and will only then be happy if he is useful to others, so too a people can only be truly happy and free if it has a feel for the well-being and freedom and reputation of other peoples; and it will in turn only be able to draw on such a feeling if it has diligently put its own house in order. True patriotism and true cosmopolitanism is the ability always to find the correct transition and the intrinsic coalescence of these vivid contradictions. Therefore mistrust every person who boasts that he knows and loves no fatherland! But also mistrust him who has boarded up the world beyond the boundaries of his country and who believes that one's chance birth into this or that people is everything and means everything and for whom the rest of the wide world is at most a great area to be plundered, in existence for the express purpose of being exploited to the utmost by his fatherland.

However, living continually in happy amazement at the fact that I have been born in this of all countries and forever praising chance for allowing this to be, is also a characteristic of a true love of my fatherland. Yet the beauty of this characteristic must be purified by love and respect for that which is foreign, and without a great and profound foundation and the happy prospect of world citizenship, patriotism is. . . a raw, infertile and moribund quality.

Keller always remained true to this conviction. We have already discussed the political stance he adopted in his younger years. During and after the 1848 Revolution he always showed a healthy mistrust of the politics pursued by Prussia, Austria and Russia. At the time of the Savoy Crisis of 1859 he was in favour of an armed struggle against Napoleon III in order to preserve Switzerland's sovereignty. He followed with great sympathy every democratic stirring throughout the world; for example, he was greatly pleased that London workers gave the Austrian General Haynau, the hangman of the Italian and Hungarian Revolutions, a thorough thrashing. He even followed the Shamil uprising against Russian Czarism in the Caucasus with sincere compassion; he participated actively in the Schiller Centenary celebrations yet he demanded that Switzerland also celebrate the centenary of the French Revolution, etc.

His basic political attitude is therefore a resolute defence of the sovereignty of Swiss democracy. The underlying principle of his convictions was, however, in the widest historical sense that of revolutionary democracy. He considered Switzerland to be a formation that had evolved by a process of historical and organic growth. He is prepared to take up arms against Germany and France, the reactionary powers that on occasion threatened Switzerland during his lifetime. He did not, however, consider any political situation to be final and repeatedly expressed hope that democracy would in the future spread and take deeper root throughout Europe, which would then also be able to exercise a decisive influence on the governmental problems of the individual peoples.

When in 1872 Gusserow, a Zurich professor, took up a chair at the newly-founded University of Strasbourg, Keller held the valedictory speech, the content of which he himself summarized as follows:

Gusserow is asked to bear greetings to the inhabitants of Strasbourg from their old friends, the people of Zurich, and to tell them that they should not feel too unhappy at being part of the new Reich. Perhaps a time will come when this German Reich will tolerate forms of government such as would be acceptable to the Swiss, at which time the latter may conceivably return to the fold. This cannot, of course, simply take the form of free cities, for these already exist, but rather must involve the recognition of larger people's republics.[11]

These thoughts, which caused general indignation at the time, are closely connected with the tradition of German democracy. In the foreword to his poem *Germany, A Winter's Tale*, Heinrich Heine expresses the same principle with respect to Alsace-Lorraine's relationship to Germany.

The depth of Keller's democratic convictions can be seen in the fact that they are closely bound up with his whole oeuvre. Everything is politics: and this was not just a deep feeling on his part, but something he had thought through. Poetry, which for him means the same as realism, could in his eyes not blossom without the concomitant blossoming of democracy in society. During his time in Heidelberg Keller wrote a small essay on the relationship of Romanticism to the present. In it he derived the historical justification for Romantic poetry from the impossibility and inability of that age to 'act diligently'. And he expected new heights of poetry to result from the social upswing caused by the revolution, from the revolutionary upsurge of life in general.

These opinions show once again Keller's close relationship to the best democratic traditions in Germany, namely to Heine's view of literature, and the convictions of his own friend, Hermann Hettner, during the latter's Feuerbachian, democratic period. He wrote his observations in the midst of the Revolution (June 1849), still uncertain as to what end it would take. Yet, he was clearly aware of the significance – in terms of both contents and perspective – of the interconnection between literature and life:

Yet come things as they may: a wealth of plots and poetry has already arisen from the friction between these different tendencies and consequently the surrogates that have existed hitherto (i.e. Romanticism, G.L.) are dispensable poetic inhabitants of our realms. The June Days in Paris, the Hungarian War, Vienna, Dresden and perhaps also Venice and Rome will serve as inexhaustible sources for the producers of all kinds of literature. A new ballad, and with it the drama, the historical novel and the novella: each will be well provided for. Yet I have seen in the Baden Revolution that they are also to be found directly in life.

Just as 'German' truly means nothing other than popular, so too it should also include the 'poetic', for the people, as soon as it has a breathing space, itself becomes poetic, in other words it becomes itself.[12]

And these observations are also very effectively supplemented in the same essay by Keller's exposure of the truth-shy philistinism in Romanticism's bourgeois-liberal afterlife:

It is solely a bloodless bourgeoisie that wishes to remain where we are and as we are, hanging with all its weight from a half dried-out branch and gnawing at its few berries, until the branch breaks and the whole lot goes tumbling into the abyss. Verily, if I did not know only too well that the philistines are just philistines then I would have to consider them the most reckless, most poetic of characters. For only such people could feel happy in such an ambiguous predicament.[13]

Keller pursues the same line of argument in his greatest and most important critical works, his essays on Jeremias Gotthelf. Keller had the greatest admiration for this significant narrative writer. He explains by means of an intricate analysis how in the case of Gotthelf 'realism' could nevertheless 'triumph', a realism despite the latter's blinkered and reactionary opinions, despite his 'short-winded world-view'. He finds that the possibility of such a triumph of realism resided in the fact that although Gotthelf's spontaneous instinct was to oppose progress, he remained deeply linked to the people and had nothing to do with the reactionary intriguers of the upper class, with the reactionary literary and political *salons*.

At the same time Keller subjects Gotthelf to merciless criticism wherever the latter violates reality by dint of his reactionary views and neglects or vulgarizes the artistic treatment of reality by means of a crude and directly propagandistic stance. Both the positive and negative sides of this dispute with his great Swiss precursor show how deeply, in the case of Keller the plebeian realist, true art is connected with plebeianism, and true poetry with democracy.

The spirit of democracy pervades the whole of Keller's thought and work.

But where, then, is one to seek the reason for the fact that in his writings this democratic spirit remained on the defensive and to a certain degree localized? The personal psychology of the author cannot furnish us with an answer here; for Keller's was, as we have seen, consistently democratic. However, the historical combination of the ensuing capitalist erosion of Swiss democracy's natural roots, the reactionary development of both Germany and France following the defeat of the 1848 Revolutions, and the reactionary form in which German national unity was achieved, all force Keller to adopt such a stance, very much against his subjective temperament and the trends of his youthful development.

Keller's early development, which climaxed in his experiencing the German revolution and his studying under Feuerbach in Heidelberg, meant that he acquired and further developed the best progressive heritage of the history of Germany in the eighteenth and nineteenth centuries. If the years 1848/1849 had brought forth revolutionary-democratic change in Germany – if, in other words, a great, progressive, democratic German cultural community had evolved in its wake, Keller would without doubt have taken up a leading position in the great German realism that would thus have ensued. The whole conception of *Green Henry* is the ideological preparation for this.

That this highly promising start should come to nought was a result of the failure of the Revolution and the German cultural crisis in the Age of Reaction: Keller was thrown back on the Swiss situation, in the narrow sense. What we mean by this is not his immediate approach and choice of material; that would, whatever the case, have been predominantly Swiss, even though decisive parts of *Green Henry* take place in Germany, even though Keller's stay and his life in a Germany in which the democratic revolution had been victorious, would have taken a completely different course and would have had completely different consequences for his writing. We have already pointed to the difference between the atmosphere surrounding Keller's life in Heidelberg and Berlin respectively.

We mean this difference in an intellectual, socio-ideological sense. Keller lost immediate literary and human contact with the major problems of massive social upheaval, which Rousseau had experienced in prerevolutionary France and had actively participated in solving; in other words, the link with those problems that Keller himself described in the Heidelberg essay just cited as the key subject matter of the great upswing in realist literature he anticipated. His work could no longer be a struggle for the victory of democratic ideals in the greater German-speaking cultural community, could no longer be the depiction of that heroic task he had dreamed of in Heidelberg during the days of the revolution. His work now concentrated on a struggle to defend the natural roots of Swiss democracy against threats from reactionary countries abroad, and against its erosion from within by capitalism.

Yet, even in this retreat Keller never became a 'provincial Swiss poet'. Admittedly, in his later work the broad and profound discussion of the major problems of German culture – as is to be found in *Green Henry* – was never to return. The social basis, and it is this that is the decisive point of departure in his later period, became ever more exclusively the particularity of Swiss democracy. But Keller approaches these problems on the basis of the developments of his younger years. That is, he presses further ahead with the problems of German Humanism; he generates a renaissance of these problems from the spirit of naturally rooted Swiss democracy. And even in the areas where Keller seemingly does not depict social but rather purely personal, human problems, this wider context, this continuity is visible: the democratic basis of German Humanism is more clearly in evidence in Keller's work than in that of any other German writer.

In many respects, Keller's historical position as an author is related to the position his teacher Ludwig Feuerbach occupies in the history of German philosophy. Just as the latter's thought signified the end of German philosophy, so Keller's work marked the end of Classical German literature. This parallelism is not just superficial. For just as Feuerbach's materialism was at the same time both continuation and dissolution of Classical German Idealism, so too Keller's realism is both fulfilment and dissolution of Germany's Classical literary traditions. Keller's realism is the fulfilment of what in Heine's case remained at the programmatic level of ironic dissolution: the end of the *Kunstperiode*.

It is not until Keller that a completely natural, a new realism emerges, which is in essence something completely different from the realism of Classicism and which represents the first German, uniquely literary counterpart to Western European realism. Keller is the first and the only German author at this time whose entry into the new period of literature signified neither shallowness of intellect nor provincialism, neither conformism to reactionary bourgeois currents nor a desperately introverted individualism.

By going beyond the traditions of the *Kunstperiode*, Keller takes up the banner of the great traditions of realism in the developed democratic countries in a manner that is neither formalistic nor artificial, but rather reaches deep enough to grasp its essence. German literature increasingly becomes directly contemporaneous with overall developments in Europe. Keller is, however, the only writer in the German language in whose work such a link to those traditions did not mean being tainted by a nascent European decadence, signs of which are clearly visible in the work of Richard Wagner, Friedrich Hebbel and Conrad Ferdinand Meyer, to name but a few major examples. Keller embeds the ideals of German Humanism in a depiction of the life of the people that is powerfully realistic. Or rather he shows with great realistic skill that these ideals are in truth the fully grown, ripe fruits of democratic popular life.

Naturally, Keller's work repeatedly shows a certain narrowness in the way the problems are posed, and its underlying tone is often one of resignation. But resignation is a general characteristic of the great realism of the nineteenth century. It demonstrates again and again both the necessary genesis and failure of the holiest ideals of bourgeois Humanism. And Keller's resignation is – for reasons that, as we will later go into in detail, have to do with the narrow Swiss basis of his writing – even milder, less despairing than that of most of the great nineteenth century realists. It is among other things milder because the destructive element in capitalist progress rages less strongly in his world of human beings than it does in that of Balzac or Dickens. Where Keller, with relentless realism, sees capitalism forging ahead and demonstrates its undermining effects, the specifically Kellerian world collapses.

As with Balzac, the picture of society Keller paints contains utopian traits that do not exist in reality; it is in many respects an unreal, exemplary world woven out of threads of the past and the future. It is not reactionary, as are Balzac's Tory utopias with their feudal-socialist characteristics; rather it grows out of Swiss democracy much more organically than Balzac's world grows out of post-revolutionary France. As a consequence, the tension between utopia and reality is much milder in the case of Keller. But precisely for that reason such tension does not lead in Keller's description of capitalism to that 'triumph of realism' which Balzac achieved. The stronger the growth of capitalism in the Swiss reality that Keller the realist is forced to perceive, the drier, the more prosaic the world he depicts, the more rigidly it is opposed to an abstract utopia. It lies beyond Keller's ability to portray the poetry of the 'intellectual jungle'. The later Keller attempts to convince himself that his struggle is not hopeless. His honesty as an author expresses itself in the fact that he fails to do so; but this struggle no longer bears fruit in literary form.

A utopia woven out of strands of the past: this links Keller with the best and most honest German realists of his age, for example with Storm or Raabe. The difference is, however, that these latter refer back to a development whose defeat is already a foregone conclusion so that writers can no longer afford to harbour any illusions on the matter. As a result, we encounter Raabe's bravely humorous pessimism in which old disillusioned veterans from the Wars of Liberation, the Polish uprising, etc., totter around like ghosts from a different world in the reactionary land of philistines, uncomprehending and misunderstood. This is also the reason why Storm restricts himself to the form of novellas of remembrance, of which he himself says:

For a writer's oeuvre to be considered Classical it is surely a prerequisite that his works reflect the essential intellectual contents of his age in an artistically perfected form. . . I, at any rate, shall have to make do with a seat in the side-boxes.[14]

Keller's realism is no such side-box. At the height of his productive powers Keller is able to harbour illusions about Swiss democracy and its natural roots, illusions that are reconcilable with a realistic reproduction of reality, indeed are even an asset, aiding him to see this reality in its essence, variety, richness, and full potential. This rich and many-sided depiction of life is one of the most important sources of Keller's humour, which – unlike that of Raabe or Reuter – does not arise from despair but, in contrast, from a confidence in his ideals, a sense of inner certainty: from the conviction that the force of a democracy rooted in nature is able to absorb all the progressive economic and cultural moments of capitalist development and process them organically, so that capitalism serves only to toughen rather than destroy it. Admittedly, this delusion of certainty cannot be maintained in the long run. Ever darker shadows fall on this wishful world of Keller's. And, because his narrative power stems from confidence rather than an embittered, malignant desire to unmask, his art now begins to decline.

The above provides an outline of the uniqueness of his literary position in both its positive sense and in its limitations. Thus, despite the fact that the significantly new traits in his work predominate, it marks the conclusion of the development of Classical German literature, rather than the beginning of a new upturn. This assertion by no means excludes, as we shall see, the fact that the poetic, social and human content of Keller's oeuvre had profound results, results that were to remain fertile for a long time.

It is precisely here that the effect of the defeat of the 1848 Revolution on intellectual developments in Germany makes its presence most felt. Once again, one need only think of Feuerbach: in Germany he signified the end of a great developmental line; after him the decline and fall of philosophy set in. Yet this downturn did not result from the contents of Feuerbach's philosophy. For in Russia his influence became the starting-point of a great upswing across the intellectual board of revolutionary democracy. The fact that nothing followed on Feuerbach's heels in Germany, whereas in Russia thinkers of the stature of Chernyshevsky and Dobrolyubov emerged, is exclusively the result of the difference in democratic developments in the two countries.

However great the parallels between the respective fates of Feuerbach and Keller may be, this comparison must not be exaggerated. For Feuerbach did not develop further philosophically; even his influence in Germany waned, and he died in almost complete isolation and obscurity. Keller's maturity as a writer occurs, by contrast, in the decades after the defeat of the Revolution, and his oeuvre receives great recognition from the outset, as we have already mentioned. Keller owes this potential for development, this ability to exercise a positive influence, to his Swiss nature. It is just as authentic and profound as that of Rousseau – though, for reasons stated above, of a less world-historical quality. Yet, here again the failure to realize the maximum potential is less attributable to the individual and more to the course of history. Keller's Swiss nature, the source of the power that drives him on, is in other words also a chapter in the life-history of German democracy, a history fraught with tragedies.

III

PLEBEIANISM

Keller's plebeianism continues the traditions of Classical German Humanism: it repeatedly shows the vivid, vital power of 'Bildung',[15] of human education through culture. German Classicism works in this sense on behalf of life. It is, however, only its greatest exponents who can maintain it at this level of profound and organic interconnection between life and education. At a very early date the problems of formative education portrayed in literature begin – as a result of the isolation of authors in backward Germany – to lose the living roots they had in society and the people. This danger is already visible in Tieck's novellas, which in some respects introduce the development of realism in Germany, and is also to be seen in Immermann's novels. This lack of roots degenerates into hollow literary intellectualism in the tendentious literature of 'Young Germany'.

On the other hand, a trend antagonistic to formative education is ever present in German plebeian literature. In Gotthelf, who was Swiss, it has its roots in his reactionary political standpoint. In the Age of Reaction, an indifference to formative education arose in Germany cloaked in humorous apparel. The writers who had remained bogged down in provincialism instinctively felt that the formative education which predominated in a politically reactionary Germany in the process of becoming capitalist was bound to be thoroughly alien to the people. They seldom, however, had the ability to counterpose a genuine form of education to this pseudo-'Bildung', and this often led to the ridiculing of formative education altogether, to its presentation as completely detached from the life of the people, as superfluous to that life. Fritz Reuter, for example, shows how Uncle Bräsig[16] tries to offer his despairing friend Hawermann distraction by providing him with reading matter. By chance he comes across a volume of Aristophanes and Reuter describes, with liberal mockery of the uneducated Mecklenburgians and the superfluousness of formative education, all the comic situations that arise from this reading.

Keller opposes both tendencies, but in order to do so adopts a narrative rather than a polemical form. For him, problems of formative education are an organic part in the growth of his figures as human beings, important factors that promote turning-points in that growth. The path from Jean Paul to Goethe, the acquaintance with Homer and in particular the appropriation of Feuerbach's philosophy play a decisive role in Henry's personal and moral development. Yet, one could argue that the hero of *Green Henry*, although a child of the people, is nevertheless an artist, a painter; the role of the problem of formative education in his life would therefore correspond to the 'Bildungsroman' in its Goethean variant. However, apart from the fact that in *Wilhelm Meister* too Shakespeare is not portrayed as a literary phenomenon but as a power in life, this 'Bildungsroman' of Keller's is decidedly 'plebianized' – in other words brought closer to the life of the broadest section of the population – compared with Goethe's.

As a result, the importance of formative education for human growth is portrayed in Keller's work even with respect to simple folk characters. For Regine, the serving girl, her acquaintance with *Des Knaben Wunderhorn* marks a new stage in her development; and Judith, the intelligent peasant in *Green Henry*, is introduced to Ariosto by her young friend, the hero of the novel, and finds the poet's work a mirror of life, rejoicing at the lucidity of its descriptions.

Keller's whole oeuvre is filled with such examples. This is a trait that exists almost in isolation in an age of nascent literary decadence. It is not until the literature of the revolutionary proletariat that the people's unbroken thirst for 'Bildung', their capacity for education, is taken up again, showing how the rediscovery of a people's great cultural heritage repeatedly signifies a profound shock that promotes growth in the human and moral development of the talented children of the people. By taking on this heritage, the great socialist realist Maxim Gorky picks up the threads of a development of which Gottfried Keller was the last German representative.

Keller's plebeianism is thus never the result of restricted provincialism. Keller is, like every true popular writer, both artist and teacher at one and the same time. His didactic intentions consist, however, in making an organic link between the authentic and the greatest forms of culture and the immediate life of the ordinary people. Consequently, he depicts the positive and negative examples of such trends, and every honest and diligent person in Keller's universe is a sort of Wilhelm Meister, albeit under disadvantageous material and cultural conditions. The intentions of Keller the pedagogue harmonize with those of the artist: a comprehensive, many-sided description of contemporary man, of the contemporary life of the people, in which for him many-sidedness means the same as the trend towards realizing man's fullest potential.

This way of presenting the problems of formative education is very closely connected with Keller's conception of the development of human society. Consequently, as a plebeian writer, he is not a simplifier, a shallow populist. He is not condescending towards the people, but has the deep conviction that everything great hitherto generated in the course of humankind's development has grown out of the life of the ordinary people and that it can therefore always be reintroduced into the life of the people. He makes no distinction between Classical literature – the literature of the educated – and popular writing, as was starting to become standard practice in his time.

The epistolary polemic that ensued between Keller and Berthold Auerbach,[17] a writer of well-loved village stories very popular at the time, over the opening lines of his novella *Romeo und Julia auf dem Dorfe* (*A Village Romeo and Juliet*) is very characteristic of this. Keller begins his story, in order to explain the reference to Shakespeare's tragedy in the title, with the following words:

To tell this story would be pointless emulation if it were not based on a real occurrence, which proves how deeply the plot is rooted in human life, a plot upon which the great old works are founded. There is but a relatively small number of such plots; but these are forever reappearing in a different guise and force one to record them.

Auerbach criticizes the novella's title. It reminds him of

that literature for the connoisseurs, a literature that does not take life as its starting-point, but rather the world of the printed word and its memories. . .

Keller's protest at this is very characteristic.

First, what we ourselves write is also printed on paper and belongs from this point of view to the world of paper, and second, even Shakespeare is, although in printed form, nothing other than life itself and not some lifeless reminiscence.[18]

In Keller's case, this rejection of trends that purported to be plebeian by virtue of their artificial distinction between the ordinary people and great literature, that failed to see the true vitality, the true plebeianism of great art and were blind to the great possibilities afforded by the life of the people, not only amounts to a stand against provincialism, but also to a defence against the decadent over-refinement and isolation of literature from life. Keller repeatedly investigated the continual reciprocity, the cross-fertilization of the highest literature from below and the enrichment of the people by the descent of such literature into their everyday lives from above. For him, cultural development is the lively dialectical interchange of this above and below. In this context, he stressed the relativity of literary originality in a letter to Hettner:

In a word, there is no such thing as sovereign, individual originality and novelty in the sense of the arbitrary genius and self-opinionated subjectivist. (The proof: Hebbel, a man of genius, yet who, precisely because of his craving for novelty, is capable of inventing such bad plots.) Only what arises from the dialectics of cultural movement is new in a profound sense. Cervantes' conception of Don Quixote was new in this sense. . .[19]

What unites didactic and artistic trends in Keller's realism is the writer's responsibility to convey to the people in literary form the totality of a progressing culture – in a readily understandable and convincing manner. In this context, Keller proceeds from the profoundly democratic presupposition that everything which is morally good will be understood by the people if it is portrayed with authentic realism. Keller the educator of the people sees with horror how skilfully the Reaction propagates its ideas demagogically and how weak the counter-propaganda provided by most of the progressive writers is, a result of their estrangement from the people. His whole literary activity is placed in the service of such a political and social, moral and emotional strengthening of the people. And his naturally democratic attitude is visible in the fact that for him human-moral progress means the same as overcoming reactionary prejudices.

Feuerbach was the decisive influence in Keller's formative education that led to the genesis of this realism. Above all because he destroyed the strand of other-worldliness in Keller, everything, that is, which went beyond the bounds of reality. The link to Feuerbach meant for Keller primarily his jettisoning all false poetry; all poetry imposed on life to ornament it rather than as something growing out of life itself. Keller is generally opposed to remnants of religious views, but is very tolerant of such residues if the persons concerned live with them in subjective honesty and without hypocrisy. He wrote the following to a friend shortly after having become familiar with Feuerbach's philosophy:

But for art and poetry there can from now on be no salvation without complete intellectual freedom and a complete, passionate grasp of nature, without any ulterior motives, and I am firmly convinced that the artist who is not willing to be completely and exclusively a mortal being has no future.[20]

Feuerbach's philosophy, with this militant worldliness in art, led Keller to follow the same path in his writing as that trodden by Goethe.

Keller never became a militant atheist, as did the Russian followers of Feuerbach, but neither did he stoop to the level of the shallow arguments of the German materialists in the eighteen fifties, such as Ludwig Büchner or Karl Vogt.[21] Feuerbach implanted in him, however, the conviction of the priority of being over consciousness; Feuerbach thus gave Keller a philosophical awareness of the practice of any true realist.

As a realist writer Keller, however, goes beyond the bounds of Feuerbachian materialism. He portrays people in terms of their social relations, and Feuerbach's contribution to Keller's understanding of the materialist basis of social life would in itself have been far too meagre to enable the latter to describe comprehensively every aspect of these relations. The mere assertion of the German materialists of this period that 'man is what he eats' becomes in this mechanistic one-sidedness not just an inadequate description but a positive fallacy with respect to life and literature.

Although this strongly emphasized material predetermination of human life forms the basis of Keller's realist practice as a writer, he depicts it in its simple crassness only in semi-comic borderline cases. A particularly witty example of this is the fairy tale 'Spiegel, das Kätzchen' ('Mirror the Cat'), in which, in a time of hunger, the wise tomcat loses his dignity and then his sanity and enters into a contract with Pineiss, the town sorcerer: he allows himself to be fattened up on condition that he then give his fat to be used for magical purposes. As soon as he is well-fed, however, his lucidity returns and he now in turn outwits the sorcerer. A similar, equally humorous portrait is to be found in *Green Henry*, when the self-confidence of the childlike hero rises in direct proportion to the amount of money he has in his pocket to spend on sweets and childish boasting.

Keller could thus be said to outline a materialist foundation for the way in which human beings are determined by their ontological basis. As soon as he concerns himself with truly social and human problems, however, Keller experiences and depicts the exceptionally complex inner interplay of being and consciousness without in so doing losing sight of the primacy of being; in other words in the concrete shape he gives his world-view he goes far beyond his teacher's philosophy.

In his initial enthusiasm for Feuerbach, Keller believed that the new world-view would cause a moral revolution in him, that humankind could aspire to even greater moral heights than before on the basis of a materialist atheism. He was soon to realize, however, that the ontological core of humankind was not reshaped by the new world-view – no more than with any change that occurs only on the level of ideas – that a transformation of life itself, a transformation of being, was necessary for such to occur. This self-restriction meant that Keller lost his militant edge as a disciple of Feuerbach's, but at the same time he distanced himself from that exaggeration which the atheist world-view tended to exhibit among those intellectuals of sensitive constitution during the second half of the nineteenth century. Jacobsen's Niels Lyhne, for example, fights a desperate heroic, subjectively exaggerated battle to affirm his atheism. This battle, however, presupposes in his case that atheism depoeticizes the world, whereas for Keller the Feuerbachian world-view signified the awakening of precisely the innate poetry of being.

Here again, we encounter the influence Swiss democracy exerted on Keller's world-view and work. The underlying connection between Feuerbachian materialism and the democratic revolution is demonstrated above all by the fact that the world is stripped of deities and this simultaneously entails the demand for a genuine, worldly, universally educated human being, the demand for the full development of the human personality. In the Germany of the Age of Reaction it soon proved to be impossible to realize this demand, and whenever a writer came face to face with capitalist society in its developed form and attempted to overcome it by intellectual and narrative means, both the innate poetry of being and the possibility of realizing the all-round human individual necessarily disappeared. This almost inevitably led to the same conclusions as Jacobsen's, and they give rise to a much better piece of literature than the shallow indifference of the German materialists.

In contrast, Swiss democracy and in particular Keller's understanding of it when he was at the height of his powers, place the demand for the all-round human being at the centre of a portrayal of both private and public life. This is why Keller's fiction is able to reflect in poetic terms that affirmation of life, that democratic optimism which was given such inspiring expression in Feuerbach's early writings.

Thus, Keller's prose becomes a poetry of real life in all its sensuousness. However, this poetry did not mean clinging on to some petty-minded factuality. In *Green Henry* Keller gives a very accurate description of the essence of what he terms poetic:

... for it is the same law that bestows poetic quality on different things or makes a reflection of their being worthwhile; but I now learned with relation to some things that I have hitherto called poetic, that the incomprehensible and the impossible, the adventurous and the rapturous are not poetic and that, as above [namely in the fine arts, G.L.], calm and tranquility in movement, so here [in literature, G.L.], simplicity and honesty must predominate in the midst of glory and description in order to engender something poetic or – which means the same – something living and rational...

... so artists differ from other people only in that they immediately see the essence of things and know how to portray it in full detail, whereas the others have first to recognize it and be amazed by it...[22]

The basic principle underlying Keller's realism is a clarity and richness with which the essential moments of life are described. This is why Keller considers the greatness of Jeremias Gotthelf's prose to reside in the latter's having always fully exhausted his material, that is, having chosen topics of essential importance to humankind and having revealed all of the factors that comprise their essence.

According to Keller, literature should affect the reader by means of this lucid reflection of the essential moments of life and not owing to some cleverly contrived points of subjective interest. In his days in Berlin, a time when Keller concerned himself very closely with the theory and practice of drama, preparing himself for a career as a dramatist, he wrote of his ideal to one of his friends:

In the meantime I have made the greatest simplicity and clarity my guiding principle: no intrigues or intricacies, no chance, etc., etc., but rather the pure effect of human passions and necessary conflicts of the soul on the characters; and I try to ensure the audience's greatest possible perspicacity and premonition of what is to come and how it will come to pass; for only this provides him with true and noble enjoyment.

These principles underlying Keller's realism also hold true for the characterization of the individual figures. When he praises in particular the fact that Gotthelf does not create characterless figures, he means this in the aesthetic sense put forward by realism and does not wish to suggest that an author is obliged to create nothing but unproblematical, positive figures. Keller hates modern psychological over-refinement which allows the human-moral contours of the figures to become blurred; he despises the German pseudo-realism of the times, which is content to portray the surface of human life and does not attempt to test man by confronting its human figures with actions in which the full content of their inner core would be revealed, be it good or evil, diligent or base.

It is precisely this that forms the font of Keller's enthusiasm for Shakespeare. In his novella *Pankraz, der Schmoller* (*Pankraz, the Sulker*), he has a Swiss petty bourgeois, who has emigrated from Switzerland to India and become a British soldier there, read Shakespeare and allows the figure to describe in direct, naïve terms the overwhelming impact of such great realism upon him. Seen from this point of view, the description is written tongue-in-cheek, yet its aesthetic content expresses such a clear profession of faith in true realism on Keller's part that we cite it at length:

This seductive false prophet really led me up the garden path. For he describes the world in all its aspects completely simply and truly as it is, but only as it is within those perfect individuals, who pursue completely and characteristically the profession of their being and their inclinations in good times and in bad; and in so doing are as clear as crystal, each of the purest water of his sort, so that, whereas bad hacks master and paint a world of mediocrity and colourless half-truths and thus lead imbeciles astray, filling them up with thousands of insignificant details, the former author by contrast leads the astute astray by means of portraying precisely the world of wholeness, of how it could succeed, in other words, how it should be, that is, when the astute view this world as the substance of life, and believe they have discovered the latter in it. Oh, but life is beautiful, but never just where we happen to be, or at the time when we live there. There are enough audacious, bad women in the world, without the beautiful somnambulance of a Lady Macbeth and her fearful rubbing of her hands. The poisoners we encounter are but insolent and show no repentance, and even write their autobiographies or put money aside for a grocery shop when they have served their sentence. . . Here we have a person of blood, without Macbeth's demonic and yet so human manliness, and there a

Richard the Third, without his wit and eloquence. . . Our Shylocks probably wish to cut our flesh from our bones but they will never dare spend
hard coin to achieve this, and our merchants of Venice do not get themselves into danger on behalf of an amusing pauper of a friend, but rather by
simply swindling with stocks and shares and by no means then hold such
beautiful, melancholic speeches but rather pull a pretty stupid face. Yet,
actually, as I have said, all such people no doubt exist in the world, but not
as beautifully assembled as in those poems; never does a real rascal encounter a man who can really defend himself, never does a complete fool come
across a happy, but decidedly clever person, so that there can be no real
tragedy or good comedy.[23]

For Keller, realism is, in other words, the exhaustive wealth of
life, its own fully developed progress to its tragic or comic conclusion. The unity of author and educator of the people in Keller's
work results from the fact that his plebeian-democratic convictions
give him an unerring scale of values by which to judge what is authentic and what is false, what is upright and what is base in man.
The exhaustive narrative treatment of plot and characterization
automatically unmasks everything hollow, affirms all human uprightness: the depiction of life as it really is, capable of unfolding
its inner dialectic unhindered, a life in which individual chance
occurrences become the driving force of the ontological dialectic of
reality.

Keller 'Shakespeareanizes' and not just in this commanding
treatment of chance, but in his unabashed use of chance as the
starting-point of the story and its poetic sublation in the exhaustive
characterization of the figures, reducing chance to a mere prompt
leading to the unveiling of the necessary essence of humankind. He
is also a pupil of Shakespeare's with respect to the tragic and comic
remorselessness of his narrative dialectic.

This remorselessness by no means signifies a preference for the
depiction of cruel or brutal scenes. Such a decadent trait appears
in the work of Keller's contemporary, Conrad Ferdinand Meyer.
Keller, however, has a deep antipathy for this affectation in a writer
whom he otherwise recognizes to be highly talented. Keller's remorselessness is the objective reflection of the fact that life and
society extend beyond the tragically implicated or comically presumptuous individual. The principle of such sociality is a humanistically idealized democracy rooted in nature. It is conceived of

artistically in the Shakespearean sense mentioned above: essence is always made to encounter essence.

Keller's realism is, in other words, by no means simply a reproduction of life in its immediate outer appearance. And not just for artistic reasons. Keller loves life in general, particularly life in its specific Swiss-democratic form. But this love is not uncritical; it by no means glorifies the status quo, not even that of Swiss democracy.

With reference to Switzerland, Keller's utopia consists only of his belief that there is an inherent energy in Swiss life enabling it to rely on its own resources in order to overcome inner social threats. He is very clearly aware both of these dangers and of the ossified and distorted social and moral traits in Swiss democracy, and describes them with remorseless realism. His enthusiasm for private and public civil virtues, for honest uprightness, is never reduced to the glorification of mere legality or of some philistine self-satisfaction with bourgeois virtues. In Keller's work, bourgeois uprightness is an intellectual and moral continuation of the ethics of the Enlightenment, its poetic opposite being not simply a crime or an 'infringement of the law' but human baseness, mendacity, hypocrisy, self-deception, etc.

This link to the socially and morally critical tradition of the Enlightenment is most clearly seen in the novella *Die drei gerechten Kammacher* (*The Three Righteous Combmakers*). Here, Keller provides a brilliant fictional refutation of Mandeville's moral theory according to which a society of virtuous people could never exist. Whereas the light-headed Seldwylers – albeit with a good deal of comical and tragi-comical friction – somehow manage to get on with one another, the humanly base, abstract 'virtuousness' of the three apprentice artisans leads to a comic catastrophe. Conversely, Keller shows how a genuinely decent person who slides into a false situation that threatens to result in complete loss of honour can extricate himself from his predicament by drawing on those reserves of human decency (*Kleider machen Leute – Clothes Make the Man*).

'Fate' in Keller's novellas, in other words, is repeatedly shown to consist of this ultimate moral core in man. Keller, Feuerbach's pupil, knows and depicts the power of social relations very accurately. At the same time, he knows that similar relations and conditions have a different effect on different people. And since he does not preempt naturalism's artistically tedious averaging out of social development, but rather portrays the concrete, dialectical interaction of society and individual, the moral core of the individual person is of decisive importance.

In the case of Keller this does not imply an individualistic relativization of morality. Rather, the remorseless stringency of a supra-individual morality turns out to facilitate true individualization. Keller's moral stringency coincides with the requirement of narrative literature that people be put to the test and judged in terms of their uprightness or baseness. Exhaustive epic treatment of the material requires that everything latent in the figures and situations be enticed out of them so that their hidden essence become visible, thus showing that the fate of the individual is dependent on his essential character. Keller's aesthetics and morality are in complete accord with one another in this realism.

Keller's humour is closely linked with the stringent morality he champions, and with his approach to narrative. It is not the maudlin 'understanding' for human weaknesses, nor the complacent embellishment of the ugliness, of the prosaicness of life that it is in the case of most of his German contemporaries. When Fritz Reuter writes a poem devoted to a comic account of his time in prison during the Age of Reaction following the Wars of Liberation and says in it, 'And I picked figs from the branches of thistles', he brings out the contrast between the German comic literature of the eighteen fifties and sixties and Keller's brand of humour. Nothing would be further from Keller's intentions than this poetic transformation of reality, this humorous embellishment of the atrocities of life, this smoothing of sharp edges. For him, a thistle always remains a thistle, however much his 'Shakespeareanization' may heighten its essence.

Keller's humour unearths the essence of particular types, exposing their concealed ridiculousness and intensifying it to monumental proportions. And he subjects every insubstantiality or baseness thus revealed to merciless Homeric laughter. In this form of mockery, Keller is just as cruel as Shakespeare, Cervantes or Molière.

He also resembles them in that he subjects the comical sides of otherwise genuine and upright characters to relentless derision, irrespective of how close to his heart the character may have grown to be and although he otherwise approves of him. Keller knows – just as Lessing had asserted in the face of Rousseau's criticism that Molière had portrayed the Misanthropist as a comic character – that this laughter is not directed at the character as a whole and certainly not at the moral principle which is his core, that this comic treatment does not detract from the human uprightness of such characters, that our laughing at them does not destroy our sympathy for them. For this sympathy rests just as much on reality, on the character's actions as we experience them, on the human qualities which become apparent in these actions, as it does on those comic traits, the remorseless portrayal of which prompts our laughter in the first place. It is precisely the all-round and realistic portrayal of a human being that enables the reader to develop such a contradictory and many-sided attitude towards the characters.

The reader can feel this way here because the author himself and his full-blooded characters love life in all its contradictoriness, in its inseparable mixture of conscientiousness and humour. It is, in particular, Keller's most important female characters that exhibit such traits. Their love is always clear-eyed, lucidly seeing through all weaknesses, passing severe judgement on human errors and yet firmly and enduringly trusting the men they have chosen with the surest of instincts. In such figures, be they Judith and Dorothea in *Green Henry*, Lucie in the *Sinngedicht*, or Marie Salander in *Martin Salander*, Keller's humour emerges as the liberating laughter of people who are morally strong and take a firm stand. It is the humour of true humanism, which is profoundly convinced that every essentially honest person can be saved, and that laughter is one of the most humane weapons which can help mankind develop to its full potential.

But, over and above this, the insistence of Keller's humour has a purely artistic side to it. Keller loves life and believes that being is just and ultimately meaningful. As a result, he not only feels justified in realist terms in making essence collide with essence, in 'Shakespeareanizing' within his small, self-created world, but this *joie de vivre* also develops into the artistic joy of portraying characteristic features.

This applies even to those traits that are characteristic of human baseness. Keller, by taking each negative quality to its logical conclusion, derives great artistic enjoyment from the grotesque and fantastic possibilities that result. Thus he invents a wide range of highly improbable and exaggerated situations in order to paint such figures in full. He is able to draw on an inexhaustible reservoir of such comic characteristics. However, even the most grotesque of fantasies never deviates from the main thrust of the story, the emphasis on what is essential. Keller never falls prey to a virtuoso Romantic indulgence in the arabesque. If Theodor Fontane compares him negatively with Arnim[24] for this reason, this shows that even as intelligent and great a writer as Fontane could lapse at times into superficial and formalist judgements.

The unity of these grotesque-fantastic exaggerations and the essential plot finds expression in the fact that Keller never gives purely picturesque descriptions of a milieu or of his characters. Such grotesque-fantastic 'stocktaking' as, for example, with the room of Züs Bünzlin, the eccentric old maid in *The Three Righteous Combmakers*, or John Kaby's equipment in *Der Schmied seines Glücks* (*The Architect of his own Fortune*), are truly narrative, novella-related means of using the action to convey character. Keller's prose achieves panoramic richness by the use of such 'exaggerations', even where he describes a socially confined and petty environment. The complete and nevertheless very complex, contradictory and varied unity of the inner and outer aspects of his figures, their exhaustive characterization through their manner, clothing, behaviour, surroundings, etc., creates – albeit often in a grotesque-fantastic manner – that picture of the completeness of life on which every truly great narrative effect rests.

IV

RESIGNATION

This special feature of Keller's, the wide-ranging narrative atmosphere in which reality is poeticized from within, must have had a very puzzling effect on his contemporaries. Indeed the nature of Keller's realism shows him to be the culmination of a line of development. His contemporaries regarded this as an affectation and a quirk. Theodor Storm, who in general held Keller's art in exceptionally high esteem, considered this an element that stood out to his detriment. In countering Keller, he quotes Goethe's claim that 'the poet also wants to have fun', and asserted that in general the reader had to wait patiently until Keller had indulged sufficiently in his whim, although, however, the reader would often be annoyed by it.[25] The example that Storm offers, the grotesque punishment and humiliation of the three rascals at the end of the novella *Die arme Baronin* (*The Poor Baroness*), is an utterly inappropriate choice. For here one encounters only Keller's above-mentioned comic ruthlessness, admittedly an aspect that understandably offended the soft and sensitive Storm. However it is Keller who stands for the true logic of art here and not Storm.

The above critical letter does, however, contain one astute and pertinent observation: Storm maintains that this characteristic of Keller's is closely allied to the sense of renunciation that forms the conclusion of almost all his major works; his favourite characters never find fulfilment, but rather play their lives out in a spirit of worthy renunciation. Storm's point specifically refers only to the reflection of the course of Keller's own life in his work. But such an important artistic feature could never be merely the expression of personal failures in love.

Renunciation in Keller's works is linked rather to the fundamental problems of his whole existence, with the impossibility of reconciling artistic activity and life, fulfilment of his personality and fulfilment of his duties as a citizen, of creating a non-compromising, perfect unity. In his early years his life at times fell into bohemian-like disorder, occasionally bordering on utter degeneration. The responsible position of poet laureate of Zurich seemingly brought his life into balance, and he appeared to complete his life as a calmly creative professional writer.

It is characteristic of Keller, however, that he always rejects those who describe themselves as professional writers; with scorn in the case of Gutzkow, with regret in the case of Heyse. And in his *Missbrauchte Liebesbriefe* (*Misused Love Letters*) he provides an annihilating caricature of the doings of men of letters as had started to emerge in the Germany of his day. The direct exploitation of life for the purposes of an author's production, observing life solely in order to valorize these observations in literature, is something that Keller rejects just as vehemently as had Goethe.[26] He repeatedly emphasizes that art and beauty must never be the final goal, the highest value in life, and he is a severe judge of the human problems in the lives of even such major writers as Heine. When Platen, the poet, proclaims in his romance criticizing Heine:

> Denn mein Herz vertrug nicht beides:
> Sänger und ein Hund zu sein!

For my heart could not endure the two: to be both singer and dog!

this could be read as a unique confession by Keller himself. Literature and art are for him but a part, just one aspect of public life, and are subordinate to the latter in all respects. The sole reason why this does not embroil Keller in a conflict is, as we have seen, that he is of the staunch conviction that the greatest art is the best means of popular enlightenment.

Despite this absence of conflict, the relationship between art and life in Keller's work is problematical both when he is the professional writer and when he is the direct organ of the democratic public sphere. In *Green Henry* the Count says the following to the hero, when the latter wants to give up art:

I too feel that you should change your profession; for a simple landscape painter your style is too wide-ranging, too full of too many twists and turns, too labyrinthine and restless; a different type of management is needed![27]

This is naturally a characterization, indeed a decisive characterization of the relation between Keller's personality and his own activity as an artist. The Count (and Keller with him) err only in believing that the public profession which the hero of this early novel decides to pursue can fully resolve this dilemma. In his function as poet laureate, Keller was conscientious to an exemplary degree, but in his inner self he was 'full of too many twists and turns, too labyrinthine and restless' even for such a position.

In this respect, Keller's life touches on the modern problem of art and life as addressed by Flaubert and Ibsen. But Keller's life is only tangential to this insoluble tragic connection, it does not yet become tragic – even without entering into any compromises – because for him art has not yet detached itself from its social context, because for him it has to exercise a social function extending to even the most profound problems of society.

But this 'for him' is the crux of the matter. The social character of Keller's art is harmonious and unproblematical to the extent that we can view it as Keller's artistic activity, as objective, completed works of art. Their artistic-didactic effectiveness, even in the context of Swiss democracy, is, by contrast, more than a little problematical. This is because, as we have seen, Keller's conception of Swiss democracy has utopian traits. It never falsifies reality, but the real trends which Keller depicts so fully, do not in reality have the future that Keller hopes they would. The real future of Swiss democracy is the dissolution of its natural roots at the hands of capitalism.

As an author, Keller is just as convinced an enlightener as were Diderot and Lessing. Yet they fought for a future that would come into being by irresistible necessity, even if not in their lifetimes; their own work as writers, their social existence as professional writers, did not therefore become problematical. The unfulfillable democratic utopia cast its shadow over Keller's self-confidence as an author even in times which contained the greatest artistic hope.

Here we again perceive the decisive impact which the defeat of the 1848 Revolution had on Keller's whole life as an author. We have cited earlier statements Keller made on the future of literature, on its future contents. We have seen that he expected the victory of a democratic revolution to be enormously invigorating. He never abandoned his opinion that democracy would in the final instance win the day; nor did he relinquish the expectations of an undreamed-of blossoming of literature associated with such a victory.

However, the doubts as to whether he himself would ever witness such an upturn, whether his own work would be fertilized by it, forced him increasingly to give up these beliefs. Naturally, these views of Keller's followed the continual ebb and flow of hope and renunciation. Yet, an observation jotted down at the beginning of the eighteen fifties paints a clear picture of the extent to which the problematics of a suppressed European, German democracy forced its way into the decisive problems connected with his work:

It is the painful resignation of an author who is forced to hear day after day that only a future age will again be able to offer poetry a beautiful reality which will enable it to unfold and thus produce great authors. The resignation of an author who accepts this and yet feels imbued with the energy and the honour with which to be able to achieve something upright in that prophetic age if he were to live in it. He has all the verve and fervour in him to lend artistic expression to a fulfilled life, but precisely because he knows that everything he might anticipate is but false idealism, he has to forswear such art, working instead within a past, long since outdated tradition, and yet he is too proud to do so. At this point he has to say to himself that he should nevertheless take up what seems closest to him and should perhaps lend beautiful form to his own situation. . . And, what is more, every age has its healthy, useful moments which can provide the material for beautiful, albeit episodic poetry.[28]

This resignation, which is not of a private but rather of a literary-universal nature, is at the core of the problem of Keller's artistic life.

This is expressed in various ways. Above all in the didactic approach Keller takes: he describes all of private life, in particular the family, love, and marriage, as the basis for public service in a democracy. He thus tackles a central problem of democracy. Such social and moral harmony between public and private life is a matter of course in every profoundly rooted democracy. This link is, however, destroyed by feudalism and capitalism; a morality of double standards arises as a social reality and a doctrine, a morality based on the impossibility of creating a harmony between the utilitarian amorality of government and the purely private and therefore petty morality of the individual.

The democratic left wing of every true bourgeois-democratic revolution made a tragic-heroic attempt, using the widest variety of ideological masks (the Old Testament in England, Sparta and Rome in France), to find a common denominator between public and private morality in a society that was becoming increasingly capitalist. Keller had very little personal sympathy for the Jacobins and the puritan sects that preceded them; but, without knowing it or wishing it, in his writings he 'placed virtue on the agenda' just as Robespierre had done in politics. His utopia of a Swiss democracy rooted in nature consists precisely in the belief that such a unification is possible. All the literature he produced was meant to serve such a unification.

At this juncture, Keller's resignation can be seen to reappear in a more profound form. His portrayal both of the educative process that leads to such citizenship and of the social and psychological problematics that prevent highly talented people from realizing such a union in their own lives is incomparable. Yet, wherever he attempts to portray the fulfilment of his ideals, the portrayal becomes sketchy (the concluding pages of his novella *Frau Regel Amrain und ihr Jüngster* [*Frau Regel Amrain and Her Youngest Son*] and of *Martin Salander* are just two examples). This failure is no coincidence, nor is it a failure of Keller as an individual or an artist. It has deep social roots. For only in a socialist democracy, not however in its bourgeois variant, can this problem be transformed into a socially topical problem which is at the same time, albeit only after a great struggle, solvable. For bourgeois democracy this remains a dream; though admittedly it is one that is, of historical necessity, dreamt by the best advocates of bourgeois democracy.

This contradiction is also to be found in Keller's depiction of individuality. As a supporter of a traditional democracy, Keller maintains that the fulfilment of individual personality and a fruitful social service must coincide harmoniously. Keller has good reason to see the wrenching apart of the link between the individual's public and private life as the social foundation of philistinism. And he states quite correctly 'that a slovenly philistine is in no way more intelligent than one who is respectable'.

Keller's humorous and satirical description of modern individualism is repeatedly slanted towards exposing the petty bourgeois nature of such individualism in its most 'sublime' and most pretentious forms. The profundity of these comic figures has until now received far too little attention. For Keller primarily describes scenes from petty bourgeois town or country life in Switzerland, and his down-at-heel petty bourgeois are the uprooted exponents of this stratum of society whose emotional and intellectual world Keller captures with such great realism. This is why so few in Germany perceived how universal these figures are, although Keller is so very conscious in his creation of such a profundity of types.

In Keller's work this twofold humorous polemic against both the sober and the drunken petty bourgeois is forever linked with a passionate and enthusiastic affirmation of true individuality, of human personality in its originality. In his descriptions, Keller overcomes the inherent contradictions: seldom did a nineteenth century author create such a gallery of truly vivid figures, 'originals' down to their very core.

Yet in terms of world-view (and thus in human terms) the question remains for him unsolved. He once says: 'A good original is one who is worthy of being copied.' But such a standard for 'normal' personality (normal in the sense that it corresponds to the norms), such a coincidence of individual originality and fulfilment of social norms is only possible in a truly perfected democracy, that is in a socialist democracy. An economy based on private property continually creates insurmountable discord which can be overcome neither by heroic, Jacobin action nor by poetic utopias.

Keller is far too great and far too honest a realist to force something upon portrayed reality that is not present in real reality; where he occasionally tries to do so, he fails as an artist. He is not utopian when expressing profound yearning that the harmonious individual should be a 'normal' phenomenon. Nor is it utopian when he depicts the struggle for such an aim as a reality; it is rather the profound recognition of the constantly recurring contradictory trends in human history. For the fulfilment of individuality in socialist democracy is not something radically new, but rather the fulfilment of the centuries-old, indeed millennia-old striving of the best representatives of the human race. The fact that Keller placed this problem at the centre of his writing is of exceptional interest and topicality to us today, in an age when socialism is being fulfilled.

However, even where the solution he provides results in successful works of art, it can never amount to more than a message of resignation. And since Keller is a profoundly authentic and original artist, this underlying tenor of his work is expressed not only in its contents but in his choice of artistic form. Because of this resignation, Keller becomes an author of novellas.

V

THE NOVELLA

Keller continues and perfects that tradition of the German novella that arose in the Classical and Romantic periods. Compared with the Old Italian and Old French variants, this represents a novella of a new type. The modern novella arose in France parallel to and in part influenced by it (for example, E.T.A. Hoffmann and Balzac). But, aside from such influences, we are dealing here with socially necessary parallel developments.

Goethe distinguished the novella from the simple story by

defining it as 'an unheard of event'.[29] The new novella cannot, how-ever, be distinguished from the old variant on the basis of this general definition. Nevertheless, in reality the novella that Goethe had in mind and that of Romanticism, above all as produced by Tieck and E.T.A. Hoffmann, are fundamentally different from the earlier form, to the extent that they remain true novellas and do not decline into purely artistic fairy tales or formless stories, into small novels that fail to give a comprehensive view of the world.

Tieck took Goethe's definition one step further:

The novella should have an outstanding climax, a focal point, in which a specific event is placed in the brightest and sharpest light. . . This event may be of the everyday, indeed of seemingly trifling importance, and yet it is nevertheless wondrous, in fact perhaps even unique, in that it can only occur under these particular conditions and can only happen to these particular individuals.[30]

The important point as far as the development of the novella is concerned is the fact that Tieck concluded from this definition that contemporary life was the most suitable material for this literary genre. He suggested that it could describe all social classes in the most complex of interactions, and that it had the widest variety of artistic means of expression at its disposal, ranging from the greatest pathos to the crudest humour. The novella was, in other words, meant to summarize life in society by focusing on an extraordinary, individual event.

This concentration on a unique, central event links the new novella to the old variant, and seen superficially it distinguishes itself from the latter merely in terms of comprehensiveness, of the degree of attention to detail that had thus become necessary and possible, and of the variety of narrative tone. Yet precisely these determinants are an expression in literature of the change in a social reality of which both forms of novella are a reflection. Boccaccio was active at the very beginning of feudal society's disintegration; the new social classes were initially formed within the framework of the feudal order, and although they were beginning to destroy the latter, the rigid social types of the old way of life were still a general social reality and thus retained their literary validity, even if pre-dominantly as the objects of satirical criticism.

However, for the narrator, the existence of fixed social types means that he is not compelled artistically to prove the authenticity of his characters, and above all their psychology, through the narrative. The facts, the deeds, the extraordinary events themselves need only to be narrated objectively, simply and visually in order to lend full validity to the social truth to be expressed. Hence the artistic economy and wonderful objectivity of the classical novella.

It would not be apposite even to hint at the historical development of the novella in the space available here, or for that matter to point to specific literary forerunners in the age of transition. We shall simply assume the basic necessity of the modern novella, namely that it is forced to derive its characters from an artistic source; that is to say, in a relatively developed bourgeois society, in which the old feudal orders have already to a great extent disintegrated, the typical is no longer directly present in society in a manner that can be used immediately for artistic purposes. As a consequence of the individualization brought into being by the development of bourgeois society, of the effect of the capitalist division of labour, permitting one's personality to unfold in professional life to an ever-decreasing extent, of the growing separation of private and public life, of the growing differentiation of erotic relationships, etc., the truly typical in characterization can only be portrayed convincingly as the product of significant artistic labour, as the concluding final result of a story, as the author's sublation of the mere individuality that originally existed.

Needless to say, this development transforms not only the novella; the new form of the modern novel also owes its existence to these factors: they create the basis for the problematics and often for the failure of bourgeois drama. They tend to cause the novella form to dissolve into a simple form of narration held together only by the contents, only by the abstract problem. Thus, the concentration of the novella in the focus of an extraordinary event as promulgated by Goethe and Tieck had the purpose, artistically speaking, of preserving the novella form from such dissolution.

However, is this simply a question of form? Indeed, are we dealing merely with a formalistic approach? In the course of later developments it certainly became reduced to such; an artificially archaicizing imitation of the Classical novella arose. But even for Tieck – leaving Goethe completely aside – the central event of the novella signified a 'dialectical turning point'. What exactly does this mean? Keller provides a clear answer in his *A Village Romeo and Juliet*. There he describes how two prosperous farmers, by progressively ploughing away more of a piece of land that lies between their fields, the legal title to which is unclear, end up as close neighbours. A struggle ensues for the outright ownership of the land which they have both illegally appropriated, in the course of which they bring each other to ruin. Keller remarks quite rightly that this is an everyday occurrence. Only because both take things to their logical conclusion with the utmost tenacity does a novella-like, wondrous event come into being in which, precisely because the individual case is brought to an out-of-the-ordinary climax, the typical social and moral determinants of the whole complex of problems are concentrated in a palpable fashion that allows them to emerge clearly. In short, the dialectical turning point of which Tieck speaks is the point at which an unusual event causes the individually-heightened, extraordinary special case to develop into something socially typical. It is not until it is formulated in terms of the exceptional case that the rule, the necessity inherent in coincidence emerges in a sensuously tangible form.

In this connection we can see the underlying reality in bourgeois society which both links the novel to the novella and yet separates them from one another. The more uniform bourgeois society becomes in economic terms and the more capitalism permeates the whole life of society, the more uniform the novel becomes. The novels of old were to a greater or lesser extent loose bundles of adventures, often indeed novella-like events, held together only by the continuity of the main characters and that of the central problem. Not until the unified pattern of social existence comes so clearly to the fore that everyone is forced to encounter it in even the most insignificant everyday events do we witness the rise of a form of narrative which expresses itself in the starkly concentrated, uniform plot of the novel. In Balzac, the experience of this unified historical pattern of social development is so profound that he has no alternative but to embark on a cycle of novels, a monumental narrative, in which uniform historical laws permeate the superficially confusing multiplicity of individual fates through and through, intellectually and artistically.

However, the great early nineteenth century realists did not yet experience this tendency to uniformity and regularity as a completed, flattening process, but rather in all its contradictoriness and variegated irregularity: more or less as a distinct but loosely-bound bundle of tragedies and comedies. When Balzac talks of the dramatic quality of the modern novel compared with that of the eighteenth century, he means by this the ineluctably novella-like quality of individual events, through which and in which the pattern of social developments is expressed. This is why it is possible for novellas to form part of Balzac's *Comédie Humaine*; this is why some of his novels are really a series of modern novellas intertwined with one another by virtue of their dramatic and psychological structure.

In his youth Keller had been deeply impressed by some of Balzac's works (*Le Chef d'oeuvre inconnu* – *The Unknown Masterpiece*). Keller's novella is, however, a completely independent continuation of the more recent trend that arose predominantly in German literature. In other words, a concentrated, unique event, which, precisely by virtue of features that deviate from the average, lends itself to a convincing, sensuous portrayal of the laws governing a typical aspect of life.

This concentration serves precisely to mark the novella off sharply from the novel: by means of the unique event in which the novella culminates, individuality stands revealed as part of a larger pattern. Yet, this is a transformation in *one point* only; the general patterns governing the course of life in society are expressed in this one point *and only here*, and elucidate from this vantage point, suddenly and surprisingly, the completely individual and unique event. As a result, the novella is not compelled to portray the whole wealth of determinants of life within society, which is what constitutes the artistic unity of the novel as the modern continuation of the great epics.

This uniqueness of the novella form is the reason for its genesis and early blossoming in the Classical and Romantic periods of German literature. In Germany, all the problems of a nascent bourgeois society were posed in the most advanced intellectual form before the capitalist economy had thoroughly permeated that country, before the contradictory unity of national life had been created as a result of this development. The novella was accordingly one of the forms in which, despite this discrepancy between social base and thought, despite this anachronistic social base in Germany, a contemporary, non-anachronistic and nevertheless realist literature could come into being. In the case of Keller, 'retreating' into Swiss topics was the socio-historical source for this – German – novella form. And for this reason, the growth of capitalism in Switzerland was bound to lead to the dissolution of that artistic form.

In French literature of the same period, by contrast, the modern novella was a supplement to the modern novel that was emerging concurrently with it (and not as a substitute for the latter's social impossibility). The novella was one of the forms in which the unevenness, the sudden, vehement and dramatic character of social transformation expressed itself.

Keller's novellas represent a unique further development of the German variant. We have already stated that the social foundations for this uniqueness – namely Switzerland's particular position with respect to the development of capitalism, the surrounding large nations and their politically reactionary tendencies – afforded Keller the opportunity to be a plebeian writer on the basis of his close link to the deep roots of Swiss democracy in a manner not open to his German contemporaries. We have also demonstrated that Keller, as a result of his deep roots in the development of German Humanism, of his leanings towards revolutionary democratism which culminated in his acceptance of Feuerbach's philosophy, was armed with the necessary intellectual defences to ensure that he did not fall prey to blinkered provincialism.

Keller was able to avoid this danger because his intellectual development was based on that of German thought from Lessing to Feuerbach. The same danger led even as important a writer as Jeremias Gotthelf to degenerate to the point of adopting reactionary positions, yet without this negating his bonds with the people; indeed, these positions were themselves, in contradiction to Gotthelf's rootedness in the people, linked to the still elemental, pre-capitalist life of the people. Owing to his intellectual development, Keller was able to overcome the provincialism of the German village story, of those German novels with nothing but local colour; one need think only of the contrast between him and Berthold Auerbach.

Keller thus stands, with all the contradictions that this entails, on the foundations of a society that is on the one hand less developed in the bourgeois, capitalist sense than in Germany, and yet on the other – in political, in national terms – forms a unity, with an ancient, traditional national past. This unique historical situation is reflected in Keller's novella form.

The uniformity of the populace to be portrayed receives an immediate, sensuously visible form in the organization of Keller's works in cycles, in cycles of novellas. However, in accordance with the loose interconnection of the elements of society, Keller's cycle is originally only held together by a common socio-historical basis. Here the uniformity of the governing social pattern is not a concrete force permeating each individual phenomenon in equally intensive measure, forming the individual fates into one unified, massive plot as in Balzac, but is rather a uniformity of timbre, of atmosphere: the uniformity of an overall framework.

This is the structure underlying the famous novella cycle *Die Leute von Seldwyla* (*The People of Seldwyla*). The patterns governing society form a general backdrop here, against which the individual novellas stand out, each giving objective form to aspects of its underlying traits. The individual stories, however, stand on their own as internally rounded-off novellas, each being complete in itself and never spilling over into one of the others. They are meant to create an overall picture of Seldwyla, but only by supplementing one another spiritually and morally. The social problematics, that is to say, the manner in which Keller visualizes the developmental potential open to traditional democracy in Switzerland, emerges in the difference between the first and second parts of the cycle. Keller determines the existence of certain tendencies in capitalism's growth in the preface to the second part. In the first novellas of this part he treats them with confident humour as teething troubles that could easily be overcome by a healthy democracy with natural roots. Yet, in the last novella (*Das verlorene Lachen – The Lost Laugh*) these questions are already beginning to arise as something objectively more developed, more serious, more dangerous, and threaten to dissolve Keller's novella form altogether.

This development is reflected in the tone of Keller's later cycles. Their structure is not so much objectively social as subjectively didactic. The overall framework, adhered to only for the first three novellas of the next cycle (the *Zurich Novellas*), is overtly and directly didactic. A young inhabitant of Zurich who wishes to be an 'eccentric'[31] at any cost is shown, using three examples both positively and negatively, of what true human originality, what true social development of the personality involves, and how this differs from its philistine petty bourgeois caricature. It is telling that the only directly social novella in this cycle, *Das Fähnlein der sieben Aufrechten* (*The Banner of the Upright Seven*), treats the great struggles for and in defence of democracy as a heroic age now long-since passed. The old fighters have a humane, educational influence on the younger generation, strengthening their moral sense, and this is depicted with a subtle balance of humour and pathos; however, the perspective for future society, for the social contents of the lives of the younger generation, remains abstract.

The overall framework in this cycle is to this extent even more artificial than in the earlier novellas. For the fiction of oral narration, the true origin of the novella, is introduced here and expanded with great artistic skill: new means in order to refurnish the modern novella with the immediacy, with the spontaneously convincing incisiveness of the older variant.

This trend in Keller's work reaches a climax in the last novella cycle, in the *Sinngedicht*. The overall frame here is itself provided by a novella which describes the love between Reinhart, a young scholar, and Lucie. The novellas built into this, without exception narrated by the actors in the framing novella, are the weapons used in a duel of love conducted in a spirit of jest and of seriousness. The questions in which this burgeoning love crystallizes are dealt with in a strong, sensuous yet unobtrusive manner; they raise the individual features of the relationship onto a high general intellectual, sociomoral plane, generalize them in poetic terms, without destroying the immediacy and the subtlety of the experience of love.

The novellas focus on the issues of what love is, of how men and women react to one another when in love, of the extent to which men are really 'superior' in love, of the 'freedom of choice' open to both, of equal rights for women, of the social and cultural equality of men and women. The contents, sequence, complementarity, and the polemics between the individual novellas – and all of this is controlled and edited through the conversation of the protagonists in the framing novella – form the individual moments, the nodal points of the action. One need only compare the contents and the tenor of the novellas narrated by Reinhart (*Regine, The Poor Baroness, Don Correa*), by Lucie (*Von einer törichten Jungfrau* [*The Mad Virgin*], *Die Berlocken*) and by her uncle (*Der Geisterseher* [*The Haunted One*]) in order clearly to perceive the socio-ideological battle of love. It is also no coincidence that each narrator commences with things he or she has experienced and observed, and that it is not until the final, grotesquely humorous climax of the duel that imagined events are narrated in which the contrasts become even more sharply contoured, indeed to be used as weapons. Thanks to the skilful intensification of these replies and rejoinders, the 'crystallization points' in Reinhart and Lucie's love for one another, to use Stendhal's term, also receive a novella-like quality and destroy any hint of rigid separation between the framing novella and the stories it frames.

The old framing form of the novella as used in the *Decameron* is thus renewed in a manner that even surpasses its Classical model in terms of artistic freedom and discipline. Admittedly, if we view the question from the standpoint of Keller's development, then we cannot but observe his increasing reluctance to choose material directly related to society and the public sphere in favour of the problematics of individual life, even though the social background even of individual problems remains vividly present. The finest gradation of experiences of love, the stages of a love that grows between two people, is never allowed to conceal the background, namely that in a democratic community love and marriage are major public affairs. Yet, this is without doubt the point in Keller's work when he comes closest to the socio-artistic form promulgated by German Classicism, and is furthest away from the path taken in his first novellas. Keller's use of the framing device takes Tieck (*Phantasus*) and Hoffmann (*Serapionsbrüder*) as its starting-point. Whereas the frame in these latter works is of an aesthetic, essayistic nature, with novella-like elements playing but an episodic role, in Keller's writings it is the features of human and moral interest that are foregrounded and rounded off to achieve epic significance in themselves.

It is therefore equally obvious that Keller's framing narration has nothing in common with that used by his contemporaries. Important writers of this period, such as Theodor Storm and Conrad Ferdinand Meyer, also showed a preference for the framing narrative; however, and this is highly significant, not in the cyclical form adopted by Keller, but as a narrative frame for each individual novella. The framing narrative serves in both cases – for different yet related reasons – to place artistic distance between the author and the narrated events. In the case of Storm, the reasons have to do with lyricism: he has a preference for narrating recollections long since past in order thus to blur the sharp contours of reality, making lyrical mood the unifying factor at the story-tellers' disposal. With Meyer, this preference stems from his conception of history. He views great men as completely isolated in their respective ages, moving enigmatically, without being understood, in the midst of events. The framing narrative – whereby the narrator is often only marginal to the plot, a character in principle incapable of understanding the hero (the Swiss crossbowman in *Der Heilige*) – serves to underline the loneliness of the main hero.

In the case of Keller, the framing narrative is adopted for utterly different reasons. It stresses – in the *Seldwyla* novellas – above all the common social background. It is also an artistic means of attesting to the fact that the narrated events actually occurred. And above all, it serves to underline forcefully Keller's popular didactic intentions, without the story itself – the purely narrative effect of the interesting events – being burdened with an overly open statement of this intention.

Keller's return to the oral tradition of story-telling is, therefore, not as artificial as that of Storm or Meyer. Keller is a decided opponent of all aestheticized stylization. He resoundingly and vehemently rejects any linguistic antiquarianism when narrating events that lie in the distant past. At the same time he is just as strict an opponent of vernacular in the epic description of local events. He strives in his fiction for a truly plebeian form of artistic generalization that originates in the whole life of the people and is thus comprehensible to the entire people.

This truly epic spirit is what he admires in the more accomplished works of Gotthelf. He is also aware, however, that such epic stature is not a question of form, but can only be achieved if the innermost issues addressed emanate from the central issues of the life of the people. And in this sense Keller's central issue is exceptionally plebeian and truly epic, consisting as it does in demonstrating how all problems of private life converge in public life, how all questions of an individual's development are a preparation, an education of the personality for public influence.

The fact that Keller's approach and the artistic form he adopted grew out of popular life in Swiss democracy lends his novellas a special, extensively epic character. The linking of private fate and public life is not merely a mental construct, a contrivance in Keller's works. It thus follows as a matter of course that each of his novellas describes private fates in such a way that they are organically linked to more or less important occurrences in the life of the Swiss people, and are bound up with the public expressions of this way of life. There is hardly a novella of Keller's in which the private, human turning point is not connected with a popular festival, with an important public event of popular life. I mention but a few, characteristic examples: the volunteer corps parade (*Frau Regel Amrain and Her Youngest Son*), the peace celebrations (*Dietegen*), the song festival (*The Lost Smile*), a Swiss Confederate marksman's contest (*The Banner of the Upright Seven*).

In considering the narrative role of these moments in Keller's work, it is to be noted that they are never merely decorative, artistic additions, but always arise from the very heart of the plot; that the wide-ranging and colourful presentation they comprise is indispensable to an exhaustive treatment of the epic material. This is most evident in *The Banner of the Upright Seven*. The growing love between Karl and Hermine meets with opposition from their fathers, the intellectual leaders of a small, radically democratic society, calling themselves the 'Upright'. Hermine's prosperous father wants to marry his daughter off to a man who will promote the continuation and the expansion of his blossoming construction business. Hediger, Karl's father and a poor tailor, an admirer of Robespierre and of the French Terror, accepts this opposition with great conviction precisely on account of his democratic standpoint. He replies to the laughter with which his humorous wife, clearly his superior, reacts to the prohibition of the marriage by saying:

... The family is where true politics begin; of course we are political friends; but in order to stay so we must be careful not to turn the families upside down and play communion with another's wealth. I'm poor and Freymann is rich and that's the way it's to be; we get all the more pleasure out of our spiritual equality. . . Fortunately there are no monstrously rich people among us; prosperity is fairly well distributed, but just let fellows with many millions spring up, who have political ambition, and you'll see what mischief they will do.[32]

He wishes to uphold the Puritan, Jacobin forms of life for himself and his family and thus supports – comically unaware of the fact – the capitalist egotism of his friend. Given such circumstances, the young couple's love is bound to triumph in this fine comedy of honourable democratic spirit, which has in part already been overtaken by real life; their love is bound to overturn such contradictory ideas. The Confederate marksman's contest of 1849 on the anniversary of the Swiss Constitution, which concluded the old struggle between reaction and democracy, uncovers in a humorous form the extent to which the 'Upright Seven' have lagged behind the times: not one of them is capable of holding the public speech which they themselves have decided shall accompany the presentation of a prize drinking-cup and a banner; all of them sense that their old way of speaking is out of place, but no one finds the right tone to suit the new situation in a changed reality. Thus, young Karl saves the day, and this proof of his social worth (in the shooting competition as well) is a means of overcoming the fathers' opposition.

One can see how deeply the description of a public festival is rooted in the individual plot: the implicit social nature of the theme becomes apparent in the public character of the solution to the conflict. The lovingly detailed portrayal of the festival is thus by no means irrelevant, a mere ornamentation, but the organically necessary development of the individual tale, the visible unravelling of all its determinants. This organic interweaving of the individual and the social, the private and the public, is even more apparent in the earlier novellas in which the capitalist problematics do not disfigure the overall democratic picture to such a degree.

In this respect Keller is, with the exception of Leo Tolstoy, the nineteenth century's greatest and most unselfconscious portrayer of the 'totality of objects',[33] the description of which Hegel rightly viewed as the essence of truly great narrative prose. With this prescription, Hegel merely gives expression to the quality that makes the major modern novels worthy successors of the ancient epic. True epic poetry depicts the whole panoramic breadth of social life. The description of human fate does not in itself suffice here. For the social interaction between people, the metabolism of society and nature is mediated through the agency of objects, institutions which function as objects, and so on. Any narrative that fails to portray these mediating instances must remain inadequate, incomplete. Yet, simply describing these 'objects' is also insufficient. Only if they become living elements of the plot, active participants in the action, only if they cease to be props or scenery, only if by means of this mediation, the essential, otherwise unrecognized aspects of human life are expressed – only then are human beings truly portrayed as social beings, in lively interaction with their social environment; only then is a 'totality of objects' created.

Keller is, alongside Tolstoy, the greatest epic portrayer of this human environment. It is only in this light that the paradoxical idiosyncrasy of his novellas becomes visible. Keller inclines socially and artistically towards the greatest epic depiction, towards a manner of narration that is unostentatious and rich, monumental and humorous, simple and intellectually demanding, and in which the 'totality of objects' has a significant effect solely through its factual importance. This propensity is, seen abstractly, that of a great novelist if we understand the novel to be the epic of the bourgeois age. The resigned tragedy of Keller's career as a writer consists in the fact that this externally comprehensive monumentality of the epic depiction of overall life could not emerge within his work. As a result of the social basis of his work, he had to restrict himself to portraying only one segment of society, i.e. confine himself to the novella, an essentially individualistic artistic form; his writing, as he himself said, remained 'episodic'.

This restriction was, however, the salvation of Keller's art, for it led to the creation in his work of a completely unique type of novella, yet to be equalled in epic stature, a stature that arises organically out of this form, that does not burst it asunder but rather expands its horizons. This is no coincidence. For precisely the form of the novella provides the bridge between the historically determined character of Keller's democratic utopia and his realism. His conviction that motifs, forms, etc., could only be artistically significant and fruitful if they lent adequate expression to the 'dialectics of cultural development' is confirmed by the example of his own creative work.

The only avenues open to Keller are either to lead his characters to the portal of empirical reality or to have them crash to tragic or comic failure before it. For that democracy of universally and culturally developed human beings whose lives – precisely because of their individuality – culminate in the democratic universality of popular life, render it fertile and are in turn rendered fertile by it, is even less a reality than the Seldwyla he describes with such humour. That the description of such processes is so true-to-life, so convincing, is precisely the result of Keller's utopian belief in the future potential of Swiss democracy. For all of this was latent in Swiss democracy as a possibility and a trend; Keller's views are utopian only to the extent that he allows these trends to achieve their real extensive and intensive fulfilment.

We have already touched on this essential quality of Keller's novellas in our brief account of *The Banner of the Upright Seven*. This is not an individual case, but rather the rule underlying his method in all his novellas. The Goethean 'unheard-of event' is a coincidental test of the character's suitability for life in society. Thus, the tailor's apprentice is mistaken for a count (*Kleider machen Leute – Clothes Make the Man*); thus Kabys, a wind-bag who is forever dreaming up schemes, is adopted by a distant, rich relative (*Der Schmied seines Glücks – The Architect of His Own Fortune*); thus the competition between the 'virtuous' apprentices results in a tragicomic contest to keep their jobs (*The Three Righteous Combmakers*), etc. These twists in life – a concentrated form of training to become a citizen which can end either positively or negatively – each take a different course; they can no longer be as simple and obvious as was the 'unheard-of event' in the Classical novella. The central, novella-like event is extended to embrace a group of individual plots that are composed as a unity, thus exposing the core of the main figures' personalities, developing each of the characteristics on which depends the question of whether they can be educated to become citizens or will fail comically. Accordingly – in the midst of deception caused unwittingly by their own doing – the human refinement and decency of the romantic tailor's apprentice from Poland in

Clothes Make the Man emerges and becomes the reason for his honourable salvation; accordingly, vacuous haughtiness and rash over-cleverness cast the 'the architect of his own fortune' back into poverty. Yet this breaking-down of the central event into a small series of interconnected plots is the full extent of the story. The question as to the purpose of such education, albeit clearly evident as an underlying social concept, is rarely portrayed, and when it is it pales to an abstraction, which inevitably contrasts sharply with the blossoming vitality of the path described.

The form of the novella, in other words, gave Keller the opportunity to concentrate on individuals and the way in which they were trained to become citizens; it allowed him to take as the crux of the novella the point of intersection between individually coincidental and socially necessary factors in their lives, and to make these the dialectical turning-point in their development. The novella form allowed Keller to incorporate the inner consequences of overall social developments in his work as mere perspective, mere horizon. In the story itself everything remains authentic and true, realistic in the deepest sense, while the utopia creates nothing but a pure, fantastic, tragic or humorous mood suspended above everyday events.

The artistic resignation inherent in the choice of the novella as his preferred literary form is also to be found in Keller's life: he repeatedly dreamed of becoming a dramatist. Keller's efforts as a playwright, of which only a few fragments remain, are a product of the literary currents of the eighteen forties, of the democratic upsurge of the day. In *Das moderne Drama* by the literary historian Hermann Hettner, to which Keller contributed, this close friend of his Heidelberg days links the future blossoming of drama with the anticipated final victory of democracy in Germany. Keller's resigned remarks on his own perspectives as an author are predominantly based on these views on the development of literature.

All the major figures in these endeavours strove to create a plebeian drama and theatre. Richard Wagner's point of departure in his theoretical and practical efforts at reform also consisted at that time in restoring the link between drama and the people. Keller too had great sympathy for this project. A closer examination, however, reveals substantial differences. Even in the writings of his revolutionary period, Wagner had already devised theories based on an abstract philosophy of history in order to justify his tragic *Gesamt-kunstwerk* as a plebeian renewal of the Greek tragedies.

Keller's hopes, by contrast, drew their sustenance from still extant plebeian traditions, local Viennese and Berlin farces, and he hoped that the democratic upsurge would generate from within these a new, contemporary – plebeian-Aristophanian – political and social comedy. For these comedies, Keller was prepared to recognize fully the linking of drama and music.

However, like Hettner, he rejected Wagner's form of tragedy; they both held the fundamental problem of tragedy to reside in the depiction of modern human individuality, in its conflict with social forces, and both maintained that the spoken word, rather than song, was indispensable in this context. Even if Keller later – in his essay 'Am Mythenstein' of 1860 – dreamed of the possibility of a Swiss popular theatre, this merely amounted to the hope that great political comedy could slowly evolve out of the crudely improvised plays performed on the occasion of popular festivals.

In other words, Keller's dramatic efforts go off in two different directions: that of major public popular comedies with choirs, music ,and so on, and that of the modern bourgeois tragedy. It is easy to understand that the first endeavour could not be realized during the Age of Reaction in Germany, and later Keller himself obviously felt that his great Swiss popular comedy was just a dream. He never attempted to fulfil his desire in practice. Yet this was a complete renunciation: he never succumbed to the temptation to trim the plebeian, the democratic *Gesamtkunstwerk* to suit the needs of the bourgeoisie of the time, with its increasingly reactionary way of thinking. He may have given up hope, but he did not compromise as did Richard Wagner.

Even the failure of his bourgeois drama is closely linked with the fate of democracy in Germany. Drama, in that great, serious sense in which Keller, an ardent admirer of Shakespeare, understands it, admittedly does not require an extensive 'totality of objects' as does major narrative prose, but it does require the portrayal of the decisive conflicts of life in society within the totality of essential determinants and relations. Here, the effect of the defeat of democracy in Germany is less palpable than in the case of comedy. The drama of the Age of Reaction forced the main general conflicts of society into the wings, with the effect that in tragedy the centre-stage was occupied by exaggerated individual problems. Keller identified this development very clearly in the work of the most significant dramatist of the time, Hebbel – whose plays written prior to 1848 he held in high esteem, albeit with critical reservations.

This sharply negative stance towards the dominant trends of the day could not, of course, give direction to his own creative work. If we consider his work on the largest of the surviving fragments, *Therese*, then we see a perpetual but vain battle to overcome the novella-like character of the draft project. Keller was unable to overcome this novella-like character – proceeding from purely individual fates to the problems of society, from the coincidence of individual events to the necessary course of events as a whole – because his point of departure did not lie in some artistic quality or in his own personality, but in the concrete form his world-view had taken. And this was determined by the boundaries of the history of his own country and those of the German cultural community as a whole. Keller's artistic self-criticism ran so deep that it prevented him from continuing to pursue this false path, even though his greatest desire as an artist was to write plays. The social determination of his world-view was, however, so strong, that he was unable to see through the fundamental theoretical mistake inherent in his dramatic efforts with any clarity, despite his otherwise extraordinarily broad and free outlook, particularly when judging drama.

What is it that constitutes this difference between the novella-like and the dramatic? What specifically determines Keller's inability to write plays, when his novellas, after all, if compared with their Classical forerunners, incorporate dramatic qualities just as consciously as do Balzac's novels compared with those of the seventeenth and eighteenth centuries? It is precisely at this juncture that we can see that there is something superimposed about the 'dramatic' quality of narrative prose in the cases of Balzac and Keller – that it is hardly an inappropriate expression with which to attempt to describe a new, but distinctively narrative form of reflecting modern reality.

Keller criticizes above all the stilted, forced, quirky and bizarre quality of the plots used by Friedrich Hebbel, the greatest of his contemporary playwrights. This weakness of Hebbel's drama – as

Keller correctly perceives – is less the result of an individual short-coming on the part of the dramatist and more a phenomenon of the times. Hebbel was never able to develop the universal, the social and the ideal essence of his conflicts organically out of the individual fates of his dramatic figures. The problems themselves, however, were perfectly clear to him. For example, he describes the general contents of his tragedy *Herodes und Mariamne*, the story of which was based on Josephus Flavius, and then says:

It rounds itself off as a tragedy almost of its own accord . . . history really did all it could here . . . Herod leaves life a monster smeared in blood . . . but did not enter the world as a monster. He appears as a young man great and noble, equipped with all the glorious qualities that go to make a hero and a man, and remains so for a long time . . . he unswervingly and daringly follows his path. . .[34]

If one now compares the beginning and the end of the tragedy then one must concur with Hebbel in saying:

There is material here for a moving tragedy of the first order, for a tragedy, namely, that describes human nature in its dependence on the forces of fate.[35]

The general conception of this tragedy is truly authentic and magnificent. Hebbel tackles – and delves more deeply into – a problem first posed and solved in modern times by Racine. Racine called his Nero (in the *Britannicus* tragedy) 'un monstre naissant', a monster in the making who – in this drama – only gradually reveals himself to be such. It is obvious in what respect Hebbel's treatment of the theme is deeper: Racine's Nero is by nature a villain; the power of relations, the court atmosphere of absolutism only bring the seeds of Evil already in him to blossom. Hebbel, by contrast, wishes to show how these relations can transform a person who is by nature good into a bloodthirsty tyrant.

Why does Racine's plan, which is the simpler, succeed, whereas Hebbel's more profound conception leads to artistic failure? Generally speaking – and we have space here only for a few general observations – because Racine develops Nero as a character in all his phases organically out of the typical relations of the absolutist court, whereas the psychology of Hebbel's Herod has to rely on other, more far-reaching, complex reasons rooted in individual biography. Thus, the former creates a closed dramatic unity, whereas in the latter's play socio-historical action and excessively individualized psychology are completely unconnected and destroy the tragic unity.

This is of course precisely the reason for Keller's constant criticism of Hebbel; and yet one must ask: to what extent was he himself free of this weakness? It has its roots in society. We have already pointed to equally inorganic components in Wagner's dramatic texts. Yet even Otto Ludwig, Hebbel's major contemporary rival and critic, was not able in his own work to avoid the fault he justly rebuked the latter for; he too sought in vain for motives and causes that were at once organic, convincing, artistically simple and streamlined, and yet would have thoroughly encapsulated the complexity of modern life.

The common reason for all these failures, for these dramaturgical problems facing highly talented playwrights, lies in the pettiness and wretchedness of social relations in Germany following the defeat of the 1848 Revolution. In the life of society, conflicts were now no longer argued out openly in public and taken through to their logical conclusion; cowardly, rotten compromises were the order of the day, from grand politics down to the social praxis of the age. Those writers whose talents drew them towards the drama were, in other words, faced with material from life which was devoid of all dramatic decisiveness and plasticity. On the other hand, as true poets they experienced the epoch in which they lived and worked as one filled with dramatic, indeed tragic contradictions. And it was these they wished to depict; as, however, the artistically concrete mediating agency of social life did not exist, in their work these conflicts were given subjectivist, psychologistic emphasis as something lying outside society. And the attempt – by Hebbel and Wagner – to forge an otherwise absent dramatic unity and objectivity by means of a mystificatory, abstract philosophy of history made the rupture between subject matter and available material all the greater.

The features that distinguish Keller from his important German contemporaries are already known to us; they enable him to perceive their faults with clarity. This by no means, however, affords him the power to overcome in his writing the dramatic fragility of his contemporary subject matter. Of course, the contents of Keller's works are of a different nature: it is Swiss democracy and not German reaction. But even Swiss democracy has in Keller's time already left its heroic age of struggle behind it; in it, too, the gradual awakening of capitalism is beginning to destroy what was humane. Given this subject matter, what great conflict of the human soul could Keller have revealed and depicted dramatically, i.e. in clear three-dimensional battles of internally and externally significant social forces? He is far too honest to conceal from himself the gradual and by no means always glorious retreat of the democratic spirit in the face of the power of money. He is far too intelligent to conduct a quixotic battle *à la* Gotthelf with the unavoidable forms of economic progress. At the same time, he has such a deep belief in bourgeois democracy's ability to prevail that he could not have given its decline, its death throes a tragic tone; for the same reason he cannot perceive the true 'hero of our times', namely the working class, in all the drama associated with its gradual ascent.

For this reason, coincidence also forms the bridge in Keller's work linking individual fate and the social meaning of the totality. Viewed abstractly, this can be seen as a rupture similar to that in Hebbel's work. (The *Therese* fragment does indeed exhibit certain Hebbel-like traits.) Yet, this is where the fundamental difference between the drama and the novella is to be found. The drama depicts, as Hebbel trenchantly puts it, 'the process of life itself'. Every coincidence must, therefore, be overcome in the drama, just as the *totality* of the life process overcomes coincidence in the necessity intrinsic to the regularity of the course taken by the whole; this *direct* reflection of the overall process within an individual occurrence is the decisive feature of the drama. The *slice* of life, by contrast, on which the novella is based, has coincidence and necessity appear in a relation governed by *individual phenomena*; the laws underlying the whole are only incorporated in a concealed fashion, as background, as a distant view of the totality; it can in fact remain unmentioned, without this disturbing the aesthetic balance of the novella.

When Keller, in other words, who found the over-exaggeration of his contemporary playwrights deeply repugnant, commenced his retreat into novella-writing, this may admittedly have amounted to a renunciation of the dreams of his early adult years, but it was simultaneously his salvation as a writer: he did not have to forego any richness in his view of life, any of its breadth or universality, nor any of his own unique form of reflection, in order to find an appropriately truthful form for his contents. Whereas Hebbel's plays are often artificial and awkward, in Keller's novella-writing one comes upon poetic inwardness living itself out freely and crystallizing organically into artistic form.

Nevertheless, the dramatic poignancy is lost in the depiction. Let us recall again Racine's 'monstre naissant' and Hebbel's failure in spite of his profundity. Keller repeatedly portrays the genesis both of ogres and of people of exemplary morals. Yet, he always portrays the *process* of genesis – as we have already demonstrated with some examples – rather than the *concrete* problems and the conflicts with reality that such a type has when fully-fledged. By thus making the actual drama a mere horizon, a distant perspective on the narrated event, Keller also beats a resigned retreat in terms of content – and in doing so saves the credibility of his utopian conception of Swiss democracy from having its utopian essence exposed, something which would have been unavoidable if the conflicts latent in the theme had been portrayed dramatically. He rescues, forever an honest thinker and writer, only what is worthy of being rescued because it is true, and for this reason his resignation again becomes the basis for the truth of the artistic form. However: it is the truth of the novella, not of the drama.

In this sense, Keller really is a 'born' novella-writer. Yet we see that this 'birth' was the result of complex socio-historical forces affecting the personal and artistic resignation of a major author.

Keller's novella-writing, which succeeds again and again in painting such rich, vivid portraits of popular life that they can be conceived of and enjoyed as the fragmented pieces of a popular epic of the modern age, is an example of how truly great writers are able to renew old forms from within and simultaneously expand them in a surprising fashion. Keller approaches the form of the novella from his central ideological viewpoint and seizes upon what is essential in ideological and artistic terms: the focus on a wondrous event, and the ability of the extraordinarily strange individual case to mirror social patterns. It is this and only this element of the traditional form of the novella that he retains: its essence, in other words that most general formal element in which the novella reflects an important and regularly recurring context of life itself. Keller, by approaching the problem from the depths of his knowledge of the world, creates a completely original and fresh novella; one could say that in his version the form of the novella is born anew, is born for the first time – and yet his very personal, very idiosyncratic manner of portrayal always complies with the essential, supra-historical laws of the novella, of novella-writing as a form of story-telling.

VI
THE NOVEL

It is only on the surface that Keller's two novels, written at the beginning and at the end of his career, would seem to contradict the novella-like character of his art. *Green Henry* became a major, monumental novel for special reasons connected with Keller's biography that were not then repeated. Firstly, the novel is a personal biographical confession. The relation between private and public life is here – as in the novellas – the basic theme. As Keller's own highly convoluted personality, full of 'nooks and crannies', served as a model for the main protagonist, it was inevitable that the presentation of the latter's educational path should receive a breadth quite unlike that in the novellas. Keller had to accept this much against his own will. The original plan stemming from the eighteen forties involved a small, elegiacal novel about his own youth with a tragic ending (that is, as we shall see below, a novella-like, irrational ending). The material grew to significant, novel-like and epic proportions very much against Keller's original intention.

Nevertheless, a truly epic totality would not have arisen but for the years in Heidelberg and the contact with Feuerbachian philosophy. It is no coincidence that even though the novel ends with the return to Switzerland, it reaches its intellectual climax in the discussion of the main problems of German culture during the spread of the democratic revolution. The about-turn in Heidelberg signified for *Green Henry* not only a flood of new insights and experiences; these also necessitated a fundamental recasting of the whole preceding Swiss autobiographical section. Keller himself wrote from Heidelberg to a friend:

. . . two thirds of which [namely *Green Henry*, G.L.] I must recast now that I have acquired a completely different standpoint and have drawn a line under my life hitherto.[36]

The narrative richness of the portrayal of the days of his youth in Zurich thus becomes, owing to his critical encounter with Feuerbachian philosophy, truly perfected, receives an ideological and poetic firmness. It is of course not coincidental that this poetic analysis of German culture came to a climax and to an end when Keller made Feuerbachian philosophy his own. He completely rejected post-revolutionary Germany, indeed he lived in Berlin at the beginning of the eighteen fifties, as we have seen, like a guest or an émigré, always on the point of striking camp, and thus there was no question of his repeating the German thematics.

The work undertaken in Berlin on *Green Henry* was perhaps the most tortuous episode in Keller's creative life – for both political and artistic reasons. He was forced to find an ending for the book; owing to his slow and rhapsodic way of writing, and hounded by material privation, he had to send a manuscript to the printer's that was in intellectual and artistic terms still incomplete. As a result, even while still working on the novel, he was highly dissatisfied with what he had so far achieved, although fully aware that his material had the potential for providing the basis for a major novel. He wrote to Hettner in 1853, by which time a large chunk of the book was already being typeset:

If I could only rewrite the book once more, I would wish now to make something of lasting value and thoroughly upright out of it.[37]

External and inner circumstances did not permit Keller to rework it as thoroughly as he had wished until decades after its publication, namely in 1879-1880.

In the case of the recasting of such famous youthful works, arguments always arise as to which version is the better work of art; has the work improved by being transformed at a more mature stage of the writer's development, or has it deteriorated? At a time when appreciation of formal perfection, mature objectivity and an elevated humanism is increasingly being cast by the wayside and the freshness of the first inspiration is indiscriminately preferred, irrespective of the overall moral-artistic composition of the work, a sentimental predilection for immature youthful works inevitably arises. When *Wilhelm Meister's Theatrical Mission* was discovered, voices were even raised claiming that this interesting draft should be accorded greater value than its subsequent version, the substantial masterpiece, *Wilhelm Meister's Apprenticeship.*[38]

This has also repeatedly been the fate of *Green Henry*. People have clung to individual episodes that were in themselves pleasing yet were then discarded, and have failed to appreciate the mature and rich humanism of Keller's later inventive talents. There is no space here to show in detail how much more refined, in a human sense, the most important components of the novel became, particularly in the second half, how much more richly Keller draws the figures, how much he strips them of their pathological one-sidedness and salvages their inner human beauty in his reworking of the text. This also applies to the main character. The second part is far less directly autobiographical than the first. Keller himself described his intentions for the plot and the characteristic features of this part as follows: '. . . this is what could have happened to me, if I had not pulled myself together.' The changes are much more decisive here than in the first part.

The ending has provoked the most debate. In the first version, the protagonist dies, whereas in the second he presses on in brave resignation to become an active citizen. And it is precisely here that Keller's greater artistic and humanistic maturity in his later years is to be seen.

The theme of the novel is the same as that of all Keller's novellas: the education a person undergoes in the process of becoming a citizen; the connection between individual life and life in society seen from the perspective of one individual who is captured in a broad and comprehensive totality comprising every kind of expression of his personality. Keller formulated the problem in a synopsis for his publisher as follows:

The moral of my book is that he who does not succeed in maintaining the secure order of his personal circumstances and those of his family is also incapable of taking up an effective position in civil life.[39]

Furthermore, Keller went on to elaborate that if the social component were emphasized as the cause for this failure, the result would be a thesis novel, whereas if it were shown to be predominantly the

fault of the individual, the work would be imbued with moral overtones; he himself had decided on the latter approach.

Keller's explanation is an implicit polemic against the superficial
thesis novels of the Young Germany movement. In reality, Keller
continued to conceive of the intertwined and complicated interaction of society and the individual – deliberately, accurately and profoundly. He at no point underestimated the social problematics of
the development of personality in bourgeois society. He wrote to
Hettner roughly at the same time as he was drawing up the synopsis
that it was his intention,

. . .to show how few guarantees even a state as enlightened and free as that
of Zurich provides for the secure education of the individual, even nowa-
days, if these guarantees are not already present in the family or individual
relations. . .[40]

This approach, so central to all of Keller's oeuvre, leads to the
death of the hero in the first version. Following great difficulties and
many obstacles, the hero eventually finds his way to a secure and
mature conception of life. His mother, however, has sacrificed herself to enable him to follow this path of development. On returning
home the first thing he encounters is her funeral procession.

Henry, who is only capable of seeing life as an interconnected whole and
who cannot therefore look to the future and play the role of utopian do-
gooder without having reconciled himself with his own past, is suddenly a
broken man. For the life of the simple, innocent woman is just as important
a part of his world as any other.[41]

This conception corresponds to Keller's general world-view.
One must ask, however, whether the death of the hero results from
this with compelling necessity, or whether this conclusion did not
stem from the passing subjective mood of the author rather than
from the objective organic dialectic of the material depicted.

At the time, major critics, such as Varnhagen, Vischer und
Hettner raised objections to the ending. Keller's defence of this
version in his letters to his friend Hettner unintentionally reveals its
purely subjective character. He refers above all to the fact that
the ending is – artistically speaking – not correctly executed; it was
written in haste and in a mood of inner conflict, 'literally scribbled
down amidst tears'. A closer analysis of the author's observations
clearly demonstrates that the ending was arbitrary and subjective.

He writes of the hero's situation following the death of the latter's mother:

> ... what is there now left for him to do? Time, philosophy and society's tolerance may well have rehabilitated him, as essentially there was no *dolus* (malevolence) in him. However, the matter struck him so swiftly and at the end of a long period of inner turmoil which had undermined his very being. This last blow may well be gratuitous, or whatever one may wish to call it. However, the affair, or the book simply had to come to an end, and I believe that this ending, in spite of its formal inadequacies, has more significance than a marital chapter would have had.[42]

Clearly, at this point Keller still presents us with a false choice of either/or. All the tragic components in the developmental path the hero takes are profoundly and faithfully drawn, yet the necessity of death – for a major narrative conception – does not follow from all this. There is no doubt that the original draft derives from a stage when Keller still wished to write a small elegiac, lyrical novel on his formative years; a novel, the basic structure of which would have been quasi-novella-like. In such a context, there may have been some artistic justification for the ending, even if only in terms of mood. However, since the basic conception changed while Keller was in Heidelberg, and an objective and total 'Bildungsroman' arose, the ending had to contain some degree of social generalization to be truly symptomatic in a human and social sense. Keller's own observations cited above demonstrate that in Berlin in the eighteen fifties he was not yet fully aware of this deeper form of social generalization. It was his social activities in Zurich and his production of richly textured novellas that led him to the truly epic second version: the hero experiences all the tragedy of the first version, yet this time survives to take on a role in society as an active citizen, resigned to the fate of humankind.

It is only this version that makes *Green Henry* a true 'Bildungsroman', like Goethe's *Wilhelm Meister* before him and Tolstoy's *War and Peace* after him.

We are referring here to the 'Bildungsroman' in the narrower, authentic sense. Conceived of more broadly and abstractly, almost every significant modern bourgeois novel is the story of an education. As the collision between individual and society and society's eventual victory (externally at any rate) provide the contents of every genuine novel, the individual always has to be led to an under-standing of social reality. Hegel too conceives of the essence of the novel as the story of an education:

> . . .in the modern world these fights are nothing more than 'apprentice-ship', the education of the individual into the realities of the present, and thereby they acquire their true significance. For the end of such apprentice-ship consists in this, that the subject sows his wild oats, builds himself with his wishes and opinions into harmony with subsisting relationships and their rationality, enters the concatenation of the world, and acquires for himself an appropriate attitude to it.[43]

The question arises, however, as to *which* individual is to be led into *which* society. The wording of the Hegelian definition of the novel presumes the complete prosaicness of capitalist life, even if it was far from Hegel's intention to see this final victory of prosaicness as something unconditionally positive. Yet he characterizes here the age and the art form typical of and appropriate to it, namely the modern novel. Balzac and Stendhal's respective works are both 'Bildungsromane' in this general, broader sense of the term. Capitalist society has already taken on its own distinctive, fully devel-oped form. What now counts is whether the individual bends or is broken, conforms or founders; Balzac's Vautrin says to Lucien de Rubempré in the decisive 'educational' dialogue:

> 'When you sit down to a game of bouillotte, do you argue about the rules? They exist, you accept them. . . Is it you who make the rules in the ambi-tion-game?. . . There are no longer any laws, merely conventions, that is to say humbug: nothing but form.'[44]

This is a baldly cynical modification of Hegel's definition of the modern novel, yet it outlines in sharp contours the essential points.

Balzac's Rastignac is 'educated' in this sense; Lucien goes under as a result of his sensitivity and weakness; Michel Chrestien falls at the barricades which the people have erected against the world of Vautrin's doctrine. Balzac is the founder of the modern novel to the extent that his work contains all the possible ways in which one can 'be educated' in capitalist society. A person who wishes to remain morally untainted can choose only between going under tragically or fleeing in resignation. A direct line leads from Fabrice del Dongo's monastery in Stendhal to Martin Arrowsmith's forest hut in Sinclair Lewis. If writers in a later age wished to bestow a positive meaning on this 'education', then they did so by dressing up this shameful capitulation in the face of capitalist society in untenable thought processes.

If one calls Goethe's *Wilhelm Meister* and Keller's *Green Henry* 'Bildungsromane' in the strict sense, then this distinction depends less on the aesthetic or moral uniqueness of the authors than on the difference in the world conditions depicted. A 'Bildungsroman' can, in Goethe's and Keller's view, only come about if individual and society do not yet irreconcilably collide, if education – the transformation of the personality, the changing of originally bestowed characteristics and desires, the overcoming of false inclinations – goes hand in hand with the hero becoming maturer and richer as an individual, with an increase in his aptitude for productive participation the life of society; if the individuals still view 'social customs' as the living result of the interaction of human beings and not as the finished, dead, amoral 'rules of the game'. The similarity between the artistic approaches adopted by Goethe and Keller has its roots in such historical constellations. This similarity is, however, of an abstract nature. For, in the work of both, the concrete narrative problems arise from the respective concrete social situation in their novels in which and for which the hero is to be educated. And the socio-historical conditions of Goethe and Keller differ radically.

Wilhelm Meister arises from a perspective, obscured by the glory and hopes of the French Revolution, which foresaw a transformation of semi-feudal, backward Germany under the influence of an inwardly rejuvenated Enlightenment. Goethe advocates the education of an elite among the nobility and bourgeoisie to undertake the tasks of the anticipated new way of life. The society to which the individual is set in relation, which educates him and for which he is educated, is thus to a large extent utopian. And the restriction of formative education to such a social and humanistically moral elite corresponds to this utopianism. The fact that, in Goethe's case, the essential group of positive heroes is free of all material worries corresponds to this conception. Their problems are of a moral and ideological nature, albeit continually directed towards the envisaged rejuvenation of society, continually interacting with the real elements and trends of a society that is in the process of renewal. Tolstoy's *War and Peace* as a 'Bildungsroman' about the intellectually and morally outstanding members of the Russian aristocracy and their path to becoming Decembrists often touches on these problems. There is insufficient space here to go into this in detail.

The whole universe of *Green Henry* is situated on a lower social stratum. The hero is plebeian – in terms of ancestry he is on the borderline between artisan and petty bourgeois with cultural leanings. The society that educates him and for which he is educated is not utopian, but is the really existing, traditional Swiss democracy, even if this, as we have seen, contains utopian traits in Keller's work. The overarching element is, nevertheless, the reality of this democracy.

The result of all this is a more down-to-earth conception of reality than that prevailing in Goethe's novel. This comparison is not based on the quality of the realism but rather on the nature of the material, which in Keller's novel is more compact, broader, firmer, more earthy and more palpable. In an intellectual and human sense, Keller is always a successor of Goethe: his more down-to-earth approach by no means signifies inferiority of intellectual stature, nor a descent into soulless mediocrity and everyday pettiness. Keller, like Goethe, places everything that is important for the moral and ideological development of humankind at the centre of his novel. That his approach is more down-to-earth simply means that he draws a clearer, more visible and palpable connection with the material basis of life, with the everyday difficulties and worries of economic existence under capitalism.

Even the experiences of a child contain an ideological and moral tussle with its social surroundings. In Keller's work, education to become a democratic citizen truly embraces the whole person. The formation of his thoughts on all world problems, his wrestling with the problem of good and bad actions – this is the focus even of the childhood world in *Green Henry*. Yet this wrestling is never allowed to become abstractly moralistic and doctrinaire; it always evolves out of the real events of life, and its intellectual heights, its human significance is always very palpable and concrete, namely the highest conceivable human and ideological point of given concrete objective and subjective conditions. In other words, the concentration of childhood development on moral and ideological problems never goes beyond the horizon of the respective development of childlikeness. Keller never endows his heroes, who are initially children, with precociously premature wisdom as is the case in so many later descriptions of youthful development. The greatness of his art is to be seen precisely in his portrayal of the ideological and moral wealth inherent in the normal development of bright children.

Keller's ever palpable and ever poetic realism is closely connected with the plebeian character of the world he depicts. It took the almost inconceivably sensuous descriptive art of a Goethe to ensure that the ideological and moral problems – which in the economically secure world of the prosperous citizen, the well-to-do nobility, necessarily appeared in a purely intellectual form – did not become abstract. Keller's novel mainly takes place among gainfully employed petty bourgeois whose problems are closely connected to their material worries and joys. He depicts the link between a person's budget and the higher problems of his or her life as accurately as Balzac.

Yet, in the Switzerland that Keller describes, the power of money has not yet taken on those demonic forms manifest in the France of the *Comédie Humaine*. Accordingly, the emphasis in the description of people and of the link between people and their surroundings, is utterly different. The testing of a man, his education to prove himself in society, the proving of his own inner integrity: in Keller all this is directly and manifestly connected with his economic situation. Yet in a traditional Swiss democracy Keller is able to 'put virtue on the agenda' and to lay the main stress on the differences between various people's moral reactions to similar economic dangers and enticements. The humanism of Goethe's world descends here into the depths of democratic popular life; the dangers, in Goethe's world purely moral and ideological, are shown here directly in the midst of the struggles of life, without thereby losing any of their moral point or ideological stature.

Keller's novel is thus to be placed between the unique and unrepeatable type of novel created by Goethe and the modern social novel of Balzac, Stendhal or Dickens. The difference one immediately notices between *Green Henry* and the modern social novel is the cheerfulness of the world Keller depicts. This arises not as a result of ignoring the dark sides of life: Henry Lee's life is in constant danger of going off the rails morally or materially. The dangers to which he is exposed are portrayed with great vividness and are always taken to their logical conclusion both morally and ideologically. Nevertheless, the hero's youth is inimitable, almost fairy tale-like in its beauty, and even the melancholy of his later failure and defeat remains humorously human; the colours Keller uses are never marred by prosaic hardness or the gloominess of despair, remaining instead always bright and poetic.

This is not Keller's 'personal touch' compared with Balzac or Dickens, nor is it a case of his 'optimism' in contrast to their 'pessimism'. Naturally, in all this the personality of the author is decisive. However, this personality is not something abstract, timeless, and purely psychological, but is based in Keller's case on the bourgeoisie of free Swiss democracy, where tradition was still intact; in the case of Balzac and Dickens it arises from the isolation of the honest artist, indeed of the honest person as such in the age of nascent capitalism.

The prosaic quality of capitalist life atomizes human beings economically. They regard the factually existing, often highly complex economic forces which determine their fate as anonymous, intangible and incomprehensible. This necessarily double-sided appearance of capitalist life leads to their inner solitude, which is so movingly portrayed by the great epic writers of capitalist prose. Even childhood is deeply invaded by this solitude. One encounters in world literature few more moving pictures of loneliness, of human isolation, than the chapters in Dickens's *Old Curiosity Shop* in which Little Nell waits alone at night for the return of her grandfather.

This loneliness, this isolation of humans from other humans, is unknown to Keller's world. Everything his hero experiences is, however sad or humiliating, experienced in some kind of community, even though it is often a problematical one. The reasons are again of a social nature. This is clearly understandable in the case of the depiction of youth in Switzerland. But the picture of Germany also exhibits certain traits of primitive development. It is no coincidence that Keller, who completed his novel in Berlin, sets the action only in Southern Germany, in a cosily provincial, petty bourgeois, artistic Munich and in the Count's castle. We also experience the organic community of artists, and later that of the artisans and workers in Munich, as well as the spontaneous alliance of true intellectuals in the Count's castle. Admittedly, threatening shadows gather everywhere: improper and unscrupulous rivalry, deception, ambition. But the element spanning all this is still the community, despite the growing dangers to its existence.

It is surely no coincidence, but rather highly characteristic of Keller's conception of democracy, that not one of the three artists whose community forms the centre of events in Munich is a German. The main hero is Swiss, Lys is Dutch and Erikson a Scandinavian; all of them originate not from politically backward, pre-revolutionary Germany, but from the neighbouring, democratic countries.

In the fate of these three, Keller depicts the conflicts inherent in an artistic calling, the contradictions of modern art, the opposition between art and life. In the presentation and processing of this problem Keller is again to be sited socio-historically between the attitude of *Wilhelm Meister* and that of *The Unknown Masterpiece* and others of Balzac's works. In the world of *Wilhelm Meister* the problematics of art itself are not yet broached. The fate of the hero's artistic career is but the failure of a dilettante. Goethe touches on the problematics of being an artist only in the secondary figures, namely Serlo and Aurelie. Balzac, by contrast, already portrays the tragic contradictions of modern art, not only in the ever deeper split between art and life under capitalism, not only its reflection in the fact that the artist's relationship to life necessarily becomes inhuman, but also in the tragic dialectics of modern art itself.

Besides the eager beavers, imposters and time-servers, Keller portrays nothing but failed artists. He also shows how certain dangerous trends in modern art necessarily result from living the life of an artist. Thus in the case of Erikson, an almost mindless naturalist routine evolves, while, especially in the case of the hero himself, it is a contemplative way of painting that increasingly loses all sensuousness. It is interesting that Keller – at that time undoubtedly with humorous exaggeration – leads his hero in the last, desperate phase of the latter's artistic activity down a path that borders on the 'abstract', 'non-representational' painting that was to rule the day many decades later.

The problematics of art and life is given a very interesting and idiosyncratic new twist in the three artists. (The failure of Römer, the teacher of Henry Lee's youth, and who has since gone mad, already contains, like a prelude, the same motif.) These three artists are, each in his own way, too rich in human terms to be fulfilled by the artistic activity open to and achievable by him. Each of them thus goes to the full extent of his own limitations, experiences a more or less deeply felt complex of problems and then gives up his artistic work in order to return to practical life.

This conflict occurs simply, indeed almost vapidly with respect to Erikson, who becomes a prosperous merchant. Lys, who later dedicates himself to an activity on behalf of society, as does Henry, forms a transition of sorts, whereby Keller very carefully expresses the differences of social ancestry and material situation in terms of artistic and human psychology. Culturally, Lys is much more developed than Henry. As a rich man he is not only able to look back on a more straightforward and thus more unproblematical development as an artist than the often erring plebeian dilettante, but also in ideological terms radically shakes off his religious prejudices at an earlier date. During the time they spend together in Munich, Lys already propounds a convinced atheism, whereas Henry still appears as a defender of God, linking religious belief to morality.

Keller shows, however, how Henry's laboriously acquired education is deeper and more valuable than the blasé superiority of the forever carefree rich, which verges on decadence. Lys is also a 'contemplative painter', yet on the basis of a technically highly-developed art. He is less sharply, less painfully aware than Henry of the problematic nature of his activity, the cul-de-sac in which he finds himself. His about-turn, his re-entry into professional life is therefore more sudden, effortless and abrupt, and has a less profound human basis than that of Henry, the son of a plebeian family. Here, as everywhere, Keller paints a very fine picture of the dialectical interaction of material possibilities and psychology. The about-turn of the two prosperous artists, Erikson and Lys, is not determined by external compulsion; on the other hand, it is more spontaneous, less profound and less ideologically grounded than in the case of Henry.

Henry's failure is a direct consequence of economic factors. However, one can see in his last artistic phase that he has gone to the limit of what is available to him, that he expresses a human richness that can in no way be given voice in his art. If he now turns, as a result of the inner necessity of his development, to a study of human beings, then he can only do so on a temporary and fragmentary basis by selling all his possessions at a ridiculously low price. The period of transition is bound to come to a rapid end, and Henry ends his career as an artist by painting flagpoles and being paid at a meagre piece rate.

All of this is authentic and true to life. If, however, Keller had stopped at this point, he would have written one of the many sentimental modern stories in which the brutality of unfavourable circumstances destroys an aspiring artist. Instead, despite this strong emphasis on the power of economic circumstance, Keller perceives Henry's failure as an inner, human tragedy. As a result, Keller has Henry, who has in the meantime worked as an artisan, arrive at the Count's castle on his arduous tramp back towards his mother country. When it emerges that the Count, a follower of Feuerbach and an art lover, has acquired Henry's works from a junk salesman, Henry's giving up of art becomes a topic of conversation between the two men. Henry stresses the similarities between his and his colleagues' turning away from art without being able to convince his older friend; indeed, the latter emphasizes that Henry, given his lack of formal artistic training, could not possibly know, as the others did, what his artistic limits were. Since Henry determinedly abides by his decision to give up work as an artist, stating as a reason that he 'had reached a modest zenith' and even 'in more favourable circumstances I should at most become a dilettante academician', the Count challenges him to take one last test:

You must not run away so ignominiously, but part with dignity from your youthful calling. . . Even what we renounce, we must renounce of our own free will, not like the fox with the grapes![45]

Henry does in fact stay in the castle and paints his last two pictures. During his stay there he has fought his way through to accepting the Feuerbachian view of the world and, in conversation with Dorothea, the Count's foster-daughter, a foundling, has matured fully as a human being; he now freely gives up the artistic leanings of his youth. Psychologically and physically liberated, he returns to political activity in his home country. What in the case of Lys was half due to the whim of a bored rentier is here the ripe fruit of a long and honest struggle.

Keller's sympathies lie, here as ever, with the plebeians; his feelings are, however, by no means one-sided or indiscriminate and do imply criticism. Lys's cultural superiority is acknowledged with the cool detachment of an impartial observer; yet there are many other cases in which Keller gives a humorous or serious description of the ineluctable interaction of higher and lower social strata. It is precisely this many-sided equilibrium that expresses Keller's truly democratic spirit: he feels so secure in this social being and consciousness that he can allow himself the most relentless criticism and self-criticism. He is far removed from the ascetic or provincial narrow-mindedness of 'pure' plebeian writers. Thus, in the castle, a small, humorous scene involves the hero being put to shame. Dorothea, the Count's foster-daughter, has read Henry's autobiography in which he prides himself on his bourgeois ancestry. She arranges a formal meal for the small company in the knight's hall, and appears dressed up as a count's lady. When, in the course of the luncheon, the conversation turns to Henry's ancestors, he plays his trump card with the pride of a burgher vis-à-vis the aristocracy, only to find, to everyone else's amusement, that the 'Count's daughter', being a foundling, has no ancestors at all. What Schiller praised in Goethe's *Wilhelm Meister*, namely that all of the descriptions of human relationships portrayed the invalidity of differences in social standing, is also the underlying characteristic of Keller's portrayal of human relations. The plot, the situations and the figures owe their creation to a truly democratic spirit.

This emphasis on balance in the novel also applies to the political-ideological relations between Switzerland and Germany. We have repeatedly indicated that it is only in Germany that Henry Lee is able to attain full ideological maturity, in the final instance as a result of his taking up the most advanced intellectual stance possible in pre-revolutionary Germany, namely his adherence to Ludwig Feuerbach's philosophy. The German section of the novel eradicates all trace of narrow provincialism in Henry. On the other hand, strong emphasis is laid on the superiority of the old traditions of Swiss democracy compared with the monarchical petty-princedoms of Germany. Again, this permeates the concrete conditions of life, changing the relations between people, and is not just described abstractly. The Count, as a Feuerbachian, is not just Henry Lee's saviour in a desperate material situation, but also his last moral and ideological educator; the Count's superiority is that of a mature, balanced person, not just the superficial cultured refinement of a Lys. Nevertheless, once Henry has been saved, and, having regained his psychological and material stability, wishes to head for home, the superiority of the Swiss democrat over the German pre-revolutionary subject 'suddenly' emerges strongly as they bid each other farewell.

I had never seen this man, ordinarily so composed, so much excited; the mere notion that I was going directly into a republic and was going to take part in its public life, appeared to awaken in him kindred ideas and revive old sores.[46]

This ever-present social element in the relations between human beings, in their psychology, morality and world-view, in their feelings, experiences, thought and action transcends the isolation of the individual known to us from modern novels; it transforms all actions, even the most isolated ruminations, into social events.

This way of viewing the world arises from Keller's firm roots in Swiss democracy and makes possible the naïve epic grandeur of his descriptive narrative, which in the nineteenth century only the work of Leo Tolstoy also exhibited.

This epic greatness is attributable to Keller's close links with the still surviving traditions of Swiss democracy. As a result, he is never forced into sentimental exaggeration or its embellishment of events; rather he reveals and then portrays the natural greatness of the popular movements themselves. He is able to describe all the bucolic practicality, and the narrow-minded limitations of his characters with a remorseless realistic humour, yet without stripping the whole story of its plebeian greatness; indeed, the epic magnificence arises precisely because this rustic, practical, down-to-earth background repeatedly becomes visible.

Thus, the peasant who acts the part of Arnold Melchtal at the Tell Festival finds the time to sell an ox on his way to the Oath on the Rütli; and similarly, the person playing the part of Tell takes advantage of the interval between the apple being pierced and Gessler being killed to persuade the governor of the province that the proposed country road simply must go right past his inn. It is this naïvely great narrative conception that causes such events to shed their purely descriptive character and become truly dramatic elements of the epic action. One need only think of the turning-point which the Tell Festival signifies in the development of Henry Lee's twofold love – for Anna and Judith; or of the influence Henry's first solemn yet playful military exercise has on the development of his renowned wasteful inclinations and on the first moral *faux pas* that then follows; or of young Henry's last meeting with Judith, after he has separated from her following Anna's death: the coach carrying the emigrants goes past with Judith in it while he is marching on the parade ground, and he is granted just one glimpse before the command to 'about turn' resounds. When he again looks towards the road Judith has vanished without trace.

Popular life has this vivacity and greatness in Keller's work because for him the people was never an abstract 'mass' to which the isolated individual is juxtaposed in some way, be it condescendingly, arrogantly or full of longing. The people here consists of vivid, individually depicted personalities, and the great festive events, in which the 'totality of objects' can be expressed, are organic, naturally evolving associations of such individuals. For this reason, the widest variety of personal interests converge in such events and, by means of the naïvely spontaneous interaction of personal and social interests, by means of the belief that a healthy public interest will ultimately prevail, a picture of traditional democracy emerges that is truly full of life. The driving force of what are often egotistical personal interests is not only depicted true to life, but also provides the basis for the narrative form: it transforms the greatest and most graphic portraits of popular life into moving, individual epic actions.

This authorial world-view animates and makes sensuous every single narrated moment. And from it evolves Keller's specific, truly epic writing: the specific innate beauty in every person and situation shines forth from it. Keller never creates beauty by the use of subjective mood, lyricism or desire. His writing liberates the objects, excavates their true essence; and the specific, otherwise concealed beauty of every individual entity, be it person, landscape or event, is made to appear in this essence. In Keller's work every human being is given a beauty specific to him or her: the ailing tenderness and frailty of Anna and Agnes just as much as the womanly maturity of Rosalie or Judith, or Dorothea's girlish, firm but flexible, witty superiority as well as the quiet but resilient, often narrow heroism of the mother. Revealing the essence of a person is in Keller's books a revelation of beauty; he shows the deep-seated wealth of life, in which we see that the essence of real people is more genuine and vivid than their outward appearance.

This material and this spirit is the source of the beauty of the Swiss world of Keller's novellas, which he creates after completing the first version of his great novel. The feeling of inner, social invulnerability of a traditional democracy forms the basis of both.

Admittedly, the more popular life is in reality disrupted by the threats to traditional democracy posed by nascent capitalism, the more aware of these dangers Keller becomes. For Keller, the possibilities of a purely Swiss novel, of attempts to condense Swiss reality into one great, complete narrative panorama, are closely connected with this problem. They thus include for him his coming to terms with the intrusion of capitalism, with the social, human and moral consequences of the gradual rise of capitalism in Switzerland. Here, Keller found himself in an insoluble dilemma, in a position of tragic resignation. As a true realist he was not able to shut his eyes to anything. At every juncture where he describes this capitalist development, he does so with ruthless realism.

Yet by so doing he himself destroys the very sources of the poetic enhancement of reality open to him. His world-view failed to provide him with an avenue for finding here the sources of a new, Shakespeareanizing poetics of reality such as Balzac and Dickens both achieved. The novella *The Lost Smile* is already problematical in many respects and is not equal to Keller's other stories. Keller himself felt this to be the case and wrote about it to F.T. Vischer:

You found the last of the Seldwyla inhabitants. . . to be too tendentious and provincial. I believe the main fault lies in the fact that the material is actually better suited to a small novel and cannot be adapted for a novella. That is why much had to be described in a deductive, summarizing manner, instead of being unravelled in anecdotal action; hence the tendentious, boring qualities. Incidentally, I believe that I should finally attempt a more serious portrait of modern culture. . .[47]

Martin Salander, Keller's last novel, written in his old age, does indeed attempt to give an overall picture of Switzerland's capitalist transformation. Unfortunately, the author's self-criticism cited above largely applies here too. Keller's great artistry is to be seen only in a few superbly-drawn characters, particularly that of Marie Salander. The narrative is otherwise on the whole dry and surprisingly sketchy for Keller; the polemic against the moral degeneration caused by capitalism remains a caricature, without ever attaining the status of truly artistic satirical distortion; the utopia is placed in dry, didactic and therefore unconvincing opposition to real life.

For this reason, Keller's greatest narrative strength, the 'totality of objects', does not come to the fore. Keller is forced to attempt to deal in his narrative with the capitalist destruction of the traditional roots of democratic popular life. The public marriage celebrations, for example, embody just such an attempt to portray the distortions to which life has subjected the declining old society within a new form of narrative prose, within a novel-like, paradoxical 'totality of objects'. This endeavour was doomed to failure because Keller's talents as a writer were inextricably bound up with the dream of a harmonious, old-style democracy, because he was no longer able to perceive the new, positive social forces that would generate a new popular life out of the destruction of the old. He at least made this attempt, whereas most of his German contemporaries fled to the 'intimacy' to be found behind the closed doors of a merely private life.

It was Maxim Gorky who was to overcome these new problems of narrative writing. In Gorky's work all the trappings, customs and morals of Old Russia are laid out before us in stirringly vivid pictures as they had been in Tolstoy's writing and as we have seen in Gottfried Keller's descriptions of Switzerland. Whereas the broad narrative presentation of birth and death, marriage, gatherings of the nobility and convivial amusement, of war and peace, etc., were an artifice for Tolstoy, by means of which he was able to attain an almost Homeric stature in terms of epic calmness and harmony, their function is almost the complete opposite in Gorky's texts. The revolutionary battle against the Czars, feudal remnants and a strengthening 'Asiatic' capitalism, and the birth pains of the new world of socialism all transform the portrait of Old Russia into that of a majestic, eery dance of death. Gorky foregrounds the customs and morals of the old, decaying world precisely because he has recognized the full profundity and the ultimately progressive nature of this process of dissolution; and by describing this world's transformation into soulless, ossified routines, cunning hypocrisy and its degeneration into barbarism, he shows the extent to which the whole of popular life is undermined by the capitalist destruction of a seemingly unmoved and allegedly immobile Old Russia.

Here, Gorky discovers a new form of epic monumentality, a completely new version of the 'totality of objects', because he is able to identify the birth pains of the new in the dissolution of the old. It was impossible for Keller to have such an insight. His greatness and his limits are to be seen in the fact that he – and he alone in his day – dared to tackle this problem, and that he necessarily had to fail in his attempts to overcome it.

Keller the great narrative writer thus had to restrict himself in resignation to the relatively minor form of the novella in order to redeem himself as an artist. Free of Romantic stylization, or from a derivative recycling of old forms, Keller created a unique fairy-tale world within modern bourgeois reality, a world which, like that of the ancient fairy tales, is profoundly realistic and true in every individual trait of humanity shown and yet describes the way in which the real desires of the best people in this reality find convincing, beautiful fulfilment.

VII
HUMANISM

We have seen that his revival of an ancient literary form, and his roots in a traditional democracy never turn Keller into a proponent of a 'return to nature', which would both reduce literary and cultural development to primitive forms and play the primitive and the old against the new. In the instances where his utopian conception of Swiss democracy draws its power and objectivity from particular characteristics of the past, this signifies for his work only that the highest human and cultural opportunities for a further development of traditional democracy appear as the depicted reality of individual lives. This can in artistic terms be reconciled – precisely by virtue of the novella's form – with an unabashed and remorseless realism. This realism is of major significance for the long-term future, in that the people portrayed stand before us as true examples of life in a democracy, and in that the real cultural, human traits of each and every democracy take on an ideal form before our eyes without losing their realism, in the Shakespearean sense. The contrast between Keller and Gotthelf, his only major Swiss precursor, is not just of a political nature. Gotthelf describes truly primitive rural conditions, and does so in terms of an ideology which idealizes the backwardness of the peasantry. As Keller demonstrates, this results in an often tendentious distortion of Swiss reality, in a tendentious slandering of progress and democracy. Keller nonetheless shows that Gotthelf achieved an incomparably epic monumentality in the description of primitive conditions.

Yet, for all his admiration for the epic stature of the artistically successful elements in Gotthelf, Keller does not continue in the latter's tradition. He cannot do so – for the simple reason that emotionally he no longer has access to the assumptions of Gotthelf's world, because for him it represents something that will always remain in the past. This is seen in Keller's treatment of love, a quality not yet present in Gotthelf's world. Admiringly, and with great artistic perception, Keller emphasizes how the absence of individual love in Gotthelf's works contributes to the monumentalization of his descriptive technique.

Keller, however, remains here the onlooker and admirer of a past epoch. The pupil of Goethe and Feuerbach, the democratic humanist who places himself at the service of the all-round development of humankind, has no use for Gotthelf's world and such a world-view. As a writer, Keller moves in Goethe's footsteps, not Gotthelf's. This profound connection between Goethe and Keller has often been recognized and stressed. However, it rests not on the superficial, formal similarities normally referred to. Naturally, *Wilhelm Meister* and *Dichtung und Wahrheit* exerted a certain influence on the form of *Green Henry*. But precisely here the contrast between the ages in question and the necessary stances adopted by the two authors is more pronounced and substantial than their similarity. The link between Goethe and Keller as authors comes to light far more in the characters they portray, in their way of organically fusing remorseless loyalty to the truth with a profound, steadfast humanism.

Dobrolyubov, the great Russian critic, pointed out in his reviews of the novels of Goncharov and Turgenev that the female figures were in every human respect on a higher plane than their male counterparts, that they were more developed, exhibited greater moral maturity and were more resolute in their actions; that the men were at most intellectually and culturally superior, in other words in terms of education. Dobrolyubov has astutely uncovered an essential element in a certain stage of nineteenth century literary development. Needless to say, such a widespread tendency, one that emerges in the works of authors of different social and artistic persuasions irrespective of the general literary influence upon them, has deep-rooted social reasons. Dobrolyubov uncovered the specific causes of this literary phenomenon in the Russia of his day.

What interests us in this context is the German stage of development in this respect. It commences in Germany with Goethe, or, to be more precise, with his work in the Weimar period, and reaches its clearest expression after the French Revolution. In the works of the youthful Goethe of the Storm and Stress period or even the beginning of his time in Weimar, during which he produced more mature versions of his early sketches, the figures of Götz, Werther, Egmont or Faust, owing to the depth of their social and human tragedy, overshadow the superbly depicted women who appear at their side. Iphigenia is the real turning-point. And this change in the relative merits of his men and women is especially discernible when Goethe, above all as a narrator, enters into concrete and practical debate with bourgeois society. One need only compare Dorothea with Hermann (in *Hermann and Dorothea*), Natalie and Philine with Wilhelm Meister, and Ottilie and Charlotte with Eduard (in *Elective Affinities*).

This change in Goethe's production is connected biographically speaking with the great disappointment of Weimar. In contrast to bourgeois literary history's usual interpretation of this disappointment, Franz Mehring provides an astute analysis of its nature and social content: it has much less to do with the tragedy of his love for Charlotte Stein than with the fact that Goethe the Enlightener went to Weimar in order to put into practice some of his socio-humanist

ideals in this small state if nowhere else, but was forced, after fierce
internal turmoil, to admit that a simple person – even if he was
Goethe – could do nothing in the face of the absolutism of the
German petty princedoms, even given a relatively 'enlightened' and
benevolent figure such as Duke Karl August.

Even though his youthful hopes were dashed, Goethe naturally
never completely gave up the idea of exerting a practical influence
on the society of his day, of introducing the ideals of humanism into
the life of bourgeois society. This problem repeatedly crops up in
his work, in various forms and with a different dosage of either hope
or resignation in each case, but his writings are now no longer conceivable without an element of resignation. The continuation of
Wilhelm Meister even bears the subtitle *Die Entsagenden*[48] and here
this renunciation means that Goethe had already acknowledged the
function of the capitalist division of labour, namely its dismembering of the all-round development of personality, to be a given fact,
to be the practical foundation of civilization in his time. And
Goethe, who just like his great contemporary Hegel – so closely
related to him in many respects – firmly championed the viewpoint
that ideal and reality, humanism and bourgeois society should
be 'reconciled', took this insight very seriously and drew human,
ideological and artistic conclusions from it.

Admittedly, the conclusions he drew with respect to his writing –
and it is this which concerns us here – were extremely contradictory.
One of these contradictions is the change of emphasis in the human
significance attached to the male and female characters. For such
time as the young Goethe was still involved in a fierce struggle
against the feudal-absolutist society, and as long as his combative
humanism was directed towards describing the latter's raw power
of human destruction, the male heroes in this humanist revolt are
imbued with that catastrophe-laden, fascinating glory, that
humanly tragic greatness, by means of which they tower over their
just as perfectly portrayed female counterparts. However, as soon as
the resigned 'reconciliation' with bourgeois society had become the
key to Goethe's realism, the contradiction of capitalist society –
namely that its development fostered individuality and necessarily
placed the demand for all-round ability on the agenda in practical
terms, on the one hand, while simultaneously, with the same socio-

economic necessity, destroying this individuality, crippling it, dismembering it on the other – had to predominate in the portrayal of human character.

Henceforth it is only in those occasional interstices that arise by curious combinations of personal and social fortune – in epicurean intercosmic spaces, intermediate realms of capitalist society as it were – that a relatively free and many-sided development of human personality is possible. Goethe himself repeatedly created such intermediate realms for himself; he was, however, far too critical, self-critical and clear-sighted as to overestimate the coincidental elements in his personal existence, elements that could not be generalized in social terms. He very clearly saw the impenetrable barrier capitalist society posed externally and internally to an all-round development of individuality as soon as he endeavoured to transform this necessary humanist ideal, which arose from within this society itself, into social activity. In the work of the more mature Goethe, the shift of emphasis in the human significance attached to his male and female figures results from a profound realistic understanding of this contradiction.

These contradictions inherent in capitalist society are, of course, also the basis for the socially necessary existence led by women. The beginnings of bourgeois society restrict their lives and their sphere of influence to the house and the family, and there is no need to comment on the fact that this amounts to a form of oppression, stunting the development of their personalities. Late nineteenth-century literature – George Sand, Hebbel and Ibsen spring to mind – depict this revolt of human personality in the case of women. For this, however, a higher stage in the development of bourgeois society is necessary than existed in the Germany of Goethe's day.

The economic underdevelopment of German capitalism at the time, combined with the blossoming of the humanist culture of the day, thus provided a few women, given particularly favourable circumstances, with such intermediate realms in which a many-sided and humanly self-confident development of personality was possible. Admittedly, the restriction of social relations to the relationship between individual people generally resulted in petty bourgeois blinkeredness, but, with the aid of a particularly happy social and personal constellation, it could sometimes lead to the interpersonal immediacy of true humanism, to a direct realization of the humanist ideals on a small scale in the relationship between individuals. Schiller's letters on aesthetic education and the conclusion of *Wilhelm Meister* as well as the illusions of the first period of Romanticism demonstrate how great the hopes of this age were with respect to these sociable intermediate realms – even though they were doomed to failure as a general phenomenon.

The immediate humanism exhibited by such women signifies that they instinctively see through fetishization, and spontaneously retranslate all social relations objectified by capitalism back into relations between human beings. The lives of women who can develop in such intercosmic spaces constitute a yardstick for measuring the human possibilities inherent in the development of bourgeois society, of the possibilities which that society constantly suppresses and cripples on a mass scale.

We are therefore clearly dealing here with a social phenomenon, albeit one that is transient and occurs only in isolated cases, and not simply with an artistic, biographical or personal idiosyncrasy of Goethe. The exceptional significance attained by women at this time, women such as Caroline von Günderode, Bettina von Arnim or Rahel Varnhagen who did not write at all, or if they did, then only sporadically and dilettantishly – a significance they owe almost exclusively to this shift in the relative weighting between the sexes – demonstrates quite transparently the general social character of this development in the Germany of the time.

Goethe's originality vis-à-vis the major female figures in past literature – including those of Shakespeare – is therefore not a question of superior or inferior writing skill, but rather a problem of socio-cultural development. Neither are we drawing an aesthetic comparison between the two authors if we now consider Gottfried Keller as having continued and further developed Goethe in this respect. Nevertheless, the fact that Keller creates quite original and significant realistic figures is the indispensable precondition for their being compared in the first place.

Keller's female characters – Judith, Dorothea, Lucie, Figura Leu and Marie Salander – continue the socio-human tradition of Goethe's portrayal of women. However, they live at a different stage of social development, in different times, in a different country, in a differently structured democratic society. As a result, they are more robust, down-to-earth and plebeian, even when they originate from a higher social stratum. Because in them human culture, the culture of emotions and of relations to other people, the culture of moral refinement and security is just as highly developed as it is in Goethe's female figures, these women accomplish a unique synthesis of the two traditions to be observed in Goethe's portrayal of humanly outstanding women.

On the one hand, Goethe portrayed women of the common people: Klärchen, Gretchen, Dorothea, Philine. The fact that the high human and moral qualities of these women could not find fulfilment on a broad scale is attributable to the nature of the age in which Goethe lived and his relationship to it. Klärchen's heroism (in *Egmont*) is expressed in her tragic self-sacrificing death; Dorothea's intelligent courage is produced by great world-historical events and once this force has manifested itself it blends back once again into everyday bourgeois life. By imposing these limitations, Goethe expresses a profound democratic wisdom: he shows that Klärchen and Dorothea are not exceptions among the people; that, on the contrary, the potential for such a simple heroism lies slumbering in very many women among the people, waiting for the great event that will awaken it and bring it forth in reality. (Walter Scott's Jeanie Deans in *The Heart of Midlothian* is the magnificent continuation of this democratic conception of the greatness of women.)

On the other hand, the women whose human essence Goethe develops and expands on a wide scale, Natalie and Ottilie, and also the princess in *Torquato Tasso*, have – on account of their potential for development in a socially higher stratum – also been endowed with particular characteristics that allow their human outline, indeed at times their social origin, to recede into the background. Only in the case of Iphigenia does Goethe succeed in creating an example of such unequalled female-human stature and authenticity, such a simple person who is the living, walking yardstick for all human action, thought and feeling. Iphigenia is to human relations what ancient logic said of truth, namely *index sui et falsi* (the measure of itself and of what is false). In order to create such a figure, Goethe had to leave the immediate social reality of his day far behind him, had to find a poetically heightened dramatic form of his own to depict this ideal image as something that really existed, a form that liberated the inspired introspection of Racine's dramas from all traces of historically determined origin. This social affinity between the plays of Goethe and Racine is quite palpable in *Torquato Tasso*, which is aesthetically similar to *Iphigenia*.

A superficial observer might find it strange that Keller, the robust and democratic realist, should be a great admirer of *tragédie classique* and even defended it against Lessing's criticism. In his estimation of Racine, whom he placed alongside Shakespeare, Keller concurs with Pushkin. Keller admires the French for the majesty of their ethical convictions, for their refined and profoundly human portrayal of characters and conflicts, for their endeavours to reduce the conflicts to their purest and simplest form; he believes they constituted a distinct form of dramatic realism.

To preempt our findings, Keller returns Iphigenia to earth, to immediate social reality, transforms her into a sensuously self-confident inhabitant of a traditional democratic society who is full of the joy of life. His major female figures exhibit – in the full breadth of human development, under the very down-to-earth relations of bourgeois everyday life, relations shot through with petty and comical traits – an apparently almost natural, seemingly effortless moral superiority, a joyful, quiet and yet iron resilience. These qualities are merely intimated in Goethe's plebeian female characters, and only emerge explosively in the face of catastrophe, or, in the case of *Iphigenia*, require an ethereal, extremely unreal atmosphere. Keller's female figures repeatedly fulfil this role accorded to Iphigenia: by virtue of their relations to the women, simply by coming into human contact with them, the men are forced to shed their one-sidedness, their inclination to individualistic eccentricity, their philistine ossification, allowing the decency, diligence, humanness and moral integrity that slumbers within them to unfold and blossom forth. Thus, in *Green Henry*, the protagonist's moral-religious prejudices are 'suddenly' abandoned once he comes into closer contact with Dorothea. Thus, through human contact with Lucie, Reinhart rids himself of the cloak of naïvely pedantic self-opinionation culled from books, the cloak of conventional, masculine superiority, and in the joy of his effortless liberation into a broader and more genuine humanness which he experiences thanks to her, he refers to his life prior to meeting her as 'ante lucem', before dawn.

This simple power, this source of light and warmth, is most intensively and entrancingly portrayed in the plebeian figure of Judith. She loves Henry, many years her junior, with the full intensity of a mature woman. At the same time she is a pitiless judge of him. Henry has committed a grave human indecency against Römer, his old teacher, one that is all the worse because it was committed in a legally and socially utterly correct form. The religious and otherwise morally very decent schoolmaster, the father of Anna, the love of Henry's youth, does not go beyond etiquette, beyond moral-religious phrases when passing judgement on the case. Judith immediately sees through to the core of the issue: the moral baseness in Henry's action and Römer's demise as the direct consequence of it. Her first feeling is pity for Römer, the feeling that he could have been saved. (Römer has gone mad and has disappeared in a Paris madhouse.)

'O, if only I had been able to look after the poor man,' she cried, 'I should certainly have cured him! I would have laughed at him and flattered him, until he came to his senses again!'

Then she stood still, looked at me, and said: 'Are you aware, Henry, that you already have a human life upon your green soul?'[49]

One would have to reproduce the conversation between Judith and Henry in its entirety in order to shed a clear light on the moral accuracy of this female plebeian figure when judging complicated human problems. She understands with instinctive certainty the contradictory unity, namely that the baseness in Henry's action cannot be made good by so-called repentance, that he must nevertheless go on living and acting and yet that his act will simultaneously embody both past and present, and, though inexpiable, will nevertheless not disturb his further actions, his further development. And when Henry, relieved by his confession and absolution, seeks the path of least resistance, she says to him:

You are a thoroughly impertinent fellow and probably think that you need only confess your shameful thoughts in order to receive my absolution. It is true that only the limited and narrow-minded never wish to confess to something; but that does not mean that the others are able to make everything good again![50]

The fundamental emotion on which all this is based is a humorously self-assured, clear-sighted love. In openly professing her love, Judith reveals the same simple moral sovereignty that also characterizes Philine's love:

'And if I love you, what is it to you?' Judith said to Henry: 'As for the rest, unfortunately I don't feel that you have been in any way hateful to me; what would we be here for, if we didn't have to love human beings as they are?'[51]

These women are the most obvious representatives of real social humanity, of those preconditions on which Keller's dream of truly democratic popular life rest. It is of no relevance whether the influence Keller's female figures have on their male counterparts constitutes a direct or only an indirect education towards their playing a part in public life. Contact with them leads to the development of that moral integrity which Keller rightly held to be the human basis for life in a democracy.

The great and liberated humanness of such women frees Keller's democratic utopia of all traits of narrow-mindedness and philistinism. If 'virtue is placed on the agenda' in humanist-Jacobin terms, then virtue signifies a broad, many-sided and free development of true human capabilities, in sharp contrast to all philistinism. And, in just such a contrast, it is characteristic that the practical democratic actions of the men (in *The Banner of the Upright Seven*, *Martin Salander*, etc.) often exhibit such apprehensive, pedantic traits. This is no coincidence, for it is in precisely such details that Keller's remorseless realism comes to bear even when realizing his favourite ideas. By depicting such female figures Keller is able to paint his democratic utopia with the colours of true reality; by virtue of their portrayal his realism rises into the higher realms of 'Shakespeareanization'.

To reiterate: it is not Goethe's and Keller's artistry in portraying people that is being juxtaposed here, but rather a stage in the path of social development from Goethe's age to that of Keller. The links and contrasts between the two cast light on a large section of German cultural history: from the after-effects of the defeat of the French Revolution to the after-effects of the defeat of the democratic revolution in Germany. For this reason, the hopeful and joyous sun of the French Revolution shines over the idyll of *Hermann and Dorothea* and over the prose epic, *Wilhelm Meister's Apprentice-*

ship. The sunset of the democratic revolution after the defeat of 1848 illuminates Judith's renunciation, in *Green Henry*, in dark elegiac colours – the greatest plebeian female figure in German literature since Goethe.

Keller's greatness lies in the fact that, despite the unfavourable socio-political and artistic conditions of his age, he nevertheless forged an art of such stature, an art as far removed from limited provincialism as it is from a self-indulgence alien to the people. The problematics of the contents and form of this art, namely its underlying tenor of resignation, is part of Germany's fate, a scene from the – hitherto tragic – life history of German democracy.

1939

Wilhelm Raabe[*]

Fame means being thought of when
an entire people is mentioned

WILHELM RAABE

Raabe's fame and popularity have an unusual history and are of an
unusual nature.

Raabe's first book, *Die Chronik der Sperlingsgasse* (*The Chronicle of
Sparrow Alley*), was very successful.[1] The works that followed were
also widely read, in particular *Der Hungerpastor* (*The Hunger Pastor*).
Not until the end of the eighteen sixties did this popularity begin to
wane. In the literary criticism of this period we hardly find any mention of Raabe; Hebbel was alone in reviewing Raabe's first book
favourably. The official organ of what was at that time Germany's
liberal bourgeoisie, Gustav Freytag's *Grenzbote*, systematically ignored him. 'I just didn't suit those gentlemen,' Raabe was later to
say. After 1870 his works fell into almost complete obscurity. When
in the early eighteen seventies the young, still pre-socialist Franz
Mehring writes about the adverse effects of the German victories[2]
on literature, the only novelists he examines are Gutzkow,
Auerbach, Reuter, Freytag and Spielhagen. He makes passing reference to Raabe as one of the writers who have since been completely forgotten. Not until the beginning of the twentieth century,
around the time of Raabe's seventieth birthday, did a new, broad
wave of popularity set in.

The nature of his popularity corresponds to its history. Raabe
always had a 'congregation' of readers and admirers. However, it is
striking that among this 'congregation' there is not a single name
which stands out as belonging to a literary or intellectual figure who
could be considered to have made a really important contribution to
Germany's ideological development. This isolation is also matched
by the course of Raabe's life. In striking contrast to important contemporaries, he had no close relations with any exceptional figure of
his epoch. Compare this with Gottfried Keller's contact with

[*] First published in *Internationale Literatur*, nos 11/12, 1940.

Freiligrath, Feuerbach, Hettner, Varnhagen, Vischer and others.[3]
The literary currents of the eighteen eighties and nineties do begin
to include Raabe among the older writers regarded as having immediate contemporary significance, yet even these critics are secondary
figures in the Naturalist movement (Michael Georg Conrad, Julius
Hart, Leo Berg).[4] Not until the advent of 'Heimatkunst', a basically
provincial and retrogressive movement that developed out of Naturalism, did the real heralds of his fame take the stage, mostly literary
and political reactionaries like Adolf Bartels, Fritz Lienhard, later
the literary historian Josef Nadler and so on.[5]

Raabe himself strongly rejected 'Heimatkunst' – both its provincialism and its artistic methods, which developed from Naturalism
and perpetuated the latter's flaws in a more shallow form.

I do not want to be a 'Heimat' writer, I want to be a *German* writer!. . .
'Heimat' literature is just so much nonsense. If one is only capable of depicting what one has experienced and witnessed oneself, then one is a mere
copier, not a true writer. The writer must possess the ability to clothe his
ideas in the garments of any age and any country.

This contradiction is characteristic of Raabe and his literary position. Viewed in themselves, such statements are not so decisive:
the important point is not what Raabe thought of 'Heimatkunst',
but rather where his work stands – objectively – in relation to it.
Raabe's intensive personal conversations with his Brunswickian
dinner-party guests and congregation are not conclusive proof of
his agreement with their aesthetic and ideological views. Nor does
his faithful vote for the National Liberal Party, the party of German
capitalism, make him a fervent supporter of the Hohenzollern-
Bismarckian establishment of the Second Reich.

It is his works that count. Nonetheless, the contradictions described here give an intimation of the basic problem in Raabe's
personality and writing – a problem which must, of course, also be
clarified through an analysis of his works.

I

The truth of what he portrays in fiction is an expression of the essential Raabe. What he himself believes is only important to the extent
that it highlights this truth and its contradictions more clearly; in all

other respects it is merely one of the problems that need solving, but cannot be cited as evidence.

Raabe's works give a clear and unmistakable conception of Germany's fate in the nineteenth century which has nothing in common with 'Heimatkunst' and its reactionary ideological representatives.

For Raabe too, German history in the nineteenth century begins with the French Revolution. The period from its beginnings until the Wars of Liberation, including the failed wars of intervention and the Napoleonic occupation and dismemberment of Germany, is the first time – since the Reformation and the Peasant Wars – that the formation of the German nation took on real contours, even though these were extremely blurred and contradictory; and it is the first time that the aspiration for national unity took on mass character, even though this mass movement was quantitatively inadequate and its consciousness very unclear. From this time onwards, the unification of the German nation was once again back on the agenda of history. Nor did the founding of the Reich in 1871 put an end to discussions as to the correctness of the means and the outcome of that unification.

Where, then, does Raabe stand on the central questions of this historical development? In his works, which most of his admirers regard as nothing more than affectionately humorous vignettes of everyday life in Germany, they play a very important, indeed a decisive role. Only a brief summary of the history of the German people in the nineteenth century as Raabe *portrays* it provides us with a basis on which to paint his portrait as a writer.

What immediately strikes us is Raabe's strongly negative attitude to the German ancien régime and his open sympathy for the French Revolution. In a brilliant chapter of *Abu Telfan*[6] he describes a typical small residential palace, indeed *the* small residence, and uses it as the setting for a bitterly satirical history of German humiliation, behind which, in his eyes, the princes were the main driving force. Little sympathy is forthcoming, even for the 'legendary' figure of Frederick of Prussia. In a historical narrative set at the time of the French Revolution (*Die Gänse von Bützow – The Geese of Bützow*) he approvingly quotes Mirabeau's devastating critique of Old Prussia: 'Rotten before it was ripe.' In his first work, *The Chronicle of Sparrow*

Alley, we already find an old explorer telling of his experiences in the battles waged against the French Revolution: with sympathy for the Revolution, with contempt for the army of intervention. And in the last work he completed, the historical novel *Hastenbeck*, we are told of the execution of the Leaseholder General, Foullai, in the Revolution, which is treated as 'late recompense' for the barbaric pillaging of the German people by the armies of French absolutism.

It is therefore a complete mistake to interpret Raabe's little masterpiece of historical satire, *The Geese of Bützow*, as a parody of the French Revolution, as many of Raabe's admirers have done. The tone of this story is indeed that of parody. The writer's irony is, however, directed against the pettiness and philistinism of German conditions. The shadows of great figures from the French Revolution obviously appear only in order to emphasize Germany's wretched backwardness more acutely. And the ironic contrast is amplified by the fact that some of the story's heroes are, in terms of their level of 'Bildung', of formative education, on a par with contemporary German humanism. Quotations from the German Classics round off the ironic contrast between being and consciousness from a different aspect. As we have already mentioned, the twist in the story, the statement of the first-person narrator with whom Raabe sympathizes most, leaves no doubts as to his true intentions.

In no respect is this contradicted by Raabe's enthusiasm for the Wars of Liberation. Most of the heroes of the older generation described by the young Raabe have taken part in the Wars of Liberation. Indeed, this experience is for Raabe the very criterion of their human worth: the decent people became soldiers, while those lacking substance stayed at home. And in Raabe's case this verdict takes on a critical plebeian accent: the peasants, the petty bourgeoisie, the intelligentsia went to war, while the noble layabouts stayed at home and did not embark on their military careers until after the victories had been won.

These judgements are not coincidental, for they correspond to Raabe's assessment of Germany's overall situation and his passionate hatred of the feudal monarchism of the petty princedoms, compared to which the foreign occupation represented a considerable advance. Thus Raabe writes in *The Hunger Pastor* on the Jewish Tax in Old Germany:

The battle of Jena, which destroyed many a degrading and senseless institution, put an end to this scandal also; but in 1815, many a loving father of his country would gladly have re-established the good old custom.[7]

And as an old man, Raabe still emphasizes the great service done by King Jérôme of Westphalia in having done away with such atrocities from Germany's past. These convictions are most clearly shown – as is always the case with Raabe – by his plebeian figures. In *The Chronicle of Sparrow Alley* he describes a master joiner who welcomes the French occupation and behaves in a comradely way towards the French soldiers. His true convictions become evident when the soldiers answer his question as to how long they intend to remain in Germany with 'forever'. He replies: 'No, not forever. You may be here now, and the likes of us can be grateful to God for having sent you, but forever. . .' It is therefore only logical that a decade later he then sends his two sons off to the War of Liberation.

Both are killed, and in the church of their home town a large plaque of honour is erected bearing the names of the dead. At first the master-joiner views it with pride and fervour. Later he cannot bear to look at it, and when the church is burnt down he is only too relieved not to have the plaque in front of him any longer. When his wife tells this story at a much later date, one of the journeymen exclaims: 'I know why Master Karsten couldn't bear to look at the plaque any more!' and Raabe adds: 'In *this* knowledge lies the future.'

This knowledge – what the princes of Germany were able to do as a result of the weakness of the people – is at the heart of Raabe's portrayal of reaction. Raabe shows very graphically how, in the aftermath of victory, the heroes of 1814 became 'superfluous' and were even looked upon with suspicion. The best of them tried to swim against the tide, but in vain. Wassertreter (in *Abu Telfan*), a member of one of the *Burschenschaft* student societies, takes part in the Wartburg celebration of 1817 and is imprisoned; Felix Götz (in *The Hunger Pastor*) later fights under Bolivar in South America, in the Polish uprising of 1830 and finally comes to grief in exile in Paris. The less passionate ones (Rudolf Götz and his friends, the Knight of Glaubigern in *Der Schüdderump – The Rumbledump*) become people 'of another world', uprooted outcasts.

Given the above, it is remarkable and striking that the year 1848 does not play a decisive part in Raabe's view of Germany. This is not for any lack of sympathy: wherever the Revolution is mentioned (the American emigrants' memory of Robert Blum[8] in *Die Leute aus dem Walde* [*The People from the Forest*], the Austrian refugee in *Gutmann's Reisen* [*Gutmann's Travels*], etc.), we clearly see Raabe's positive stance towards it, so that the documentary evidence of statements in which Raabe takes sides with the 1848 Revolution is only of secondary interest. However, the 1848 Revolution is not an important element in Raabe's overall view of Germany as portrayed in his writings.

The reasons for this are directly biographical. At the time of the Revolution, Raabe was still very young, and nothing significant happened in Brunswick, where he was living at the time. His first major experience is the period of reaction in Berlin, to which his first work is a passionate response. However, the fact that he harks back to the Wars of Liberation and indeed even further back in time, to the old free towns of the Middle Ages, the fact that it is here that he seeks his model for the future rather than in the decidedly revolutionary democratic movement of 1848, sheds light on the central weaknesses of his entire ideology.

His predilection for Germany's former greatness is not remarkable in itself, least of all in the period of struggle for national unity, at a time when, following the unsuccessful attempts of 1815 and 1848 a different kind of national unity was going through new birth pains. Raabe follows a literary tradition that began with Goethe's *Götz von Berlichingen*. Admittedly, almost a full century has passed since then. Lassalle's tragedy *Franz von Sickingen* – which appeared at almost the same time as Raabe first began to write – is set in the same period, but the spirit behind it is already different, though less historically authentic than Goethe's subject. Raabe's poetic-historical sense of reality is stronger than Lassalle's, although he is of course politically much less radical. He does not invent a Sickingen who conflicts with reality, but returns to the real struggles of the German cities against emerging petty princedoms, which he judges and rejects much more accurately than Lassalle. The prelude to *Unseres Herrgotts Kanzlei* (*Our Lord God's Chancellory*) (1862) is the unsuccessful siege of the town of Brunswick by the Duke, and the story then goes on to describe the struggle of various princes under the leadership of Moritz of Saxony waged against the town of Magdeburg. The story is a heroic eulogy to the courage of the bourgeoisie and their military and political superiority over the princes and their mercenaries.

Raabe retains this enthusiasm for the rest of his life, and no doubt it does have a positive aspect. Raabe possesses very acute bourgeois, anti-aristocratic self-confidence and is always derisive in his rejection of the byzantinism of the German intelligentsia preceding and following the founding of the Reich. At an advanced age, when he too was overwhelmed with official honours (medals, honorary doctorates, honorary citizenships), he said:

The free communities of proud citizens that existed during the Middle Ages have always been my ideal. The Brunswickians of 1671, for example, who slammed the door in the face of their local duke. I would be twice as proud to have been an honorary citizen of that Brunswick as I am of today's honorary citizenship.

Important though this staunchness, this defence against capitulation and servility may have been, it does also have a negative side. Raabe constructs his politico-historical world-view around a utopia, around a dream of reviving the free medieval towns. It naturally follows that this utopian attitude makes him less impartial towards the distant past than he is towards the Wars of Liberation, in which he very carefully weighs up both sides. In his treatment of the medieval cities he does not criticize their local narrowness, their provincial politics, which were an important cause of the failure of the Peasant Uprisings. Apart from occasional episodes (*Lorenz Scheibenhart*, 1858), his view of the class nature of the medieval city regime is very vague. Whenever he depicts the contrast between the higher and lower orders, he does so only out of pity with the oppressed plebeian strata, on the assumption that this oppression also has a detrimental effect on the politics and morals of the ruling class. However, he adopts a disapproving stance vis-à-vis the active ideological and political representatives of the plebeians, such as the Mennonite preacher in the Magdeburg novella.

In this way Raabe blocks up his own exit from a social situation which he himself condemns. (Seen in this light, his attitude towards the French Revolution is no more than one of sympathy, of no concrete consequence for Germany's current reality.) Among the German plebeians Raabe recognizes at a very early date – again with strong sympathy – the decisive element for a possible transformation of Germany from below: the proletariat. In his youth he not only harbours sympathy for the oppressed, for their mutual solidarity, for the 'charity of the streets' by contrast to the egotism of the rich, but also has a premonition of their future power. Admittedly, this premonition is full of dread. In his early novel *Ein Frühling* (*One Springtime*) he speaks of three great universal disasters: the Flood, the Migration of Nations – and the future proletarian revolution.

Later this dread ceases. He welcomes the development of control from below through organized labour; but this is as far as his understanding goes.

More than this cannot be expected and certainly not demanded of him, bourgeois writer that he was. Dickens – on whom Raabe modelled many aspects of his literary social criticism – did not have a much higher level of understanding of the revolutionary side of the workers' movement, even though he lived in the midst of the Chartist uprisings and not, like the young Raabe, in industrially backward Germany. Whatever the reason for this lack of understanding, the fact remains that it cuts Raabe off from any perspective of democratic rebirth in Germany. As a fervent patriot he participates in all movements that further the cause of national unity (joining the small-German 'National Association'[9] in 1860), is inspired by the Prussian victories of 1866 and 1870/71 which bring national unity into being, and continues, as we have seen, to be a faithful electoral supporter of the National Liberal Party, the party of Bismarck and the Hohenzollerns.

However, an abyss which he was to remain incapable of bridging lies between these political convictions of Raabe's and his appraisal of life itself as expressed in his literary portrayal of it. The faithful supporter of the capitalist National Liberal Party criticizes with increasing harshness and bitterness the political, social and moral degradation which has resulted from the interaction between capitalism, which is gaining in momentum, and the Bismarck-Hohenzollern Reich.

This inner dichotomy very quickly becomes evident. As early as October 1870 he writes to a friend:

I shall not be writing a great novel of the age, as you constantly urge me to do. I am either too stupid or too clever for such an undertaking, and shall leave you to decide which – but only after 15 years have elapsed.

Nor was Raabe's attitude to change at a later date, if anything it merely became harsher and more embittered. In 1875 Raabe wrote *Der Horacker*, a story set in the time immediately following the great victories over Austria. Here the genuine people of Old Germany are contrasted with the type that has come to the fore and achieved leading positions as a result of the Prussian victories. Raabe has one of his positive figures say:

They're always going on about how the schoolmaster won the recent Battle of Königgrätz, but now I'm asking you . . . which kind of schoolmaster? The old one or the young one? From what I've heard, the answer can only be: the old one! . . . It remains to be seen what kind of a race of victors the new ones are bringing up with their

> Stand firm, firm, firm,
> See everything in the same terms.[10]

In a letter dating from the eighteen eighties Raabe expresses his satisfaction at having at the time of the great German victories written a story about the Schiller Centenary celebrations of 1859 in which he describes the struggle of the idealists against dull-witted philistinism. In the foreword to the second edition of *Christoph Pechlin* (the story dates from 1871/72, the foreword from 1890) he writes of the *Gründerperiode*, the Founding Years of the German Reich which followed the victories of 1870/71:

The wounds of the heroes had not yet healed over, the tears of the children, mothers, wives, fiancées and sisters had not yet dried, grass had not yet grown over the graves of the war dead. But peculiar things were already happening in Germany, such a short time after the terrible wars and the costly victories. It was as though a barrel of treacle had burst during or after a great fire and the rabble and the urchins had begun to slurp up the sweet syrup: in Germany the money bags had come undone and the coins were rolling in the streets too, where there were more than enough hands ready to grab for them. It almost seemed as though this was the greatest gain in world history which the newly united Fatherland could extract from its great successes.[11]

It is not difficult to guess whom Raabe means by 'rabble'. In the most subjective of his later novels (*Stopfkuchen*), he has the hero, who bears some of his own features, say:

Just one look into any courtroom, any classroom or pulpit, into any regional parliament or especially into the German Reichstag is enough to show you what our leading educated social classes have turned out to be like.[12]

However, this strongly plebeian bitterness no longer crystallizes in the form of an oppositional figure, nor in such open and strong criticism as was expressed of the petty princedoms in *Abu Telfan*. Above all, this is shown by the fact that the plots of the novels become increasingly private, that the effect of major public events on the fates of the characters becomes more episodic and less frequent than in earlier works. The dichotomy we have examined here is the real reason for Raabe's well-known 'pessimism', Schopenhauer's influence on which has been the subject of much superfluous writing. Although he did not understand, and was certainly not able to uncover the real cause of the unease which the present day inspired in him, Raabe himself did give a clear statement of the reason for his disillusionment. In 1909 he looks back on the foundation of the National Association and says: 'It was better in those days. In those days we had hope – and what do we have now?'

The utopia of the free medieval town community is merely an intellectual and literary symbol for the fact that Raabe could not find a plebeian-democratic current in his own Germany which he felt able to join; and that his social world-view stood in the way of his earnestly searching for one. This lack of clarity, this political and social hopelessness – made all the more confusing by his personal statements – has given the reactionaries the ostensible right to claim Raabe as one of their own.

II

The consequence of the dichotomy in Raabe's socio-historical world-view is that he is only able to conceive of individual solutions to social contradictions. In *Abu Telfan* we already find the statement: 'We are few against a million, we are defending a small realm against the whole wild world. . .' And this realm is defined as something 'the world knows nothing of'. The basic line of Raabe's work points towards uncovering educational paths by means of people and life's events – individual paths which are suited to preserving and bringing to fruition that genuine seed in people which makes them true human beings and which links their lives with the best traditions of Germany.

From the beginning, Raabe feels that this humanity, this Germanism is under threat from superior enemy forces. What he describes is from the start a defensive battle, the highest objective of which is no more than to find a niche in which the true forces of inner humanity can develop without distortion or interruption.

Raabe's heroes do not set out to conquer the world like the heroes of Goethe, Balzac or Stendhal. They only want to preserve their human integrity in the face of the impending dangers of modern life. In the end, therefore, their path always takes the form of 'renunciation', as was already the case, incidentally, in Goethe's later works. This 'renunciation' may under certain circumstances mean a retreat into a remote, peaceful corner, a resigned happiness in this kind of idyll, but very often it simply means inner self-preservation in the face of outward decline.

Who is the enemy? Because of Germany's historical situation, the outline is blurred in the case of the younger Raabe. It is on the one hand the old feudal-monarchist, reactionary, fragmented Germany, in which everyone with a true sense of decency and justice is bound to be treated with contempt as an 'undesirable'. On the other hand, it is capitalism, permeating these obsolescent social forms, partly destroying them and partly adapting to them. Raabe was doubtless unaware of Marx's verdict on German capitalism during this period, and even if he had been aware of it, he would doubtless not have understood it. Nonetheless, Raabe's view of Germany corresponds in many respects to Marxian definitions; for him too, the dead takes a grip on the living.

This similarity must of course be seen in very limited terms. Raabe sees only the outward symptoms of the economic process of Germany's advancing capitalism: the destruction of old towns and landscapes; proletarianization; emigration; former personal relationships between human beings replaced by fetishized, inhuman forms of capitalism based on naked exploitation and domination. In the period following 1870, the features of capitalism occur in Raabe's works with ever greater frequency and are ever more pronounced.

In addition to this, like his great idol Dickens, Raabe is less interested in the development of capitalism itself than in the spiritual and moral disfigurement it causes in exploiters and exploited alike. Whereas Balzac acquaints us with the precise financial physiognomy of Nucingen, Keller, du Tillet or Gobseck, Dickens – for example in the figure of Dombey – merely depicts the process of spiritual petrifaction and the prospect of a humanitarian way out. Raabe takes the same course.

Both Dickens and Raabe develop two different styles with which to portray the top and bottom layers of society respectively. The former is a caricaturist and satirist, the latter a humorist and sympathetic realist. Raabe of course differs from Dickens because of the substantial difference between Britain and Germany in the mid-nineteenth century. Dickens's caricatures are often of a standard comparable with the best of Hogarth or Daumier, and are – precisely because of their satirical power – very realistic. (The Circumlocution Office in *Little Dorrit*, legal practice in *Bleak House*, capitalist and political dealings in *Hard Times*, etc.) Images of such uncanny greatness are not to be found in Raabe. Only the description of the courts of the petty princedoms in *Abu Telfan* might be said to approach this level. However, the satirical hatred of the capitalist upper class does indeed run along the same lines as Dickens's. In his youthful novel, *The People from the Forest*, Raabe uses the style of a stock market report to describe a soirée with the moneyed aristocracy:

Before we go into detail, we can start by conveying the general impression in the language of the day, namely that of the stock market. We find the mood of the assembled guests generally stable, with the business of conversation being conducted along the firm lines of steady progress. Compliments and flattery were met in kind by eager takers offering compliments in return. There was a run on scandal; demand for local gossip, however, remained unchanged, though still popular. Politics fluctuating, brisk trading in music and the theatre, favourable climate for the latest novel; scientific questions and truth fared poorly. The older ladies were in very firm hands, whereas the younger ones fluctuated. The older gentlemen remained unchanged – retail trade. Quotations for the younger gentlemen were slack. After 2 o'clock the value of the conversation plummeted; we have not received any quotations from the final hour of business.[13]

Raabe's weakness, like that of Dickens, although almost always on an inferior level, lies in his portrayal of the inner life and external fate of capitalists. Raabe looks on the commercial adventures and inhumanities, the sexual excesses of high society, with the naïve, shocked romanticism of a German petty bourgeois.

Raabe is only able to produce a significant picture of this side of life when describing the inner tragedy of deformed humanity, how it is stifled and perverted by greed and the thirst for power. When describing the frigid emptiness of the lives of such people, for example the career of the lawyer Hahnenberg (*Drei Federn – Three Pens*), Raabe reaches Dickensian heights. And his strong, explicit and conscious partisanship for the bottom of society does not distort his vision when it comes to showing how greed and selfishness can pervert the character of members of the lower classes.

However, for Raabe, as for Dickens, all this merely serves as a basis, a background and a means of contrast. Raabe sees it as his main task to portray the ways in which people can be educated to lead lives befitting human beings, and the inner and outward nature of these lives. We are already acquainted with the general picture: it can only mean withdrawal from the great mechanisms of state and commerce. Resignation in lyrical or ironical, stoic or epicurean form, from motives which differ according to the social and ideological attitudes of different individuals. Human freedom in the society of his day consisted for Raabe in renouncing power, riches and prestige. 'In the end, power only turns us into greater slaves' (Hagenheim in *One Springtime*).

The nature of this renunciation is at once both very simple and very complicated. Simple, because the great veracity of Raabe's portrayal of his figures and their fates enables us to identify clearly the ultimate social reason behind their renunciation: helplessness, the weakness of the individual in the face of powerful social currents, the impotence of individual morality when confronted by the facts of German society under expanding capitalism.

This helplessness in Raabe, however, has a very interesting, diversified, intrinsic, moral and ideological dialectic, in which the main questions admittedly do not so much concern whether renunciation or struggle is the correct path to take, but rather the possibilities of revealing the internal how and why of such renunciation. Raabe's novels are full of vital, highly differentiated figures, whose lives, development, feelings, reflections, etc., present us with many variations of this dialectic. It would be a mistake to overlook the fact that, in the course of time, Raabe's response to the essential problems of his life underwent significant changes. These changes may not have had sufficient impact to alter the basic nature of his writing, but they are sufficient to make his world rich and complex.

This complexity is greatly enhanced by Raabe's realistic incisiveness. For although the ideologically decisive factor, indeed the final word of humanness necessarily lies more in reflection on events than in the events themselves, and although the figures are set off from each other and from their background more by their thoughts and feelings than by their deeds, every one of Raabe's stories has an interesting and often exciting plot.

Here too, Raabe follows in Dickens's footsteps. Yet Raabe is neither a disciple nor an imitator: rather the two writers are linked by an inner relationship based on their ultimate positions regarding humankind.

Raabe the moralist wants to put people to the test in his works, to expose their inner core and separate the core from the outer shell. The dialectical reflexes of such transformations, their morally positive and negative aspects, are provided in colourful form by Raabe's highly characteristic conversations, full of emotion, with humorous ambiguity, yet at the same time on a very high intellectual level and with refined ideological individualization. Yet the trigger is always *the deed*; a vital decision with which the figure is faced and in which – in the course of his or her interaction with the outside world – a move is made inwardly towards the person's own centre or away from it. In spite of the fact that feelings, reflexes, reflections, and the humorous ideological 'for and against' remain in the foreground, Raabe is obliged to develop a complicated, surprising plot forged from a chain of abrupt changes in order to realize his intentions in literary form.

Raabe's masterly treatment of chance, a quality he shares with many important narrators, results from this ideological and compositional treatment of the plot. With Raabe, though, this takes on a very specific note. On the one hand, chance plays an extremely important role in his whole conception of the world. In one of his novels we read that chance 'is, and always will be, our lord and master'. The more Raabe reduces social events to the personal destiny of particular individuals and the more socio-historical categories are reduced to general variations of background, the greater the role he has to assign to chance in the objective course of events.

This is also reflected in the feelings and opinions of his characters. The deep-seated experience of the insecurity and inexplicability of social life prevents Raabe from completely renouncing religion. He always retains a certain sense of religion, yet at the same time his aversion to it is unmistakably evident, despite being masked by humorous reservations. This humour leads him to anticipate something of the socio-psychological roots of modern bourgeois religiosity (including his own). In the novel *Kloster Lugau*, for example, he writes:

There is no such thing as a person who does not believe in some kind of God. Every man and woman clings onto one particular God right up until their very last breath on this earth, so full of trouble and strife: the *Deus ex machina!* Belief in His divine intervention in matters great and small is shared by the atheist, the pantheist, the deist and even the theist. It is to Him that everyone reaches out in a desperate situation, be it a nation in ruins, family life in decay, or a foundering ship about to go under. . . Yet if there is one God that seldom allows Himself to be claimed as a personal God, it is the Deus ex machina.[14]

On the other hand, the role of chance in Raabe derives its full literary justification from the basic problems of the 'Bildungsroman'. Chance is the litmus test that reveals the true character, the real structure at the core of the individual figures. Only so much, not more. Since the inner necessity, the literary coherence, of all of Raabe's stories is based on the social and individual truth of such developments, it is quite legitimate to regard the pragmatic side to those incidents which in part give rise to the individual nodal points as being of secondary importance. A minimum of causal possibility is perfectly adequate for these incidents; as was already pointed out by Schelling, literary necessity can never be the result of a mere causal link, no matter how logical this link might be. These more or less chance incidents make convincing literature because of the reactions they evoke, because of the energy with which they bring to light the inner core of the human beings in question. In the novel *Alte Nester* (*Old Nests*), Raabe has his hero say:

There are times when nothing is more helpful to a person than to turn him completely inside out. Only when his innermost substance is brought into the open does he realize what has been lurking inside him and what has been but a passing, superficial attribute.[15]

If Raabe's accumulation of chance occurrences sometimes seems contrived and 'novella-like', it is because there are individual passages – particularly those portraying the upper classes – in which the characters' emotional reactions are false, romantic in the negative sense, or simply vacuous.

Raabe's chosen path of constantly reformulating the substance of his resignation, is – all things considered – a brave way of coming to terms with illusions that have become untenable. Admittedly, the actual room for manoeuvre left open to this fearlessness is limited socially. However, there is no doubt that by the war of 1870 he had developed considerably from the gentle lyricism of his early works, full of the spirit of renunciation (*The Chronicle of Sparrow Alley*, 1856; *One Springtime*, 1857; *The People from the Forest*, 1862/63), and this development is expressed in the vastly increased power of the social and historical indictment contained in the later works (*Three Pens*, 1865, according to Raabe his first truly independent work; *Abu Telfan*, 1867; and *The Rumbledump*, 1869/70).

In bourgeois literary history, Raabe's indictment of society is also classed as 'pessimism' *à la* Schopenhauer. But what exactly is the true nature of this 'pessimism'?

Raabe is vehement in condemning the mentality of the German petty princedoms and their feudal-monarchist character. He regards it as a mire of the most petty philistinism, opposed to every decent feeling, whether individual or social. In this world, every person of any significance, indeed every strictly moral person becomes a pariah, an outcast.

All the same, Raabe does not believe that the development of capitalism in Germany is a change for the better. Capitalism represents for him the destruction and corruption of all that is best in the world and in humankind. He realizes at a very early date that the new power of money may be destroying the old world whose passing he laments, yet at the same time keeps in power the petty, degenerate, faint-heartedly arrogant aristocratic upper class of the petty states that he detests so much. In all of Raabe's works from *One Springtime* to *The Rumbledump* we find an alliance of the old aristocracy with the new financial magnates.

We are already familiar with Raabe's overall view of possible individual salvation from these two enemies. As in *Wilhelm Meister's Apprenticeship*, there even emerges a circle of like-minded individuals, and a didactic, propagandistic perspective is also in evidence (*Abu Telfan*). It would be too abstract, however, to draw far-reaching conclusions from the fact that the perspective of Goethe's 'Bildungsroman' is also utopian, and to overestimate Raabe's affinity to Goethe's example, by which Raabe always set great store. Goethe's utopia is located amidst the world upheaval brought about by the French Revolution. Its social basis, despite all its utopian features, was an ostensibly visible path of development. Raabe's perspective is not only fraught with scepticism, is not only a resigned retreat from the path which 'the entire world' had taken at that time, not only the desperate attempt to create peaceful 'intercosmic spaces' amidst a reality inimical both to the intellect and to humankind, but – and this demonstrates Raabe's great literary honesty – his perspective is constantly contradicted, or at least called into doubt, by the plot itself. Raabe's positive heroes represent the spirit of a bygone epoch, of spiritual uprising at the time of the Wars of Liberation and, when they can muster the extreme heroism of resistance, stand like 'sabre-rattling ghosts', like so many Don Quixotes confronting a victorious external reality.

We have seen that the war of 1870 marks an important transformation in Raabe; we are also familiar with his – ambiguous – reaction to these events. Once again, this time under fundamentally different conditions, Raabe attempts to keep alive the best elements during this transitional period, salvaging them for the future. Thus he defends the enthusiasm of the Schiller Centenary of 1859 against the egotistic 'realism' of the philistines (*Der Dräumling* [*The Dräumling Swamp*], 1872). And he now feels obliged to tackle in his writings the true ruler of Germany, namely capitalism. In this he suffers a literary defeat, precisely because he tries to find a middle-of-the-road approach, a 'reconciliation' at any price. Raabe tries to invent characters in whom capitalist activity can be reconciled with the spirit of German traditions that he wishes to preserve. However, neither Schönow, the kind-hearted eccentric and entrepreneur from Berlin (*Villa Schönow*, 1884), nor the chemist, Asche – who becomes a capitalist himself and yet wants to create a spiritual 'intercosmic space' for himself in a marriage of love and in humanistic studies (*Pfisters Mühle* [*Pfister's Mill*], 1884) – contains the truth of typicality. They are at best, like Schönow, figures of individually eccentric authenticity. When old Pfister, whose forefathers have run the mill and the inn for centuries, capitulates in the face of the new world in a spirit of self-denying understanding, saying, 'The Lord probably thinks it'll be for the best in the next few years', he is expressing Raabe's dream of reconciliation and demonstrates the social limitations of his creator. But fortunately for Raabe's work, this attempt at reconciliation was only a passing episode in his life.

Raabe's faith in this middle road was never all that strong. His sense of reality was much too clear to allow him to believe such figures to be genuine and significant typical representatives, either of the epoch or of his own desire for the future. His opposition to the new world of capitalism did not diminish, even though he welcomed the national unity brought about by the new Reich. However, this opposition became more and more individualistic and apolitical. The result was a cycle of novels concerning the 'victory of the past', a 'childhood paradise' lost and regained (*Old Nests*, 1879; *Stopfkuchen* [*Stuffcake*], 1888/90; *Die Akten des Vogelsangs* [*The Documents of the Birdsong*], 1896; *Altershausen*, started 1899, unfinished).

Here the flight to a spiritual 'intercosmic space' predominates – the salvation of humankind by entering a world of childhood dreams recreated on earth, or even, as in his last, unfinished work, the world of childhood dreams itself. This emphasis on the importance of the past and of memory is characteristic of Raabe's whole career. In his first book we already find the statement:

The true, pure source of all virtue, of all true sacrifice, is the past in its sad sweetness, with its faded images, its deeds and dreams wholly or partially forgotten.

And in *Pfister's Mill* Raabe puts the exigency of the age into the mouth of a semi-degenerate poet: 'Follow our advice and you will have something to look forward to.' But he immediately adds: 'But don't look back on what you might have left behind you.' And what man loses, leaves behind him in the process of adapting to capitalist life, is precisely what Raabe considers to be of greatest human value. In the later novels, this lost something is searched for – either in vain or successfully.

Raabe's approach is genuinely German and grows organically out of the clash between his world-view and the rapid expansion of capitalism. This is by no means the private problem of an eccentric writer. On the contrary, Raabe's popularity is based largely on the fact that his rejection of capitalism was passionate, yet purely emotional and subjective.

That Raabe's specific formulation of the problem is typically German does not alter the fact that it is also an international phenomenon in the second half of the nineteenth century. The poetry of childhood is one of the ancient treasures from which literature can draw. However, in the case of the eighteenth century English realists, of Goethe and of Gottfried Keller, the great latecomer of democratic literature, this poetry was still able to grow out of the feeling – not yet interrupted by social constraints – that Marx clearly conceptualizes, together with all its social and historical roots:

An adult cannot become a child again, or he becomes childish. But does not the naïveté of the child give him pleasure, and must he not himself endeavour to reproduce the child's veracity on a higher level? Does not the specific character of every epoch come to life again in its natural veracity in the child's nature?[16]

Here Marx is also indicating the social preconditions by which this feeling could persist without being interrupted or becoming problematic. Whether the individual is able 'to reproduce veracity on a higher level' is very much dependent on whether, and to what extent, the specific character of an epoch is able to find and realize its natural truth in life itself. If this is possible, then important writers can attain the normal relationship to childhood that Marx describes. If, on the other hand, as a result of the socio-historical structure of a period, the 'normal' development of the individual leads to paralysis, to an ossification of humanity, then the individual relationship to childhood also appears in a different light. We know how Raabe viewed the possibilities of individual development in capitalist society; we have also seen that in this he was expressing a typical truth about the social situation in the second half of the nineteenth century. In his works he repeatedly provides both concrete and generalized descriptions of these processes. Let us cite one such example of typical generalization (from *Fabian and Sebastian*):

Truth does not always fall upon one's heart, crushing it as would a stone. In the ordinary way it trickles down like sand; its flying atoms are hardly noticeable to begin with, but they gradually build up, grain by grain, day and night; treated at first with derision, it seems as though it could be blown away with a single puff, not worthy of provoking serious thought, let alone physical unease. How attentive you must be to notice how the twilight looms, how light turns to darkness!. . . How grey the world becomes! Your life, your spirit is covered in a layer of dust!. . . Powerless against the trickling sand, woe betide you when you start to brood over the time when you first caught the taste of earth on your tongue!. . . and today you know. . . that the dust, the grey, gloomy coating on all your pleasures, your opinions, your ideas, will continue to grow forever; that the shadow and the dust are bound to be your masters accompanying you on your distant path through life. . . You feel – and indeed you are – alone in a grey desert. Why not count the grains of sand? Keep counting, but count backwards! Now you have come to count on the dust which has gathered on your world and which can never be blown away again. . .[17]

Is it not self-evident that in a world of this nature, viewed from this ideological standpoint, childhood and youth are no longer merely the sun-filled, magically radiant start to life, but appear to be the lost paradise of truth, of nature and of human existence?

Dickens is the first great writer to portray childhood in this light. At the end of Flaubert's most subjective novel (*A Sentimental Education*) the two main characters, both of whose lives have been wasted and squandered, converse about small, insignificant episodes in their youth, and both consider these memories to be the best thing that life has bestowed upon them. And Baudelaire sings (in 'Moesta et Errabunda'):

> Mais le vert paradis des amours enfantines,
> . . .
> L'innocent paradis, plein de plaisirs furtifs,
> Est-il déjà plus loin que l'Inde et que la Chine?
> – Peut-on le rappeler avec des cris plaintifs
> Et l'animer encore d'une voix argentine,
> L'innocent paradis plein de plaisirs furtifs?

But the green paradise of childhood's loves. . .The innocent paradise of secret pleasures, is it really farther away than India or China? Can we ever call it back with plaintive cries, make it alive again with silvery voices, that innocent paradise, full of furtive pleasures.[18]

Raabe's late works form an original German counterpart to these international trends. What makes Raabe's works special – and specifically modern – is that these journeys back into the paradise of childhood occupy a much more central position in his novels than in Dickens or Flaubert. They form the main contents of the late works and accordingly also determine the style. Raabe's whimsicality which always bears a lively, interactive relation to the strictly narrative structure of the plot, transforms itself more and more into an interplay of past and present, of reminiscence and experience, with the childhood memories that well up coming to dominate the increasingly sparse experiences of the present to an ever greater extent.

However, if Raabe had carried this juxtaposition straight through to its logical conclusion, if he had unconditionally and rigorously opted against 'adult' life and in favour of childhood, there would have been no room left for the complicated dialectical 'for and against' of such feelings and attitudes towards life – and the ageing Raabe would either have descended to the level of writing sentimental, trivial literature or would have degenerated into a subjectivist decadent. (In his poorer works and in the weaker sections of the better works of his late period he comes close to both.)

Yet Raabe the writer remains highly critical of his own dreams. He portrays them with genuine realism, which is to say that he always sees the dream and its realization in terms of its living base in reality. What are its origins? In which direction does it lead? What is its purpose? He always asks these questions with an unshakable regard for truth and does not confuse his evaluation of reality with reality itself, indeed he is constantly uncovering the real roots of his value judgements, of his dreams.

For this reason – even in his earlier novels – dreams are contrasted with reality; this is why he exposes the quixotic character of dreamers, their merely playful (and to a certain extent unscrupulous) intervention in the lives of others; this is why, in every period of his work, Raabe's dreamers are contrasted with realistic, healthy female characters, who are sometimes so down-to-earth as to be almost philistine. Raabe's subtle dialectic is shown by the fact that this good sense only superficially borders on the 'worldly wisdom' of the philistine, yet at its innermost core represents a different, higher, resigned form of seeing through reality. Such women are aware of the unreality of these dreams and dreamers, yet are at the same time sufficiently just to recognize their profound existential necessity. They smile – sometimes sadly, sometimes with benevolent irony – at the unrealistic foundations on which the lives of most contemporary people are based, and try to keep them from coming into fruitless conflict with vulgar reality. At the same time, however, they are proud of being different from the simple, 'organic' products of the present age, the philistines. These women act like Sancho Panza, who, in spite of his frequently vindicated foresight, is constantly aware emotionally of Don Quixote's superiority. The only difference is that their 'Sancho-Panza-ism' contains more insight, puts more emphasis on feelings, is more ironical and self-ironical than, for historical reasons, their classical model could be.

In Raabe's late works, this complicated contradictory relationship between dreams and real life, ideal and reality, becomes increasingly introverted and dialectical. A new kind of world-view arises – because there is now even a subjective awareness that ideals no longer have any impact on real life; because the dreamer no longer confuses his dream with reality, nor does he desire to struggle to impose it on reality; because amidst his dreaming he knows that he is only dreaming, that he has placed himself outside the reality of life. What in Raabe's early novels the others knew about the quixotic heroes, these heroes now know themselves.

This change of consciousness is, however, at the same time a transformation of contents and evaluation. Raabe's late works necessarily contain Ibsen's problem of the life lie. In a relatively early work (*Vom alten Proteus*, 1875) we find: 'Give us this day our daily self-deception'; and two years later in *Old Nests* we can read:

How insignificant is that stupid, worthless phrase, 'My home is my castle!' compared to that so thoroughly unpolitical, so seldom spoken yet so deeply and firmly held conviction, indeed sometimes clung onto with the fear of despair, namely: 'My castle-in-the-air is my home!'[19]

And in the late novel, *Documents of the Birdsong*, Raabe offers an interesting parallel to the death of Peer Gynt's old mother in Ibsen, who (thanks to an imaginative act of deception) dies contented and with a sense of fulfilment. (An episode in *Villa Schönow* contains a short prelude to this.) Just as in Ibsen's play Solveig waits all her life for Peer Gynt, so the strong-willed, imaginative, sensible mother waits for the return of the son who set out to force reality to conform to his ideals. She too knows something of Raabe's late wisdom with respect to the connection between ideals and illusions: 'Illusions are simply another means of making the earth green and keeping it beautiful,' she once says. Amidst an environment which is becoming increasingly prosaic and hostile, she preserves in unsullied form the son's youthful paradise for him. He now returns, broken and disillusioned. He finds his dying, but still loyal mother and acts out for her a comedy of 'unlost illusions'; thus, like Peer Gynt, he gently rocks her, with fantastic lies, into a contented death.

It is no coincidence that this relativity of ideals, of living lies and self-deceptions that have lost their social roots, should be a theme common to the later Ibsen and the later Raabe. The desire to preserve ideals dating back to the age of an ascendent bourgeoisie inevitably leads perceptive psychologists to this problem and to the realization of its insolubility (on bourgeois terrain, which was of course something that these writers could not have known). Raabe's heroes stand alone against capitalist reality. If their flight to a 'castle in the air' fails – and self-deception and life lies cast their shadow on every castle in the air – they are forced to conform to reality or perish. And Raabe depicts with melancholic irony a whole series of lives in which the inability to distinguish dream from reality finally leads, by slow but remorseless logic, to the land of the philistines.

Thus the later Raabe portrays a deeply sad world, full of disillusionment, of people who have gone astray, have been ruined or who are forced to live a lie. Yet even here he does not shy away from the most extreme consequences of his position, and is prepared to call escapism and castles in the air by their true names. In spite of this, the world-view that emerges is not one of pessimistic despair – even though Raabe can see no real way out of his dilemma – because of Raabe's strong bonds with the people. In 1843 Marx calls Arnold Ruge's 'funeral song' unpolitical. The reason he gives is this:

No people wholly despairs, and even if for a long time it goes on hoping merely out of stupidity, yet one day, after many years it will suddenly become wise and fulfil all its pious wishes.[20]

And the case of Raabe is no exception: behind the all-consuming dialectic of illusions stands this 'stupidity' of the people. He feels that it is impossible for the human core of a great people really and ultimately to become rotten, to lose its essence, to disintegrate. This 'stupidity', by means of which Raabe is able to remain affirmative 'in spite of everything' (Ibsen's last words, incidentally) is his humour.

III

The defeat of revolutionary democracy in Germany in the 1848/49 Revolution and the subsequent humiliation of the German people form the socio-political basis of this humour. Even before Raabe appeared on the scene, Gottfried Keller prophesied that a new comic literature would emerge from the events following the shattered revolution.

Keller's political pessimism with regard to the course of events in Germany proved to be correct, and his literary prediction also came true. What he was not able to foresee was the fact that an independent reviver of the comic attitude of Sterne and Jean Paul should be a genuinely plebeian German writer of this period.

Sterne and Jean Paul, mentioned by Keller, are not called to mind here in order to indicate any direct literary influence, not even in the sense of a literary historical succession. Mehring has pointed out certain contrasts in style between Jean Paul and Raabe; and – in an essay on Gottfried Keller – I too have shown their dissimilarity from a different standpoint.

Raabe's humour is quite idiosyncratic and, despite his frequently expressed admiration for Sterne and Jean Paul, is independent of both of them. Of course, when an important writer attempts to create a comic novel under the new conditions in Germany following the defeat of the democratic revolution, it is inevitable that certain common features will crop up linking his work to that of his great predecessors.

The reasons for this are not purely literary. Humour is – as Hegel rightly observed – essentially modern. It was unknown to Classical Antiquity. It first appears with the birth pangs of bourgeois society; it reflects certain new social phenomena and attests to certain new spiritual reactions to them, which were either completely unknown to earlier stages of history or at least played an insignificant part in them. These elements of humour common to a whole epoch are naturally bound to recur, allowing of course for individual and historical differences, in various representatives of humorous literature.

It would go beyond the scope of the present study to proffer even a tentative theory of humour or a history of humorists. We shall confine ourselves to pointing out a few essential features: those which are particularly characteristic of Raabe's idiosyncratic approach.

What must be mentioned above all in this context is the universal applicability of factors viewed in microcosm. The more developed modern life becomes, the deeper important humorists delve into the smallest events in the unspectacular lives of insignificant people. Despite the mass of minute details, this has nothing to do with Naturalism. On the contrary. Humorists in particular never give a mere detail, an observation for the sake of observation, for the sake of stating facts. Humorists always show an intensive inner connection between the major factors determining society and the apparently insignificant fates of apparently insignificant people. The more sharply public and private life seem to be separated from one another in the capitalist world, and the more it appears that personal destinies, subject as they are to chance, are simply abstract examples subsumed under abstract laws, the greater the efforts of the humorists to demonstrate the overall trends inherent in social development, the laws governing human life compressed into the form of small events. Expressing this methodological creed, Raabe correctly says:

What is a humorist? A person who knocks the tiniest of nails into the wall or into the skulls of his honourable readers and then hangs upon it the entire wardrobe of the age and of all past ages.[21]

It is certainly true that in the process public life often receives too little attention. This is not only true in the case of Raabe, although here the flaw is particularly pronounced. Dickens too, with only a few exceptions, allows public life to be overwhelmed by the private. This results from the belief that the public life of developed bourgeois society has little to do with the real, major interests of the people, that the really significant social processes take place not on the widely visible surface of parliaments and tribunals, but rather deep down in remote alleyways, in humble dwellings.

As a result of the German situation and Raabe's reaction to it, as described above, this general trend in modern humorous writing is particularly accentuated in Raabe. Even when he allows public events not only to enter into the plot but even to become the actual subject (as he does with the Schiller Centenary celebrations mentioned above and with the founding of the National Association in *Gutmann's Travels*), it is the microcosmic realm of the small, private, individual life that always remains the hub of the narrative; the public event only serves as a humorous, contrasting backdrop. Raabe's clearest expression of this attitude is in *The Rumbledump*, when he declares that the Olympian gods were more concerned about the war between frogs and mice than about the Trojan War.

This attitude undoubtedly contained an element of philistinism which wreaked severe artistic vengeance on Raabe as a novelist. The introversion of his social world-view and his retreat from public life endow the world he created with a certain narrowness and mustiness. Raabe is an excellent, graphic and highly discerning portrayer of all objects and events in external life. However, his view of society dictates that he develop plots from which the objects and events of major public life are bound to be absent and which are predominantly set in smoke-filled bachelor apartments, at the regulars' table in the local pub, etc. His own portrayals, the broad, free, many-sided world he creates in numerous historical narratives set in pre-capitalist times, testify to the artistic and epic loss that this represented. That Raabe chose this path is evidence of his unshakable honesty and his refusal to settle for literary compromise. It should also be pointed out that this tendency, with all the negative consequences it entails, is by no means an individual idiosyncrasy of Raabe and by no means exclusively bound up with Raabe's humour. Rather it is the overall current that prevailed in Western European literature in the second half of the nineteenth century and is to be found – in very varied forms, of course – in most of the outstanding writers of the period. These historical considerations, however, do not alter the qualitative difference that meets the eye when one compares the narrow and scanty nature of Raabe's overall picture of social life (despite its richness of detail) with the 'totality of objects' created by, say, Keller or Dickens.

We repeat: there is a dash of philistinism in Raabe's humour. In his day, Chernyshevsky showed very clearly in his analysis of some of E.T.A. Hoffmann's figures how their philistinism is connected to the fact that their psychology is lacking in public aspects. After what has already been said, it is not necessary to emphasize the fact that such a complete lack cannot be attributed to either Raabe's positive figures, nor indeed to Raabe himself. It is merely a question of the degree to which such traits are present and of the force with which they are able to find expression in life.

Raabe himself was clearly aware of this side to his modern characters. In the historical story, *Our Lord God's Chancellory*, a careworn woman is envious of her equally troubled husband: 'He talks and thinks and busies himself about the health or otherwise of society and loses sight of his own troubles.' Raabe knows that it would be impossible in the Germany of his time for any of his heroines to talk in this manner about their husbands. But this social development invariably reflects back on the writer too; the general devaluation of public life, the way in which the characters do not participate in public life, is reflected in the structure of the works themselves.

This is why the humorous portrayal of the dialectic of ideal, dream, living lie and reality, the humorous dialectic of Raabe's reconciliation or non-reconciliation with reality, is always necessarily linked to the twofold question: What is philistinism? Who is a philistine?

Raabe is constantly aware – even in his late period – of the philistine traits of his positive figures: the philistine side to the way in which they solve the problems of their lives. Yet he is incapable of answering these problems in a way that can satisfy his honesty both as a human being and as a writer.

It is not all that difficult to discern the reason for this. With his sharp eyes and keen awareness, Raabe observes the basic dilemma facing humankind in capitalist society, which Lenin expressed thus: 'The old society was based on the principle: rob or be robbed; work for others or make others work for you; be a slave-owner or a slave.'[22] In accordance with his whole social horizon and sense of the world Raabe endeavours to answer this question with a 'neither-nor'. This is a harmful, anti-progressive illusion commonly held by the bourgeois intelligentsia. And Raabe would be of little interest to us if he had given us nothing more than this illusion, and if his novels did nothing more than foist this ideal onto an 'evil reality' or demonstrate its tragic failure in face of it.

However, Raabe is unrelentingly aware *in every single case* of the problem involved in each of the chosen solutions, even though he is unable to recognize the general incorrectness of this attempt to answer the dilemma of capitalism. It is because of this that almost all of Raabe's important books are populated by a whole group of contrasting figures, who in their lives and thoughts adopt various stances on this same question, namely whether and how the problem of reconciliation or non-reconciliation with capitalist society is to be achieved. The different positive characters, who vary in their closeness to Raabe's heart, are always in search of an individual, human way out of both the dilemma of capitalism and the descent into philistinism, which constantly threatens to befall them on account of the illusory nature of their middle-of-the-road position. And Raabe's humour consists in the fact that he refuses to recognize any of these solutions as being really successful, exposing the philistine elements in all of them. At the same time, admittedly, he also demonstrates – in most of his positive figures – those elements or tendencies which go beyond philistinism or at least strive to do so, and which score a modest, problematic, partial success in averting its strangulating effects.

Raabe was not blind to this affinity to philistinism not only of his world but also his world-view. In *Abu Telfan* he draws an interesting comparison between the German and the Western European classics in which he points to the philistine elements in Goethe, Luther, Jean Paul etc. as a national peculiarity. These observations are very interesting, but essentially wrong. Above all, Raabe confuses philistinism with having a down-to-earth attitude and roots in the daily life of the working people; moreover, he underestimates the degree to which the great foreign writers are truly down-to-earth. The incorrectness of his arguments is most blatantly expressed in his regard for Schiller as the German writer furthest removed from philistinism. Yet in spite of all these inaccuracies, the instinct behind Raabe's assessment of German literature is correct. Marx and Engels frequently referred to the philistine traits of the greatest Germans, namely Goethe and Heine; they recognized, however, that this philistinism was expressed in the way in which, for example, Goethe and Hegel reconcile themselves with reality.

But Raabe's practical work as a writer stands on a higher plane than his theoretical observations and is at the same time more closely linked to the great currents of world literature which led to humorous world-views finding literary form.

Here too, space permits us to point to only a few instances. Particularly characteristic of Raabe's humour is his ceaseless positing and then overcoming of relativity, the relative justification and un- tenability of various ways of dealing with reality. Sterne's *Tristram Shandy* is the first classical work to arise out of this attitude. Hettner is right in noting that the basic idea behind Sterne's composition is the relativization of the relationship between Don Quixote and Sancho Panza; each of the Shandy brothers thinks he is Don Quixote and the other is Sancho Panza.

This is the literary model for Raabe's dialectic of philistinism. But Raabe is more introverted. Many of his characters incorporate both aspects, which fight out their battle within the individual char- acter. However, even when adopting Sterne's method, he always depicts an objectively insoluble problem (insoluble from his social standpoint, that is) in its dynamism and self-reproduction. His humour is the compositional concession to the insolubility of the problem, which is why this humour can never be judged in purely formal terms: its depth always depends on the extent to which a real problem is portrayed in its real insolubility.

This ceaseless relativization of individual positions, this ceaseless positing and sublation of what has been posited, is reflected in all the stylistic problems in Raabe's art. He had from the very begin- ning a strong propensity for symbolic description. As with most of his contemporaries, these arise out of weakness and out of the problem of combining the individual with the universal, out of the attempt to substitute the symbol for the lack of inherent unity. But at the same time Raabe also tends to use humour to criticize and undermine his symbols. In *Three Pens* he describes the process of creating symbols as follows:

How we twist and turn things, how we rearrange our life to suit ourselves once there is no longer any chance of really changing it! We try to turn the commonplace into a symbol in an attempt to gain some sort of feeble satisfaction out of it after all. Just as poets and storytellers like to seek and find profound, far-reaching motives for the deeds of their heroes, so we too seek and find the motives behind the development of our own personality and the more subjectively we wrap our dressing-gown around our old bones and the more comfortable we have made ourselves in our rocking-chair, the more objective we believe ourselves to be.[23]

In this humorous way, Raabe himself sublates his own symbols.

But that is only one side of the coin. Raabe never abstains sceptically from passing judgement. He always takes sides, albeit with humorous reservations. An important literary technique for this is the creation of 'originals', eccentrics.

This too is an old subject of comedy and humour. Shakespeare's contemporary Ben Jonson defined humour as the absolute predominance of one characteristic in a person over all emotions, spirits and forces. This predominance of a single characteristic as the source of comedy is very old. It develops out of the distortion of humankind in and by class society. However, as long as the distortion of a person is only depicted as such, seen from the outside and from a purely negative point of view, the result can only be comedy, irony or satire but not humour. Not until man's struggle to retain his health and equilibrium when confronted by a society that tries to distort him and reduce him to a single function is transformed into a problem of introversion, does specifically modern humour develop.

Now it is precisely this desire to achieve inner harmony that is the main concern of the people created by Raabe. 'Measure for measure' is what the hero of *The Hunger Pastor* is searching for, and in *Abu Telfan* the desire for human harmony is expressed as a demand linked closely to social existence: 'It is a truly great pleasure still to feel so alive in one's body and in one's nation.' We know that this desire felt by Raabe's positive heroes is unattainable; life inevitably distorts them. However, this takes on a special accent in the case of the positive figures: the distortion is not foreign to the inner core of the person, it is not simply a perversion of his essential being, but rather the person *seeks asylum in the distortion*, the salvation of his human worth, indeed the most valuable part of him, from the influence of capitalist society. The eccentricity of Raabe's positive figures is therefore a fence to prevent the ravages of the world from intruding into the hidden garden of their soul. That this protection is highly problematic is expressed precisely in the humorous illumination of the characters' eccentricity.

We already encounter this positive aspect of modern humour in Jean Paul; the eighteenth century put even greater emphasis on aggressive social criticism and ridicule. In his observations on Don Quixote, Heine gives a truly clear appraisal of this new attitude:

> Those cool-headed, wise philosophers! How sympathetic are their condescending smiles at poor Don Quixote's self-torment and madness, yet for all their scholastic wisdom they fail to notice that this Don Quixotism is nonetheless the most praiseworthy thing there is in life, that it is indeed life itself. . .[24]

This is also the position held by Raabe, who always declared Heine to be his favourite writer: the poetic relativization of philistinism, demonstrating its presence even in those 'perfect' individuals who appear to have overcome it, and at the same time demonstrating what is humanly valuable in the philistine eccentrics.

Admittedly, Raabe generally uses a moralistic yardstick: the need to keep humanity alive in the capitalist world. The humour of his writing constantly relativizes vitality by turning to the fantastic. But even here Raabe the humorist does not fall into the trap of relativism. He knows exactly what is vital and what is a mere phantom. 'When vitality appears among the dead, people are all too inclined to mistake the former for the ghost.' When investigating how human beings become distorted by society, the important question for Raabe is whether they are led away from life into the sham life of phantoms, or towards the problematical salvation of life's inner core in the form of eccentricity. This is the reason why (as with E.T.A. Hoffmann, though without the latter's fairy-tale fantasy) such an important role is played in Raabe by the fantastic in the deadly, fatal distortions of capitalist existence – this ghostly appearance of genuine humanity in the dead and rotten mire of ossified philistinism, though without the external reality of everyday life being transcended.

Moreover, vitality in Raabe always has a plebeian oppositional accent which permeates even the smallest, apparently most coincidental aspects of life, or indeed – in the absence of major public conflicts – finds its clearest expression precisely in these trivia. Thus Raabe never tires of deriding the empty, inconsequential, detached enthusiasm of the philistines for the beauty of nature. In one instance, the hero of his *Stuffcake* says of the beautiful evening sun:

Of course it is beautiful; it is absolutely enchanting that we should be permitted. . . to enjoy this longed-for freedom to be truly human. Look yonder, the sun's reflection is gleaming in the windows. . . of the provincial gaol. Fairy-tale magic of the purest kind![25]

And, above all, it should not be forgotten that Raabe's whole conception of the 'childhood paradise' exhibits this plebeian oppositional accent: the children of high society have, so to speak, no childhood at all; their ossification begins to set in from the very moment their education commences.

The humorous affirmation of the positive figures in Raabe is the self-affirmation of those good, humanly moral qualities of the German people which, somewhere along the tortuous and contradictory path to its unification as a people and its acquisition of capitalist civilization, have been preserved in various hiding places under the camouflage of eccentricity. As a tireless uncoverer of these concealed elements of – historically relative – permanence in the national character, Raabe is a fundamentally plebeian writer.

Of course, describing Raabe as a writer of the people should not be understood metaphysically, as a mark of ideological 'infallibility', but rather as a concrete characteristic which requires elucidatory analysis in every case. In class society, the unified people is but a reactionary legend. However, repeated instances of more or less universally national problems and solutions are to be found precisely in the concrete forms of class development and class struggle. Every plebeian writer approaches the people from the being and consciousness of a specific class; in Raabe's case, as a petty bourgeois intellectual. It now depends on whether class viewpoints remain within the confines of narrow interests or whether they reach out to embrace major national problems; on what, from the concrete standpoint of a specific writer (belonging to a class at a specific stage of development), is regarded as a major national problem in the first place; on how writers give literary expression to these problems; and on the extent to which they are able, in typical form, to intervene in the life of the people, reflect it and generalize the relevance of its problems. All this – let it once more be emphasized – within the limits of class and history.

There are, of course, literary bureaucrats who believe that Balzac or Tolstoy would necessarily have been better writers if they had had a different, objectively more advanced world-view. This only proves how little they know about the genuine bonds to the people that may exist in a writer and the interaction between this and the writer's world-view and method of writing. Every plebeian writer is an Antaeus whose strength is derived from constant contact with Mother Earth. And this earth is not always as pure as the freshly swept pavement on Nevsky Prospect. Both in his thoughts and in the act of literary production, the writer can and should rise above his class base, but if he were to detach himself completely from this base he would lose the literary force that is *specific to him alone*. Thus Tolstoy is linked to the strengths and weaknesses of the Russian peasantry, and Raabe with those of the German petty bourgeoisie of his time. This sort of literary bureaucrat, however, confuses Tolstoy with himself, who is capable of writing from any standpoint at random. And writes accordingly.

By exposing the class roots of Raabe's plebeianism, we have concretized his stature as a writer. But at the same time: plebeianism is not like a medal that can be awarded, not even for the highest level of artistic perfection. Raabe's position in relation to the peaks of German literature may be modest, but he nonetheless remains an important plebeian writer.

Raabe himself always demanded of literature that it point the way forward. However, his portrayal of the great way forward for humankind never approaches the heights attained by Balzac, Tolstoy, Dickens or Keller. He is able to avert the dangers of despair, of treading water, petrifaction, compromises and capitulations, but the way forward he depicts lacks any clear direction. It is the 'hope born out of stupidity' as defined by Marx in the earlier quotation.

Even his plebeianism is unable to give his work direction. Raabe's positive figures never find their place in public life, and this detail is – despite Raabe's limitations – motivated by good plebeian considerations and is convincing. It is also evident that such people, if they do make the effort to participate in a public activity, would only ever do so out of honest enthusiasm. Yet Raabe's world-view, and to an even greater extent that of his characters, are completely devoid of a compass that could show them that *righteous* commitment to a cause means commitment to the *right* cause, that of the true liberation of humankind. Raabe himself made the right choice of battlefields for his positive figures: be it with Bolivar, in the 1830 Polish Uprising or in Grant's camp in the North American war against slavery, they never fight on the wrong side of the barricades. However, the reasons for these choices are not given the clarity needed to provide a categorical, unequivocal perspective for the future. (Bartels, Nadler and the like are able to make use of this lack of clarity to claim Raabe as one of their own.)

These figures are simply 'vacillating petty bourgeois', the schematist would say, shrugging his shoulders. And many an epigone of the Enlightenment, having forgotten that *Rameau's Nephew* and *Tristram Shandy* represented the pinnacle of Enlightenment literature, repeats this schematic interpretation and is at times even prepared to abandon the whole petty bourgeoisie, lock, stock and barrel to the forces of reaction. Thus the well known progressive writer Oscar Maria Graf writes in his novel *Anton Sittinger*:

They embody all the cleverness and craftiness, all the unbelief and all the wretchedness of a class in decline. . . They appear harmless, and their venomous egotism is always cloaked in respectability. They are the most blatant, the most devastating nihilists under the sun. You have to take them into account politically if you want to change the world, but you must never succumb to the crazy idea that they might be useful for the struggle to achieve a better future. They do not even belong to the fermenting present, they belong solely to the past, which is why they are the most invulnerable gravediggers of any just social order.

It is not only Raabe's greatness as a writer which stands in opposition to such verdicts, but also the social progressiveness and current relevance of his perplexity and 'stupidity'. The ways of peoples are labyrinthine, until they find their true selves in the act of their real liberation. The historic destiny of the German people has chosen a particularly tortuous path since the Peasant Wars and the Reformation. In Arnold Zweig's novel *Erziehung vor Verdun (Education at Verdun)*, the poet Christoph Kroysing, who is killed at an early stage, writes of the way German writers take root in the people:

But these roots seem to me to be like long, stringy fibrous roots, winding their way around many an obstacle, waiting a long time before sending a flower up towards the light somewhere far away.

Raabe is not mentioned by name, but it is equally his present and future potential influence that is correctly characterized here. He will never be accorded the same rank in German literature as Hoffmann or Keller. Yet flowers and fruits will grow out of his roots, and he will be accorded the fame he sought to achieve.

1939

The Later Fontane[*]

> Our literary production. . . corresponds
> to our *nature* but not necessarily to our
> *taste*. . . If our taste. . . determines our
> *production*, our nature, having taken a
> different course, leaves us in the lurch,
> and we come to grief. We have had our
> way, but the outcome is a stillbirth.
>
> THEODOR FONTANE

Fontane is an almost unique phenomenon in literary history. The most important period in his career as a writer began when he was sixty, and reached its climax when he was at the grand old age of nearly eighty. Thomas Mann has provided a very good description of this phenomenon:

Just as there are born adolescents, those early developers who never reach full maturity, let alone old age, without outliving themselves, so there are evidently people for whom, by nature, old age is the only appropriate stage of life, classical old men so to speak, whose calling is to bring to the attention of humankind the ideal merits of this time of life in their most perfect form, merits such as gentleness, kindness, fairness, a sense of humour, cunning wisdom, in short, the return to childlike freedom and innocence on a higher plane.[1]

There is no doubt as to the truth of all this. Nonetheless, Thomas Mann is only describing the Fontane phenomenon, not explaining it. This cannot be achieved solely from Fontane's individual biography. For ability – even within the individual – is a complicated and intricate interaction of aesthetic, moral, intellectual and other components and cannot be defined at all without an analysis of the reciprocal relationship between the gifted individual and the concrete society in which his talent develops. It is well known that a particular epoch can bring forth or suppress talents. It would be wrong to maintain that the lieutenants or non-commissioned officers suddenly developed great military ability at the time of the French Revolution. The psychological and other preconditions for

* First published in *Sinn und Form*, vol.3, no.2, 1951.

such abilities also existed in certain individuals or indeed en masse before and after the Revolutionary Wars, which merely put these latent talents to use and allowed them to flower. In order to illustrate this point with counter-examples, it is worth reading Balzac and Stendhal to see what the Age of Restoration did to people's abilities.

However, it would be mechanistic to reduce the question to one of talent coming to fruition. The inter-relationship involved is much closer than is generally imagined. The problem of just such an inter-relationship is always the root cause determining whether a talent reaches its climax in youth, adulthood or old age, whether an ability blossoms, stagnates or even wanes. The inborn qualities of the respective personality (as well as those acquired through membership of a certain class in a specific society) obviously play a major role. They are, however, never the sole decisive factor, but rather one factor within this inter-relationship.

It has been said – quite rightly – that certain periods are more likely than others to favour the development of artistic talent. However, in order not to distort the concept of period, one must hasten to add that it makes a difference whether one lived through, say, the French Revolution as an aristocrat or as a Parisian plebeian. And this difference is not merely static and direct, seen from an existentially determining standpoint, but above all dynamic and indirect, relying, namely, on the objective development determining the vectors of subjective development. Nonetheless, even accounting for all the ensuing differentiations, there exists an abstract, general framework capable of exercising considerable influence on the concrete and the individual – the favourable or unfavourable conditions of the period. The crucial question is whether talent is borne along by its epoch or constrained by it, whether its development takes place with or against the stream.

This is by no means tantamount to saying that the gifted individual is merely a product of his epoch, of the social structure and of his class position. Every individual is born with specific characteristics whose specific structure and proportions are dynamic. Through interaction with their social environment, major or indeed decisive transformations and rearrangements can occur, a complete reverse may even take place; nevertheless, certain basic tendencies and proportions remain constant. With respect to talent, such socially determined conditions may have either a stimulating or a constraining effect. Herwegh, for example, was a great, abstractly rhetorical, lyrical talent. This coincided highly opportunely with the socio-ideological conditions in Germany during the first preparatory period in the early eighteen forties leading up to the democratic revolution. This kind of ability was no longer able to cope with the concretization of these tasks in the revolution itself and after its defeat. Herwegh's stagnation cannot, therefore, be explained solely by the subjective nature of his talent nor by the conditions of the time seen in isolation, but is only explicable in terms of the concrete interaction of both.

Having said this, it should always be borne in mind that the subjective factor – ability – is not something entire of itself, given for all time, but rather the result of the highly complex interaction of the emotional forces within the individual himself and at the same time that of the individual with his constantly changing social environment. Conversely, the way in which a talent reacts to the changing times, whether these further its development or condemn it to infertility, cannot be divorced from inborn possibilities. We stress the word 'possibilities'. For the sharpest turn of the path, the abruptest change of direction, presupposes that individuals possess certain possibilities, in other words emotional, intellectual, moral, etc., reserves, even if they have been totally unaware of them up until that point. (One need only think of Thomas Mann's development following the first imperialist world war.)

I

The phenomenon of the later Fontane must be approached bearing these aspects in mind. That means asking not only: what is the nature of the later Fontane, how does he differ from the early Fontane, but also: how did Fontane as an old man come to be what he was, which objective and subjective forces were at work?

Thomas Mann gives a vivid description of the contrast:

A comparison between the pallid, febrile, neophyte-like and rather nondescript countenance of the early pictures and the magnificent, firm, kindly and cheerful features of the old man. . . leaves no doubt as to when the man and his intellect were at their peak, as to when his personality had attained perfection.[2]

If, taking this as our point of departure, we are to inquire as to the cause of this nondescript appearance, we are forced to alter the way in which we state the facts: namely that the young Fontane, despite his amiability and his talent, did not rise above the – hardly very outstanding – average for pre-1848 youth. The fact that he was prevented from studying owing to his irregular family situation and that he entered journalism as a failed pharmacist gave him a number of advantages over many of his peers: a greater and richer experience of life; the obligation to observe the world of high 'society' from below; close, personal relationships with a plebeian – though admittedly mostly petty-bourgeois – world.

Through his lack of deep emotional roots in any class or stratum of society, and because society always influences him indirectly and without his being conscious of it, the young Fontane's world-view falls into a frightening crisis of instability. In this he often seems to be a typical intellectual, yet with the advantage (and at the same time, the disadvantage) that his development debars him from ever being a typical representative of the intelligentsia. His personal qualities thus become blurred as they simply drift along, borne by currents of the day that are often diametrically opposed to one another. Initially, the young Fontane, like so many of his peers, follows and parrots Herwegh's revolutionary poetry. Membership of the Berlin writers' association 'The Tunnel'[3] may have put an end to this extremely rhetorical style, bringing out a certain feature of Fontane's work that is to remain decisive for a long time: the poetry of the ballad. Yet the profile of the writer that emerges still contains just as many derivative characteristics, which is not surprising when one considers that the leading lights of the 'Tunnel', Geibel or Heyse, were themselves no more than epigones. As early as 1854, in a healthily self-critical letter to Theodor Storm, Fontane writes of this period: 'My predilection and – if I may say so – my strong point is description. Inwardly there may occasionally be something lacking, but external appearance is at my command.'[4] Such self-criticisms recur, despite the fact that, even at an advanced age, he occasionally believes of his poetry that 'much will live on'.

Thus while 'The Tunnel' may have meant a certain degree of

progress in literary terms, a certain stabilization of Fontane's literary ideas, his youthful detachment from real life became even greater, although it took a different direction than during his Herwegh period. In his autobiography, written as a very old man, Fontane says of himself and his close friend at that time, Bernhard von Lepel:

Right from the earliest years of our friendship we identified with the saying: 'All events were only valuable and important to us inasmuch as they provided us with subject matter.'[5]

The consequences of this attitude become apparent in the March Days of 1848. Fontane, who was in fact nearly thirty years old and therefore no longer really a youth, took part in the battles with youthful enthusiasm and youthful naïvety – and his conclusions following the victory of the people of Berlin also reflect the political innocence of a young member of the German intelligentsia at that time. He gives a very clear description of this mood in his autobiography, making no attempt to gloss over the past:

I could never rid myself of the feeling that everything that passed for victory in those days was no more than a small something granted by the powers on high, yet which was unjustifiably given the aura of a great triumph that had been gained by the people. I, for my part, was more deeply convinced than ever of the invincibility of well-disciplined troops when confronted with a horde of common people, no matter how courageous the latter might be. The will of the people counted for nothing, royal power was everything. And this was my view for forty years.[6]

With the same honesty he admits to having begun to revise this opinion at a very late date (1891) after reading General von Gerlach's *Memorabilia*, and to having reached conclusions diametrically opposed to those he had drawn from his immediate impressions and experiences at the time. Fontane makes some astute comments on the street battles, on the tactical advantages of the barricade fighters over the regular troops, and on the inevitability of their morale waning in the course of such skirmishes. He summarizes his later views thus:

It is inevitable that they [the struggles, G.L.] – provided that a great, universally felt sentiment is expressed in the uprising – will always end in the victory of the revolution. For a people in revolt, even if it has nothing but its bare hands to fight with, is ultimately stronger than even the most heavily armed power.[7]

As an old man, Fontane often revised the opinions of his youth, and we shall return to some of them later. For the present, however, it is important to note that the Fontane of 1848 was a fervent, albeit extremely confused, supporter of the revolution and yet at the same time profoundly convinced of the invincibility of the Hohenzollern regime. This last view is much more than revolutionary defeatism on his part. The young Fontane's literary production largely consists of a glorification of the House of Hohenzollern. His most important and most popular ballads deal with the 'great period' of Prussia, the time up until the death of Frederick II. And on this question his critical reappraisal of the past is never able to get to the roots of these old opinions. This is especially true of his literary works. Fontane not only perpetuates this theme in poetry (poems on Bismarck, even after the latter's death, when Fontane himself was very old), but also writes great popularizing works on the wars of 1864, 1866, 1870/71 and his *Wanderings in the Brandenburg Marches*.

Behind this lies, of course, much more than Fontane's lack of social direction. To be more precise: this is, in many of its essential features, merely the ideological reflex of the German people's irresistible, economically determined impulse to achieve economic and political unity. Bismarck and the Hohenzollerns were no more than the executive agents of this impulse, following the ultimate demise of all tendencies that promoted a democratic form of German unity. Despite Fontane's later criticisms of Bismarck's personality, to which we shall later return in more detail, this is the objective, social source of his continued admiration for Bismarck. Fontane writes of this in his autobiography:

That Bismarck was later able to celebrate such phenomenal triumphs was above all, with due respect to his genius, the result of his placing his stupendous power at the service of the idea that fires the soul of the German people.[8]

This disorientation of Fontane's, an expression of the immaturity of the German petty bourgeoisie and the German intelligentsia, embroiled him in serious conflicts – a situation made all the worse by his utterly insecure financial position. These conflicts initially concerned his profession as a writer. Fontane writes to Lepel in 1849, at the time of his engagement:

Indeed I would not have the courage to sally forth into the wide world for six months in search of material for my writing, while the girl that I profess to love sees the passing of a fourth year without coming any closer to her goal than she was on the very first day. Such hardship must at least be borne together; but the thought of merrymaking and composing tercets while a loving heart is weeping and breaking is more than I can bear.[9]

Existential reasons force him, only a short time after the revolution, to join the counter-revolutionary press corps of the Prussian government, where he even had to write poems in praise of Manteuffel. This transition is not without its moral convulsions. In July 1850, Fontane writes to Lepel: 'The only thing that sets one above the average blackguards is that, like Wittenberg-educated Hamlet, one is fully aware of one's blackguardism.'[10] And in November 1851, also to Lepel:

No matter which way I look at it – it remains deceit, betrayal, cruelty. I simply cannot accept the absolution that the beastly depravity of this world and *these times* have accorded me. Fat old Ernst Schultze said to his wife: 'Come on, Jotte, that little bit of suffering for your convictions is nothing compared with the sufferings of other people!' – 'My tables, My tables!' calls Hamlet. If it should at some point become necessary to give our times a title, then I submit that these great words be given the prominence they deserve.[11]

It is not the purpose of our essay to depict Fontane's path of suffering, both as a writer and as a human being, from his time as a reporter in London, via the *Kreuzzeitung* through to the *Vossische Zeitung* (with a short interlude in the secretariat of an academy). Our question – our search for the emotional foundations and resources of the later Fontane – is limited to the following: how is it possible that such a life, such a life-style, did not turn Fontane into a degenerate ideological scoundrel like so many former veterans of 1848 who landed in the Prussian camp (from Miquel[12] down to common police spies)? How is it that in precisely this way, in spite of all the potential dangers to his moral and literary character, he became what he finally was – the later Fontane?

Fontane's only defence against the moral decay that seemed so near at hand was to divorce his public activities from his private life; to attempt to distance his politically highly dubious profession as far as possible from his individual morality, to create an area of individual morality within himself in which he could more or less maintain his human integrity – the basis his writing needed in order to mature. This is why the subject of independence increasingly became the focus of his moral and literary life-style. Fontane stated this clearly as early as the eighteen fifties. In 1870, during a material crisis, he writes to his wife:

Don't you agree that this amount will be enough to save us from humilia-tion and compromise? And *that* is, after all, the only important thing. Independence above all else! Anything else is just humbug.[13]

It requires no detailed analysis to realize that dismissing the external circumstances as 'humbug' was an illusion on Fontane's part. We shall deal later with the artistic consequences of his illusions about his own path to salvation.

This retreat into privacy is a general symptom of the post-1848 period, especially in Germany. I have already described in detail the variation of this in the case of Raabe, which was very different from that of Fontane. In Raabe's case, however, turning his back on public life was simpler, more direct, less problematic; it entailed a radical indictment of the Prussianization of contemporary public life, a pessimistically humorous eulogy on the distant past.

This course was not open to Fontane in that material need forced him to take part in politics as a journalist – on the side of Reaction. In order to avoid going under, both morally and as a human being, he had to attempt to distance his activities from his personal exist-ence. The first precondition for this was that brutally frank self-criticism of which we have just cited some examples. The second: rigorous propriety in his private life, even and indeed especially when this was connected with his public life. In 1858, for example, when Manteuffel was deposed and an old-style liberal government took the helm, Fontane did not defect to the victors despite material disadvantages and although he himself admitted: 'if the past eight years of my life had taken a completely normal course, that is, one based on my own nature, I would very likely be on the side of the party now in power.' In a letter to Lepel he gives a characteristic reason for this conduct:

This is the way things look when viewed by the light of day: I am neither a *Kreuzzeitung* man, nor a follower of Manteuffel, nor a particular friend of the new administration under Bethmann-Hollweg, Patow and the like. I am just Fontane, plain and simple, and I don't happen to feel like attacking

Manteuffel immediately after his downfall, because the said Manteuffel (whose torch under our backsides and whose police regime were abhorrent to me) has done me, the said Fontane, *personal favours*. What I have done and said is nothing more than that which common decency and gratitude demands.[14]

Twelve years later he breaks with the *Kreuzzeitung* for basically similar motives.

This form of self-preservation is, however, extremely precarious in every respect. In a late retrospective comment, Fontane talks of a 'ride over Lake Constance'[15] although he was admittedly referring more to his material living conditions. Nonetheless, the comparison holds good for his inner development as a writer. For the strict division between his private integrity and his lack of political principles can only be reconciled by means of a nihilistic scepticism in Fontane's personality. Here too, Fontane is not alone in post-1848 Germany. One need only think of Wilhelm Busch.[16]

Fontane gradually comes to adopt a stance, albeit a rather eccentric one, and this eccentricity provides the key to understanding why he did not find himself as a writer until in his old age. In 1879, at the age of sixty, he writes:

... but, ridiculous though it may sound, I can say of myself – unfortunately, perhaps: *'I'm only just beginning.'* I have nothing behind me, everything lies ahead of me, which is my good and ill fortune at one and the same time.[17]

Here Fontane perceives and emphasizes the ambiguity in his strange situation. He is naturally thinking of its external aspect; yet we shall see in the course of our observations that, in all questions of principle and of detail concerning his writing, this ambiguity became a determining factor in every area.

Above all it means the inextricable interlinking of extreme scepticism and the most naïve credulity in questions of public life. Because Fontane has become accustomed to making a sharp distinction between the personal and the universal, he is ultimately able to maintain his 'loyal', safe standpoint while exercising far-reaching and often judicious and perceptive criticisms of individuals and even of overall situations and trends.

Of course, it is the objective developmental trends of German capitalism that lie behind this individual stand. Above all, that of German unity. We have already seen that Fontane, owing to his superficial, wavering attitude, was carried along on the post-1848 wave of 'Freedom through Unity' among the German bourgeoisie which led to the Prussian-Bismarckian foundation of the Reich. We are also aware of the fact that he swam with this tide in spite of his personal critical misgivings.

A stronger conflict sets in following the foundation of the Reich, once the patriotic wave which has hitherto carried Fontane and so many others along finally subsides. The external pomp of the new Reich, coupled with the increasingly evident problems of its internal structure, the lack of political freedom, the cultural stagnation, was bound to cause ever greater doubt and concern in the minds of all but the staunchest supporters of the Bismarck System. The growth of such doubts and concerns in Fontane's mind was a complex, contradictory process. Yet it was only through the interaction of these new impressions, experiences and insights with his ideological and artistic development that the later Fontane was able to mature. In view of his overall development, this turning-point was bound to be of a predominantly private, moralistic nature. The turning-point in his views, the maturing of that quality that formed the basis of his work as an old man, is first and most clearly evident in his letters. It is remarkable that, both as far as the development towards the later Fontane and as far as his insuperable limitations are concerned, Fontane maintains the divide between public and private spheres – although it gradually becomes more and more undermined.

This development is particularly strong in Fontane's harsh criticism of Bismarck. As early as 1880, Fontane wrote in a letter:

A storm of resentment against Bismarck is gradually gathering amongst the people. . . He overestimates his popularity. It used to be enormous, but those days are gone. Every day hundreds, maybe thousands desert him. . . Even if he makes a grandiose display of the increasingly evident examples of his pettiness, that does not turn his pettiness into something grand.[18]

And he states even more harshly after Bismarck's fall from grace:

There has never been anyone with such little regard for principles as Bismarck, and it was a 'principle' which eventually brought his defeat and his downfall – that same principle that he always purported to stand by and which he never lived up to. . . He bears a great resemblance to *Schiller's* Wallenstein (the historical figure was different): a genius, a saviour of his nation, and a sentimental traitor. I must always come first, even if that holds up the course of history – complaints of ingratitude and tears of North German sentimentality.[19]

And equally so following Bismarck's reconciliation with Wilhelm II:

This mixture of superman and smart aleck, of founding statesman and stable-owning tax-evader. . ., of hero and cry-baby who looks as though butter wouldn't melt in his mouth, instills mixed feelings in me, preventing me from feeling pure admiration. He lacks a certain something, namely that vital ingredient that makes for true greatness.[20]

These verdicts, echoed in the conversations on Bismarck in novels written during Fontane's gradual maturing as a writer – and which should always be seen in conjunction with his enthusiastic poems in order to appreciate the deep-seated conflict within him – are still of a predominantly personal, moral nature, and are a drastic expression of the ambiguity, the sharp division between the public and the private, that we have already described. The older he becomes, however, and the deeper the impression made on him by the reactionary development of Germany following the foundation of the Reich, the more Fontane's criticism is directed towards public life. In his autobiography, the ageing Fontane refers to himself as a National Liberal who was never able to strike up a proper relationship with the party itself. And he adds that he has become increasingly democratic in his old age. This is true enough, yet it needs elaboration if the characteristics specific to Fontane are to become clear.

To start with: National Liberalism. One should not confuse the initial effect of the general National Liberal Party ideology prior to the foundation of the Reich, particularly on intellectuals, with the party itself, especially under Bismarck and above all under Wilhelm II. National Liberalism acted as a catch-all ideology for German unity without democratic revolution. Thus Raabe was also able to be a National Liberal in spite of his burning hatred and profound disdain for the emerging capitalist regime especially after the foundation of the Reich. For Fontane this question is both simpler and yet more complex. An important feature of his intellectual physiognomy is that, unlike Raabe, he was never a *laudator temporis acti*.[21] In his youth he underwent far too much suffering at the hands of the petty philistinism of Old Germany to hanker after this past time in any form whatsoever. And – again in contrast to Raabe, who was more provincial – he was too familiar with and too appreciative of the civilized capitalist world, especially England, not to welcome the expansion of Berlin, his permanent home in Germany, into a major city. He says in his autobiography:

It is so much nonsense to keep on talking about the 'good old days' or even of their 'virtues'; on the contrary, everything has got much better.

Implicit in this – again in contrast to Raabe – is an affirmation of the capitalist development of Germany. Admittedly, it is a peculiar kind of affirmation; a peculiarly Prussian kind, one might say. Fontane is essentially in favour of the capitalist development of Germany, but at the same time opposed to the bourgeoisie. 'The bourgeois as I see him,' says Fontane in his autobiography, sounding somewhat Lassallian, 'is not really, or at least not exclusively, rooted in bags of money.' Fontane adds his private, moralizing nuance to this view:

They all profess to have ideals; they never cease to chatter on about 'beauty, virtue and truth', yet all they ever do is bow down to the golden calf, either by actually seizing any opportunity that promises to bring in money and property or at least inwardly bleeding themselves white in their yearning for suchlike. These secret bourgeois. . . are by far the worse of the two because their lives are simply one big lie.[22]

Whereas, therefore, Lassalle's concept of the bourgeois is a shallow and mechanistic 'politicization' of the socio-economic existence of the bourgeoisie, Fontane, as we have already seen, also turns this question into a moral one, making it a struggle against hypocrisy and lies, thus criticizing one side of bourgeois existence without dealing with the central problems of capitalism. On this question, in the struggle against self-deception and hypocrisy, his position increasingly overlaps with that of Ibsen. We shall discuss the complexities of his relationship to the latter in more detail below.

This ambiguous position is, however, of great significance for Fontane's development, for it enables him to incorporate, albeit in an extremely contradictory way, his affection for Old Prussia and the Prussian aristocracy into his changing world-view in which progress is seen as something positive. Conversely, it would be completely wrong to assume that Fontane adhered to a romantic anti-capitalism, a yearning for a return to a pre-capitalist age or to primitive capitalism. And it would show just as much ignorance of his life to view him as a simple or indeed uncritical admirer of the Prussian aristocracy. His personal, intimate statements and – much more important – the works of his most mature period, contain scathing criticism of *Junkerism*. Nonetheless, this criticism is shot through with a profoundly felt personal attachment, with a strong aesthetic and ethical preference for the good specimens of Prussian aristocracy, especially those from the Brandenburg Marches. Fontane often expresses this 'human sympathy' for certain types of *Junkerism*. His autobiography gives a clearly formulated summary of his inwardly ambiguous position:

The shining examples among them – and there are more than a few – do indeed shine, and it would be stupid not to want to love them; but even those who do not shine – and their number is great, I admit – still have, despite their egotism and quixotism, or perhaps because of both, a peculiar charm, and I consider myself lucky to be able to sense this. Their reactionary principles as such are not at all to my taste, but I do have a liking for the chance representatives of these principles, now as ever.[23]

Thus Fontane is prone to widely ranging vacillations with thoroughly blurred boundaries between the various extremes: affirmation of capitalist development, yet disdain for the bourgeoisie; a predilection for the aristocracy, yet (at times) a clear insight into its historical obsolescence. Obviously this is only a more concrete, extended and heightened form of the conflict we have already observed between the public and the private. However, Fontane is obliged, despite his deep scepticism and his constant self-criticism, to look for a certain orientation in his way of life, even if it can never be straightforward. Precisely because of this, he gains a sixth sense for still vague, nascent developments and at times has a more than critical attitude to the official views of the time.

Again we must confine ourselves to the most characteristic examples. Immediately after the German victories over France, after the meeting of the Austrian, German and Russian emperors in 1872, Fontane believes the state of the new and apparently so mighty Germany to be extremely precarious and insecure:

I sense more than I can prove that a deep feeling of discontent, be it justified or unjustified, is brewing among broad sections of the people. . . There is certainly enough tinder to set the world ablaze again without any oil being poured over it.[24]

And twenty years later, in much harsher tones:

The collapse of all the splendour that was built up between 1864 and 1870 is being discussed openly. . . . no one is. . . at all convinced of the stability of our circumstances. What has been conquered can be lost again. Bavaria is able to stand entirely on its own feet once more. The Rhine provinces have gone down the drain, so have West and East Prussia, and an independent state of Poland (which I consider a distinct probability sooner or later) is re-emerging.[25]

Fontane harboured similar doubts about the stability of British rule in India, etc. In the last year of his life he sums up his views to an English friend:

Governments are still in control, not the passions of the people. But when *these* do have their say, we will experience terrible struggles, after which the world and its maps will look different from today.[26]

This last statement shows how justified Fontane was in speaking of a democratization of his views; even in the March Days of 1848 he had already recognized the fact that the workers were the only serious, really courageous fighters. His understanding of the working class increases in proportion to his experience of life. As early as 1878, at the time of the Anti-Socialist Law, he writes to his wife about the workers:

All these people are our equals in every respect. They cannot be fobbed off with claims that 'politics are not for the likes of them', nor can they be kept down by force of arms. It is not true that they only stand for chaos and rebellion, they also stand for *ideas* which are partly justified and which cannot be beaten to death or eradicated by dealing out prison sentences.[27]

And the words he chooses when writing to his English friend (1896) are even more determined:

All interest lies with the fourth estate. The bourgeoisie are dreadful people, the aristocracy and the clergy are behind the times, and always the same. Hope for a new, better world starts with the fourth estate. This would be true even if things were only at the stage of aims, of first attempts. Yet this is not the case. What the workers think, say and write has actually overtaken the thought, speeches and writings of the old ruling classes. Everything is much more genuine, more valid, more full of life. They, the workers, have a new approach to everything, they not only have new aims, but also new *methods*.[28]

Nevertheless – and this rounds off the picture of how he came to become the later Fontane – none of this is capable of bringing about a decisive transformation in his world-view as a whole, indeed it has no revolutionary impact on the basis and structure of his ideas. Fontane's sympathy for the working class and for all plebeian strata remains coupled with his attachment to the old *Junkers* of the Brandenburg Marches. For example, in his old age he once hears a young sales girl recite one of his poems very well, and writes to his daughter about this:

I am becoming more and more democratic and only have any respect left for true aristocracy. I have little time for everything in between: philistines, bourgeois, officials and self-professed 'scholars'.[29]

Thus Fontane becomes – and the more he matures, the more this applies – a wavering figure, a person and a writer who feels he cannot rely on any of the rival classes or parties. By virtue of the emotional tradition of his development and his aesthetic and moral sympathies he feels closest to the *Junkers* of the eastern borderlands (the Mark). His works, however, in which his sceptical irony is given free rein to develop, objectively upset or even destroy this intimate bond, which is subjectively so strong. Fontane wrote Prussian ballads, three great war books, the *Wanderings in the Brandenburg Marches* in vain – classes cannot be deceived. At his seventieth birthday celebrations, those very people he had praised all his life were absent. He writes about this in a letter:

People have made a tremendous fuss of me – and then again, not at all. Modern Berlin treated me like a minor deity, but Old Prussia, which I have been glorifying for the past forty years or more in my war books, biographies, descriptions of the countryside and the people and in folk poetry, this 'Old Prussia' hardly stirred. . .[30]

In an ironical, indeed self-ironical poem Fontane provides a vivid description of the celebrations and his feelings.

And as Fontane's cosmopolitan-Berlin self-irony becomes stronger, richer, more subtle, we find an expression of what he occasionally noticed when observing his environment and the history of his country without, of course, being able to draw any decisive conclusions that might have affected his way of life and his writing. In the *Wanderings* he says of Berlin irony:

The irony itself was self-defence, a natural consequence of the fact that a whole number of important intellectual forces were wrongfully excluded from the main arenas of public life. Freedom of speech has finally proved to be the death of irony.

This final sentence is, of course, a grave self-deception, although it is one which Fontane himself occasionally manages to dispel by using irony. Thus, in the last year of his life he writes on the German elections:

> . . . in our country, where behind every voter there stands a policeman, and then a battalion, and then an artillery battery, it all seems to me to be a complete waste of time. The power of the people has to stand behind a popular election; if it does not, then everything is just a farce.[31]

Fontane is therefore aware of what lies behind the German façade of freedom. The Brandenburg *Junkers* had every reason – in spite of his ballads, war books and the *Wanderings* – to consider him unreliable: the more so, the older he became. The more Fontane developed in this direction, the richer his writing became and the more he became the later Fontane.

In his mature period Fontane's specific qualities as a writer stand out with particular clarity; as do his specific limitations, however. That it was the later Fontane who was to become the true Fontane is therefore the result of the furthest possible development of these contradictions in alliance with the interaction of his natural disposition and the social development of Germany. These contradictions expressed themselves in his youth in the form of crude opposites which, because they were mutually exclusive, hurled Fontane as a person helplessly from one extreme to the other without leaving him anything to cling to. Because of the class basis of his existence, these antagonisms could never be resolved, nor even relieved to any great extent. The tendency within his privatized scepticism that furthered his development lay in the fact that these opposites permeated one another and, without objectively blunting each other, emerged in the form of increasingly concrete contradictions. The way in which this process was stimulated by his scepticism, irony and self-irony shows us clearly the nature of the personal attributes which formed the basis of Fontane's late maturity.

However, it would be one-sided and wrong to see this as no more than a problem of individual psychology. Fontane's inner growth, the structural transformation of his behaviour towards himself and his environment is – in a complicated, indirect way, of course – essentially a reflection of what was taking place in Germany from the time of his youth up until his death. The immaturity of the revolutionary movement in Germany was responsible for the crude extremism of the contradictions of his youth. The wave of nationalism leading up to the foundation of the Reich prevented his inner development from progressing quickly. It fixed and consolidated all the weaker aspects of his world-view. This is not contradicted by the fact that his increasing knowledge of the world did have a positive effect below the surface, indeed it only serves to heighten the antagonisms within his views. Not until the Bismarck-Wilhelminian period, when the contradictions of the false, anti-democratic foundation of the Reich became increasingly evident, did that fertile interaction develop in which Fontane's positive qualities as a writer were gradually able to come to the fore. As we have seen, he correctly believed that at the beginning of the eighteen seventies his career as a writer was really only just beginning, and the reason for this phenomenon lay only partly in his personality. As indicated above, it can only be fully understood from the point of view of the interaction of that personality with the course of German history.

II

We have seen that a kind of scepticism, at times bordering on nihilism, is Fontane's solution, and indeed the motivating force behind his growth. However, a word like doubt tells us very little in itself. We have to ask ourselves what this doubt was directed against. This question must include the subjective aspect: do scepticism, irony and self-irony undermine the personality of the writer himself, depriving him of stability and direction, or do they rather provide the personality with a form of camouflage, a cover to see him through unfavourable times? And on the other hand, what does this doubt signify from an objective, socio-historical standpoint? Does it point forwards or backwards?

It is important to make a distinction here that is vital for our assessment of Fontane's historical position and the identification of where his limitations lay. In this kind of situation it is always necessary to ask: is the solution to that problem which has given rise to doubt in the mind of the person wrestling with it already objectively available to him, having been born out of society's womb; has it indeed already been clearly formulated? Although Georg Büchner, with his irony, pathos and criticisms, was searching for something higher than 1793, something that in social terms surpassed the democratic revolution, the Germany of his day completely lacked even the abstract possibility of its realization. However, in Fontane's day, clear solutions had already been found to the problems he faced. To put it oversimply, he need only have gone into a bookshop to find in the works of Marx and Engels clearly formulated answers to all his questions.

Of course, considering the totality of Fontane the person, that would be an oversimplification. For it was no coincidence that he did not go in search of these books (ignoring for the moment any other possibilities besides books). Nonetheless, this simplification does imply a judgement: namely that Fontane, because of his personal and his class position, lacked the concrete opportunity to acquire insights that were already the property of a great mass of his contemporaries. Even in those few moments when such insights did vaguely occur to him, or even clearly presented themselves to him, he lacked any means of incorporating them usefully in his attitude to life, in his world-view. Thus, the social facts behind what Fontane regards as objectively insoluble problems have already become the dynamic, future-oriented contradictions of social development, and are recognized as such by many.

It is not simply a case of Fontane being a bourgeois writer. For the writer of this epoch, so Chekhov maintains, the main task of literary practice is to delve deep into problems and to portray them in an appropriate artistic form. Tolstoy was also a bourgeois writer, yet just as Swift and Fielding, Balzac and Stendhal had done before him, Tolstoy approached and demonstrated in literary form the conflicts of his time on a much higher level than Fontane was ever capable of. One of the decisive factors leading to these different levels is that of doubt: how and where it arises and what it is directed towards; what is accepted and what is undermined and destroyed in the act of writing; whether scepticism, irony and self-irony provide literary weapons with which to attack the existing capitalist social order (which the writer, from a purely cognitive point of view, may not fully comprehend or interpret correctly), or whether they are merely a lifebelt to save the writer from drowning in the floodwaters of unfavourable times.

There can be no doubt that Fontane belongs in the second category. His letters in particular contain more than a few comments that come quite close to the decadent movements which only developed in Germany after Fontane's death. I shall confine myself to citing one letter to his daughter in which his scepticism seems to have intensified to the level of nihilistic pessimism:

I know full well that 'life is but an illusion and death is the truth' – the most profound statement ever made about humanity and all things human. Not only the most profound, however, but also the saddest. . . What we call faith is nothing but fraud or deception or stupidity; what we call loyalty is nothing but calculation; what we call love can be all sorts of things, but it is not usually love; what we call adherence to a creed is nothing but dogmatism. . . It is true that the highest and holiest only occurs once in a lifetime, or, to put it more accurately, there are serious, heartfelt convictions (which certainly does not make them necessarily true) for which individuals are occasionally prepared to die an honest death. But these individuals are like a drop of true ink in the ocean. The ocean is a meaningless, indifferent stretch of water. And humanity is not even water, but merely a swamp, with micro-organisms in every drop that would make your blood curdle if you could see them. . . All we have is a bit of art and science that, in honest toil, is able to elevate us above ourselves, and the best thing we have is – Nature. All the rest is rubbish, and the more so, the more fuss and political turmoil there is. It's all a waste of time.[32]

This feature of Fontane's character should not be ignored, nor played down as a passing fit of emotion. For these emotions occur by objective, social necessity in any person whose consciousness undertakes the vain attempt to detach individual being from the social base, to exist in complete independence of it in private life. The nihilism that is bound to develop in such cases rapidly went on to take its toll on subsequent generations of German writers. A comparatively early example of utter self-disintegration can clearly be seen in Hugo von Hofmannsthal's famous *Lord Chandos Letter to Francis Bacon, Lord Verulam.*

There is virtually no evidence of Fontane going to this introverted, self-tormenting extreme, and this clearly distinguishes him from his decadent successors. As a writer, Fontane falls between two periods. Although he only becomes a central figure of modern German literature through the emergence of the Naturalist movement in the eighteen eighties and nineties and in spite of his enthusiastic support for Ibsen and particularly Hauptmann, he nonetheless has serious theoretical and practical reservations with respect to the movement as a whole. He would not dream of identifying himself with it, either on an artistic or an ideological level. He does, however, recognize the Naturalist movement as one that points the way forward in literary terms; just as he regards the age in which he lives, for all his criticisms of it, as representing progress when compared with the periods preceding and following 1848, so too he regards naturalism as progress, especially compared to the barren period following the foundation of the Reich.

Fontane by no means underestimates the progress inherent in the observation of human phenomena, even in its most superficial, purely descriptive form, in comparison to the dead conventions of his contemporaries. On the occasion of a novel by Alexander Kielland, he writes:

I acknowledge the immense literary progress represented by the recourse to exact reporting, which has delivered us at a stroke from the dull chatter of past decades, during which time average and sometimes even good writers were constantly writing 'from the depths of their moral awareness' about things they had never seen.[33]

He is, however, equally vehement in his demand that literature should go further than this.

However, it is not the task of the novel simply to depict things that occur, or at least that *could* occur any day. It seems to me that the task of the modern novel is to depict a way of life, a society, a group of people who provide an undistorted reflection of the very life that we lead. The best novel is the one whose characters can take their place among the characters of real life, so that when we think back on a particular epoch we are no longer quite sure whether they were living or fictitious figures. . .[34]

Consistent with this is the way he mocks his 'admirers' who enthusiastically praise the photographic and historical accuracy of his detailed descriptions. Thus, in a letter, he writes of the details contained in *Schach von Wuthenow*[35] that 'everything, down to the last straw, was my own invention'; and in another letter he lists with irony all the inaccurate details contained in his Berlin novels, adding that they are nonetheless essentially realistic.

In the main, therefore, Fontane's literary leaning is towards realism, not naturalism. One might even say that his basic aesthetic premisses are rooted in the classical period of bourgeois realism.

It is no coincidence that he remains throughout his life a faithful follower of the art of Walter Scott. And it is characteristic of his view of art that a novel like *Heart of Midlothian* should affect him so strongly. In this connection, he writes to his wife:

Quite apart from all the hundred other merits, one senses running through the whole novel a gift of being able to make people always say the most natural, the most appropriate thing, a gift shared by no other, apart from Shakespeare and Goethe. I consider this to be the greatest gift of all.[36]

He repeatedly expresses this conviction – especially with regard to Zola, whose skill as a writer he otherwise admires – by stating his resistance to any kind of exaggeration, and his intention as a novelist 'to leave everything in the proportions and percentages bestowed upon phenomena by life itself'.

These remarks are enough to show that for Fontane moderation and proportion were concepts not of form but of content, which should be taken from life and applied to art, rather than imposed on life by art. His particular aversion to exaggeration is for Fontane a primary principle of life. He hates what he calls 'emotional noise'. Following the death of his oldest son he turns against those people who expect of him 'besides stupendous courage and stupendous love . . . stupendous sadness as well'. 'Moderation is not only a thing of beauty, but it is also the truth.'

This standpoint determines his judgement of writers and works. He is a close friend of Storm and Heyse, but he is very critical of the latter, 'because his senses are not accurate enough', and makes fun of the former, whose poetry he greatly admires, because of the contrived erotic scenes for which Fontane calls him the 'monopolist of the solemn kiss'. Occasionally Fontane raises this kind of criticism to the level of principle:

There can be no work of art without poetry, to which it only remains to be added that perfect *reproduction of nature* is most certainly an expression of the highest degree of poetic representation. Nothing is rarer than this highest degree, which signifies absolute objectivity. As a rule, the artist who reproduces reality is not a God, but a mere human being, an ego, and he projects part of this ego into his creative work. From the moment this takes place, everything revolves around the question, 'What is the nature of this ego?'[37]

Here Fontane is concerned with what is correct, moderate, healthy and normal. In this his standpoint is the opposite of most of his contemporaries; he once again finds himself in agreement with the old realists. Criticizing the poet's ego, he says of Freiligrath:

There is something strange about him. There is something in his soul that is not healthy. That is why his images are more sensational than poetic. Even those that are poetic are at least a little sickly.[38]

Fontane's life struggle, the radically private orientation of his world-view, his irony and self-irony as guidelines for self-preservation, all served the following purpose: to protect this sense of moderation and proportion, of what is normal and healthy, from the unhealthy tendencies of the times, and to allow it to develop within him.

We have seen that for Fontane – as a result of his personal characteristics, his class situation and the development of Germany – the only possible way of realizing this was to retreat into privacy. There is no question that, objectively speaking, this represents an ideologically reactionary tendency, and subjectively an almost philistine one, and on the other hand, closely connected with this, a loss in literary terms, namely the disappearance of directly social factors from plot and characterization.

Seen in the context of the development of bourgeois literature in this period, this latter trend is by no means exclusive to Germany. In mid-nineteenth century France we can observe a passionate, and in many cases fruitless struggle to preserve the old richness of literature, its capacity to encompass all social phenomena, especially on the part of Flaubert and Zola. In England, Thackeray – one of Fontane's favourite authors – openly admits defeat in this fight against capitalist reality. He incorporates a lengthy reflection on this into his novel *The Virginians* in which he clearly states that people's actual working activities only provide a very small part of the 'novelist's budget'.

What can a story-teller say about the professional existence of these men?. . . All authors can do, is to depict men *out* of their business – in their passions, loves, laughters, amusements, hatreds, and what not. . .[39]

Therefore, although all these figures follow a profession, the writer is only able to give them literary form in situations in which they are free from their work.

It would go beyond our present scope to give even the most

cursory description of this struggle waged by bourgeois writers. We would like to mention in this context the ignominious, philistine failure of Fontane's contemporary, Gustav Freytag, who set out to 'look for the German people at work'. That this failure should take on such an extremely philistine form is not at all coincidental, but is the inevitable consequence of the insurmountably dreary prosaic quality of that bourgeois professional efficiency which liberals like to hold up as such a virtue. As a mature writer, Fontane essentially takes the same course as Thackeray.

This runs parallel to the change in his view of history and historical heroism, which contrasts with Fontane's youthful ballads and the subject matter of his early period – a tragedy set in the English Revolution and a Barbarossa epos – and with many poems dating from the later period. And of course this change is not confined to the level of subject matter, but in the mature novels is emphasized as a polemic against the official, traditional concept of history. In *Unwiederbringlich* (*Beyond Recall*) the grand style of history and its portrayal in literature is discussed. Ebba Rosenberg, the intelligent lady-in-waiting, says: 'But what does grand style really mean? Grand style means ignoring everything that really interests people.' The extent to which this corresponds to Fontane's own standpoint is shown by the fact that, in *Frau Jenny Treibel*, Professor Schmidt, who shares a number of features with the author, makes a very similar observation:

The incidental, that much is right, doesn't count if it is merely incidental, if there is nothing in it. But if there is something in it, then it's the main thing, because it always reveals the human essence.[40]

On the other hand, in a letter to his wife, Fontane gives a fairly clear indication of the degree to which this attitude is a reflection of the times:

I treat the small with the same loving attention as I do the great, because I refuse to recognize the distinction between great and small. . . Herwegh concludes one of his sonnets 'An die Dichter' ['To the Poets'] with the following lines:

> Und wenn einmal ein *Löwe* vor euch steht,
> Sollt ihr nicht das *Insekt* auf ihn besingen.

> 'And if one day a *lion* should stand before you,
> Do not sing about the *insect* that crawls upon him.'

By these standards I am, I admit, literally a lousy poet, indeed passionately so at times; but one of the reasons for that is the absence of a lion.[41]

The last remark shows clearly the strength with which Fontane
felt his view to be a stand against the Prusso-German status quo.
However, it was only a feeling, and even then it was not always
present. Fontane's standpoint thereby acquired a twofold character. As we shall see when analysing his works, he is only progressive
and productive as a writer to the extent that the anti-Prussian
tendency gains the upper hand. This kind of polemic against the
Prussian concept of heroism occurs with relative frequency. In the
semi-autobiographical novel, *Der Stechlin* (*Lake Stechlin*), we read:

If a battalion is called to the front and I'm caught right in the middle of it,
what am I supposed to do? I just have to go. And then – bang – there I am
on the ground. And now I'm a hero. But I'm not really a hero. I'm only
there because I have to be, and compulsory heroes like that are two a
penny. That's what I call the great wars.

Similarly in *Irrungen, Wirrungen* (*Errors, Entanglements*) Fontane
discovers ironic parallels between German aristocrats who were
killed in the Seven Years' War and Scottish horse-thieves who were
hanged by the English in connection with clan feuds. There is of
course a very serious view behind all this irony. In his autobiography
Fontane speaks of the true and the false heroes of the March
struggles. He says:

Heroism is a wonderful thing, just about the most beautiful thing there is,
but it has to be genuine. And in order for it to be genuine, even in such
matters, there has to be meaning and rationality. If these elements are
missing, then I have very mixed feelings with regard to such heroism.[42]

Otherwise Fontane restricts himself to counterposing individual
morality, which takes on a quietistic, fatalistic character in this context, to Prussian discipline, to Prussian ambition, to the capitalist
'fight for survival'. This attitude is clearly evident in his later poetry:

> Nur als Furioso nichts erstreben
> Und fechten, bis der Säbel bricht;
> Es muß sich dir von *selber* geben –
> Man hat es oder hat es nicht.
> Der Weg zu jedem höchsten Glücke,
> Wär das Gedräng auch noch so dicht,
> Ist keine Beresina-Brücke –
> Man hat es oder hat es nicht.

Don't strive for things like a madman, or fight until your sabre is shattered; things have to succeed of *themselves* – either you have the knack, or you don't. The road to the greatest success, however great the throng may be, is no Beresina Bridge – either you have the knack or you don't.

The inevitable conclusion to be drawn from this is that standing on the sidelines, adopting the pose of a resigned and sceptical observer, is the correct way to behave in life:

> Ein Chinese ('s sind schon an 200 Jahr)
> In Frankreich auf einem Hofball war.
> Und die einen frugen ihn, ob er das kenne?
> Und die anderen frugen ihn, wie man es nenne?
> 'Wir nennen es tanzen,' sprach er mit Lachen,
> 'Aber wir lassen es *andere* machen.'

A Chinaman – some 200 years ago – went to a ball in France. Some asked him whether he had ever seen such a thing before. Others asked him whether he had a word for it? 'We call it "dancing",' he said with a smile, 'but we get *others* to do it.'

The scepticism of the old Fontane, his famous willingness to 'turn a blind eye', vacillates between these two poles. As we have seen, it is not at all a case of nihilism standing in opposition to any kind of morality. On the contrary. Without being able (or indeed wishing) to define morality in terms of its content, i.e. from a social point of view, Fontane nonetheless has a strong sense of human integrity which he admires wherever it occurs, regardless of its social content. Admittedly, as soon as he even tries to generalize his affirmation he inevitably falls into the trap of moral formalism. Thus his view of heroism as expressed in *Der Stechlin* is socially nihilistic:

The only really important thing is that a person is able to say, 'That's what I'm prepared to die for'. And then goes on to do so. It doesn't really matter what for.

Implicit in this attitude is an instinctive recognition of the priority of being over consciousness: a method of composition, in which people's behaviour is consistently determined by their social existence; opinions, feelings or moods that come into conflict with that existence are always treated as secondary, superficial phases. When in *Frau Jenny Treibel* the heroine, a conceited bourgeois lady, becomes hysterical on hearing that her son intends to form a 'misalliance' with Professor Schmidt's daughter, she is violently reproached by her husband:

Everything you've blared out here is firstly nonsensical and secondly disgusting. And what else besides – blind, forgetful, arrogant – I don't even want to talk about. . .[43]

This is the tone in which Treibel, a distinguished businessman, addresses his wife, who is at first extremely taken aback, but is then contented and relieved because she knows that her husband, having said his piece, will think quite differently about the matter the following day.

Like many other details, this is well observed, and is accurately portrayed so that the inevitable social hypocrisy is exposed. This method of portrayal equally inevitably results in Fontane's plebeian figures enjoying intellectual or at least moral superiority over the *Junkers* or the bourgeoisie. However, this superiority is never rebellious; it only means that Fontane's plebeian figures do not harbour dishonest illusions or self-delusions, that they accept the society of the day the way it is. (At this point it should once again be stressed that this takes place at a time of advanced class struggles of which, as we have seen, Fontane was an attentive observer. That these struggles find absolutely no expression in his works, not even in the form of moralistic reflections, is a further sign of his limitations.) The behaviour of Fontane's plebeian figures is best exemplified by Widow Pittelkow in *Stine*. When the young Count Haldern wishes to marry her sister, she says to her:

Everyone has their place, and there's nothing you or that young Count fellow can do to alter that. I couldn't give two hoots for the counts, young or old, you've seen that often enough. But I can hoot as much as I want and I still can't blow them away, neither them nor the difference between us. They're just there, and they are the way they are, and they're dolled up different from the likes of us, and they can't change their spots. And if one of them does want to change his spots, the others don't let him and don't let up until they've got him back where he belongs.

This world-view also lies behind Fontane's ambiguous position on his important contemporaries, Gottfried Keller and Henrik Ibsen – a mixture of enthusiasm and rejection. Generally, Fontane is a fine, discerning judge of literature. Yet in his opinion of Keller he fails miserably. He considers him lacking in style, and compares him with affected Romantics such as Arnim. Thomas Mann shows with great elegance that this objection concerning an absence of style, which Fontane raises in connection with Keller's writing, would apply first and foremost to Fontane himself. It is hardly coincidental that Fontane levels this criticism, namely that the terse, personal mode of writing lacks style because it violates the concrete subject matter and robs it of all contours, only against Keller.

I believe that Fontane's essential disagreement with Keller lies deeply rooted in his own personality. Precisely because he was only able to preserve his individuality as a human being and a writer by 'turning a blind eye', he felt the cruelty of the humorist Keller as a self-indictment. Fontane also attempts to draw logical conclusions from the lives of his figures and their situation. However, his scepticism shrouds every conflict in a mild, conciliatory, comprehending atmosphere, whereas Keller employs all the cruelty of the great old humorists to drive the philistine characters he so despises to their comic destruction. With Keller, this is based on the radical democrat's stable scale of values, on the Jacobin attitude of 'putting virtue on the agenda', as I have discussed in my essay on Keller. In the final analysis it is precisely this to which Fontane objects in him.

Fontane's much more frequent, more comprehensive and more forthright criticisms of Ibsen are quite a different matter. Fontane admires Ibsen as a great innovator of the theatre, as a 'blessed revolutionary' of drama and theatre in terms of his realism, simplicity, lack of rhetoric, and of his criticism of the falseness of bourgeois ideals (*The Wild Duck*). However here too, the praise is not without reservation. When Gerhart Hauptmann appears on the scene, his enthusiasm is less muted. Hauptmann, he writes, is 'a completely unrhetorical Ibsen, in other words, he is what Ibsen would merely like to be but never can . . .'[44] Fontane does however add that he would not wish to see Hauptmann's way of writing become the single predominant style of the future.[45]

His main objection to Ibsen, as formulated in the previously quoted letter to his daughter, is that Ibsen

is more or less mad, and in his heightened fits of madness degenerates into utterly empty phrase-mongering. Not phrase-mongering in the verbal sense, but rather in the sense of emotions, of outlook.[46]

The principle behind this criticism is already familiar to us from

Fontane's critique of Heyse and Storm. This critique touches upon one of the most important aspects of Fontane's position on art and life: the struggle for normality. Fontane rejects Ibsen's subjective-idealistic, abstractly moralistic critique of bourgeois society, particularly of bourgeois marriage. This colours his view of Ibsen's art, and he thus finds many of Ibsen's conflicts and solutions contrived and mathematical. He writes to Otto Brahm on the ending of *Little Eyolf*, which he admires as a 'colossal achievement': 'Its proportions are false. Of course, if one chooses to calculate, one runs the risk of miscalculating. The simple, stupid cow always finds the right grass.'[47] And he prophesies to Paul Schlenther: 'In thirty years (at the latest) Ibsen's comedy will have become outdated.'

At the centre of this passionate rejection, always accompanied by admiration, was what Fontane refers to as Ibsen's 'marriage nonsense'. Fontane and Ibsen occupy positions at opposite extremes of the spectrum of bourgeois attitudes to the question of love and marriage in bourgeois society. As is well known, Ibsen was a radical advocate of individual love – created by bourgeois society, but constantly undermined by it in the practical reality of everyday life – and he adamantly rejects any form of marriage not based exclusively on love. Fontane rejects this as exaggerated, unrealistic and pathological. He demands recognition of the exigences of reality, and even – to use the terminology of German Classical philosophy – reconciliation with them. He believes that love will come sooner or later under normal social circumstances, and '*if it does not come, then no harm has been done*'. He adopts a standpoint which, in spite of its conservative tone, is apparently more realistic, more faithful to social existence, than that of Ibsen. And in opposing bourgeois-decadent, blind glorification of any kind of passion, he is thus able, to a certain extent, to salvage his call for human normality as the basis of moderation and beauty in art. But only to a certain extent. For in this polemic, which is of central significance to him, Fontane firstly overlooks the fact that individual love is just as much a product of the laws of bourgeois society as is its prevention by these laws, and secondly, that – particularly in terms of the human normality to which Fontane aspires – under no circumstances can meek acceptance of the facts of capitalist life be considered humanly normal.

Fortunately for Fontane, his literary portrayal of life does not always, and not entirely, follow the line of his – in many respects justified – critique of Ibsen. Wherever this is the case, he descends to the level of mere, albeit good, belles lettres. That Fontane's works were in constant danger of this is just as characteristic of his limitations as are, respectively, Ibsen's lapses into sophistries bordering on decadence. Fontane and Ibsen are simply two extreme examples of the limited nature of the bourgeois view of social problems.

III

What is the cause of this lapse into mere belles lettres? Fontane sets himself the highest artistic standards, re-writing his works and polishing them with the greatest of care; he possesses an extremely keen stylistic awareness, from major questions of composition down to the linguistic refinement of the smallest detail; he works hard to maintain the highest level of which he is capable. (A very interesting example of this can be found in the observations in his correspondence on the connection between the variation of narrative tone and the use or avoidance of 'and' at the beginning of a sentence.) Nor is Fontane prepared to make any concessions to current taste. He horrifies the older generation with his frank discussion of moral problems and his realistic portrayal of facts of life which had previously been taboo for these readers. At the same time, he is equally averse to making concessions to the tastes of the younger generation, i.e. to the Naturalist movement.

We have already seen that Fontane rejects a naturalistic, photographic attention to detail. In his writings he makes no concessions to the crassness of subject matter and method of description which can also be ascribed to naturalism and which is particularly striking in its portrayal of sexuality. When it appears necessary, Fontane never shies away from examining even the physiological basis of love or non-love. However, he does so with such elevated artistic discretion and so sparingly, always confining himself so strictly to what is absolutely necessary in human terms, that neither the decadent lovers of sexualism nor those of naturalist brutality find what they are looking for in his works. (Take, for example, the depiction of married life in *Effi Briest*.)

In the later Fontane, this restraint does not lead to dullness or monotony. On the contrary. It is a necessary consequence of his compositional form, which – in his successful works – is tight and yet at the same time appears free, loose and unfettered in the spirit of truly epic writing. In this respect too, Fontane could be seen as a German parallel to Thackeray, in that both writers try to combine modernity of content and form with a strong regard for the traditions of the classic realist novel. The decisive factor in this is the provision of an extensive and uninhibited survey of the relationships between the various characters. On this point, the old-style novel paid very little attention to naturalistic probability. Its main concern was to paint a picture of life in which the true lives of the characters, the real social significance of their destinies found expression in socially and therefore humanly correct proportions. Fontane uses this typically 'old' method with great awareness. For example, when describing the discovery of Effi's unfaithfulness to her husband, he deliberately chooses a banal option, the chance discovery of love-letters, simply to avoid introducing an image that might appear somehow far-fetched or contrived.

From Thackeray's remarks quoted earlier we know that his essential method of composition was determined by the material, the subject matter, namely the impoverishment of bourgeois life as a result of the capitalist division of labour, the privatization of the emotional life of the bourgeois individual, and his forced or voluntary withdrawal from public life. (The particular nature of this subject matter is a natural consequence of viewing advanced capitalism from a bourgeois class standpoint.)

With Fontane, this tendency is if anything even more pronounced and consistent than with Thackeray. It is no coincidence that Fontane's novels always contain a relatively narrow circle of characters, and that, despite the apparently loosely-knit composition, they are often clustered around a single decisive event, as in a novella or ballad. Fontane is aware of this novella-like tendency in the structure of his novels, and also that by excluding professional activities and even all forms of public life from the portrayal of his characters, he runs the risk of over-restricting the terrain in which they can act out their destinies – the risk of creating a portrayal based on bloodless psychologism.

For this reason, Fontane is always at pains to overcome these restrictions by including the intellectual and moral reflections of those areas of life that lie beyond the limits of composition, allowing them to exert a decisive influence on the fates of the characters. This accounts for the major role played by conversations in Fontane's novels. This compositional method, of course, reflects the dichotomy of his position, proving that the retreat from public life is not a true retreat, merely the illusion of the bourgeois intellectual at the beginning of capitalism's period of decline. In these conversations, Fontane displays the full force of his mastery as a writer. They are without exception on a high intellectual level, very different from the naturalistic barrenness of dialogue which Lafargue criticizes in Zola.[48] Although every figure is imbued with Fontane's spirit and possesses his distinctive powers of articulation, each one still expresses his or her own personal class psychology. The form of expression is always finely individualized, not, of course, in the naturalistic sense of dialect, choice of words, recurring 'characteristic' expressions, etc., but in terms of their content, of the political and social, the intellectual and moral physiognomy of the speakers.

On the other hand, Fontane always endeavours to give his narratives that objective completeness, that 'totality of objects', necessary for the convincing portrayal of any narrative world, any palpable interaction between the individual and society. For Fontane, of course, this presents an extremely difficult, indeed almost insoluble problem. One need only think of his great contemporaries to appreciate the significance in terms of the totality of objects of festivals, public events (the Tell celebrations in *Green Henry*, etc.) in Gottfried Keller, for example. Fontane's subject matter, the Prussian Germany of his time, and of course, amplifying this, his attitude to this social reality, precludes such richness. Fontane is only able to employ small, fragmentary moments of urban private life, such as excursions, social functions, visits to the theatre, in order to show his characters in palpable interaction with their fellow human beings and their environment. This is obviously a very narrow base, a meagre source of material compared to the richness and variety of what Gottfried Keller – not to mention Tolstoy – is able to incorporate into his works. Fontane's great art consists in his ability to make maximum use of this scant material element, to conjure up – in his successful works – the appearance of objective plenitude.

This is closely linked to the above-mentioned high intellectual level of his works. The intellectual richness of the conversations that take place on such occasions, their at times disguised, always loosely conceived connection with the decisive twists of fate in the lives of the novel's characters are therefore able nevertheless to transform what are essentially but the socially insubstantial remnants of a once more plentiful totality of objects into effective building-blocks with which to construct a genuinely epic world.

If this is the case, why does Fontane relatively frequently lapse from realistic novel writing into mere – albeit stylistically cultivated – belles lettres? Our analysis so far has already shown that his composition is based on an extremely unstable equilibrium of elements of content and world-view, balancing on a knife's edge, where the slightest slip can lead to his sense of realism becoming distorted to an artistically catastrophic extent.

There are relatively simple cases of Fontane allowing himself to be carried away by his own virtuosity as an author of dialogues, cases in which intellectual conversation becomes an end in itself, thus ceasing to be a driving force behind the essential plot and the continuing exposition of central conflicts. Among the examples of this are the conversations about Old Prussian history in *Cécile*; and also, in part – because of its disproportionate length – the contrast, amusing enough in itself, between the Berlin and the Hamburg bourgeoisie in *Frau Jenny Treibel*.

However, the phenomenon we have in mind here is by no means adequately described by citing such examples of the occasional misjudgement. Not least because there generally lies a deeper problem behind such cases. Namely: how does Fontane's life's principle of 'turning a blind eye' affect the structure of his plots, the internal organization of his chosen subject? As a polemic against the hypocritical rigidity of bourgeois morality and as sympathy with its victims, or as an understanding tolerance, a forgiving registration of the facts of life of the ruling classes, against whom the material itself demands a firmer stance?

This kind of exaggerated, all too complacent attitude of 'tout comprendre, tout pardonner' nearly reduces *Frau Jenny Treibel*, for all its brilliant observations and excellent satirical details, to the level of mere belles lettres. In other cases, especially in extreme old age, Fontane shows an inclination, also caused by his scepticism, not to follow a problem through to its final, severest conclusion, and instead breaks the plot off at the very point where the opposites are approaching their supreme satirical poignancy, allowing a pragmatically more or less justifiable coincidence to direct the course of events towards a kind of ideological 'happy ending'. This occurs in *The Poggenpuhl Family*.

In this story Fontane starts by describing how an impoverished *Junker* officer's family slowly has to come to terms with the dominance of Jewish high finance, but goes on to save the Poggenpuhl 'dynasty' from this 'ignominious fate' in the nick of time by the death of a wealthy uncle. The same is true of the posthumously published story *Mathilde Möhring*. Here too, Fontane lays the foundations for what would have been a promising satire if it had been carried through to its logical conclusion. A thoroughly mediocre patrician's son marries a moderately intelligent petty-bourgeois local innkeeper's daughter in Berlin. She coaches him through his state examinations, procures him a job as mayor of a small provincial town, where she turns him into a 'reformer', placing him at the centre of 'society'. Fontane then interrupts the story with a *deus ex machina* – the death of the man – at the very point at which the satire would have begun, namely with the actual career of an amiable but totally incompetent man furthered by his wife's simple manipulations, thus bringing the story to a – from a ruling class standpoint – 'emotionally spiritualized' happy ending. It is abundantly evident that in these cases Fontane's fear of the final consequences, his rejection of Keller's humorous cruelty, his 'turning a blind eye', reduces substantial or at least interesting projects to a level approaching that of mere belles lettres.

The later Fontane is a very deliberate artist. Whereas in his youth this deliberateness was applied only to the formal aspects of writing, the later Fontane is able to broaden his understanding of artistic activity to include the whole, to concentrate more and more on the reciprocal relationship between the subject-matter and the form adopted. It is no coincidence that Fontane first poses the question as to the complicated relationship between 'nature' and 'taste' – which we chose as a motto to introduce this essay and which is the central dialectic question for his work – in his first great novel, *Vor dem Sturm* (*Before the Storm*), written at the end of the eighteen seventies. If we wish to investigate this dialectic in the later Fontane more closely, we naturally have to keep in mind the fact that neither 'nature' nor 'taste' are unalterable, metaphysical powers but, on the contrary, are in a constant state of flux, and that, as we have tried to show, the later Fontane's 'nature' is the gradually emerging, constantly changing product of highly complex social and emotional processes.

Foremost among these tendencies of growth and refinement is Fontane's steadily increasing progressiveness, his democratization. We have already quoted statements confirming this development; they refer primarily to his realization that the true future lies with the working class. The most extensive literary reflection of this change of direction is Fontane's plan to write a novel – set in the fifteenth century – about Klaus Störtebeker (*Die Likedeeler*).[49] Fontane himself emphasizes that, besides the picturesque romanticism of the milieu, it was the 'social democratic modernity' of the subject matter that attracted him. This plan occupied Fontane's mind for years (we find references to it in his letters between 1887 and 1896). Thomas Mann calls it an 'ambitious plan', and there is no doubt that ambition did play some part in it. In one of the letters mentioning it, Fontane actually writes that people would see that he was not only capable of portraying present-day Berlin, but also a great and eventful past, that he was not just a specialist in the subject matter for which he was best known.

Nonetheless, we do not believe that ambition was the decisive factor behind the plan. Rather it was Fontane's 'taste' that had also undergone a change. *Errors, Entanglements, Stine*, as well as the Roswitha episode in *Effi Briest*, etc., display this fault-line in his work. However, it was only in Fontane's 'nature' to show the moral and intellectual superiority of plebeian figures in such a way that they could react to the same bourgeois society – which he portrayed as being unalterable – in a morally superior manner by virtue of their being better able to uphold the individuality of their human core, above all without resorting to illusions, hypocrisy or pseudo-tragedy. Fontane's 'taste' often admires revolutionary sublation at an aesthetic or intellectual level, and yet he is no longer able to identify with it sufficiently to be able to portray it in literature, to incorporate it into his 'nature'. No matter how sharp his insight into the fragility of bourgeois existence may have been at times, this same existence lays down an unrelenting veto when it comes to giving it literary form.

Similarly it is a question of 'taste', admittedly a more episodic one, when, in order to make the petty baseness of the German bourgeoisie of his day seem even more despicable, the later Fontane occasionally enthuses, not without self-irony, over American multimillionaires. The later Fontane's 'nature' always rejected the victors and rulers of modern bourgeois life; as a writer he did not even draw passing inspiration from them. This rejection, however, also applies to the *Junkers*. Fontane remarks in his last, highly subjective novel, *Der Stechlin*, that the power of the Prussian aristocracy has, if anything, grown rather than diminished. Yet despite this, his works are devoid of representatives of the victorious *Junker* class, except perhaps for the occasional secondary character who is treated in ironic fashion.

The later Fontane's 'nature' and 'taste' are only in harmony when, in a temporary conflict between social being and consciousness, he depicts the triumph of the former, such that resistance to the exigences of class stems from the best, most genuine, human instincts of the individual and yet inevitably suffers defeat at the hands of the irresistible forces of class. Society thus reigns supreme, yet has in such cases ceased to be a moral force. For Fontane, the apparently perfect *Junker* or bourgeois is therefore only a product of this struggle; he is broken as a human being in order to become, or remain, a true representative of his class. Fontane regards people who undergo this process without a struggle as sad caricatures; hypocrisy and self-deception have already become the instinctive principles of their lives (see Jenny Treibel, for example).

In the opinion of the later Fontane, all these class-based views have long since come to contradict the principles of a simple but nevertheless at least human existence. The basic vital instincts of any human being who has not become utterly numb are therefore bound constantly to collide with the objective social basis of his life. What determines the specific character of such conflicts is that Fontane's 'heroes' stop well short of calling into question the basis of their social existence, of rebelling against the views of their class, of even seriously considering breaking with this class. The young, ailing Count Haldern, the 'hero' of the story *Stine*, is very clear on this point:

I respect the dominant views. But sometimes one finds oneself in a situation in which one is in conflict with what one normally holds to be correct. That is my present situation.

And his partner in conversation, himself an aristocrat, gives an equally clear characterization of their whole milieu when he concludes:

The freer one is in theory, the more tied one is in practice, the more constrained and apprehensive when applying the theory to one's own self.

The later Fontane is in this respect the first writer in Germany to pose one of the central questions facing literature at the beginning of the period of decline of the bourgeois class. He stands here – despite or because of the Prusso-German way in which he poses the concrete questions – on common European ground, and is thus one of the first to liberate German literature in the second half of the nineteenth century from the constraints of provincialism. In this respect he stands in the tradition of Turgenev and Goncharov, Jens Peter Jacobsen and Pontoppidan, Flaubert and Thackeray, without having been influenced by these writers to any great extent, indeed without even having heard of some of them. This grouping is of course based on the similarity of central themes rather than literary style: they are all portrayers of a half-way house, which took on different forms in different countries at various historical stages of development, and yet became a typical phenomenon everywhere at the onset of the decline of the bourgeois class. We stress the onset of the decline because at this stage the socially necessary half-way house has not yet, in the humanly decent specimens of the ruling class at any rate, acquired that coquetry, egocentricity and complacency that, at a later stage, characterize the types to be found in decadent literature.

IV

With respect to a specific type of literary portrayal, the standard of works and authors is always dependent on the degree of social generalization they are able to attain, on the extent to which the half-way house is shown as being a necessary consequence of social developments and class struggles. This need to generalize is also present in Fontane, yet it can develop in two different directions: extensively or intensively. The former appears as an extension of the milieu portrayed to include areas beyond Prussian Germany. Fontane doubtless intends this to imply that the phenomenon he has observed is one common to the whole of Europe; thus *Count Petöfy* is set in Vienna and Hungary, *Beyond Recall* in Denmark, the second half of *Quitt* even in North America.

The danger of his work degenerating to the level of mere belles lettres is particularly glaring here. Not only because most of the details are inevitably secondhand and thus often superficial. (The second part of *Quitt* is a prime example of the contrived and artificial trivial novel and, for example, even the title of *Count Petöfy* sounds as strange as if one were to talk of Count Büchner, Comte Béranger, Lord Burns.) More important, though, when on foreign soil Fontane is unable to establish the necessary level of generalization in the concrete fates of his heroes. His theoretical grasp of the viable course is correct: the half-heartedness of the figures must appear as the necessary effect of their entire social being on their overall individuality. Only if portrayed in this way does the dramatic conflict – which for obvious reasons mainly takes the direct form of a marital or lovers' disagreement – caused by the character's half-heartedness appear not to be purely personal, coincidental, eccentric, even pathological, but for all its individuality to be socially necessary.

Fontane attempts this kind of generalization in both of the marital novels mentioned here. Thus his Count Petöfy is supposed to stand as a Hungarian aristocrat between dynasty and nation, unable to decide resolutely which party to fight for. Count Holk in *Beyond Recall*, on the other hand, is a Schleswig separatist (the novel takes place before the war of 1864), yet at the same time a gentleman of the Danish court. In both cases, however, Fontane – apparently only because of his superficial familiarity with the society and history of the countries concerned – is incapable of combining these traits organically with the half-heartedness of the erotic relationships around which the plots revolve, of portraying this link in directly palpable form. In both cases the main plot – despite socio-historical episodes – thus remains on a purely psychological plane, almost reducing both novels, especially *Count Petöfy* with its rather contrived assumptions, to the level of mere belles lettres.

However, even the greater refinement shown in the emotional lines drawn in *Beyond Recall*, which C.F. Meyer so admired, is not able to offset this basic flaw. Here Fontane attempts to approximate his novel to the type represented by Goethe's *Elective Affinities*, but, for one thing, the latter chooses a marital conflict that was in itself much more general and thus much more directly social, and for another, Goethe was still able to work within the abstract milieu created by eighteenth century literature. That Fontane should recognize the necessity of concretization in describing the environment is an admission: the marital conflict requires a determinate socio-historical background in order to achieve adequate literary generalization at the level of his portraits of human beings. However, Fontane is not capable of providing this.

This is no coincidence. For – and this returns us to the problem we discussed earlier – only the intensive generalization of a conflict can bear literary fruit. No matter how universally bourgeois, how European this conflict may be, its concrete manifestation remains inseparably bound up with a specific social situation. The literary generalization consists precisely in tracing and elaborating the underlying determining factors contained within this socio-historical concreteness. Thanks to his portrayal of the life of the Russian aristocracy, Goncharov has become a writer of world significance. And for Fontane too, truly literary generalization of his problems can only be achieved by means of the concretely intensive, of a critique of Prussianism.

However, it is here that the contradiction between Fontane's 'taste' and his 'nature' is at its sharpest, thus resulting in diametrically opposite solutions in his writings. At the beginning and the end of the later Fontane's career as an author we find works in which he approaches this question according to his subjective inclinations, sympathies and 'taste' and – in widely differing ways – fails. *Before the Storm* (1879) and *Der Stechlin* (1898) are examples of this.

In the historical novel (*Before the Storm*), which marks the beginning of his output of major narrative prose, he is attracted, as had

been Willibald Alexis at an earlier date, to the eccentric individualistic figure of the reactionary *Junker*, Marwitz, around whom he
attempts to arrange the preparatory period leading up to the Wars
of Liberation. However, this – false, Prusso-conservative – subjectivism results in Fontane completely neglecting the most important
factor of this period, the Scharnhorst-Gneisenau faction, in favour
of the reactionary *Junkers*. Fontane's intention at that time, namely
to pose genuine patriotism as an alternative to purely sloganizing
patriotism, is bound to fail because the social reality in which this
genuine patriotism, albeit in very confused form, was actually
present, is absent from the narrative, revolving as it does around a
false centre, the uncritically treated central figure of the reactionary
Junker.

Raabe is right in sensing that there would have been nothing
plebeian about the Wars of Liberation, nothing even approaching
greatness, had it not been for the after-effects of the French Revolution and the plebeian elements that it brought to life. Based on his
false premisses, Fontane creates a picture bereft of atmosphere in
which the fates of the most important individual characters are only
loosely and often arbitrarily linked to the historical background they
were actually intended to inject with life. Towards the end of the
novel, Fontane himself becomes aware of this weakness in the historical structure of his subject and has his eccentric character, retired General Bamme, say: 'So far as I'm concerned it's the human
being that counts, and if this general and universal *homo* – of whom
as a good Latinist I am entitled to speak – has really grown a head
taller since they made the poor king a head shorter, then it does not
seem to me to have been purchased at too high a price. *Le jeu vaut
la chandelle*.'[50] Nonetheless, individual exclamations of this sort,
especially coming from a minor figure, are obviously not enough to
provide a retroactive correction of the false structure and the resultant vacuousness. It is with good reason that Fontane says of this
novel some years later that it is one 'I keep forgetting I ever wrote'.

Fontane's last novel, *Der Stechlin* was published twenty years
later. This is yet another work resulting from 'taste', i.e. from the
author's subjective sympathies for the best specimens of the *Junker*
class. Admittedly, twenty years have since passed and his sympathies have become much more critical, much more ambiguous.

Fontane even admits to the exaggeratedly subjective way in which he approached this topic when he says of the novel: 'It is a comparison between what our aristocracy *should* be and what it *is*.' The lyrical-psychological realization of this 'should' takes place unconsciously: a series of personally likable traits exhibited by Fontane as an old man are loosely and inorganically combined with the figure of a somewhat whimsical old *Junker* who has been condemned to the wings of history, set in an all too loosely constructed plot that does not reveal anything of great significance. The admirers of the later Fontane value this work precisely for these personal characteristics, ignoring the fact that these contradictions, which do not combine with one another but coexist side by side, ultimately render the all-important protagonist featureless. When a secondary figure says of old Stechlin that 'he has. . . in his heart something common to all true *Junkers*: an element of Social Democracy; when provoked, they are even prepared to admit it themselves', this aptly captures certain moods of Fontane himself, but from the standpoint of the figure of old Stechlin these episodes are incongruous because they contradict the genuine contours of his character. Compositional disintegration is therefore not the real weakness of the later works, as some critics would have us believe. The main flaw in these works is that here Fontane does not, as in his earlier works, take actual social existence as the point of departure for his composition, but rather a very confused, and utterly inaccurate concept of the way things should be. Even the wittiest of dialogues is not able to bend this distorted structure back into shape.

The later Fontane proves himself to be a writer of importance in those works in which he succeeds in allowing this half-heartedness of his figures to grow out of the specific development of Prussian Germany, in which he is able to show that the triumph of this social being over his figures' consciousness, inclinations and career ambitions is rooted in the specific conditions of this form of existence. Because, in so doing, expression is given to the specificity of this being and consciousness; the people and their fates achieve an intensive and concrete literary generalization. Precisely because their characters and fates are shown to be specifically Prusso-German, these figures attain the status of types in a sense that has general validity beyond Prussian Germany.

It is no coincidence that the important literary critics of this German development – Raabe as well as the later Fontane – repeatedly refer to Mirabeau's verdict that Prussia is a fruit that had begun to rot before it had even ripened. For this trenchant observation is not only true of Frederick the Great's Prussia. The Reich, as it developed towards imperialism, and especially the Germany of the age of imperialism, also display these characteristics only too clearly. And it is also no coincidence that later outstanding critics of Germany – above all Heinrich and Thomas Mann – are also of the same opinion, even if they do not actually cite Mirabeau. In the case of Thomas Mann, one can even make out a direct connection to the later Fontane.

The crucial factor from a literary point of view, and at the same time the very point at which a correct grasp of the specifically Prussian element develops directly, and apparently without its conscious generalization, into a valid criticism of modern bourgeois society as a whole, is the relentlessness with which an already utterly conventional society holds sway over the lives of individuals. This society has unlimited power over life and death, yet has ceased to be an inwardly binding moral force, in other words, a power that not only determines people's outward dealings but intellectually and emotionally dominates their attitudes and convictions. There is, of course, a considerable difference here between members of the ruling class, even though they might be impoverished, and those of the oppressed classes. The latter – we are not talking about the proletariat, which is absent from Fontane's works – accept external compulsion as something purely external, relying on it in roughly the same way as one relies on the departure times of trains, without the slightest inner emotional involvement. However, with the former, as we have already indicated, the evaluation of this power develops an inner automatism: the inner horizon of these people is irresistibly limited by these views; at the same time, with every conflict – which is the inevitable consequence as soon as anyone, even within the narrowest confines of intimately private life, is not prepared to allow himself to be swallowed up hook, line and sinker by this class automatism – the relentless necessity arises of capitulating before these commandments, commandments which those involved have come to regard as pointless.

The importance of the later Fontane results from his having recognized this structure in the old and the new Prussia and having given it literary expression. Not until he does so can his 'nature', which took time to mature during his long life, be said to have outgrown his 'taste', i.e. his sympathy for Frederick II and Bismarck, in his literary production – even though he seldom gave thought to this transformation of his 'nature' and still less drew conscious logical conclusions from it.

Schach von Wuthenow (*A Man of Honour*) (1893) is a small masterpiece in terms of this critique of historical Prussia, a solitary peak of German historical narrative art, the full significance of which has yet to be recognized. Here Fontane succeeds in giving a brilliant illustration of the reasons for the destruction of Frederick's Prussia at the Battle of Jena by means of the ups and downs of a love story set in Berlin 'society'. It is a Prussia whose officers, particularly the 'hero' of the story, are convinced that

the world rests no more securely on the shoulders of Atlas than does Prussia on those of her army.[51]

The general atmosphere is characterized by the sad remark of an old officer at a parade:

Let us fix this scene in our memory, ladies, for trust an old man's presentiment, we shan't live to see so much splendour again. This is the valedictory parade of the Frederickian army.[52]

The discontented *Junker* officer, von Bülow, who is very familiar with other countries, even speaks of a 'Prussian episode' in world history and elaborates on this criticism by calling the Prussian state religion, Lutheranism, episodic too.

What has Prussia done for the good of the world? What's the sum total I arrive at when I add it all up? The tall regimentals in blue of King Frederick William I, the iron ramrod, the pigtail, and that magnificent ethos that coined the phrase, 'I tied him to the crib, why wouldn't he eat?'[53]

And he asks of Luther:

What did he really bequeath to the world? Intolerance and witchhunts, lack of imagination and boredom. Not the kind of cement to weather the millennia of ages.[54]

The artistic perfection of this work lies in the fact that its concrete content, the love story, despite its individualized and at times even bizarre features, is a typical expression of this socio-historical base. The 'hero' of the story, Schach von Wuthenow, is a well-mannered, average man, characterized by Victoire von Carayon as 'neither a man of outstanding intellectual significance nor of superior character'; his abilities essentially befit the role of a 'demi-god at a prince's court'. The story of his love and marriage is comparatively simple; Schach has for a long time been courting Josephine von Carayon. One evening a love affair develops between him and her daughter Victoire, an intelligent young girl robbed of her former beauty by the scars of illness.

The facts are simple. They are only complicated on a psychological level by the fact that shortly beforehand, at a soirée at Prince Louis Ferdinand's, conversation had been directed towards Victoire, and the Prince had referred to her 'beauté du diable'. And – strangely, or rather naturally – the Prince's casual paradoxical remark plays a crucial role in the seduction scene. Before the decisive crescendo in the love scene begins, Fontane notes in typically discreet fashion: 'Schach looked at her in astonishment. Much of what the Prince had said about her was going through his mind.' And the critical von Bülow makes a similar remark after the catastrophe. This consists in the fact that the Prince's casual remark is too slender a basis for marriage, even for a man like Schach. He fears appearing ridiculous at the side of such an ugly, disfigured woman and beats a retreat. However, because Frau von Carayon takes the matter to the King, who orders the officer Schach von Wuthenow to marry, he does wed Victoire, only to shoot himself as soon as the marriage has been formally sealed. He obeys, therefore – again using Bülow's formulation – 'only to commit the most blatant breach of discipline in the very moment of obedience'.

Bülow now comments on the general significance of this false concept of honour in Frederick's army 'which in place of honour has only arrogance, and in place of a soul has only the works of a clock – a clock that will soon have run down'. And he generalizes this observation to include the prophecy of inevitable defeat for a nation in which this kind of morality holds sway.

There you have the quintessence of hollow honour. It puts us at the mercy of the most unstable and capricious elements there are, the quicksand on which the criteria of social opinions are based, and makes us sacrifice the most sacrosanct precepts and our finest and most natural impulses on the altar of this very idol of society. And on this cult of hollow honour, which is nothing but vanity and aberration, Schach foundered, and bigger fish than he will follow suit. Mark my words. We have, ostrich-like, buried our heads in the sand so as to shut our eyes and ears. But such ostrich-like caution has never yet led to salvation. . . War has been declared. And what this portends I can clearly envisage in my mind's eye. We shall be destroyed by the same world of appearances that destroyed Schach.[55]

What Fontane uncovers here by literary means is the frailty of any people and social system whose morality is based on this kind of false honour, on the formalistic recognition of a convention which is no longer a moral force even in its own social reality. The only work prior to Fontane in which a vague notion of this relationship can occasionally be detected is in Kleist's *The Prince of Homburg* – although here it occurs totally unconsciously. Later it is to appear in an intellectually much more advanced form in Thomas Mann's *Death in Venice*. The literary documentation of this relationship forms the basis of Fontane's most important contemporary novels: *Errors, Entanglements* and, above all, *Effi Briest*.

It follows from the nature of the subject matter, as well as from the manner in which the later Fontane regards the age he lives in, that there is no direct reference to an impending catastrophe or even to the socio-historical perspectives of these tragedies of love and marriage. The inner connection, however, which in pre-Jena Prussia has made these perspectives visible and describable, is clearly present in the composition itself. This is why these stories – particularly the far more important novel about married life, *Effi Briest* – rise above the zone in which Fontane, in spite of his prose style, which remains consistently literary and well-balanced, comes close to producing mere belles lettres. *Effi Briest* belongs in the category of great bourgeois novels, alongside *Madame Bovary* and *Anna Karenina*, in which the simple description of a marriage and its inevitable breakdown develops into a portrayal of the general contradictions of bourgeois society in its entirety.

The inner stature of *Errors, Entanglements* is more modest. This is determined above all by the subject matter: marriage is a much more central theme than the pre-marital love affair, which conflicts with the – materially determined – compulsion to enter a marriage 'of equals'. The general applicability of this conflict is restricted to the ruling class, although Fontane's portrayal of the moral, humanist superiority of the plebeian figures over the ruling class is of a clarity unparalleled in any of his other works – with the exception of the related story *Stine*, which is insipid by comparison. However, the totality of social determining forces is in itself given a much firmer footing in the novel of married life, *Effi Briest*.

It is highly instructive that the subject matter should play such an important role in the success of these novels. It shows the extent to which, particularly in the case of Fontane and despite, or rather because of, his heightened artistic awareness, success or failure depends on fortunate or unfortunate coincidences, on the subject matter that happens to present itself to him. This is – directly – connected with the constantly increasing degree to which the artistic awareness of late bourgeois writers is directed towards formal questions, a shift that begins with Flaubert. The late bourgeois writers regard the subject matter as a given quantity, a gift from the gods, so to speak, the result of chance. The further this trend develops, the further it is from the writers' minds to train their artistic sensibility to shed light on the dialectic of subject and form, as was still possible in the case of Goethe and Schiller. Of course, Fontane is by no means a formalist: he tries to fashion the form of each work out of the concrete possibilities afforded by the material. He senses – and often says as much – that he gives his best as a conscientious worker but that success does not come easy to him. This is a direct reflection of the role played by chance in finding an appropriate subject matter.

The main problem, however, is not a lack of aesthetic awareness. Fontane's failure to recognize the true dialectic connection between subject and form indicates that in the final analysis he is – socially speaking – no longer able to assess accurately the crucial possibilities of content presented by his subject matter. This is the reason for the lack of concrete links between subject and form. In view of the weakness and the confused nature of his relationship to contemporary German society, it is a matter of chance whether his world-view happens to coincide with a fitting subject that at the same time reflects essential social relationships.

This element of chance can be seen very clearly in the genesis of a masterpiece like *Schach von Wuthenow*. Fontane already knew the anecdote behind the love story but was unsure whether it should be set in the time before or after the Battle of Jena, and in order to aid his decision he tried to find out exactly when the affair actually took place. For, he writes:

Each of the two epochs lend themselves well; each has, from a novelistic point of view, particular advantages.[56]

Thus the factor that makes this a great novel, the atmosphere of decay in the time before Jena, owes its existence to a semi-coincidence. Even after completion, Fontane was by no means aware of its decisive content. In a letter to his publisher in which he deals with the question of the book's title, he writes of the period immediately preceding Jena: 'After all, the times were not nearly as bad as they were made out to be . . .'[57] Here we see how unaware, how spontaneous, how prone to coincidences a writer with Fontane's degree of awareness was when it came to subject matter, to the content inherent in a particular subject. *Schach von Wuthenow* is a gift of chance.

This is also true of *Errors, Entanglements* and, to an even greater degree, of *Effi Briest*. The content of both works is easy to summarize. In the former: a humanly fulfilling relationship is broken off for the sake of a marriage of convention. In the latter: a mediocre marriage, unfaithfulness out of boredom and frustration, exposure of the affair, a duel resulting in the death of the lover, divorce, etc. The figures and their fates almost never rise above a respectable ordinariness and it is only Fontane's dialogue that elevates every scene to the highest possible concrete level of self-awareness and articulation.

As with many modern writers, this human mediocrity shows up more clearly in the male than in the female characters. The former only emerge from the eternal blandness of mediocrity by virtue of their ability to articulate, by their – in practice impotent – capacity for clearly expressing the dialectic of their capitulation in the face of the relentless norms of their class. Lene Nimptsch, the heroine of *Errors, Entanglements*, however, elevates herself, morally speaking, far above the novel's other figures in an unpretentious, utterly unrhetorical way, utterly free of illusions. Since we simply have to accept that Fontane is not capable of portraying rebellious people, this plebeian embodies the best human being that his literary world has to offer. Just as Philine introduced Goethe's Spinozan ethics into everyday life, so Lene Nimptsch embodies and brings to life the best of Fontane's morality and world-view, indeed she even goes beyond their general horizon: Goethe's hatred of philistinism may generally be much stronger, more powerful and more incisive than Fontane's, but here hatred of the fact that individual life is dominated by fear and hope – especially in Lene Nimptsch's unpretentious lack of rhetoric – is given body and immediacy in an exemplary way. She is the most important figure ever created by Fontane; as with Goethe and Keller – who were intellectually superior – a triumph of the popular-plebeian over bourgeois mediocrity.

Effi Briest is Fontane's most likable character. She remains not only intellectually but also morally within the respectable average for a girl and a young woman of the nobility. What makes her an unforgettable character is her simple vitality which she makes use of in every situation, be it idyllic, dangerous or tragic, in order to find the form of human expression best suited to her character and her abilities. Despite certain social ambitions, her needs are more than modest. Yet in this society they are bound to be trampled underfoot. And the fact that this vitality constantly reasserts itself, though the flame may become weaker, that Effi can only be put down but never humanly corrupted, is, precisely because of its quietness and modesty, a powerful indictment of a society which does not allow human needs even this modicum of freedom. At the same time, however, Effi's inner resilience is evidence of that human reservoir of strength which this society uselessly squanders and corrupts and yet which could spontaneously give rise to a simple and pleasant life in a different society, one which cultivated humanist values. Here Fontane, like all great, authentic portrayers of people in bourgeois literature, is – without consciously wanting to be, or indeed even without being aware of the fact – an accuser.

But where is the literary generalization in these novels, the generalization of the critique of Old Prussia in terms of the present day? Fontane shows here, precisely by means of the mediocrity of his figures and their fates, how the social morality of Bismarck's Prussian Germany affects private everyday life. He shows that every person in whom even the slightest desire for a humanly dignified life stirs is bound to come into conflict with this morality. The conflict is carried out in the way we have already described: outwardly by conforming to all the formal requirements of convention; inwardly by each of the parties involved becoming more or less broken individuals who are only able to carry on by resorting to 'makeshift expedients', as they are called in *Effi Briest*. Although outwardly everything appears to be in order and despite a reasonably or at times even an outstandingly successful career, each person loses all real moral power of resistance, and becomes incapable of performing a true deed. And those who do not even make it as far as this kind of conflict are – from a social point of view – of an even worse sort.

Why do people live and die, why do they kill in this world? Innstetten, Effi's husband, has shot and killed his wife's lover in a duel. Even before the duel the question arises in conversation with his friend Wüllersdorf: is there any point in duelling over an affair that occurred six years previously? After the duel Innstetten is unable to rid his mind of this thought:

There must be a time limit, because a time limit is the only sensible thing and it doesn't matter whether it's prosaic as well; what's sensible usually is prosaic. I am forty-five now. If I'd found the letter twenty-five years later, I'd be seventy. Then Wüllersdorf would have said: 'Innstetten, don't be a fool!'. . . But where does it begin? Where is the limit? A ten-year interval makes a duel still necessary and then it's called honour, and after eleven years, or perhaps even ten-and-a-half, it's called nonsense. The limit, the limit! Was that what it was? Had it already been passed? When I think of his last look, resigned and yet smiling in his misery, it seemed to be saying: 'Innstetten, always standing on principle. . . You might have spared me that and yourself as well.'[58]

Innstetten is therefore fully aware that he has not killed out of vengeance, nor a sense of moral outrage, nor in fulfilment of a sincerely felt duty:

So it was all done merely to support a fantasy, an abstraction, it was just a made-up story, a bit of play-acting. And now I must continue to play-act and send Effi away and ruin her life and mine as well.[59]

And here Fontane emphasizes even more powerfully the emptiness of this convention of honour which has destroyed a whole series of lives. For the idea that the period in which a crime could be punished can 'expire', brought up by Wüllersdorf, arises even before the duel, and immediately makes a strong impression on Innstetten, though not sufficiently to make him change his mind. Again as a result of the automatism of a 'morality' that dominates without being a true force. In this conversation Innstetten says:

Six hours ago, I'll grant you this in advance, the cards were still in my hand and I could have done one thing or another, there was still a way out. But not any longer, I'm in an impasse. I've only myself to blame, if you like, I should have been more guarded and shown more self-control, I should have kept everything to myself, fought it all out in my own mind. But it came so suddenly and so violently. . . I went to your place and wrote you a note, and by doing that the game passed out of my hands. From that moment onwards, there was someone else who knew something of my misfortune and, what is more important, of the stain on my honour; and as soon as we had exchanged our first few words, there was someone else who knew all about it. And, because there is such a person, I can't go back.[60]

And yet this destruction and self-destruction of human lives continues with relentless logic. Innstetten is able to build a career, but his life has become morbid and inwardly incapable of resistance. It does nonetheless continue to run its deadly, automatic course. In spite of the reflections we have just described following the duel, Innstetten consistently carries out the process set in motion by the duel. He removes their only child from its mother, and when she – thanks to the intervention of a minister's wife – does finally manage to arrange a meeting with her child, that same automatism that has now been bred into the child is expressed so violently that the passionately longed-for reunion turns into a tragicomic catastrophe which eventually threatens Effi's life. And even Effi's parents, although they honestly love their daughter – in their own way – behave in a similar manner after the 'scandal'. Only when she is dying is Effi able to return home to them.

And in this world of mechanical conventions, of the destruction of all expressions of humanity, only Effi's uneducated, superstitious servant Roswitha shows any human feeling for the fate of human beings. In a very naïve letter she asks Innstetten at least to allow Effi to keep her old dog, her only companion. Innstetten subsequently has a highly characteristic conversation with his friend Wüllersdorf, on the very day when he has been promoted to a high position:

'Yes,' said Wüllersdorf, folding up the letter, 'she's worth more than we are.' – 'I think so too.' – 'And that's why you feel so doubtful about everything else.' – 'You're quite correct. I've been thinking about it for a long time now, and these simple words with their deliberate or perhaps quite unintentional accusation have quite upset me. It's been tormenting me for years, and now I'd like to get out of the whole business. I've lost all pleasure in everything. The more distinctions I earn, the more I feel it's been value-less. I've made a mess of my life. . .'[61]

And in the course of this conversation Wüllersdorf says that it is quite impossible to lead one's life to its conclusion without 'make-shift expedients'.

An important part of the unity of ideas in this work and of its artistic perfection is the fact that its long-suffering heroine, Effi, a wonderfully vital female character, is also incapable of seeing beyond the horizon of this 'morality'. For all her genuinely human spontaneity of feeling and her vitality, for all her sensitive wisdom and her practical cunning she remains, both in fortune and in mis-fortune, totally a creature of this aristocratic world. Her emotional protest against the most harshly inhuman treatment never rises to even a vague notion of real protest against this system. The inevita-bility of her victimization has such a profound and moving effect for precisely this reason.

In all of this, the later Fontane is prophesying a new Jena for his Bismarckian Prussian Germany – without the slightest awareness of it. It is of course a passive, a sceptically pessimistic prophecy. The forces of German renewal lie totally beyond his literary horizon. Lene Nimptsch, Stine and other plebeian figures are ultimately just as much passive victims as Effi Briest. In none of these figures do we detect the unconscious human seeds of those forces which could turn the desert into fertile soil.

Here it is not only a question of the social situation of the charac-ters, but particularly of the way Fontane himself sees and portrays them. Because Tolstoy – particularly as a writer – was able to see and reflect the ferment among the Russian peasantry, some of his aristo-cratic figures, the best of them, have something instinctively rebel-lious about them. They are not content to lead the lives of broken men, are not prone from the start to impotent resignation. Of course they are not able to break their social chains. And when they do strive for liberation it is a purely individual liberation, only for their own person. (Pierre Bezukhov's links with the preparations leading up to the December Revolt is an exception.) Nonetheless, a figure like Anna Karenina rattles mightily at the chains that make her, too, a slave to rotting conventions.

Fontane is one of the important realists of the second half of the nineteenth century. First, because he portrays what is odious about his times in the way it deserves; second because – although his world-view remains confined to the private and the personal – he does not succumb to the temptation of appearing to 'deepen' these inevitable conflicts while actually distracting attention from the main idea by treating them as pathological. For any conflict can only be generalized in social and therefore human terms if the normal social determinants of being (no matter how extreme the forms in which they appear) come into collision with normal human characters (no matter how extreme they may be as representatives of their type). Every pathological feature of a figure, when it affects their essential nature, helps to reduce that figure to the singularity of social eccentricity; the completely pathological individual is a unique clinical case who can at best be subsumed under general medical laws, but must never appear as a type, as a representative of literary generalization. That is why any pathological character trait is a – conscious or unconscious – avoidance of the social nature of literature, of the social and therefore human generalization of the characters and their collisions.

This appreciation of normality as the basis of true literature is one of Tolstoy's greatest qualities. However, like Tolstoy, the later Fontane also sees that his characters collide with society all the more strongly and authentically when he centres on inwardly healthy and normal people with the right instincts towards life. The difference between Fontane's and Tolstoy's literary stature is not only attributable to their differing ability. This too was able to develop in Tolstoy and was impeded in Fontane by the social developments in Russia and in Prussian Germany respectively. The relationship of *Anna Karenina* to *Effi Briest* is comparable with that of the Great October Revolution of 1917 to the German November Revolution of 1918. That this comparison is at all possible, and that it should give this result, is a mark – in both a positive and negative sense – of the literary stature of the later Fontane.

1950

Notes

FOREWORD

1. *Goethe and his Age*, translated by Robert Anchor, London, 1968.
2. Karl Marx & Frederick Engels, *Collected Works*, London, 1975, vol. 3, p.176.
3. ibid., p.180.
4. Letter to Karl Ludwig Knebel, 14 December 1822, in *Goethes Briefe*, Hamburg, 1967, vol. IV, pp.54–6.
5. *Kunstperiode* (literally: 'art period'), a term coined by Heine to describe the 'Age of Goethe', is of considerable importance for German intellectual history. It signifies an era in which art could portray 'the beautiful objective world' in Goethean fashion, without concerning itself with political issues. It is the idea of art as an autonomous practice. Heine partly defends Goethe from attacks by liberals and nationalists, but joins in the criticism of a traditional art divorced from reality. By signalling the 'end of the art period' Heine clearly echoes Hegel's thesis of the end of art as such. But he goes beyond Hegel, who had argued that art would be superseded by philosophy, by proclaiming a new, modern art in which the 'egoism' of the age of art gives way to an art which is both socially responsible and experimental in its attitude to form. For Lukács's discussion see p.133.
6. Karl Marx, op. cit., p.183.
7. The concept of 'decadence' has a complex history in German. Marx used the ordinary word 'Verfall' (decay, decline), but Lukács talks of 'Dekadenz' which introduces the connotations of the French 'décadence', a term used to refer to the aesthetic movement from Gautier and Baudelaire down to the symbolists of the *fin du siècle*. The word was introduced into German in a positive sense by the Austrian critic Hermann Bahr in 1894 to describe an artistic programme. As a negative term, it was popularized by Max Nordau in his novel *Entartung* in 1892–3, a book with which Lukács was familiar. This term suggests biological degeneration, and Nordau described the avant-garde as 'a mental disease of the nation'. His quasi-racist usage later influenced the Nazis. A third powerful influence was Nietzsche with his savage attack on German cultural decadence under the Bismarckian Empire. Lukács's arguments are based on his thesis that the European bourgeoisie went into decline after the failure of the 1848 Revolutions. In effect he provides a traditionalist idea of aesthetic decline with a Marxist underpinning and confers intellectual respectability on the vulgar Marxist talk of the 'decadent bourgeoisie'.

8. *Conversations of Goethe with Eckermann*, translated by John Oxenford, introduction by Havelock Ellis, London, 1930, p.395. *Agnes Bernauerin* and *Otto von Wittelsbach* are long-forgotten plays by Joseph August von Törring (1780) and Joseph Maria von Babo (1785) respectively.

9. Karl Immermann (1796–1840) was a Prussian civil servant and a judge who made a reputation as a prolific writer. He is best known for his novels *Die Epigonen* (1836), which introduced that eponymous term to define the difficulty his generation felt in continuing a literary tradition in Goethe's shadow; and *Münchhausen* (1838–9), which uses the tall stories characteristic of its progenitor to satirize the aristocracy and contemporary fashionable writers. The so-called 'Oberhof' episode contrasts this decadent society with a rural world viewed as a refuge of uncorrupted traditional values.

10. *Die Judenbuche* (*The Jew's Beech*) (1842) by Annette von Droste-Hülshoff is an early realistic novella which describes the murder of a Jew. Having shown the growth of the power of evil, Droste-Hülshoff goes on to depict the equally great sense of guilt that drives the murderer, Friedrich Mergel, to take his own life.

11. Willibald Alexis (1798–1871) wrote historical novels set in Brandenburg-Prussia. Although strongly influenced by Scott, he dispensed with the latter's Romanticism, strong dramatic sense and epic breadth, replacing them with a more episodic narrative style with an eye for detail. His works were neglected for a long time, but some (*Die Hosen des Herren von Bredow* and *Ruhe ist die erste Bürgerpflicht*) have recently been republished because of their liberal ideology and solid realist values.

12. Karl Marx & Frederick Engels, *Collected Works*, op. cit., vol. 16, pp.465–6.

13. Heinrich Heine, *Aufzeichnungen* (*Notes*), in *Sämtliche Schriften*, edited by Klaus Briegleb, Hanser, Munich, 1970–4, vol. 6/1, p.649. Heine referred to his late, bed-ridden period as his 'mattress grave'.

14. The law by which Bismarck proscribed the German Social Democratic Party in 1878.

15. Gerhart Hauptmann's novel *Der Narr in Christo Emanuel Quint* (*Emanuel Quint, The Holy Fool*) (1910) tells the story of a man who determines to relive the life of Christ in the modern world. He ends up persecuted and alone on the St Gotthard pass, where he perishes in a snowstorm. Hauptmann treats both his naive hero and his sceptical opponents with irony.

16. *German Literature in the Age of Imperialism*, East Berlin, 1945. This (untranslated) study forms the theoretical backbone for the work on the German realists as well as on Mann and Goethe.

17. Translated by Stanley Mitchell, London, 1964.

18. V. Lenin, *Collected Works*, London, 1961, vol. 38 , p.144.

THE TRAGEDY OF HEINRICH VON KLEIST

1. *Die Famile Schroffenstein* (*The Schroffenstein Family*) Act II, sc. 3, lines 1213–14.
2. Letter to O.A. Rühle von Lilienstern, 31 August 1806, in Heinrich von Kleist, *Sämtliche Werke und Briefe*, edited by Helmut Sembdner, vol. 2, Munich 1984, p.768 (cited henceforth as Sembdner).
3. 'Hermann's Battle', known in history as the Battle of the Teutoburg Forest, where Hermann, the Cheruscan (Germanic) king defeated the Romans under Varus in 9 AD.
4. *Die Hermannsschlacht*, Act V, sc. 4.
5. Letter to Karoline Schlieben, 18 July 1801, Sembdner, op. cit., pp.659–60.
6. Letter to his sister, Ulrike von Kleist, 23 March 1801, Sembdner, op. cit., p.636.
7. Letter to his fiancée, Wilhelmine von Zenge, 21 July 1801, Sembdner, op. cit., p.669.
8. Letter to O.A Rühle von Lilienstern, 31 August 1806, Sembdner, op. cit., p.769–70.
9. See 'Schillers Briefwechsel mit Körner', in Friedrich Hebbel, *Sämtliche Werke*, edited by Richard Werner, Berlin, 1904 vol. 1/12, pp.193–4. See also *Tagebücher*, 9 April 1844, op. cit., vol. 3/2, p.391.
10. Zacharias Werner (1768–1823) was the principal exponent of the Romantic fate tragedy, a genre which goes back to K.P. Moritz's *Blunt, oder der Gast* of 1781. Werner's *Der vierundzwanzigste Februar* (1806), which was clearly influenced by Schiller's *The Bride of Messina* (1803), set a fashion which lasted over a decade.
11. In Strindberg's *The Father*.
12. *Penthesilea*, Scene 9.
13. *The Prince of Homburg*, Act IV, scene 1, in Heinrich von Kleist, *Five Plays*, translated, with an introduction, by Martin Greenberg, New Haven and London, 1988, p.321.
14. Friedrich Gundolf (1880–1931) was a disciple of Stefan George and a professor of German literature in Heidelberg from 1920. He was one of the leading literary scholars of his day, noted for his books on Shakespeare, George, Goethe, Kleist and others. His approach is an extreme example of the late-Romantic worship of genius and the idea of the poet as hero. See his *Heinrich von Kleist*, Berlin, 1922, pp.61 and 63.
15. Lukács is referring to Theodor Körner's sentimental drama *Toni* of 1813. Hebbel does not refer explicitly to this play in his essay *Über Theodor Körner und Heinrich von Kleist* of 1835, but he writes dismissively of Körner's talents as a writer of comedies. See Friedrich Hebbel, *Sämtliche Werke*, op. cit., vol. 9, pp.31–60.
16. *Amphitryon*, Act III, scene 1, in Kleist, op. cit., p.29.

17. J.W. von Goethe, 'Ludwig Tieck, Dramaturgische Blätter', 1826 (printed 1833), in Helmut Sembdner, *Heinrich von Kleists Nachruhm*, vol. 2, Frankfurt, 1984, p.208.

EICHENDORFF

1. F. Engels , 'Antwort an Paul Ernst', in Karl Marx/ Friedrich Engels, *Werke*, Berlin, 1970, vol. 22, pp 81–2.
2. *Ahnung und Gegenwart*, in *Werke und Schriften*, Stuttgart 1957, vol. 2, p.40.
3. ibid.
4. ibid., p.31.
5. ibid., p.141.
6. ibid.
7. ibid., p.30.
8. *Des Knaben Wunderhorn*, a collection of folksongs edited by Clemens Brentano and Achim von Arnim between 1805 and 1808.
9. K. Marx & F. Engels, 'Value, Price and Profit', in *Collected Works*, vol. 20, London, 1985, p.142.
10. *Capital*, vol. III, London, 1959, p.820.
11. *Lucinde*, in Friedrich Schlegel, *Kritische Ausgabe*, edited by Hans Eichner, Munich, Paderborn, Vienna, 1962, vol. 5, p.25ff.
12. ibid., p.27.
13. ibid., p.29.
14. *Memoirs of a Good-for-Nothing*, translated by Bayard Quincey Morgan, New York, 1955, p.61–2.
15. ibid, p.22.
16. Friedrich Schiller, *Über naive und sentimentalische Dichtung*, in *Sämtliche Werke*, edited by G. Fricke & H.G. Göpfert, Munich, 1959, vol. 5, p.707.
17. ibid., p.715.

THE REAL GEORG BÜCHNER
AND HIS FASCIST MISREPRESENTATION

1. F. Gundolf, *Romantiker. Fünf Aufsätze*, Berlin, 1930, vol. 1, pp.375–95.
2. Karl Viëtor, 'Die Tragödie des heldischen Pessimismus', in *Deutsche Vierteljahrschrift* 12 (1934), pp.173–209; Arthur Pfeiffer, *Georg Büchner. Vom Wesen der Geschichte des Dämonischen und Dramatischen*, Frankfurt, 1934.
3. Letter of February 1834 to his family, in *Werke und Briefe*, edited by Werner Lehmann, Munich, 1980, p.254.
4. Letter of 5 April 1833, in Georg Büchner, *The Complete Plays together*

with other prose writings, edited and introduced by Michael Patterson, Letters translated by Michael Patterson, London, 1987, p.286.

5. August Becker (1814–71), Büchner's closest friend in Giessen, was, like him, a member of the revolutionary 'Society of Human Rights'. While Büchner was able to flee when the authorities cracked down in 1835, Becker was arrested and remained in prison until he was amnestied in 1839. He then joined Wilhelm Weitling's communist group in Switzerland. He also contributed to Karl Marx's *Rheinische Zeitung*, and later to *Vorwärts* in Paris. In the 1848 Revolution he served as a deputy in the Hesse *Landtag*. He died in the United States.

6. Letter to his family of June 1833, in Büchner, *The Complete Plays*, op. cit., p.207.

7. Undated letter to Gutzkow, ibid., p.294.

8. ibid.

9. ibid., p.297.

10. ibid.

11. Act I, scene 2, in Georg Büchner, *Danton's Death, Leonce and Lena, Woyzeck*, translated with an introduction by Victor Price, Oxford and New York, 1988, p.10. The 'veto' is the king.

12. Act I, scene 6, in ibid., p.22.

13. In *The German Ideology*, in *Collected Works*, vol. 5, London, 1976, p.410.

14. *Danton's Death*, Act I, scene 5, in Büchner, trans. Price, op. cit., p.21.

15. ibid., p.27.

16. ibid., p.59.

17. Büchner, trans. Price, op. cit., p.51.

18. ibid., p.55.

19. ibid., p.52.

20. Büchner, *The Complete Plays*, op. cit., p.290.

21. Büchner, trans. Price, op. cit., p.7.

22. Heinrich Heine, *Die Romantische Schule, Sämtliche Schriften*, edited by Klaus Briegleb, Munich, 1971–4, vol. 3, p.370.

23. Georg Büchner, *Leonce and Lena, Lenz, Woyzeck*, translated with an introduction by Michael Hamburger, Chicago and London, 1972, p.66.

24. ibid., p.46.

25. Lenin, *Collected Works*, London, 1961, vol. 26, p.212.

26. The reference is to Georgi Dimitrov's speech at the Seventh World Congress of the Communist International, held in Moscow in 1935.

27. *Niels Lyhne*, by Jens Peter Jacobsen (1880), a psychological novel of the Naturalist school which tells the story of its eponymous hero's defeats and death. Lyhne is unable to harmonize his over-fertile imagination with reality and ends in resignation.

HEINRICH HEINE AS NATIONAL POET

1. Heine planned to publish his *Neue Gedichte* in 1838, but was deterred by a letter from Gutzkow of 6 August 1838, warning him that he had already offended public taste with his love poems to Paris street beauties and that further publication would risk alienating his few remaining friends. When Heine subsequently received a savagely mutilated copy of his poems from the censor he decided not to go ahead. The volume finally appeared in 1844. In the case of Heine's book on Börne, *Ludwig Börne: eine Denkschrift* ('Ludwig Börne: A Memoir'), Heine's publisher Campe, who was anxious to intensify the rivalry between the two men, changed the title to 'Heinrich Heine on [*über*, which also means 'over' or 'above'] Ludwig Börne', the title page graphically showing Heine's superiority. Heine was infuriated by the gratuitous insult towards Börne. (For Börne see note 17, below.)

2. Heinrich Heine, *Complete Poems: A Modern English Version*, translated by Hal Draper, New York and Oxford, 1984, p.708 (cited henceforth as 'Draper').

3. *Dieses ist mein Testament. Spätere Nachschrift, Sämtliche Schriften*, edited by Klaus Briegleb, Munich, 1971–4, vol. 6/1, p.536 (cited subsequently as 'Briegleb').

4. Draper, op. cit., pp.787–89.

5. Draper, op. cit., p.789.

6. Karl Marx, in Marx and Engels, *Collected Works*, vol. 39, London, 1983, p.509.

7. Marx and Engels, op. cit., vol. 42, p.340. 'Vultus instantis tyrannis': 'nor the face of a tyrant before his very eyes, can shake him in his steady purpose' (Horace, *Odes*, Bk.III, 3).

8. *Französische Zustände* (*Conditions in France*), Briegleb, op. cit., vol. 3, pp.232–3.

9. Letter to Heinrich Laube, 23 November 1835, in Heine Säkularausgabe, Berlin and Paris, 1970ff., vol. 21, p.125 (cited subsequently as HSA).

10. Letter of 7 November 1842, HSA, op. cit., vol. 22, p.36.

11. In his letter of 21 April 1832. See the discussion in Heinrich Heine, *Briefe*, edited by F. Hirth, Mainz, 1950, vol. 5, p.53.

12. Heinrich Heine, *Deutschland. A Winter's Tale*, translated with an introduction and notes by T.J. Reed, London, 1986, p.56.

13. Karl Varnhagen von Ense (1785–1858) fought against Napoleon as an officer in the Austrian army and subsequently served as a Prussian diplomat. He settled in Berlin after 1819 where, with his much more celebrated wife, Rahel Levin, his apartment became a centre of literary social life. Though not a major writer his diaries and his correspondence with Rahel are an invaluable source for the period.

14. For Immermann, see note 9 on p.336.

15. Heinrich Laube (1806–64), writer and journalist, one of the principal members of the Young German movement. When they were proscribed in 1835 he was sentenced to seven years' detention, later reduced on appeal to eighteen months, which he was allowed to spend in comfortable circumstances on the estate of his friend Prince Pückler-Muskau, another member of the group. Laube made his name with a socio-political novel, *Das junge Europa*, and six volumes of travel stories (*Reisenovellen*).

16. Alfred Meissner (1822–85) was a liberal from Bavaria, a friend of Heine's last years.

17. Ludwig Börne (1786–1837) was a radical writer and journalist. After the July Revolution in France in 1830 he moved to Paris where he made his name as a witty political commentator whose style was not unlike Heine's in some respects. He was best known for his *Briefe aus Paris* (1832–4) and *Menzel der Franzosenfresser* (1837). Although not named in the banning of the Young German movement he sympathized with their views and aims.

18. Heine, trans. Reed, op. cit., p.75.

19. See *Begegnungen mit Heine*, edited by Michael Werner, Hamburg, 1973, vol. I, p.210. Ludwig Wienbarg (1802–72) was one of the most prominent of the so-called Young Germans.

20. Draper, op. cit., p.649.

21. Karl Marx, '*Contribution to the Critique of Hegel's Philosophy of Law*', in Marx and Engels, op. cit., vol. 3, 1975, p.176.

22. ibid., p.180.

23. *Geständnisse (Confessions)*, in Briegleb, op. cit., vol. 6/1, p.466.

24. *Memoiren*, ibid., p.608.

25. Letter to Varnhagen von Ense, 19 November 1830, HSA, op. cit., vol. 20, p.422.

26. *Ludwig Börne, Eine Denkschrift (Ludwig Börne, A Memoir)*, in Briegleb, op. cit., vol. 4, p.60.

27. *Conditions in France*, Briegleb, op. cit., vol. 3, p.191.

28. ibid, pp.192–3.

29. *Die Nordsee. Dritte Abteilung*, in *Reisebilder (Travel Pictures)* Part II, Briegleb, vol. 2, op. cit., pp.214–5.

30. *Ludwig Börne*, in Briegleb, op. cit., vol. 4, p.29.

31. *Lutetia*, in Briegleb, op. cit., vol. 5, pp.333–4.

32. On 5 and 6 June 1832, during the funeral of the popular General Lamarque, a rebellion broke out against the regime of Louis Philippe. According to Heine, some republicans defended themselves with great valour and were killed by the National Guard; others took refuge in the Church of St Méry and, rather than surrendering, took their own lives. See *Conditions in France*, Briegleb, op. cit., vol. 3, pp.218–9. Lukács often refers to this episode which is also described in Balzac's, *Les Secrets de la Princesse de Cadignan*. Balzac's character, Michel Chrétien, who died during the siege, seemed to him to be the very model of civic heroism.

33. *Conditions in France*, Briegleb, op. cit., p.126.

34. ibid., p.127.

35. ibid., p.103.

36. *Germany, A Winter's Tale*, Briegleb, op. cit., vol. 4, p.574.

37. *Ludwig Börne*, Briegleb, op. cit., vol. 4, p.90.

38. Wolfgang Menzel (1798–1873), was one of the leading literary critics of his day. His *Die deutsche Literatur* (1827) was written in a liberal spirit which Heine found congenial, although he criticized Menzel's over-savage treatment of Goethe. By the eighteen-thirties Menzel had moved decisively to the right. His criticism became markedly anti-Semitic and his attack on Gutzkow's mildly erotic novel, *Wally die Zweiflerin* (1835), was used by the censors as a pretext to proscribe the entire Young German movement. For this reason Menzel was attacked both by Börne (*Menzel der Franzosenfresser*), and Heine (in the long Preface to *Salon* III). Heine's scurrilous onslaught was written with the aim, ineffectual as it turned out, of provoking Menzel into challenging him to a duel.

39. Marx in Karl Marx and Frederick Engels, op. cit., vol. 11, 1979, p.111.

40. *Lutetia*, Briegleb, op. cit., vol. 5, p.414.

41. Draper, op. cit., p.783.

42. Letter to Julius Campe, 24 August 1852, HSA, op. cit., vol 23, p.230.

43. *Knotentum*, a word derived from student slang to refer to clumsy rustics or apprentices. It is often used by Marx and Engels to denote the backward-looking German handicraftsmen in an age of rising capitalism.

44. *Zur Geschichte der Religion und Philosophie in Deutschland (The History of Religion and Philosophy in Germany)*, Briegleb, op. cit., vol. 3, p.570.

45. Heine, *Deutschland, A Winter's Tale*, trans. Reed, op. cit., p.30.

46. Preface to *Lutetia*, Briegleb, op. cit., vol. 5, p.237.

47. ibid., pp.232–3.

48. ibid. p.233.

49. F. Engels in *Ludwig Feuerbach and the End of Classical German Philosophy*, in Marx and Engels, *Selected Works in One Volume*, London, 1970, p.586.

50. i.e. *Die Posaune des jüngsten Gerichts*. Bruno Bauer (1809–82) was a theologian and a student of Hegel. He lectured first in Berlin and then in Bonn. He moved from a criticism of the historicity of Jesus to a critique of religion in general, and this in turn led to his dismissal from his post in 1842. His contribution to the Young Hegelians ended in 1844, but had made a great impact by then. Karl Marx took issue with his views both in *The Jewish Question* and *The Holy Family*.

51. *Briefe über Deutschland (Letters about Germany)*, Briegleb, op. cit., vol. 5, p.197.

52. *Confessions*, Briegleb, op. cit., vol. 6/1, pp.473–4.

53. *Letters about Germany*, Briegleb, op. cit., vol. 5, pp.195–198.

54. *The Romantic School*, Briegleb, op. cit., vol. 3, p.370.

55. *The History of Philosophy and Religion in Germany*, Briegleb, op. cit., vol. 3, p.519.

56. ibid., p.570.

57. F. Engels, *Ludwig Feuerbach and the End of Classical German Philosophy*, in Karl Marx & Frederick Engels, *Selected Works in One Volume*, London, 1970, p.596.

58. ibid., p.592.

59. *Confessions*, Briegleb, op. cit., vol. 6/1, p.474.

60. ibid., p.476.

61. H.H. Houben, *Gespräche mit Heine*, Potsdam 1948, p.771.

62. *Begegnungen mit Heine*, 1847–1856, edited by Michael Werner, Hamburg, 1973, p.122.

63. Draper, op. cit., pp.714–15.

64. ibid., p.813.

65. Houben, op. cit., p.685.

66. Draper, op. cit., p.709.

67. Houben, op. cit., p.970.

68. Draper, op. cit., p.647.

69. Franz Dingelstedt (1814–81) and Georg Herwegh (1817–75) were among the leading radical poets of the eighteen forties (others were Ferdinand Freiligrath and Hoffmann von Fallersleben, the author of *Deutschland über alles*). Heine viewed them with mixed feelings, regarding them as rivals rather than allies, although he was on friendly terms with, for example, Dingelstedt. In general he criticizes them for writing bad poetry.

70. Draper, op. cit., p.634.

71. ibid., p.700.

72. Karl Marx, *Capital*, vol. 1, translated by Samuel Moore, London, 1967, p.79.

73. *Confessions*, Briegleb, op. cit., vol. 6/1, p.447.

74. See p.335 note 5.

75. *Französische Maler* (*French Painters*), Briegleb, op. cit., vol. 3, p.72.

76. ibid., pp.72–3.

77. 'The Wars of Liberation' (1813–15) is the name given to the campaigns against Napoleon following the retreat from Moscow. The initial campaign culminated in the battle of Leipzig in October 1813, which is known in Germany as the Battle of the Nations. Ideologically, the wars left an ambivalent legacy in Germany. They appeared progressive because Metternich was alarmed by the threat to the Restoration posed by the popular response to the King of Prussia's appeal 'An mein Volk' ('To my people'). At the same time German nationalism received a powerful boost. In time the nationalistic mythology came to outweigh the popular and progressive element of hostility to tyranny.

78. *The Romantic School*, Briegleb, op. cit., vol. 3, p.379.

79. The Swabian School of German Romanticism was known for its cultivation of the ballad and more generally, poetry with folk-song affinities. Its adherents developed an interest in medieval literature and German legend. Its leading members, apart from Ludwig Uhland (1787–1862), included Gustav Schwab, Justinus Kerner and Wilhelm Hauff.

80. *Deutschland. A Winter's Tale*, trans. Reed, op. cit., p.69.

81. *The History of Religion and Philosophy in Germany*, Briegleb, op. cit., vol. 3, p.619.

82. Preface to *Travel Pictures*, Briegleb, op. cit., vol. 2, p.209.

83. F. Engels, in Karl Marx and Frederick Engels, *Collected Works*, op. cit., vol. 6, p.244.

84. Karl Wilhelm Ferdinand Solger (1780–1817) was a philosopher who specialized in aesthetics. In 1811 he became one of the two professors of philosophy at the newly established University of Berlin (Fichte was the other). He is one of the central exponents of the concept of Romantic Irony. His aesthetics revolve round the twin concepts of irony and tragedy. Tragedy in his view is concerned with the ultimate comprehension of human suffering against a background in which universal forces are responsible for the hero's plight in adversity. Tragedy builds up a mounting sense of incomprehension which must be sustained until the hero's death. However, at the moment of death the hero has a fleeting illumination of the true nature of the universe. Solger terms this the 'divine idea'. He regards it as ironical that such insight can only be obtained in death. Hegel wrote an important essay on his work (*Über Solgers nachgelassene Schriften und Briefe*).

85. Letter to Friederike Robert, 12 October 1825, in HSA, op. cit., vol. 20, p.219. Ludwig Robert (1778–1832) was the brother of Rahel von Varnhagen and a well-known dramatist. Heine frequently quotes from his play *Die Macht der Verhältnisse* (*The Force of Circumstances*).

86. Karl Marx, *Capital*, vol. 1, translated by Samuel Moore, London, 1967, pp.103–4.

87. F. Hebbel, *Ernst, Freiherr von Feuchtersleben*, in *Sämtliche Werke*, edited by R.M. Werner, I/12, p.61.

88. Johann Heinrich Voss (1751–1826) was a poet of lowly origins now remembered for his verse idyll *Luise* and, especially, his translation of Homer's *Odyssey* into German hexameters. Gottfried August Bürger (1747–94) achieved fame for his popular ballad *Lenore* which helped to establish the ballad tradition in Germany, but which was severely criticized by Schiller for its over-simple, inartistic language and lack of refinement. Heine vigorously defends them both in *The Romantic School*.

89. Letter to Wilhelm Müller, 7 June 1826, HSA, op. cit., vol. 20, p.250.

90. August, Count von Platen (1796–1835) was the impoverished descendant of an ancient family. Having first served in the army he later lived (mainly in Italy) on a pension granted him by the King of Bavaria. After he had published a clumsy satire on Immermann, *Der romantische Ödipus*

(1829), a play which contained a number of anti-Semitic jibes about Heine, the latter responded ferociously in the same year with *The Baths of Lucca*.

91. Emanuel Geibel (1815–84), a minor poet celebrated in his day as the apostle of a refined beauty, but forgotten now apart from a few poems which survive in settings by Hugo Wolf.

92. Draper, op. cit., p.552.

93. ibid., p.400.

94. *Ludwig Börne*, Briegleb, op. cit., vol. 4, p.129.

95. Houben, op. cit., p.196.

96. *Über die französische Bühne* ('The French Theatre'), Briegleb, op. cit., vol. 3, p.304.

97. The *feuilleton*, i.e. the literary review section of the newspaper, developed in the course of the nineteenth century. Its practitioners often cultivated a witty or facetious style and commonly regarded Heine or the Austrian Moritz Saphir as the originators of the genre. It was because of this that Karl Kraus launched his savage attack on Heine in his essay *Heine und die Folgen* ('Heine and the Consequences').

98. Draper, op. cit., p.392.

99. *Confessions*, Briegleb, op. cit., vol. 6/1, p.472.

100. Draper, op. cit., p.154.

101. Draper, op. cit., p.748.

102. In Ibsen's *Hedda Gabler*, the heroine feels stifled by the life of bourgeois security she has chosen. She longs to inspire Eilert Lövborg, a genius half-destroyed by alcohol. He is now a teetotaller, but Hedda taunts him for his fear of drink and encourages him to join her husband and a friend in a stag party. She imagines that he will return triumphant over his vice and appear before her 'with vineleaves in his hair'. This becomes the symbol of a powerful, free, non-bourgeois way of life.

103. Draper, op. cit., p.646.

104. ibid., p.575–6.

105. Georg Weerth (1822–56), a political journalist associated with Marx and Engels. Forced to flee after the 1848 Revolution he settled for a time in Bradford. He wrote satirical fiction and political poetry.

106. Eduard Mörike (1804–75), long regarded as Germany's major lyric poet after Goethe and perhaps Hölderlin; his poetry is admired for its truth of feeling and subtlety of perception. Heine's reputation in contrast has undergone many vicissitudes, not least because of the Nazis who had proscribed his works at the time Lukács was writing this essay. Lukács's dismissive phrase '*niedliche Zwerge*', 'quaint little dwarfs', was intended to be provocative and caused considerable offence. In his eyes Mörike is the prime example of that 'inwardness' which Thomas Mann described as 'machtgeschützt', 'protected by power', and which turned the eyes of the educated German away from the brutal realities of politics. Lukács sees Mörike as the antipode of Heine, the greatest German political poet. Ernst

Bloch, who greatly objected to this dismissive judgement of Mörike, suggests that here as elsewhere Lukács has turned against a man he has previously admired (see Ernst Bloch and Georg Lukács, *Dokumente Zum 100 Geburtstag*, Budapest, 1984, p.316).

GOTTFRIED KELLER

1. For Karl Immermann see note 9, p.336. The 'Oberhof' episode in *Münchhausen* is a realist narrative running parallel to the comic satire on the lunacy of the aristocracy. It is a solid story of Westfalian country life which relishes the description of the farm, its inhabitants and their customs, especially a rural wedding. Within this framework it tells the story of the love of a young couple who overcome misunderstandings and the opposition of the village magistrate.

2. Karl Gutzkow (1811–78) was one of the leading figures of the Young German movement. It was the scandal attending his mildly erotic novel *Wally die Zweiflerin* (1835), which triggered the persecution of the entire group. In the same year he was forced to serve a month in prison for obscenity and blasphemy. Apart from his own extremely varied literary activities, he was notable for his encouragement of Büchner, some of whose work he published. Gustav Freytag (1816–95) was a novelist in the realist tradition, best known for his extremely popular novel *Soll und Haben* (1855). Friedrich Spielhagen (1829–1911) was a popular writer who dealt with contemporary issues from a liberal point of view. His works are now mainly forgotten, but they are interesting documents of the development of Germany in the second half of the century. Paul Lindau (1839–1919) was a dramatist and novelist. He was director of the Berlin Theatre and then the *Deutsches Theater*. He was a prolific writer of Berlin stories with a strong social emphasis.

3. Otto Ludwig (1813–65) started life as a musician and studied under Mendelssohn, but soon turned to literature and made his name as a playwright. He is now remembered for a single novella, *Zwischen Himmel und Erde* (1856) which explores the terrain between normality and pathology.

4. Fritz Reuter (1810–74) was a realist novelist whose main works (*Ut mine Stromtid*, 1862–4) were set in North Germany and written in Low German dialect, of which he remains the foremost literary exponent.

5. The so-called Punctuation of Olmütz of 29 November 1850 was an agreement between Otto von Manteuffel, the Prussian Foreign Minister, and Prince Felix Schwarzenberg, the Austrian Minister-President, according to which Prussia would abandon its efforts to create a German federation excluding German Austria. In effect the Prussians agreed to accept the continued domination of Germany by Austria. However, Schwarzenberg's attempts to consolidate his victory by securing the inclusion of the non-German provinces of Habsburg Empire in the Confederation suffered a

setback in the Dresden Conference of early 1851, when Prussia showed unexpected firmness and received support from France and Russia.

6. In the course of arguing that Wagner was a mere actor, incapable of creating a true dramatic action, Nietzsche in *The Case of Wagner* suggests that the much vaunted 'mythic contents' of his operas can best be tested by translating them into bourgeois reality.

7. Jeremias Gotthelf (1797–1854), a parson who became famous as the author of novels and stories dealing with Swiss country life. His best known story is *Die schwarze Spinne* (1842).

8. Letter to Ferdinand Freiligrath, 30 April 1857, in J. Baechtold, *Gottfried Kellers Leben*, Stuttgart & Berlin 1903, vol. 2, p.383.

9. *Der grüne Heinrich*, in Gottfried Keller, *Sämtliche Werke und Ausgewählte Briefe*, edited by C. Heselhaus, Munich, 1958, vol. 1, p.43 (cited subsequently as Heselhaus).

10. 'Jeremias Gotthelf' in *Sämtliche Werke*, edited by J. Fränkel & C. Helbling, Bern, 1948, vol. 22, p.88.

11. Letter to the *Basler Nachrichten*, 30 March 1872, in Gottfried Keller, *Leben, Briefe und Tagebücher*, edited by Emil Ermatinger, Stuttgart & Berlin, 1925, vol. 3, p.45.

12. 'Die Romantik und die Gegenwart', *Sämtliche Werke*, edited by J. Fränkel & C. Helbling, Bern, 1948, Volume 22, p.314.

13. ibid.

14. *Briefwechsel Theodor Storm and Emil Kuh*, *Westermanns illustrierte deutsche Monatshefte*, 67, 1889–90, p.107.

15. The German word 'Bildung' denotes the process of education in the broader sense. The term 'Bildungsroman' has been retained here (Lukács actually uses the more or less synomymous 'Erziehungsroman') to refer to the tradition, established by Wieland in the eighteenth century and continued throughout the nineteenth century, of novels in which the central character, after a number of false starts or wrong choices, is led to follow the right path and develop into a mature and well-balanced person. The phrase 'formative education' has been generally used to render 'Bildung'.

16. Uncle Bräsig, i.e. Zacharias Bräsig, the central figure of Fritz Reuter's *Ut mine Stromtid* (*My Farming Days*), a novel which describes Reuter's life as a farmer in Mecklenburg, where he went after spending seven years in gaol for taking part in an uprising in Frankfurt. Uncle Bräsig personifies modern, enlightened ideas, is an advocate of progress and has a youthful, enthusiastic heart.

17. Berthold Auerbach (1812–82) a German-Jewish writer associated at first with the *Burschenschaften* and the Young Germans. He made his name with the *Schwarzwälder Dorfgeschichten* (*Village Stories from the Black Forest*, 1849–53) which praise the simplicities of rural life at the expense of the complexities and insincerities of the town.

18. Letter to Auerbach, 3 June 1856, in Heselhaus, op. cit., vol. 3,

pp.1167–8. Auerbach had reviewed the collection of stories in *Die Leute von Seldwyla* in the literary supplement of the *Augsburger Allgemeine Zeitung* (17 April 1856).

19. Letter to Hettner, 26 June 1854, in Heselhaus, op. cit., vol. 3, p.1139. Hermann Hettner (1821–82) became friendly with Keller while a lecturer in Heidelberg. Subsequently he became a professor in literature and philosophy in Jena, and in 1855 a museum director in Dresden. He wrote a stimulating study on the modern drama (1852), but his reputation rested mainly on his monumental history of German literature in the eighteenth century. He was known for his liberal views.

20. Letter to Wilhelm Baumgartner, 27 March 1851, in Gottfried Keller, *Werke, Briefe und Tagebücher*, edited by Emil Ermatinger, Stuttgart & Berlin, 1925, vol. 2, p.275.

21. Ludwig Büchner (1824–99), the playwright Georg's younger brother, was a doctor in Darmstadt who wrote an influential book, *Kraft und Stoff* (*Energy and Matter*, 1855), a popularizing exposition of materialism. In his view nothing existed apart from energy and matter. The soul was no more than the function of the brain described in physiological terms. He later helped to popularize Darwinism in Germany. Karl Vogt (1817–95), a scientist who worked at first in Liebig's laboratory in Giessen and later took part in the glacier expedition of Desor and Agassiz in Neuenburg, became professor in Giessen in 1847. During the 1848 Revolution he played a role on the far left of the Frankfurt *Vorparlament* and the National Assembly, becoming one of the five Imperial Regents in 1849. He was later a professor of geology and zoology in Geneva. He was a vigorous exponent of materialism and Darwinism. Marx attacked him at great length in his polemic *Herr Vogt*.

22. *Der grüne Heinrich*, Book III, chapter I, in Gottfried Keller, *Werke*, introduced by Robert Faesi, Zurich, 1951, vol. II, p.467.

23. *Pankraz der Schmoller*, in Heselhaus, op. cit., vol. 2, pp.40–1.

24. Achim von Arnim (1781–1831), known mainly for his role in collecting German folk poetry; *Des Knaben Wunderhorn*, which he published with Clemens Brentano, is the classical anthology of folk poems. Arnim's own writings are decorative and anecdotal, a patchwork quilt which often borders on the formless. The Romantic concept of the 'arabesque' is often applied to this playful technique. In recent years attempts have been made to reclaim some of his writings from oblivion.

25. Storm's view was expressed in a letter to Keller written on 15 May 1881; Keller's reply on 16 August 1881. See Heselhaus, op. cit., vol. 3, pp.1256–7.

26. Keller, *Der Apotheker von Chamonix*, in Heselhaus, Munich, 1958, vol. 3, p.475.

27. *Der grüne Heinrich*, G. Keller, *Werke*, introduced by Robert Faesi, Book IV, Chapter II, vol. II, p.701.

28. Keller *Sämtliche Werke*, edited by J. Fränkel & C. Helbling, Bern, 1925, vol. 22, p.337.

29. Goethe defined the novella as 'eine sich ereignete, unerhörte Begebenheit', ('an event which is unheard of, but has taken place') (*Conversations with Eckermann*, 29 January 1827). 'Unerhört' can mean either that the event is unfamiliar to the reader or that it is unprecedented, extraordinary, 'surprising' or 'novel'. The true meaning and importance of the definition has been the subject of much debate.

30. Similar formulation in *Dichter über ihre Dichtungen, Ludwig Tieck*, edited by U. Schweikert, Munich, 1971, Volume 9/3, pp.214–6 & 244–5.

31. The German 'Original' means 'eccentric', but also has the less derogatory meaning of someone who stands out owing to one of his idiosyncrasies or character traits predominating in the way he presents himself. Lukács elsewhere uses the term '*Exzentriker*'.

32. *The Banner of the Upright Seven*, New York, 1972, p.290.

33. The idea of the 'totality of objects' is of central importance in Lukács's concept of realism. It derives from Hegel, for whom the epic is a unified totality. 'The contents of the epic. . . are the entirety of a world in which an individual action happens. Consequently this involves the greatest variety of topics belonging to the views, deeds and situations of such a world . . . all the detail of what can be regarded as the poetry of human existence' (*Aesthetics*, translated by T.M. Knox, Oxford, 1975, vol. 2, p.1078). In his discussion of the *Odyssey* Hegel stresses the interweaving of the particular and the general. Lukács takes up these ideas but moves beyond them with his claim that the realist novel contains such a totality of objects which is not just an aggregate of surface phenomena such as are found in the naturalist descriptions of Zola, but a meaningful totality in which superficial appearances are related to the broad historical processes which give rise to them.

34. Hebbel's review of *Ludovico*, Deinhardstein's version of Massinger's *The Duke of Milan*, an earlier version of the story of Herod and Mariamne, in *Sämtliche Werke*, edited by R. Werner, op. cit., vol. I/11, pp.247–8.

35. ibid., p.248.

36. Letter to Eduard Dössekel, 8 February 1849, in *Dichter über ihre Dichtungen: Gottfried Keller*, edited by Klaus Jerziorkowski, Munich, 1969, p.78.

37. Letter to Hermann Hettner, 3 August 1853, in *Keller in seinen Briefen*, edited by Heinz Amelung, Berlin, n.d., p.118.

38. A manuscript of this earlier version of Goethe's *Wilhelm Meister* was discovered only in 1910.

39. Letter to Eduard Vieweg, 3 May 1850, *Keller in seinen Briefen*, op. cit., p.83.

40. Letter to Hermann Hettner, 4 March 1851, ibid., p.95.

41. Letter to Hermann Hettner, 5 January 1854, ibid., p.122.

42. Letter to Hermann Hettner, 25 June 1855, ibid., p.139.

43. G.W. Hegel, *Aesthetics. Lectures on Fine Art*, translated by T.M. Knox, Oxford, 1975, vol. I, p.593.

44. Honoré de Balzac, *Lost Illusions*, translated by Herbert J. Hunt, Harmondsworth, 1976, pp.648–9.

45. *Der grüne Heinrich*, Book IV, chapter 10, G. Keller, *Werke*, introduced by Robert Faesi, op. cit., volume 2, p.697 (this and most subsequent passages are quoted from the abridged English-language edition, *Green Henry*, translated by A.M. Holt, London, 1960).

46. *Der grüne Heinrich*, Book IV, chapter 14, ibid., Volume II, p.744.

47. Letter to F.T. Vischer, 29 June 1875, in *Keller in seinen Briefen*, op. cit., pp.174–5.

48. *Wilhelm Meisters Wanderjahre (Years of Travel) oder die Entsagenden* is the full title of the continuation of *Wilhelm Meister's Apprenticeship*. 'Entsagen' is the German for 'to renounce'.

49. *Der grüne Heinrich*, Book III, chapter 6, Keller, *Werke*, introduced by Robert Faesi, op. cit., p.495.

50. ibid., p.497.

51. ibid., p.496.

WILHELM RAABE

1. The English titles of Raabe's works, few of which have been translated into English, have been taken from those used by Jeffrey Sammons in his recent study, *Wilhelm Raabe, The Fiction of the Alternative Community*, Princeton, 1987.

2. In the Franco-Prussian War of 1870–71.

3. Ferdinand Freiligrath (1810–76), one of the generation of political poets to emerge in the eighteen forties. In 1845, as a radical, he emigrated to Brussels, where he became friendly with Marx, and then to Zurich where he became acquainted with Keller. He later worked on the *Neue Rheinische Zeitung* and moved to London where he lived until his return to Germany in 1868, following an amnesty. Friedrich Theodor Vischer (1807–87) was a leading philosopher of aesthetics in Tübingen and Zurich. A moderate liberal in the 1848 Revolution, he was a deputy in the Frankfurt Parliament. He is remembered for his *Aesthetics* (1846–57), his autobiographical novel *Auch Einer* (1879) and his parody of Goethe's *Faust*.

4. Michael Georg Conrad (1846–1927) was a member of the Naturalist school of writers. Although a prolific writer he is known principally as the founder and editor of *Die Gesellschaft*, the chief organ of the movement. Julius Hart (1857–1930) was a drama critic best known for his critical pamphlet *Kritische Waffengänge*, written with his brother Heinrich, which paved the way for Naturalism by denouncing the literature of the eighteen seventies. Leo Berg (1862–1908) was a journalist and founding-member of *Durch*, an avant-garde literary society in Berlin in the eighteen eighties, and

the *Freie Bühne*, a private society that mounted plays banned by the censor. Both were influential in establishing Naturalism in Germany.

5. Adolf Bartels (1862–1945) was a literary historian and a popular writer of regional novels. He had extreme conservative and anti-Semitic views which led at a later date to an association with the Nazis. Fritz Lienhard (1865–1929) was a prolific regional writer from Alsace. Under the influence of the proto-fascist ideas of Julius Langbehn, he wrote books which defended the healthy countryside against the decadent town, and denounced modernity and the dominance of Berlin. Josef Nadler (1884–1963) was a literary historian closely associated with the Nazis. Under the influence of racist ideas he wrote a literary history of Germany in which writers are classifed according to the Germanic tribes they came from.

6. *Abu Telfan oder die Heimkehr vom Mondgebirge (Abu Telfan; or the Return from the Mountains of the Moon)*.

7. Wilhelm Raabe, *The Hunger Pastor*, translated by Arnold, London, 1885, p.58.

8. Robert Blum (1807–48) was a radical democrat, a deputy, and one of the leaders of the 1848 Revolution. He was executed as such, in Vienna in November 1848.

9. A group interested in the creation of Germany as an entity which did not include Austria and the Sudetenland, hence 'small-German'.

10. Wilhelm Raabe, *Horacker*, in *Sämtliche Werke*, Braunschweiger Ausgabe, edited by Karl Hoppe, Freiburg and Braunschweig, 1955, vol. 12, p.398. (cited henceforth as Hoppe).

11. *Christoph Pechlin*, Hoppe, op. cit., vol. 10, p.205.

12. *Stopfkuchen*, Hoppe, op. cit., vol. 18, p.130.

13. *People from the Forest*, Hoppe, op. cit., vol. 5, p.63–4.

14. *Kloster Lugau*, Hoppe, op. cit., vol. 19, pp.72–3.

15. *Alte Nester,(Old Nests)* Hoppe, op. cit., vol.14.

16. Karl Marx and Frederick Engels, *Collected Works*, vol. 28, London, 1986, pp.47–8.

17. *Fabian and Sebastian*, Hoppe, op. cit., vol. 15., pp.87–8.

18. Charles Baudelaire, *Les Fleurs du Mal, (Flowers of Evil)*, in *The Complete Verse*, edited and translated by Francis Scarfe, London, 1986, p.14.

19. *Old Nests*, Hoppe, op. cit., vol 14, p.148.

20. Karl Marx and Frederick Engels, op. cit., vol. 3, p.134.

21. Karl Hoppe, *'Aphorismen Raabes: chronologisch geordnet'*, *Wilhelm Raabe: Beiträge zum Verständnis seiner Person und seines Werkes*, Göttingen, 1967, p.97.

22. V. Lenin, *Collected Works*, vol. 31, 1966, p.293.

23. *Three Pens*, Hoppe, op. cit., vol. 9/1, p.373.

24. Heine, *Travel Pictures IV, The Town of Lucca*, Briegleb, op. cit., vol. 2., p.521.

25. *Stuffcake*, Hoppe, op. cit., vol. 18, p.46.

THE LATER FONTANE

1. Thomas Mann, 'Der alte Fontane', in *Gesammelte Werke*, Frankfurt, 1974, vol. IX, p.9.

2. ibid., p.10.

3. The full name was the '*Tunnel über der Spree*' – 'Tunnel over the Spree'.

4. Letter to Theodor Storm, in Fontane, *Werke, Schriften und Briefe*, edited by W. Keitel and H. Nürnberger (Hanser edition) Munich, 1976, IV,1, p.376 (cited hereafter as 'Hanser').

5. Fontane, *Von Zwanzig bis Dreissig*, in *Sämtliche Werke*, Munich, 1967, vol. XV, p.275.

6. ibid., p.347.

7. ibid., p.348.

8. ibid., p.331.

9. Letter to Bernhard von Lepel, 7 April 1849, Hanser, op. cit., IV, 1, p.64.

10. Letter to Bernhard von Lepel, 28 July 1850, Hanser, op. cit., IV, 1, p.127.

11. Letter to Bernhard von Lepel, 3 November 1851, Hanser, op. cit., IV, 1, p.195.

12. Johannes von Miquel (1828–1901), once a member of the Communist League, became a National Liberal, and ended his political career as Prussian Minister of Finance.

13. Letter to Emilie Fontane, 28 May 1870, Hanser, op. cit., IV, 2, p.320.

14. Letter to Bernhard von Lepel, 1 December 1858, Hanser, op. cit., IV, 1, pp.635–6.

15. 'Ritt über den Bodensee', is a phrase taken from a legend about a man who rides across the frozen Lake Constance by night, only realizing on his arrival what a narrow escape he has had.

16. Wilhelm Busch (1832–1908), Germany's best-known and loved comic poet. His most famous works include *Max und Moritz* and *Die fromme Helene*. They are written in doggerel verse and accompanied by grotesque line drawings. The other side of Busch is his pessimism in which he was strongly influenced by the philosophy of Arthur Schopenhauer.

17. Letter to Wilhelm Hertz, 18 August 1879, Hanser, op. cit., IV, 3, p.41.

18. Letter to Philipp zu Eulenburg, 23 April 1881, Hanser, op. cit., IV, 3, p.131.

19. Letter to Martha Fontane, 29 January 1894, Hanser, op. cit., IV, 4, p.326.

20. Letter to Marthe Fontane, 1 April 1895, Hanser, op. cit., IV, 4, p.440.

21. Literally, a person who praises times past – or harks back to the good old days (see Horace, *Ars Poetica*, 173).

22. *Von Zwanzig bis Dreissig*, *Sämtliche Werke*, op. cit., vol. XV, p.14.

23. ibid., p.270.

24. *Von Zwanzig bis Dreissig*, Hanser, op. cit., III, 4, p.430.

25. Letter to August von Heyden, 5 August 1893, Hanser, op. cit., IV, 4, p.272.

26. Letter to James Morris, 6 January 1898, Hanser, op. cit., IV, 4, p.688. Fontane's English friend and correspondent was a London doctor who had taken German lessons with Fontane in 1862 when Fontane was a journalist in England, and who kept in touch with him till his death.

27. Letter to Emilie Fontane, 5 June 1878, Hanser, op. cit., IV, 2, p.581.

28. Letter to James Morris, 22 February 1896, Hanser, op. cit., IV, 4, p.539.

29. Letter to Martha Fontane, 16 February 1894, Hanser, op. cit., IV, 4, p.335.

30. Letter to Heinrich Jacobi, 23 January 1890, Hanser, op. cit., IV, 4, p.18. The poem referred to in the next paragraph is 'An meinen Fünfundsiebzigsten' ('On my Seventy-Fifth Birthday'), in which Fontane contrasts those with aristocratic names who did not come to his birthday celebrations with the non-aristocratic, Polish, Jewish, etc., names of those who did.

31. Letter to Friedrich Fontane, 16 June 1898, Hanser, op. cit., IV, 4, p.728.

32. Letter to Martha Fontane, 13 March 1888, Hanser, op. cit., IV, 3, p.590.

33. On Alexander Kielland, *Arbeiter* (Workers), in Hanser, op. cit., III, 1, p.528.

34. On Paul Lindau, *Der Zug nach dem Westen (Nachlassfassung)*, Hanser, op. cit., III, 1, p.568.

35. Translated by E.M. Valk, as *A Man of Honor*, New York, 1975.

36. Letter to Emilie Fontane, 2 September 1868, Hanser, op. cit., IV, 2, p.209.

37. Letter to Emil Dominik, Hanser, op. cit., IV, 3, pp.177–8.

38. ibid., p.178.

39. W. M. Thackeray, *The Virginians*, London, 1900, vol. 2, p.86.

40. *Jenny Treibel*, translated with an introduction by Ulf Zimmermann, New York, 1976, p.70.

41. Letter to Emilie Fontane, 8 August 1883, Hanser, op. cit., IV, 3, p.278.

42. *Von Zwanzig bis Dreissig, Sämtliche Werke*, op. cit., Volume XV, p.336.

43. *Jenny Treibel*, op. cit., p.152.

44. Letter to Martha Fontane, 14 September 1889, Hanser, op. cit., IV, 3, p.725.

45. Letter to Friedrich Stephany, 10 October 1889, Hanser, op. cit., IV, 3, p.729.

46. Letter to Martha Fontane, Hanser, op. cit., p.725.

47. Letter to Otto Brahm, 14 January 1985, Hanser, op. cit., IV, 4, pp.416–7.

48. See Paul Lafargue, '*Das Geld* von Zola', *Die neue Zeit* (Stuttgart), X, no. 1, 1891–2, pp.4–10, 41–6, 76–86, 101–10.

49. Klaus Störtebeker was a pirate in the Middle Ages who led a gang called the *Vitalienbrüder*, which was said to have communist aspirations. Fontane's novel on this subject intended to underline the parallels with his own day. Its title, *Die Likedeeler*, means 'fairsharers'.

50. *Before the Storm*, translated with an introduction by R.J. Hollingdale, Oxford, 1985, p.561.

51. *A Man of Honor*, op. cit., p.43.

52. ibid., p.85.

53. ibid., p.16.

54. ibid.

55. ibid., pp.187–8.

56. Letter to Mathilde von Rohr, 11 August 1878, Hanser, op. cit., IV, 2, p.612.

57. Letter to Wilhelm Friedrich, 5 November 1882, Hanser, op. cit., IV, 3, p.217.

58. *Effi Briest*, translated with an introduction by Douglas Parmée, Harmondsworth, 1967, p.221.

59. ibid., p.222.

60. ibid., pp.215–6.

61. ibid., p.259.

Index

DATE DUE

DEMCO 38-297